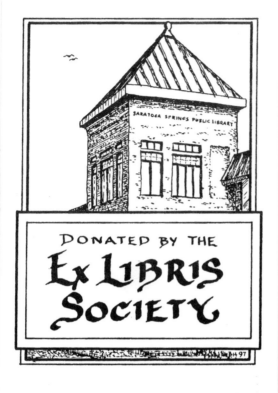

INEZ

The Life and Times of Inez Milholland

Inez Milholland, ca. 1910. *Courtesy of Library of Congress.*

INEZ
The Life and Times of Inez Milholland

Linda J. Lumsden

Indiana University Press
Bloomington and Indianapolis

Library of Congress Cataloging-in-Publication Data

Lumsden, Linda J., date
 Inez : the life and times of Inez Milholland /
Linda J. Lumsden.
    p. cm.
 Includes bibliographical references and index.
 ISBN 0-253-34418-2 (alk. paper)
   1. Milholland, Inez. 2. Feminists—United
States—Biography. 3. Suffragists—United States—
Biography. 4. Women social reformers—United
States—Biography.
 I. Title.
 HQ1413.M55L86 2004
 324.6'23'092—dc22
                                              2003027308

This book is a publication of

1 2 3 4 5 09 08 07 06 05 04

Indiana University Press
601 North Morton Street
Bloomington, IN 47404-3797 USA

http://iupress.indiana.edu

Telephone orders 800-842-6796
Fax orders 812-855-7931
Orders by e-mail iuporder@indiana.edu

The paper used in this publication meets the minimum
requirements of American National Standard for Information Sciences—Permanence of Paper for Printed Library Materials, ANSI Z39.48-1984.

Manufactured in the United States of America

To Georgann Roche

CONTENTS

ILLUSTRATIONS

ACKNOWLEDGMENTS

This is the best part. My deepest thanks go to the many people who helped transform an idea into the lovely, tangible form of a book. Even across the gap of nearly a century, I discovered during my research, Inez Milholland continues to inspire people. I am deeply obliged to everyone who shared with me their enthusiasm and expertise.

Ace librarians Debra Day and Selina Langford at Western Kentucky University's Helm Library obtained hundreds of items through interlibrary loan without which I would have been unable to complete the book. The staff at all of the archives I visited were helpful and professional, especially Dean Rogers at Vassar College. The Ticonderoga Historical Society let me settle in for a summer to read the diaries and family papers of John E. Milholland, an invaluable resource. John and Olivia Milholland graciously invited me into their home and lent me family papers. John Tepper Marlin, great nephew of Eugen Boissevain, generously volunteered some of the family papers he has collected for his own work about Inez. Kristen Jaconi shared her unpublished paper on Milholland's final trip west. Mona Mulholland of Tamlaghtduff invited me, a strange Yank at her door, to spend the night in her Northern Ireland cottage. Barbara Page let me read her unpublished biographical sketch of Inez. Elizabeth Barnett, director of the Edna St. Vincent Millay Society, granted permission to quote from Millay's sonnet "To Inez Milholland."

Susan Doolittle of the Essex County Historical Society located information about the region and transcribed an 1894 article. Felicia Lassk put me up with class in Boston. Karin Egloff translated letters from French. Claire Jentsch, Patricia Walker, Sandra Weber, and Richard Weigel provided fruitful research tips. Tom Coleco answered questions about the Underground Railroad in the Adirondacks. Bob and Edith Scott of Croton gave me an enlightening tour of the village. Jane R. Bramham, M.D., helped explain pernicious anemia. Katherine Sweatt, Lewis town historian, opened her records. Judith Galamian told me tales of Meadowmount and shared old photographs. George B. Stoneman, M.D., unearthed an old photograph of Good Samaritan Hospital in Los Angeles. Margaret Blanchard once again served as an encouraging mentor.

Jo-Ann Albers, retired director of WKU's School of Journalism and Broadcasting, enthusiastically supported my research agenda, as did Potter College Dean David Lee. I especially want to thank the various committees of the college's Department of Graduates Studies and Research for a generous array of grants that enabled me to visit archives in New York, Washington, D.C., North Carolina, Boston, London, Belfast, and elsewhere.

Lois Rudnick offered astute insights on the complexity of New Women that made the book better. Kathryn Abbott ably checked the manuscript for historical accuracy. Laura Simpson cheerfully helped proofread it. Staff at Indiana University Press shepherded it to publication. I am indebted to their insights but assume responsibility for any errors.

Karen and Brian Delaney provided me with a beautiful setting and energetic company while I edited the manuscript. Jessalee Lumsden Landfried and Mason Rhodes checked several important facts. Samuel Lumsden Landfried provided expert technical support. My sister Laurie "Kayak" Kamuda was always good for a laugh. My parents, Len and Margaret Lumsden, as ever, made me feel that since I was writing this book, it must be good.

INEZ

The Life and Times of Inez Milholland

Introduction

"The full, reliant, audacious way in which they go about"

"No."

No one will talk about votes for women at Vassar College, repeated the portly man whose handlebar mustache drooped below the waddles of his chin. The mere sound of the word irked the young woman standing before this ancient walrus, Vassar president James Monroe Taylor. Inez Milholland was no small personage herself at Vassar in spring 1908: She was president of the junior class, captain of the field hockey team, former star of *Romeo and Juliet* (as the male lead), president of the socialist club, holder of the school shot-put record, bane of the administration, and idol of the student body.

"Why should there not be a lecture on suffrage," she shot back, "if Vassar claims to be a modern institution?"[1] She found it ludicrous to try to keep college women from discussing the seminal question of their generation. The twentieth century already was eight years old, and she was sure the era would go down in history as woman's century.[2] The president remained unmoved. Taylor would not subject his charges to propaganda and would expel Inez if she persisted with her plans to expose students to suffrage.

One May afternoon soon after, Milholland led a line of young women across the lawn leading from Vassar's Main Building to a narrow ribbon of trees and into a modest cemetery adjacent to campus. They settled themselves as if on a picnic on the grass under shade trees in a corner of the graveyard while Milholland helped four older women set up a canary-colored banner amid the tombstones. She believed the message embroidered on it in big black letters held the answer to all of the world's woes: "Come, let us reason together." Then this feminist pied piper introduced the first of the remarkable quartet she had assembled for her defiant suffrage rally.

Harriot Stanton Blatch, Vassar class of 1878, had suckled on the radical ideas of her mother, pioneer suffragist Elizabeth Cady Stanton. Blatch was a fan of the militant British suffragette theatrics and had determined to drag the phlegmatic American suffrage movement into the streets in the spectacular style of their colleagues across the Atlantic. Novelist and economist Charlotte Perkins Gilman lent the gathering a dash of glamour. College women across the nation quoted her *Women and Economics* like the Bible; its call for communal kitchens and childcare offered their ambitious generation a map of the virtually uncharted territory that combined career and family. Gilman also wrote every line in her feminist magazine, *The Forerunner*. Doubtless her listeners also knew Gilman's nightmarish, autobiographical short story, "The Yellow Wall-Paper," detailing the hell of a woman driven mad by marriage. "Work—then love," Gilman privately admonished herself, advice Milholland also struggled to follow.[3] Labor organizer Rose Schneiderman appeared as intense as Gilman seemed cool. The Russian émigré had worked for years in a cap factory for pennies a day. The socialist began challenging male bosses and burly scabs when she was a teenager, persuading thousands of tentative factory workers to follow her onto union picket lines. Her speech on the travails of factory women won the most applause at the cemetery, even though in her typically abrasive manner she called the students spineless. The fourth speaker was fresh-faced Helen Hoy, Vassar '99, one of the squadron of young feminist lawyers Milholland so admired.

Milholland drank in the scene of smart, brave women creatively defying male authority. At least two dozen students had followed Milholland despite the president's stormy edict to punish anyone who attended. Just the day before, Taylor had blasted inklings of radicalism on campus. The audaciousness of Milholland's scheme was magnified by the fact that no suffrage club even existed in Poughkeepsie. Besides the renegade students, ten alumna and two men followed her to the forbidden meeting. Milholland joined them in the bursts of applause that punctuated each speaker's message. No one present, however, was truly aware that the sound heralded the arrival of twentieth-century feminism in the United States.[4]

Not that American women hadn't been fighting for equal rights. When several hundred women had attended the first woman's rights conference in Seneca Falls, New York, in 1848, the lack of the ballot was just one grievance in their laundry list of civil rights denied women. The rare woman who owned a house and earned money for her produce, for instance, lost her property and earnings if she married. If her husband beat her and she divorced him (practically unheard of), she lost her children. Blatch's mother and her indefatigable comrade Susan B. Anthony railed against such injustice. Stanton even penned a sacrilegious *Woman's Bible*. As the most appalling inequities slowly began to topple one by one, women focused on the vote. But Civil War cannons silenced them, and Reconstruction politics cleaved the political alliance between white women and African Americans, whose men at least emerged from the fray clutching the ballot. The split over the Fifteenth Amendment fractured the woman suffrage movement, which shattered totally after Victoria Woodhull picked up its banner and ran for president in 1872, her reputation as "high priestess" of free love wafting around her like cheap perfume.[5] It took nearly two decades for shell-shocked suffragists to regroup as the National American Woman Suffrage Association (NAWSA) in 1890, when only the newly admitted state of Wyoming let women vote. By the time Milholland turned ten years old in 1896, women also voted in Colorado, Utah, and Idaho. The tally remained stuck there on this sunny afternoon when students at the first real college for women had to skulk off to a graveyard to talk about suffrage.[6]

Just a couple of weeks earlier, Blatch had embarked on the nation's first "open air" suffrage campaign. The British import was so called because meetings involved preaching suffrage outdoors on the unpredictable streets. Blatch was accompanied on her upstate trolley tour by Maud Malone, a fervent, feminist librarian who shocked Manhattan when she conducted the nation's first open-air meeting balanced atop a wooden box in Madison Square the previous New Year's Eve.[7] Sensible as their publicity tactics sound today, they threatened the very fabric of society. By planting themselves on public streets, Blatch and Malone challenged deeply inscribed cultural rules that reserved for men the public, political sphere and relegated women to the private, domestic sphere.[8] This divide between the sexes arguably cut deeper than either race or class.[9] The notion of a woman at the polls exploded this neat dichotomy: If women voted, suffrage's many critics guffawed, would men nurse babies?[10] Voting women threatened the family by contaminating women through contact with the vile world, a perpetual fear of middle-class Americans of both sexes.[11] Yet women were swarming into man's world by the 1900s, elbowing into factories, offices, universities, department stores, reform clubs, baseball games, and amusement parks.[12] One keen observer declared women's migration from the private to public sphere marked change "as startling in its way as the abolition of slavery or the coming of the machine age."[13]

So Milholland's illicit little rally quivered with political and cultural portent. The rally helped launch not only the lively last decade of the suffrage movement but also Milholland's rise as its most glamorous and

celebrated messenger. Milholland became an icon of the suffrage movement who symbolized its idealism and influenced its most spectacular
campaigns, most notably the unprecedented picketing of the White
House in 1917. Although her significance nearly a century ago has van-
ished like a ripple in a pond, when prewar Americans beheld Milholland
she seemed to reflect back their highest hopes for the modern, twentieth-
century woman. The luminous warrior for women's rights idolized in the
nation's periodicals symbolized her generation's desire to lead free and
full lives. In the hands of the acolyte press, Milholland's exploits assumed
mythic proportions: going to jail alongside striking shirtwaist workers; charging a drunken mob astride her white horse to make headway for a suffrage
parade; fighting to get a convicted murderer off Death Row; trekking to
the Italian front to cover the war; sailing with Henry Ford to try to stop the
carnage; declaring herself a devotee of free love. Her classic looks—a
mane of dark hair, searching blue-gray eyes, a robust physique—captivated
the press, lurching into its twentieth-century love affair with celebrity.
Her popularity benefited from this trend in the burgeoning print media,
and she proved adept at manipulating the journalistic gaze. Reporters
anointed her the most beautiful suffragist in the land. Men called her a
goddess, an Amazon.

Amazons were a race of female warriors in Greek mythology that caught
the public imagination in the 1910s. Gilman's feminist utopia in *Herland*,
for instance, was populated by an Amazonian tribe of beautiful, peaceful,
and noble women needless of men. Allen Churchill was among Greenwich Village chroniclers who recalled Milholland's "Amazonian beauty."[14]
A typical newspaper account called her the "ideal figure of the typical
American woman."[15] A suitor wrote her, "One only approaches a goddess
with awe and reverence and I have put you on so high a pedestal that I
cannot reach you unless you stoop a little."[16] After witnessing a Milholland speech, even crusty *Evening Post* publisher Oscar Garrison Villard
fell under the spell of the "young goddess."[17] The play between her sex
appeal and the confident way she comported herself in the public sphere—
as comfortable and assertive as any man—conjured a new kind of femininity. Everything about Milholland, in fact, radiated newness, the totem
of modernity. One member of the adulatory press asserted that she symbolized the feminist ideal because she represented "the highest reach of
the 'new freedom,' as she goes riding a spirited steed down the street at the
head of a demonstration, with her eyes flashing, calm, self-confident, but
thoroughly feminine."[18] Always she seemed to be in motion, an apt meta-
phor for her times. The aura of freedom enveloping Milholland made her

the epitome of the "New Woman" who came into her own in the early twentieth century.

Because she was an ideal, interpretations of the New Woman were malleable. Yet all possessed certain innate characteristics: They demanded full engagement with the world and believed gender no impediment to following one's bliss. In contrast, the nineteenth-century Victorian middle-class woman's constricted life was ruled by gender, and she was supposed to live for everyone but herself. The notion that self-fulfillment existed beyond the self-negating "true woman's" parlor was unthinkable.[19] Any inkling of independence constituted the sin of selfishness.

The first generation of New Women that came of age in the 1890s challenged those constrictions. They were the first American women to attend college in significant numbers, and they stayed single at an unprecedented rate.[20] The female institutions they built, such as settlement houses, nurtured both female community and autonomy.[21] They entered the professions and created new ones that addressed women's issues, broadly defined today as social services.[22] As their interest in reform drew them into the supremely male domain of politics, gaining the vote became a high priority. Meaningful work was central to this New Woman's self-image. Work meant more than financial independence, which New Women were keenly aware held the key to escaping marriage and other cultural expectations. Working outside the home was psychologically liberating for middle-class and upper-class white women smothered by over-protectiveness. Jane Addams, an exemplar of this first generation, spoke of being "sickened by advantages" before she broke free of her family and began her life's work at Hull House.[23] Significantly, she chose work that she believed would make the world a better place.

Addams's experience highlights the prominent role economic privilege played in the creation of the New Woman. Millions of working-class women who labored in factories or as domestics in the nineteenth century viewed their monotonous toil as anything but liberating. Racism reduced even further the career options of women of color. Whether physicians or laundresses, however, all women faced sex discrimination on the job and were tainted by the cultural prejudice that working outside the home made them less than ladies. All shared the indignity and injustice of belonging to the allegedly inferior sex. Another commonality among nineteenth-century women, no matter their class or race, was the lack of agency in their lives.

Agency was a defining trait of the second generation of New Women such as Milholland that came of age in the decade before World War I.

Independence was another. These New Women cherished choice and abhorred limits. Even the most elite possessed a dash of the rebel. They determined to make their own decisions about how to live their lives. One fan, Greenwich Village intellectual Randolph Bourne, enthused, "[T]he full, reliant, audacious way in which they go about makes you wonder if the new woman isn't to be a very splendid sort of person."[24] These qualities were constant among the variations of the New Woman in the 1910s, linking such diverse individuals as conservative suffrage leader Carrie Chapman Catt, union organizer Elizabeth "Rebel Girl" Gurley Flynn, African American journalist Ida Wells-Barnett, and glamorous Inez Milholland, whose advocacy of socialism and free love perched her at the radical end of the New Woman spectrum.

Scholars' analyses underscore the decade's many stripes of New Woman in image and reality. Lois Rudnick described the Progressive New Woman, the Literary New Woman, and the Radical New Woman. Martha Banta said mass-media images of New Women evolved from three types of the turn-of-the-century ideal "American Girl": the Beautiful Charmer, the New England Woman, and the Outdoors Pal. Leila Rupp categorized New Women in media images as "the 'charity girl,' the flapper, the Greenwich Village bohemian, the Androgyne, the career woman, the Mythic Mannish Lesbian." Martha Patterson discussed the aspirations of the "New Negro Woman," while Elizabeth Ammons analyzed how racism limited the options of Asian and African American New Women. Kathy Peiss admired the feisty working-class variant of the New Woman, and Marjorie Spruill Wheeler pondered the blend of conservatism and rebellion in southern New Women.[25] The quality that united the broad range of individuals who called themselves New Women was a determination to create selves that relied not on dusty rules but on their richly imagined vision for the future.

The move from the Victorian woman's self-sacrifice to the New Woman's self-realization in the 1910s was a critical step in the evolution of twentieth-century women. Nancy Cott says these New Women were the first Americans to call themselves feminists.[26] Christine Stansell calls Milholland's generation of New Women "icons of modernity," the era's sweeping call for cultural freedoms that signified the nation's break with Victorianism and the succession of twentieth-century sensibilities.[27] Not the least of New Women's qualities was playfulness, what Lois Banner called "a desire for pleasure that flew in the face of Victorian canons of duty and submissiveness."[28] These New Women clamored for "feminine individualism," unheard-of a generation earlier. "The young woman of today is supplementing a certain old-fashioned word, *duty*, by two other words," wrote a Milholland contemporary, "'to myself.'"[29]

Milholland would have agreed with a hearty laugh that this characterization fit her. She loved to laugh and flirt. Like other New Women, she placed high priority on creating a rewarding personal life. The more radical New Women such as Milholland envisioned a new sexual politics that they struggled to put into practice. They sought a more equitable economic and social order in which everyone could realize their potential. Much of their agenda remains relevant. "Their concerns," Rudnick observed, "led them to reimagine society and the state and to raise questions feminists are still grappling with."[30] New Women's quest for self-fulfillment mattered because it triggered cultural tremors in four key sectors of American society: education, work, politics, and sex.[31]

By the 1910s, Inez Milholland—Vassar graduate, lawyer, suffragist, libertine—personified the popular image of this willful, shirtwaisted foremother of the 1960s women's liberationists. It was Inez Milholland whom many Americans imagined when talk turned, as it inevitably did, to the New Woman. An examination of her life illuminates this important chapter of American feminism. Her life intrigues in part because the joys and challenges encountered by the "most famous feminist of her day" make vivid what was arguably American women's most exciting decade. This New Woman's life is instructive because it reflects the values and goals of the cadre of "restless women" eager to experience all life had to offer celebrated by lawyer Elinor Byrns in 1916: "I believe that we restless women here in New York this minute . . . are having a better time than any women in the world ever had before."[32] The restless Milholland's liberal views on diverse issues made her the quintessential symbol of the radical strain of New Woman: She advocated gender equity, birth control, sexual fulfillment, labor unions, socialism, pacifism, freedom of expression; she opposed war, censorship, all forms of sex and race discrimination, corporate greed, and capital punishment.

Milholland's life also reveals much about the complexities of New Women. Casting off cultural expectations proved daunting and constructing new identities could be confusing.[33] Well-entrenched social, economic, and political restrictions on women conspired against their success. New Women themselves had internalized restrictive stereotypes about gender. Cautionary tales abounded: New Women portrayed in contemporary theatre and fiction, for example, often were lonely, punished, or committed suicide.[34] Detractors decried their ego and condemned them as socially deviant.[35] Asserting their sexuality proved tricky in a society awash in sexual double standards for women and men. Their vaunted independence could be dearly won or more illusionary than portrayed by the mass media. Although they prided themselves on their empowerment, New Women functioned in a world dominated by men. Compromise was sometimes an unavoidable survival tool. The fact that the elite Milholland—white, wealthy, well-educated, professional, heterosexual—came to symbolize the ideal New Woman highlights the exclusionary nature of the dominant image popularized by the mass media.

Milholland's uniqueness—notably her unprecedented ability to make votes for American women look and sound exciting and glamorous—makes her a particularly fascinating case study. This quintessential New Woman also was a distinct individual. Contradictions between her public persona and private self are revelatory. The socialist-feminist savored sipping champagne in society ballrooms surrounded by male admirers. More than most New Women, she struggled to balance her hedonism with her sense of social responsibility. Neither was Milholland always the free spirit glorified in the press. The public never knew that the Amazon so often flashing a confident grin at them from newspaper photographs feared she was a failure. Reporters never encountered Milholland's dark moods and self-doubt and overlooked her self-indulgence. She hid her physical frailty, which embarrassed the young beauty so proud of her Amazonian image. Private papers reveal she was not an Amazon but a mere woman, an infinitely more interesting creature. She was, however, indisputably a New Woman, determined to forge a full life that mattered. Her example inspired countless others. In the 1910s, Americans found themselves drawn to Milholland's passion, courage, and beauty like metal filings to a magnet.

Childhood

*"He sings to the wide world,
she to her nest"*

1

An inkling of six-year-old Inez's destiny as champion of the underdog surfaced one day as she played in Madison Square, the fashionable oasis of greenery at the lively junction of Twenty-third Street, Fifth Avenue, and Broadway where the Milhollands moved after her father's career took off. A band of immigrant children that had roamed up from the Lower East Side gathered around Inez. Her rich playmates announced they would not play with tenement children. "All right for you," Inez replied, as her bemused nanny looked on. "You don't have to play with me." Then she skipped off with her new friends.[1]

Inez's mother liked to tell this story in an exasperated tone that failed to hide her pride in her daughter's independence and kindness. Inez inherited her affinity for the underdog from her father, the biggest influence upon her life. John Elmer Milholland was a contradictory crusader who rose from his birth in a mountain shack to become an international entrepreneur. Inez heard the tale many times: Her grandfather immigrated to America in the 1840s from an emerald slice of undulating Northern Ireland townland called Tamlaghtduff. John Mulholland, born on the summer solstice in 1819, undoubtedly learned hard lessons in prejudice because his father was Protestant and his mother Catholic. John, his three brothers, and three sisters were raised as Protestants but had many Catholic relatives in the vicinity of their rented thatched-roof stone cottage.[2] The seven-acre farm kept the smallholders, near the bottom of Ulster's highly stratified social pyramid, too busy to worry much about religion.[3] Despite their hard work, John Mulholland knew he never would own land. He could read, unlike most Ulstermen, and had left Ulster at least once, crossing to Scotland to make extra money during its harvest.[4] America's natural rights rhetoric beckoned such ambitious, bright young men. More than a third of immigrants to the United States in the 1820s were Irish, and the exodus nearly quadrupled in the 1830s, even before the great potato famine.[5] Twenty-two-year-old John Mulholland followed in 1841.[6]

The four pounds he scraped together for his fare bought him a bed along a triple tier of bunks lining the innards of a wooden sailing ship that Herman Melville, who made the trip in 1839, likened to dog kennels.[7] Mulholland settled in the upstate New York hamlet of Lewis on the fringe of the wild Adirondack Mountains.[8] He signed on as a laborer for fellow Londonderry natives Alexander and Robert Moore, who in 1828 had realized every immigrant's ambition, when for one hundred dollars they bought their own fifty-acre farm.[9] Mulholland married the widowed Robert's daughter, Mary Ann, and their first child, Mary, arrived in 1847, followed the next year by Emily Ann. When the couple gained title to their own hundred acres in 1854, John signed the deed "John Milholland," signaling his change of identity from Ulsterman to American.[10] Crops and children multiplied. The one-room red schoolhouse the children attended down the dirt road housed their parents' desire for their children to live an even better life.[11] Ulster's senseless religious prejudice echoing in his ears, John stood firmly with the rest of the county in the North's swelling abolitionist ranks, a link in the Underground Railroad. Abraham Lincoln swept the county in 1860, the year the couple's sixth child, John Elmer Milholland, was born.[12]

Their American dream seemed nearly realized when a kerosene lantern tipped over and burned down the house, a common hazard of pioneer life. A visiting neighbor scooped sleeping three-year-old John out of his bed and rushed him to safety, but seventeen-year-old Mary and her mother became trapped by the flames. The children raced to a neighbor's home where they spent the horrible night. Several days later, the toddler joined the funeral procession to the Congregational Church, whose bell tolled the ages of his mother and sister as a long line of people filed by.[13]

The tragedy set off a series of events that lifted John Elmer Milholland into a world of ideas and money inconceivable to his parents, a world that allowed his daughter Inez to grow up amid privilege and power. With a hardscrabble pioneer's resolve, John's father wasted no time erecting a gray clapboard house on the ashes of the first. Overnight, fifteen-year-old Emily became woman of the house and a second mother to young John. He loved the farm, especially the top of a big hill from which he could see Lake Champlain and dream of what lay beyond.[14] His father, however, was unable to keep his farm or family together. When he sold the farm in 1869, he left behind Fred, aged fourteen, as an apprentice printer for the *Elizabethtown Post*, probably immensely pleased his oldest son was learning a trade.[15]

Emily, twenty, and Martha, seventeen, like most nineteenth-century women, faced duller prospects.[16] They remained in Elizabethtown, working as live-in maids for a judge. Eleven-year-old Alice's whereabouts are unrecorded. Milholland took his namesake back to Tamlaghtduff for two years. When they returned to America,[17] the siblings were reunited in crowded Paterson, New Jersey, where their father opened a confectioner's shop that soon expanded into a grocery store where John E. worked after school.[18] He proved a precocious student at Paterson High School, praised for his speaking and writing skills, and graduated with a dozen other students in 1878. The Milholland family joined the local Presbyterian church, whose Calvinist creed appealed to the ambitious but resourceless teen.[19] Even more critical to Milholland's future, a powerful mentor took notice of him.

Congressman William Walter Phelps was the scion of local New Jersey gentry, and his estate stretched from Hackensack to the Hudson River. He held degrees from Yale and Columbia University Law School but valued ability over pedigree. As Phelps did for other promising boys from his district, he may have helped pay for John to begin college.[20] After a year of boning up on the classics, John passed the entrance exam for New York University, the first Milholland to attend college. Although one of the ablest debaters on campus, he collapsed from overwork and dropped out after his second year.[21] He apparently worked for local newspapers for the next couple of years to pay off college debts before buying the *Ticonderoga Sentinel* and moving back to the Adirondacks. As he lacked the capital to make such a purchase, Phelps likely financed the venture.[22] "[A]n Essex County boy takes the helm," wrote publisher R. R. Stevenson upon turning over his Republican weekly to Milholland. "He is a young man of ability, backed up with energy which is so essential. He has the 'push' in him and has come here to stay."[23]

The roots of Inez Milholland's individualism can be discerned in her father's early editorials. They reveal the maverick political streak that became the hallmark of his life. The days of blind party fealty were over, he declared in his first editorial: "This is simply the result of the growth and dominance of Individualism—the outcome of our great thinking age."[24] The moralistic Milholland campaigned for whipping wife beaters and locking up drunks and brawlers. He also issued some of the earliest calls to preserve the Adirondack wilderness and restore crumbling Fort Ticonderoga.[25]

Not all of the energies of the tall, handsome newspaperman with a dashing mustache were devoted to journalism. He met a raven-haired Scottish beauty in Jersey City the previous winter. After Jean Torry's father drowned off a Boston pier, her mother remarried, and the family ended up in Jersey City. The young editor intrigued the cultured Jean enough for her to invite him to call.[26] Soon after, at the end of a sermon on marriage they heard at the Broadway Tabernacle, Milholland blurted out a proposal. Two days later, March 11, 1884, the couple married. The newlyweds splurged on a carriage ride to Grand Central Station to catch the Montrealer Express, so excited they forgot to eat dinner. Barely had the newlyweds settled into Ticonderoga, however, than Milholland sold the *Sentinel* for triple what he paid for it and, a recommendation letter from Phelps in hand, landed a job as a political writer for the *New York Tribune*.[27] Whitelaw Reid's aggressively Republican *New York Tribune* served as the city's "Great Moral Organ" during the turbulent Gilded Age, when newspapers were synonymous with party politics. Milholland's flair for the era's high-spirited prose made him a natural as the *Tribune*'s chief editorial writer, and he jockeyed into position as Reid's right-hand man on the business end of the paper and in politics. Both were righteous Presbyterians but otherwise made an odd couple: Egalitarian Milholland expected the party of Lincoln to promote civil rights for blacks; Reid was elitist and racist. Both, however, were optimists who believed economic growth resulted in social good.[28] The job moved Milholland into national Republican circles, where he helped Reid choreograph candidates and campaigns.

Inez's birth on August 6, 1886, thrilled her parents. Another daughter, Vida, followed on January 17, 1888. The little girls would fly out the door to throw their arms around their father's neck on his nightly return from Manhattan to the family's modest bungalow at 179 Bainbridge Street, a commute eased by the recent completion of the Brooklyn Bridge.[29] But his wife and daughters' charms could not compete with the adrenalin of Manhattan politics and journalism. One Christmas Eve, John abandoned Jean and the girls to race back into Manhattan.[30] He moved his prospering family to more capacious quarters at bustling Madison Square in 1892, a few months before the birth of John Angus Milholland, nicknamed Jack. In a five-minute stroll from home, the Milhollands could ogle jewelry at Tiffany's, browse among bestsellers such as *Quo Vadis* at Brentano's, indulge in fantasy at F.A.O. Schwarz Toy Bazaar, or clap for the elephants at the circus at Madison Square Gardens. They shopped for dresses along Fifth Avenue at Gimbel Brothers, Siegel Cooper Co., and the twenty-six-acre R. H. Macy & Co., early temples to burgeoning twentieth-century consumerism.[31] The Milhollands' growing fondness for middle-class indulgences did not replace church as the center of their family life. Inez received her own child-sized Bible as soon as she could read. The children attended nearby Madison Square Presbyterian Church presided over

Childhood photograph of Inez, left, and Vida Milholland.
Courtesy of John Tepper Marlin.

by Rev. Charles H. Parkhurst, president of the new Society for the Prevention of Crime. John Milholland, a church deacon, admired the crusading pastor's secular preaching against gambling, prostitution, and city officials who looked the other way, although detractors joked that Parkhurst wanted to run Manhattan like a Sunday school.[32]

Inez was weaned on talk about reform, as her father played an active role in the wave of reform sentiment rolling across the nation. Parkhurst was just one reformer who visited the Milholland home, where Inez absorbed the example of his successful tirades against the powerful. Her father's political career had received a boost when Republican Benjamin Harrison moved into the White House in 1889. Publisher Reid advised his friend the president, another pious Presbyterian, to appoint Milholland chief inspector of immigration for the Port of New York.[33] When Harrison appointed Reid ambassador to France, Reid left Milholland in charge of tough negotiations with the New York Typographical Union Number Six, which Reid had warred with for fifteen years.[34] Settling the strife became imperative when Reid emerged as a contender for the 1892 vice presidential nomination.[35] Milholland played an instrumental role in securing Reid's nomination by producing the leaders of Big Six at the GOP convention in Minneapolis, where they dramatically announced the union had settled with the *Tribune*.[36] As a reward for his savvy political choreography, Milholland was named an assistant secretary of the National Republican Committee.[37] His political star seemed to be rising, but Milholland fared less well in city politics. Although in coming years Inez's rebellious streak perplexed her father, he had to look no farther for its seeds than his own example as an ebullient rabble-rouser.

Within weeks after moving into Manhattan, he brashly tried to take over the Eleventh Assembly District from conservative GOP stalwarts. Although Milholland enjoyed a loyal local following, he had provoked powerful enemies.[38] He not only failed but also was forced to resign his immigration post.[39] His hubris and inability to compromise proved a fatal political flaw. He further sabotaged his political future when he created a renegade city Republican committee, reigning for a short, shining season in 1894 as the "young Napoleon of ward politics."[40] "Fellow rebels, traitors, revolters, dissensionists," a beaming Milholland addressed fourteen hundred "Milhollandites" who squeezed into Cooper Union for an organizing rally. Jean looked on supportively from a section near the podium from which she and a dozen other women watched the proceedings, her presence in this male enclave an indication of her willingness to test the limits of woman's place.[41] Milholland's organization, however, disbanded within months after state GOP boss Thomas Platt backed the old guard.[42] Although Platt mingled among guests the next month when Rev. Parkhurst christened Inez, Vida, and Jack at home on the Milhollands' tenth wedding anniversary, Milholland's political career was over.[43] The hole in anti-machine politics remained gaping until an equally brash Theodore Roosevelt returned to the city the next year.[44] While Police Commissioner Roosevelt's exploits filled the headlines, Milholland suffered a final political setback when William McKinley's managers named a conservative to the Republican National Executive Committee in 1896 instead of Milholland, even though he had organized the first club supporting McKinley's presidential candidacy. Milholland forever resented the twist in the political fortunes between himself and Roosevelt, the assassinated McKinley's successor to the White House. "My hold was firmer; my following larger," he said of Roosevelt when he looked back at the 1890s from middle age, memory inflating his political importance. "My prospects far brighter."[45]

In contrast to John's politicking, Jean's vocation was her children, and she directed her considerable energy to the domestic sphere. "'He sings to the wide world, she to her nest,' says the poet" she once wrote, "and as one who has enjoyed the latter privilege, I fully believe it is the better part."[46] For all her domesticity, however, Jean showed signs she had broken with the asphyxiating Victorian creed that trapped middle-class women in their homes. Jean was ambitious for her daughters. Inez and Vida enrolled in the private Comstock School, and Jean expected them to have some sort of career, still suspect for girls.[47] Notwithstanding Queen Victoria, completing her half-century of rule over the British Empire the year Inez was born, women held precious little power or freedom in the late nineteenth century. Just weeks after Inez's birth, in fact, suffragists protested the dedication of the nearby Statue of Liberty as mocking women's lack of civil rights.[48] Jean quietly supported votes for women; she probably had been too preoccupied with five-month-old Inez, however, to pay much attention when woman suffrage first came up for a vote in the U.S. Senate in 1887. It lost 16 to 34, harbinger of the long road ahead.

Such serious matters did not yet preoccupy Inez. Always tall for her age, "Nan," as her family called her, was a natural leader, with plump Vida, nicknamed "Tub," usually trailing a few steps behind her. Her mother believed in the novel notion that fresh air and freedom benefited girls as well as boys, so Inez and Vida roamed the Lake Champlain beach where they summered barefoot in plain frocks and shaggy tam o'shanters.[49] Their mother ignored the stares they drew, more evidence that this content housewife was no slave to convention and was quietly nurturing her daughters' independence.

John Milholland refocused on business pursuits he began before his bitter political defeat. He headed a pneumatic mail tubes business, encouraged by one of Milholland's influential friends from the Harrison administration, former postmaster general John Wanamaker. Pneumatic mail tubes were the e-mail of the turn of the century. *Harper's Weekly* predicted tubes would make a greater impact on the twentieth century

John and Jean Milholland at a resort in Lakewood, N.J., 1909.
Courtesy of Ticonderoga Historical Society.

than trolley cars; others said the underground tubes' "instantaneous" delivery made them as revolutionary as the telephone.[50] The technology used vacuums to propel metal canisters eight inches in diameter and two feet long along tubes installed between post office branches beneath city streets increasingly clogged by cars.[51] Wanamaker department store clerks sent money to cash rooms through twenty miles of tubes connecting 250 stations.[52] As postmaster general, Wanamaker had authorized installation of the first American mail tubes in Philadelphia, sure they would revolutionize communication.[53]

The tubes may not have revolutionized the mail, but they profoundly changed Inez's life. Her father's firm broke ground for New York's first pneumatic mail tubes line at the corner of Park Row and Beekman Street on August 2, 1897.[54] The company built the lines and ran the machinery, making money by renting use of the system to its sole customer, the United States Post Office. The inaugural run in October featured the Milholland family Bible wrapped in an American flag that zipped into the Produce Exchange forty seconds after John sent it from the central post—versus the seventeen minutes it took a messenger boy to make the trip.[55] Over the next few years, Inez, Vida, and Jack watched wide-eyed at official openings of new spurs as their father sent kittens, puppies, and even a bowl of six goldfish whooshing along the tubes.[56] Eventually, fifty-four miles of mail tubes in New York City handled more than five million letters daily, about a quarter of the total load.[57] Milholland expanded operations to Boston, Philadelphia, St. Louis, Chicago, and Europe. By the turn of the century, Milholland was worth a half million dollars—a pittance to a Rockefeller but, in the days before graduated income taxes, still making Inez and her siblings richer than 99 percent of all Americans.[58]

Her father made two decisions on how to spend his new wealth that symbolized the basic contradiction in his nature: his need to do good versus his desire to live well. Inez inherited both traits. In 1898 he bought back the family farm, gradually accumulating four thousand Adirondack acres around Mt. Discovery that he called Meadowmount.[59] His dream was to someday use the property to help the poor. Over the next decade, he replaced the gray house his father built with a green cottage and added six more, plus stables, barns, and offices. Ducks quacked and geese honked on the two-acre trout pond; horses, a donkey, cattle, and sheep grazed in the meadow; chickens scratched in the barnyard; and a couple of drooling St. Bernards chased off strangers. Inez loved all of the animals. Her father even snaked some five miles of eight-foot-high fencing around Mt. Discovery and filled it with deer, elk, and a moose.[60] Eventually, he built the thirty-six room, green-and-white "Big House" on a bluff that backed up to the base of the mountain. Milholland likened his sojourns to Meadowmount to Christ's pilgrimages in the wilderness. "The mountains mean so much to me in things spiritual," he mused atop his favorite boyhood hill, which he named Mt. Jacob.[61] He often spent the night alone at the summit, praying until the sun rose before the stone altar he erected. "I could stay and meditate week in and week out," he wrote. "No place just like it—nowhere I go."[62]

But go he did. John seemed incapable of staying still, another inherited trait that cursed as well as blessed Inez. No sooner did her father buy Meadowmount than the Milhollands moved to London. His growing pneumatic tube business enabled restless John and Jean to fulfill their dream of living in Europe, where he hoped to expand operations.[63] They wanted to expose their children to culture and tolerance they found lacking in the United States.[64] The Spanish-American War appalled them, as did the racially chauvinist call for manifest destiny.

The fin de siècle preoccupation with the potential for rebirth in the new century also stoked the Milhollands' desire to begin a new life overseas. Besides revealing their Victorian reverence for history, their desire said something about the value the Milhollands placed on culture that they moved to England while the rest of the country focused on the Wild West. London represented a life of the mind, an opportunity to bathe their senses in great art, literature, and history less revered in increasingly materialistic America. The Milhollands wanted to impress upon their children that intellectual and cultural pursuits, not the acquisition of money, were worthy goals in life. Inez had just turned thirteen when the family sailed aboard the *Lucania* on August 12, 1899, launching a lifelong pattern of motion. Before settling into London life, the family undertook the obligatory grand tour of Europe, following in the footsteps of Henry James's "Daisy Miller." They touched down in Edinborough, Paris, Berlin, Budapest, Antwerp, and Vienna before settling into a four-story townhouse within hailing distance of Kensington Palace just as the new century snapped open like an English Christmas cracker.[65]

Inez's father built this 34-room mansion, "The Big House," at Meadowmount, the family's 1,600-acre estate, on the site of the farm where he was born in Lewis, N.Y. *Courtesy of Meadowmount School of Music.*

London

"Hard to find a more interesting family"

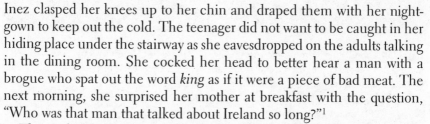

Inez clasped her knees up to her chin and draped them with her night-gown to keep out the cold. The teenager did not want to be caught in her hiding place under the stairway as she eavesdropped on the adults talking in the dining room. She cocked her head to better hear a man with a brogue who spat out the word *king* as if it were a piece of bad meat. The next morning, she surprised her mother at breakfast with the question, "Who was that man that talked about Ireland so long?"[1]

The six heady years Inez spent in London pushed her politically and socially beyond her American peers. "Because of her father's interest in the underdog our house was always full of leaders of unpopular causes," her mother recalled.[2] Bureaucrats, diplomats, educators, and reformers of all races made up the guest lists at the Milhollands' elaborate dinner parties at 4 Prince of Wales Terrace, a cul-de-sac off fashionable Kensington High Street across from Hyde Park and within sight of the golden gates at Kensington Palace. The four-story, white stone townhouse quickly earned a reputation as a "hotbed of humanitarianism."[3] Inez saw dissenters as heroes, despite her privileged upbringing, through the prism of the bombastic father she idolized. John vocally opposed the Boer War, once scandalizing his dinner hosts by pointedly refusing to toast a British victory over the Boers.[4] One evening Inez listened in as guests debated her father's idealistic scheme for a global string of clubs to fight war and racism. The short-lived pacifist International Union that John co-founded with radical publisher William Stead anticipated the United Nations by a half century.[5]

Politics was only one of myriad diversions at the terrace. The Milhollands were ardent Gilbert and Sullivan fans who never missed a production of *Pirates of Penzance*.[6] The children delighted in *The Mikado* at the Savoy Theatre and *Twelfth Night*, but only Inez was allowed to attend the

Four-story town home in London at 4 Prince of Wales Terrace, where young Inez and her family moved in 1899. *Courtesy of The Royal Borough of Kensington & Chelsea Libraries and Arts Service.*

darker *Hamlet* with her parents.[7] At home, where several servants kept the household running smoothly, the family played charades, checkers, chess, and wildly competitive rounds of ping-pong, the new vogue in games. Inez could hold her own boxing with her brother, her height compensating for his technique. The family often gathered to sing songs around Jean, who knew all of the Scottish ballads, and the Milhollands rang in every New Year by holding hands and belting out chorus after chorus of "Auld Lang Syne."[8]

Her London studies were instrumental in inclining Inez to dedicate her life to working for social justice. Kensington High School for Girls, just a few blocks from the terrace, was the oldest in a string of thirty-eight private girls' schools. The Girls Public Day School Trust was created in the 1870s by a tenacious quartet of women who believed its charges should be educated "not as graceful playthings or useful drudges, but as the possessors of a power which society must, at its peril, teach them to use for its benefit." The nondenominational school ignored class distinctions, so daughters of shopkeepers took lessons alongside daughters of earls.[9] Academics were more rigorous than in New York, and Inez struggled to maintain Ds her first semester. Literature was her favorite subject. "I love it!" she gushed.[10] The avid reader stole hours from her studies lost in the books that lined her parents' library. She devoured the works of Edmund Burke. "[O]nce I am in one of the 'library, etc.' books I cannot stop, so it is yourself to blame and not I," she chided her father, "for having such interesting books."[11]

Outside the classroom, Inez learned to play tennis, a lifelong passion, and competed in track. Inez played Theseus and Vida played Helena in the school production of *A Midsummer Night's Dream*. Both girls sang in the choir, performing once for the Prince of Wales.[12] Service to the poor was part of the curriculum. Inez caught an early glimpse of poverty volunteering at a soup kitchen with the school. She credited the experience with stirring her feminist inklings by forging in her mind the first link between financial independence and equal rights for women.[13]

Inez's mother also nurtured her social conscience. Jean started a branch of the International Sunshine Society, in which Inez, Vida, and their young club mates performed good deeds.[14] The lessons in charity at home and school rubbed off. One afternoon, after Inez failed to return home, her worried family finally found her helping a Salvation Army volunteer at Charing Cross.[15] Jean subscribed to the relatively new notion that childhood required a mother's constant attentiveness to ensure that youngsters became productive adults. Jean shepherded her adolescents, a new term, with enriching excursions to museums and concerts, morally uplifting charitable activities, exercise outdoors, and good schools.[16] As strong-willed as her husband, Jean gave Inez a role model for challenging male authority. She called suffrage the most critical demand of the "New Woman Movement" that was crystallizing in the United States as Inez came of age in London.[17] Jean also passed on her sense of fun. She liked gossip and dancing. Beautiful and chic, she showed Inez the power of style. More importantly, Inez's dignified mother also continued to display a healthy disregard for convention amid London society. She ignored, for instance, the gasps of London friends shocked that Inez and Vida galloped their horses astride instead of sedately riding sidesaddle along Hyde Park's Rotten Row.[18] The Milhollands' American sensibilities also prized qualities such as independence and resourcefulness in their children. That independence also could be irksome, as when Inez refused to be presented at the British court, ignoring her mother's entreaties that all of her friends' daughters would be presented. "Pooh! Why should she kiss a king's hand?" her mother recalled. "She wouldn't be seen with a king, she would say, and dash off to some radical meeting."[19]

Jean and John shared their enthusiasm for new ideas with the children. They extended an invitation to tea to African American feminist Mary Church Terrell as soon as they heard the educator was in town, for instance, an invitation that also demonstrated their unusual commitment to racial and sexual equality. Terrell gave the "strikingly handsome" sixteen-year-old Inez and her family a first-hand account of the International Congress of Women she had just attended in Berlin, giving Inez a glimpse into the excitement and commitment of the mushrooming worldwide woman's movement. Terrell recalled, "It would have been hard to find a more interesting family than Mr. Milholland's."[20]

One interesting but well-hidden fact about the Milhollands was their precarious finances. On paper John appeared to be close to a millionaire, but in reality he constantly dodged loan deadlines and used his considerable pile of tube stocks to pay off debts despite their dubious value.[21] His tube stocks' inflated value hinged upon their anticipated sale to the United States post office, which rented the mail tube systems, and their official adoption by Parliament and other European governments. Politics and changing technology conspired against sealing the sales. Money woes strained his marriage. "I haven't felt this poor since I lived in Brooklyn," Jean fretted after a 1903 setback.[22] Yet the family's lavish lifestyle seemed unaffected despite Jean's frequent talk of economizing. John, however, complained all his life that business was a "prison" as he scrambled to stay solvent.[23] One of his biggest struggles was to reconcile Christianity with business. He observed, "To take the Golden Rule with you into everyday trading and bargaining is not easy."[24] He still dreamed of converting Meadowmount into a center for training the poor and degenerate in farming and worship.[25] He had befriended Salvation Army "General" William Booth. The seventy-five-year-old, biblically bearded former Methodist minister's army of street evangelists ran soup kitchens and sent out brass bands to attract converts. John Milholland hoped to replicate Booth's experiment at Hadleigh, where several hundred ex-convicts, homeless, and alcoholic men tended pastures and fruit trees on three thousand acres on a Thames River estuary.[26] The two fervent men immediately clicked and ended their meeting by dropping to their knees to pray together.[27]

The Meadowmount experiment never happened, one of a string of altruistic Milholland dreams that never materialized. "How I hate myself," he scribbled in 1904.[28] He chided himself for his anger, greed, and impatience. His wife and children saw more flashes of his righteous temper as they grew older. Even he admitted he was a "terror to live with."[29] The teens began to challenge their freedom-spouting father's personally rigid code of conduct. Besides attending Emperors Gate Presbyterian Church Sunday mornings, for instance, the family studied the Bible for hours in the evening, a ritual that Inez, who also taught Sunday school, especially chafed against.[30] John's generosity helped Inez sometimes overlook what she called his "bad habit of thinking the world can't go round without his advice."[31] But as she grew older, they clashed more. One visitor described the Milholland household as a battlefield save for "an inexhaustible flow of Irish wit and laughter in which all wounds would be frequently washed."[32] Another huge stress upon family life was John's frequent, extended separations from home. Business kept him in New York for up to six months at a time, and he felt compelled to battle political oppression wherever it sprouted. He rang in the new century at The Hague, trying to muster support for the Boers. Alone in Kensington on January 1, 1900, Jean gathered her rambunctious brood around her on her bed and unsuccessfully tried to impress upon them the solemn significance of the date.[33]

Much of the teenaged Inez's relationship with her dashing but demanding father unfolded in letters. She sent him riddles and reminded him to bring home American treats such as apples and the humor magazines *Life* and *Puck*. "It's getting pretty near Christmas you know, and not a word of coming over," one plaintive missive began. For weeks at a time, every Wednesday and Saturday, when the big liners arrived from New York, the children crossed their fingers John would cross the threshold and join them to share the traditional plum pudding. Another Christmas Eve, she wrote, "[W]e expected you would 'surprise' us up to the last moment."[34] Her father's distance surely affected the daughter who so wanted to please him with her cheery accounts of school activities and grades. The family usually managed to squeeze a couple weeks together at Meadowmount, either for Fourth of July baseball and fireworks or in late August before school resumed in London. But the farm became another source of family friction.

Neither Jean nor her worldly daughters found Meadowmount as charming as did her nostalgic husband, although Inez loved the mountains and animals.[35] Jean and the girls did not get along with John's provincial siblings, who summered there. Jean believed they mooched off their generous brother, and she thought he wasted time and energy on the remote farm. Family feuds blew in as unpredictably as mountain showers.[36] John began to spend increasingly large chunks of time alone at Meadowmount, reviving himself in the farm's earthy tasks.[37] John's evangelism more than Meadowmount estranged him from the rest of the family. Innumerable times over the years, he prayed on his knees until daylight for divine help with his latest financial crisis or "life battle against sin."[38] Immediately after consummating one six-figure deal, he took the night train north and climbed little Mt. Jacob to thank God for blessing "poor, wicked, unworthy John E. Milholland."[39]

The windfall enabled him to accelerate his lifelong ambition to fight racism, an almost unheard-of cause among whites at the time. John Milholland's courageous civil rights efforts are the most significant accomplishment of his life. Initially a Booker T. Washington supporter, Milholland came to believe the "Wizard of Tuskegee" too accommodating. In 1903 Milholland created a virtual one-man entity called the Constitution League that campaigned against the onerous new "Jim Crow" laws that codified segregation.[40] The league's combative approach in the courts and media served as the model for the National Association for the Advancement of Colored People.[41] Given her father's reverence for constitutional rights, it is no surprise John Milholland's daughter grew up to fight for a constitutional amendment to grant women the vote. He offered her a role model for fighting injustice in the league's most famous battle, when it challenged the discharge without honor of a battalion of 167 black soldiers stationed at Brownsville, Texas.[42] The league's investigation failed to reverse the decision, but the Brownsville Affair sparked nationwide debate on race.[43] Such crusades, however, ate up Milholland's time and money.

Other factors also may have strained the Milholland marriage. John worked closely with New York race reformer Mary White Ovington over several years.[44] They met for lunch and tea and, Ovington's biographer speculates, lovemaking.[45] His diary implies Milholland struggled against infidelity: When he climbed Mt. Jacob on his forty-fifth birthday, he prayed for love to conquer sensuality.[46] Back at Meadowmount two weeks later, he recorded, "I prayed for grace to subdue the flesh, the sins that so easily beset me." A few days later found him again on his knees, asking God, "To purify my filthy imagination, to subdue sensuality, to make Sense subject to Soul."[47] Whether or not the two zealots became lovers, John and Jean's tempestuous marriage continued. Their bond is apparent in Jean's 1903 plea to her absent husband that they abandon the London highlife for a simpler life together: "I want to be with you to fight it out together. . . . We never were so happy as when we had none."[48] More than twenty years after marrying, in between days of quarrels and stony silence, John and Jean could still enjoy a passionate tryst uniting "brain, heart and body in conjugal relations."[49]

Inez undoubtedly inherited her parents' passion; she enjoyed sex and the power of the role of seductress. As soon as she hit adolescence, men began buzzing around her like bees around honeysuckle. An early admirer was thirtyish Guglielmo Marconi, inventor of wireless telegraphy. As a youth in 1895, he scored a coup over scientists in laboratories around the world when he transmitted the first message without wires on his father's Bologna estate. "Billy" became a close family friend after meeting Jean and the children aboard the *Lucania* while crossing from New York to London in October 1903. They became engrossed in Marconi's shipboard experiments; at one point he was able to transmit signals to both North America and Europe. When the ship was in the mid-Atlantic, Jean and the children discovered a cheerful "Marconi-gram" from John back in New York posted on the ship's bulletin board, supposedly the first wireless message ever received by a passenger. Inez said they felt like the ship's wireless was their own "special property."[50]

Marconi, who routinely lost his heart to beautiful young women, became a frequent caller at 4 Prince of Wales Terrace. He enjoyed explaining the intricacies of his latest invention to his apt audience—swearing them to secrecy—and the girls thrilled at his promise to show them some radium.[51] Although Inez was only seventeen, Marconi proposed marriage. The engagement seems to have been fairly whimsical, as the next summer, Marconi fell in love with a nineteen-year-old Irish baroness and broke off the engagement. "My heart isn't broken," Inez said when she learned he was marrying Beatrice O'Brien. Although she couldn't resist sniping to Vida that Beatrice looked like a "dinky doo" in her wedding photograph, Inez and Marconi maintained a lifelong friendship, and he would play a pivotal role at more than one milestone in her life. Years later, he lamented they never married.[52]

More suitors followed, but the modern Milhollands wanted sheepskins, not trousseaus, for their daughters.[53] They investigated the women's colleges at Cambridge, but Inez resisted the idea.[54] "I'm hanged if I'll be what the term 'college girl' implies," Inez insisted. She considered them uptight bookworms. If she had to go to college, it would be Bryn Mawr or Vassar College in the United States. "They are rotten," she said of British universities. "And if I went there and then to American [*sic*] afterwards, I would be 100 before I came out."[55] When her parents learned Vassar would not accept Kensington's higher certificate, they whisked their protesting daughter after graduation to the strict Willard School for Girls in Berlin despite its "decidedly American" atmosphere.[56] Willard students made their own beds in the big house they shared at 27 Luitpold Strasse and spoke German at all meals except on Sundays. After a cold bath at 7:00 a.m., breakfast, and prayers, Inez attended class, huddled with a Latin tutor, and hunched over homework until 10:00 p.m. "I've never worked so hard in my life," she wrote home.[57] It paid off, however, when the brusque headmistress called her aside after the first semester to declare her an able scholar. "I was never so dumbfounded!" Inez reported home.[58] She could thank the school's strict rules forbidding its young women to go out unchaperoned for helping to maintain her focus as well as her parents' edict that she could only go out on Friday and Saturday nights. "Why I might as well be in a German village," she complained.[59] Her most joyous reprieve was the operas the students attended most Friday nights. "It was perfect," she said of a performance of her favorite, *Carmen.*[60]

Inez's letters home reveal her mischievous streak. One evening when most of the other girls went to a concert, she and another student sprinkled breadcrumbs and sugar in their beds and sewed up their nightgowns. Another night she sneaked out to buy sweets at the *patisserie*. When a teacher denied her request to smoke cigarettes, Inez retorted, "Why not?" Her nickname was "der Teuflin"—little devil. Unabashedly self-centered, it peeved Inez when she was mistakenly singled out for altruism. She once gave an unwanted concert ticket to a classmate. "This morning I have heard nothing but my unselfishness dinned in to my ears," she informed her mother, "and I feel absolutely ridiculous. Wouldn't it give you the willies?" She was full of herself. She thanked her mother for sending her a red blouse. "I look ripping in it—modest maiden aren't I?"[61]

Teasing banter with her parents showed their affection despite their differences. She signed a letter to her mother, "Your baddest daughter," following her return to Berlin after Christmas. "Pity I'm not always an angel, when I'm home, isn't it? But I'll do better next time."[62] She teased her father she was becoming a socialist. He kept her up-to-date on the world beyond Berlin by clipping and mailing her articles on current events, while her mother sent snapshots of the animals at Meadowmount.[63] And after she moved back to London in May, Inez found her little brother to be an athletic teenager who wore a top hat and Eton jacket to classes at the exclusive Westminster School. Cheerful Vida was finishing her junior year at high school and showing promise as a singer. Inez made up for her lost time in the cloistered boarding school. The "butterfly of fashion" reveled in four days at Cambridge up to her neck in men, canoeing on the Cam River or playing tennis in the day and dancing outdoors under fairy lamps until dawn.[64] July found all three Milholland women taking in the Henley Regatta aboard a launch with twenty sunburned friends. Vida had a wild time throwing cakes, making even her mother laugh. Inez joked the display was "simply disgraceful."[65] One night, Inez danced at the annual American Ball until 4:00 a.m.[66]

Inez felt no need to apologize for her self-indulgence. The independent teenager's emergence as a New Woman determined to please herself began in the cocoon of her protective yet progressive family. June Sochen believes New Women drew their energy and will from supportive families and a circle of like-minded friends.[67] In Inez's case, both Jean and John Milholland encouraged their daughter to develop her talents. Jean instilled respect for education and service to others. But in addition to her emphasis on self-discipline, Jean appreciated her daughter's spirit, perhaps even more important in helping her bloom. "She is young—and loves life—and should make the most of her time, I suppose," Jean admitted.[68] Her father's reform work—and rhetoric—served as a powerful role model for Inez's independent thinking. His example of fighting for underdogs branded her, as did his penchant for inflammatory rhetoric. It is more difficult to assess the impact of her parents' stormy relationship on Inez. Perhaps an awareness of her pious father's hypocrisy inclined her to be brutally frank with lovers and made her wary of marriage. The free-love creed may have appealed because she had witnessed the impotency of a marriage certificate to guarantee fidelity. Yet Inez also had to be aware of John and Jean's emotional commitment and physical intimacy, and to this partly may be attributed the all-consuming intensity she sought in relationships with men all her life.

Coming of age in London left an indelible stamp upon Milholland. Mingling among aristocratic reformers made her idealistic, questioning, confident, and sophisticated. Her schooling inclined her to serve others, and her progressive parents encouraged her to contribute to society. Besides acquiring a cultured British accent that added to the allure of her low, resonant voice, the experience exposed her to people and ideas that gave her a broader outlook in life than most of her American peers. Inez told her father an ocean away, "I am beginning to really think, and I find the employment very profitable."[69] She finally was ready to return to America for college. In September 1905, her mother shepherded her north to Poughkeepsie to dive into three days of entrance exams for Vassar. Wednesday she plowed through five hours of testing in English and Latin; the next day, geography and history; and the next, Greek and German.[70] She passed. Milholland was about to take the next step to becoming a New Woman.

Vassar

"Fascinating, — but a trifle dangerous"

3

Matthew Vassar brewed beer like his father before him but wanted more. By the time he became president of the Hudson River Railroad Co., he desired to do something constructive with his money: create a women's college.[1] Vassar's proposal was revolutionary, as no women's college comparable to men's existed in the mid-nineteenth century; doctors even proclaimed that education made women infertile.[2] The immigrant brewer-turned-banker, however, disliked limits. "It occurred to me," Vassar told the newly installed Board of Trustees of Vassar Female College on February 26, 1861, "that woman, having received from her Creator the same intellectual constitution as man, has the same right as man to intellectual culture and development." Then he handed them $408,000 in securities and the deed to two hundred acres.[3] The generous visionary, however, failed to comprehend the ramifications of creating a new breed of woman, the college graduate. The 353 young women who paid $350 for a year's tuition and room when the college opened in 1865 formed a new elite. Their entry across the portal of Main Building marked their first step toward challenging ideas about womanhood.[4] Vassar had created a breeding ground for rebels.

One rebel in the bud was nineteen-year-old Inez Milholland. Her four years in the bucolic haven where ideas percolated alongside Casper's Kill forged the intellectual and political beliefs that served as beacons for the rest of her life. Her Vassar experience helped transform Milholland into a New Woman. She joined the flood of women enrolling in college after the turn of the century, encouraged in part by research by women psychologists challenging the scientific dogma that women's brains differed from men's.[5] College women more than tripled in the first two decades of the twentieth century; even though only 5 percent of Americans attended college in 1910, 40 percent were women. That surge in female education was requisite to the emergence of the New Woman.[6]

Inez, center of top row, was captain of Vassar's field hockey team.
Courtesy of Archives & Special Collections, Vassar College Library.

Milholland struggled with the college's liberal arts fare, which for her included English, French, German, Latin, mathematics, history, and economics. Outside of the classroom, she radiated fire. Tall and sturdy, she excelled at all athletics. She was lucky to be entering college just as society was beginning to accept physically active women. Mass media portrayed the prototypical New Woman riding a bicycle or swinging a tennis racquet. Women on the move became desirable. Bloomers, baggy trousers cut at the knee, which were worn in the new sport of basketball—Milholland proved a natural—encouraged movement and breeched the taboo against exposing the female body. Outdoor games such as golf and tennis were becoming popular among the affluent.[7] Milholland enjoyed both. She played right fullback on Vassar's fledgling field hockey team.[8] Standing arms akimbo in her baggy, shin-length shorts and V-neck sweater on Vassar's Field Day, she projected an ease with her body foreign to women a generation earlier.

Her day began with morning classes, followed after lunch by a lesson in interpreting Shakespeare and another before dinner in elocution. Then came play rehearsals, chapel, and dress rehearsal until nine o'clock, leaving only an hour before lights out to squeeze in studying. Milholland so impressed seniors in the student drama club that they broke with tradition to cast the freshman as Romeo. She cut a handsome figure in tights, dark cape, and roguish thigh-high boots, her long hair crammed under a cap.[9] The student magazine applauded the passion she threw into the balcony scene.[10] She joined the Current Topics Club, the College Settlement, the German Club, and the debating team.[11] She even found time to help organize a children's court in Poughkeepsie. The city appointed her and several other students as probation officers, an experience that fueled her interest in criminal law and court reform.[12] She chomped on apples as part of her training for the shot put, the sole Field Day event advisers allowed her to add to her killing schedule. Not for the last time, Milholland pushed herself too hard. "[I]f there weren't such absurd rules now I could drop some of my work," she complained to her mother. "But they are furious if they don't get first-class work in the play, and expect similar work in all lessons."[13]

Vida joined her older sister at Vassar the following year but dropped out after freshman year to study singing.[14] Relations between the sisters sometimes were strained, as Inez was so much more willful and Vida may have felt overshadowed on campus by her sister's overpowering personality. Although she lacked Inez's magnetism, Vida's sweet face and bubbly personality attracted friends of both sexes. Before Vida left Vassar, she played King Leontes opposite the "calm strength and sweetness" of Inez as Queen Hermione in *The Winter's Tale*. Braids hanging like ropes to her hips, the gowned and crowned Inez looked every inch like royalty in the soft light of the Japanese lanterns that lit the production amid the apple blossoms perfuming Sunset Hill.[15] For Inez, it must have seemed that, as a contemporary wrote of college's influence upon young women, Vassar sang to her: "Look! The heavens and earth and water that are under the earth are yours! . . . The very winds of God are blowing for your sails! You—*you*—YOU—"[16]

Milholland got involved in the British suffragette movement the summer before or after her sophomore year, an experience that profoundly shaped her ideas about female activism. As a freshman, she was so naive about votes for women that she turned to her father for advice when assigned the pro-suffrage side in a debating team match. Her line of questioning indicated someone had introduced her to the standard anti-suffrage argument of the day: "[T]ell me why women should have suffrage when politics are already in such a turmoil. Would not the corruption be increased? And even if women should have suffrage, is it expedient just at present?"[17] Her questions were answered after Milholland met the widowed

Inez, with braids, portraying "Hermione" in *The Winter's Tale* during her senior year at Vassar. *Courtesy of Archives & Special Collections, Vassar College Library.*

aristocratic radical Emmeline Pankhurst in London, where her militant Women's Social and Political Union was shaking up the establishment. The WSPU "suffragettes'" motto "Deeds Not Words" signified their aggressive new approach to British women's forty-year struggle for the vote. Emmeline and her supporters began to march on Parliament in 1906, although their tactics had yet to escalate to their infamous rock-throwing and arson campaigns. The WSPU's civil disobedience began with the arrest of Pankhurst's daughter Christabel and Annie Kenney in 1905 after the pair heckled a politician. They were the first of more than a thousand British suffragettes jailed before World War I, and the sentence was the first of five Christabel served for the cause. Beautiful Christabel also was a brilliant lawyer who won an international prize for law, another reason Milholland admired her.[18]

Christabel Pankhurst undoubtedly served as a role model for Milholland, who described her as "so pretty."[19] The WSPU's theatrical call to arms for women's rights naturally drew Milholland. She persuaded her reluctant mother to host a WSPU parlor meeting featuring Emmeline Pankhurst in the drawing room at 4 Prince of Wales Terrace. "It cost me two of my best friends, too," Jean recalled of the meeting, attended by several members of Parliament. "But I couldn't stop Inez any more than one could stop the lightning."[20] Inez joined the suffragette soap boxers who defied police in Hyde Park, slipping from them through the crowd like fish in the sea.[21] When she returned to Vassar for her junior year, she wrote assuredly about England's suffragettes in the campus newspaper, remarking that Americans' tepid efforts made her a "bit ashamed."[22] The British example showed her the value of public spectacle.

By her junior year at Vassar, Milholland enjoyed a loyal following willing to defy Vassar president Taylor. The "idol of the whole undergraduate body" was president of her class and captain of the field hockey team.[23] She had earned her first varsity letter "V" for her sweater as a sophomore by setting the school shot-put record, and the next year she captured the college cup as best all-around athlete, adding basketball and track to her crowded schedule.[24] When Harriot Stanton Blatch's trolley tour hit the rails, she was winding up a run as Benedick in *Much Ado about Nothing*— "charmingly boyish, egotistic and impressionable."[25] Not only her mother but also strangers who saw her perform, in fact, urged her to consider a stage career.[26] Milholland also was notorious for nonconformity. She smoked cigarettes and favored sensual accessories such as yards of beads, turbans, and potent perfume.[27] But what most bedazzled her classmates was her political activism.[28] She finally persuaded President Taylor to permit a suffrage debate in spring 1909 on the condition that no outsiders be involved and no faculty speak. Due to a misunderstanding, seven faculty members did speak for suffrage. Taylor was livid. Several faculty blasted back that the president was obstructing academic freedom and freedom of speech.[29] Milholland tweaked him once more before graduation. At dusk, three quarters of the student body waited in line outside Main Hall to walk through a series of rooms in which Milholland and others staged a series of "living tableaux" in which silent, motionless young women posed in scenes illustrating various arguments for suffrage.[30] The antic reinforced Milholland's reputation as campus leader and rebel.

President Taylor narrowly interpreted the college's mission "not to reform society but to educate women."[31] He believed his role was to shelter students from propaganda. The paternalistic Baptist minister's ban showed the conflicting messages female college students received at the turn of the century. On an academic plane, women within Vassar's ivy-covered walls were encouraged to fly high; in reality, their wings remained closely clipped. The hypocrisy grated on Milholland and her peers. "Many college women," Debra Herman wrote of this conundrum, "found they were rebellious almost despite themselves."[32] Vassar's ban on suffrage talks was especially onerous. Faculty forced to go off campus to discuss votes for women bristled at the infringement upon their freedom of speech. They blanched when Taylor refused to let Jane Addams visit in spring 1908.[33]

Inez throwing the shot put at Vassar's Field Day. She held the school record. *Courtesy of Archives & Special Collections, Vassar College Library.*

Yet no one had defied the president's archaic policy before junior Inez Milholland. The New York City press reveled in the irony of a women's school that banned suffrage talk. "Revolution, not evolution . . . is brewing at the college," wrote one reporter of the cemetery rally, "for forty girls openly defied the commands of President Taylor in order to attend the meeting of the ballot brigade."[34] A *New York American* headline scoffed, "Suffragists Invade Vassar. How Rude!"[35] Taylor responded that he would not let outsiders "exploit" students and blamed the rally on certain unnamed students out to get his goat because he had forbidden Addams's visit.[36] The suffrage weekly *Woman's Journal* scolded him, predicting, "The suffrage movement at Vassar will profit by his mistake."[37]

That summer, open-air suffrage meetings popped up across New York like mushrooms after rain.[38] The move into the streets revitalized the suffrage movement, thanks largely to the Equality League of Self-Supporting Women that Blatch had formed in January 1907. Milholland joined the league, which united working-class women with professional and independently wealthy women in the fight for votes for women. The organization crystallized Blatch's view that earning a living held the key to female independence. It helped introduce the militant style of the U.S. labor movement and the theatrical approach of English suffragettes into the anemic American suffrage movement.[39] Blatch served as an important mentor to Milholland both in political activism and the uses of publicity. Milholland advocated the league's techniques and creed; she, too, believed economics lay at the heart of female autonomy. Both women, of course, owed their financial independence to their ties to wealthy men, which perhaps made the concept sound deceptively easy to them.

Fresh from her heady success in the cemetery, that summer Milholland participated in the British suffragettes' biggest protest ever. She carried a big yellow banner emblazoned with the words, "Votes for Women" in London's first "monster" suffrage rally, the spectacular "Women's Sunday" on June 21, 1908. She was the first American, at least according to the *New York Times*, to parade with the London suffragettes.[40] Thirty thousand women converged from seven directions on Hyde Park, where a quarter million people blanketed every inch of its grass.[41] When buglers signaled the speeches' end, Milholland joined in the multitude's roar: "Votes for Women! Votes for Women! Votes for Women!" The near-religious exaltation of the spectacle intoxicated Milholland, as it did thousands of Englishwomen. "Self was forgotten," wrote Sylvia Pankhurst, "personality seemed minute, the movement so big, so splendid."[42]

Milholland returned home eager to help import this euphoria to New York. She laughed when waiting reporters asked as she walked off the *Lusitania* if the London mass meetings scared her. "When you are in the company of these earnest women," she said, "you haven't time to be nervous."[43] She and Vida passed out suffrage literature at the polls.[44] The sisters ushered a performance of the rousing suffrage play "Votes for Women!" whose finale featured a monster suffrage rally.[45] Milholland and Blatch soon discovered the dramatic effect Milholland worked upon the male public. Just before the Republicans' election parade, the Equality League rented a second-floor room over a Fifth Avenue store with huge windows that swung open. Milholland helped drop from them hundreds of yellow "Votes for Women" balloons, hollering "Votes for Women" through a megaphone. One contingent stopped when it spotted her, a few members breaking ranks and sprinting upstairs. "Helen of Troy was not more upsetting," Blatch recalled. Milholland lectured the rowdies for twenty minutes on suffrage before calmly announcing, "Gentlemen, I thank you for your attention. May I ask you kindly to clear the room?" Clutching suffrage fliers, the men obediently filed downstairs.[46]

Early on election morning, Milholland rendezvoused with a handful of women outside Blatch's house at 103 East Nineteenth Street. Blatch handed each a pile of leaflets seeking a state suffrage referendum before the women roared off in her car to distribute them at the polls. "We must seek on the highways the unconverted," Blatch explained of the novel public campaign techniques that had been evolving over the past year. The notoriously anti-suffrage *New York Times* demonstrated the shrewdness of this approach when its Sunday magazine featured Blatch's colorful Election Day efforts in a respectful five-column, four-photo spread.[47] The "old gray lady's" editorials might rail against votes for women, but the newspaper of record was honor bound to report impartially when suffragists made news. Milholland, as her cemetery rally showed, possessed a special flair for winning headlines, in part because the press favored her good looks, perhaps in part because of lessons she absorbed at the knee of her journalist father. When she and fellow members of the College Women's Equal Suffrage League heard that anti-suffragists had rented the Berkeley Theater, for instance, they rented the theatre for that evening. Before the antis arrived, the students plastered the hall with college flags and suffrage posters, forcing the antis' speaker to decry the ballot beneath the reproachful gaze of a portrait of Susan B. Anthony. That night, Milholland and other students in college gowns worked as ushers for their talk by an English suffragette. The fresh-faced young women contradicted the afternoon speaker's condemnation of that "horrible unfeminine creature, the new woman."[48]

Milholland ventured out on her own over Christmas break to address an East Side suffrage club.[49] Back at Vassar, she helped organize a suffrage rally under the auspices of the city's Socialist Club, joining labor organizer Rose Schneiderman and three local suffragists on the podium. Milholland's defense of the English suffragettes—by then smashing windows—displayed her understanding of sexual double standards. "Why is it so terrible if women adopt the methods by which men have attained liberty," she asked her audience, "when all other methods fail so utterly to achieve it? [B]ecause they are doing just what men did in the American War of Independence when they threw the Boston tea into the harbor, they are called unwomanly, undignified . . . though we say that violence is unfortunate and wasteful and will be unnecessary when women have something to say about government, still we take matters and men as we find them—and fight."[50]

John Milholland slumped in his seat in the audience as Inez defended the suffragettes' violence. Yet her parents' public support never flagged; John only counseled that she avoid militant rhetoric. "[O]nly the dynamite of sound ideas is required," he told her.[51] When press accounts mistakenly reported Inez was arrested in London, Jean dashed off a note to the *New York Times* to correct that error as well as the paper's mistaken assumption Inez was English. Jean defended her daughter's work for suffrage and child labor reform.[52] Inez and her common-sense mother were close even if their reform styles differed. When Jean worried about her exploits, Inez teased that if her mother did not relax, she would "paint Poughkeepsie a Socialist red."[53]

Milholland was, in fact, president of the campus Intercollegiate Socialist Society.[54] Socialism was for Milholland "a vital means to correct the monster evils under the sun," her father recalled.[55] "Socialism has become a craze with her. She is almost a monomaniac."[56] Socialism was in part a response to the chasm between the giant trusts symbolized by U.S. Steel, whose capitalization at $1.4 billion in 1901 made it the biggest business ever, and the poverty of millions of immigrants flooding New York, packed as many as two thousand people in a single tenement block.[57] The socialist platform of public ownership of utilities and equalizing wealth appeared promising to the modernist vision of a more humane society. Young socialists also reflected the moderns' alienation from mainstream American values. The "socialist" label's cache of danger that attracted Milholland frightened many Americans. When Milholland was a sophomore, for instance, socialist Bill Haywood narrowly won acquittal as an accomplice in the murder of the ex-governor of Idaho. Nonetheless, 1,150 socialists held office in thirty-six states by 1911, and the party drew nearly 6 percent of the vote in the 1912 election.[58] Milholland belonged to the reform wing of socialists who emphasized education, voting, and trade unions. Her comfortable station in life placed her in the ranks of what Theodore Roosevelt dismissed as "parlor socialists," because their contribution to class struggle was confined largely to sympathetic conversation over sherry and cigars.[59] Milholland recruited classmates to join her at socialist meetings in Poughkeepsie and New York City, alarming administrators who refused to grasp that the critical thinking they encouraged inevitably pushed their charges to challenge the status quo.[60] Women dominated the Intercollegiate Socialist Society, reflecting their identification with the oppressed and the reformist spirit drummed into them in their liberal studies.[61] Milholland's affinity for the socialist experiment also reflected her passion for personal growth, an important goal among New Women.[62]

Milholland found a bit of this growth painful during one of her earliest speeches—and most disastrous. The incident before the Manhattan chapter of the Intercollegiate Socialist Society in January of her senior year revealed her intensity and vulnerability. The society sponsored Friday night "one-dollar dinners" at Kalil's Restaurant on Park Place, a popular bohemian hangout. Still a novice at public speaking, Milholland memorized her talk on a panel headed by prominent socialist reformer and journalist Charles Edward Russell.[63] She was so nervous her parents had begged her to cancel. Just after a Wellesley professor scolded college women for materialism and apathy, however, Russell called upon Milholland to rise from the table where she sat with her mother and two dozen Vassar representatives. She stepped gingerly to the front of the room and gamely challenged the professor.[64] When she returned to her prepared remarks, her mind went blank at the part where she explained the college woman needs "integration." She repeated the word three or four times. A few giggles sputtered from the tables. "Wait a minute," she said, "I have forgotten what I was talking about." The audience waited a minute—then two. Laughter broke out at one table, then another. People shouted suggestions. Through it all she stood, flushed and scowling, as one observer observed, "forgetful of everything in the world but her determination to remember that speech." After three minutes, she said, "Well, I can't take any more of your time," and sat down. A typhoon of applause followed her back to her seat.[65] Despite her public spunk, she sank into a depression that left her "tense and forlorn."[66]

Depression stalked Milholland throughout her life. More than youthful moodiness made her ponder in London that "[s]ometimes I feel as if there was nothing so lovely as life, and other times as though life were not worth living, for everything seems so empty."[67] The public never had an inkling of the insecurities that occasionally crippled the luminous, confident crusader who shined on stage and in the newspaper columns. Its source is difficult to pinpoint, and she may have been genetically predisposed to the condition, as her father also seemed inclined to depression, and it surfaced later in other family members. Milholland also set nearly impossible standards for herself, in part because of expectations instilled in her by her parents and teachers, and in part because she wanted to live up to her evolving image as an Amazon. So highly independent, she also unjustly blamed herself for failures more rightly attributed to institutional sex discrimination.

Another aspect of Milholland that contradicted her public persona was a preoccupation with creature comforts. When she invited eight classmates to Meadowmount, she fretted to her parents: "I do want to live as in England, and have everything conventional and nice. I am noted for that here at college, and as people can't see us in London, I don't want them to judge us by the farm. We may not be the Four Hundred, but we certainly are representative of culture. . . . I should hate to have this, my first house party at Meadowmount, a failure."[68] She once apologized for bringing guests home on short notice to the Hotel Manhattan. The Milhol-lands had leased a large luxury flat in the Forty-second Street and Fifth Avenue hotel, its grand portico and Italian Renaissance façade of Indiana limestone making it one of the statelier examples of the new "apartment hotels" creeping up the avenue.[69] She added, "You could hire a butler for the night, and a maid to bring hot water, tea and prepare our guests' bath in the morning."[70] Society simultaneously repulsed and attracted her. During her social exile in Berlin, an account of a big New York ball made her "mouth water." She continued, "Not that I care so much for such extravagances and luxury, but I want to be in a position to refuse, and to condemn without having 'sour grapes' said to you."[71] John Milholland also understood his daughter's contradictions, so like his own. "Poor kid! She is so fond of what she doesn't want!"[72]

The young Inez Milholland who bubbled about dates and dresses in her letters home is barely discernable as the politically charged, altruistic heroine portrayed in press accounts of her suffrage and socialism activities. "Life is particularly pleasant for me just now, Little Mum, so much so, in fact that I am growing more selfish and self-centered than ever."[73] As her career as a suffrage orator grew, so did her clothing bill. Jean admonished her daughter to be less extravagant, but Inez insisted her wardrobe was indispensable to her public role. She explained to her mother, "One magazine said lately I was one of the most artistically gowned public women in America. Now mother, don't you see that there are heaps of people who will come to hear me, because I am reported a beauty, magnetic, artistic, up to date."[74] He father would add that Inez was "strong in mind and will, impulsive in disposition; passionate in devotion; beautiful in face and form." In less charitable moments, however, her stubbornness angered him. He reported to Jean in London, "Nan and I have gone nearly 24 hours without breaking *one bit* of China!"[75]

One of their greatest sources of friction was her rejection of religion. Like many other New Women, she disparaged faith in an unknown higher being as one more constricting Victorian relic. The irony of higher education's secularizing influence on his daughter hit John on a visit to campus. He fell asleep at the college inn thanking God for giving him the means to educate his children well, but the next morning after chapel, Inez trashed the Episcopal sermon. At dinner she declared God dead. John tossed and turned in bed that night as he lamented Vassar's "pernicious influences."[76] By summer Inez refused to take part in family prayers.[77] Father and daughter briefly reconciled when she became the first Milholland to graduate from college. John beamed as she delivered a light-hearted speech during the outdoor Class Day festivities. Jean, Vida, and John Jr. were in London, but Inez clasped the bouquet her father presented her of red roses, her favorite flower.[78] After a woman sitting next to John in the chapel at graduation ceremonies the next day praised Inez, he thought, Inez may not be a genius, but she possessed priceless passion and unbounded enthusiasm.[79] Her yearbook portrait revealed a classical profile of a thick-browed brunette in a high-necked lace blouse, resting her cheek on her hand as if deep in thought. The signature phrase beneath read, "Fascinating, — but a trifle dangerous for household use."[80]

Milholland's professional goals and political beliefs had coalesced by the time she clasped her diploma. As early as her year in Germany, Milholland had decided to become a lawyer. Although she entered Vassar ignorant about suffrage, by the time she left she had refined her career goal to practice law to advance women's rights. During college she demonstrated her commitment to criminal and children's rights by working as a probation officer. Intellectual dalliances with the socialists in Greenwich Village had honed her sense of class injustice and radicalized her politics. Her experiences with the Pankhursts in England and Blatch in New York solidified her desire to be in the front ranks of the suffrage movement. She had proved courageous and creative in challenging patriarchy, the hallmark of the entire movement in the decade to follow. Vassar's one-time stage Romeo especially enjoyed the media spotlight.

By the time Milholland graduated from Vassar, the press already had begun to spin its image of her as the ideal New Woman. Several factors fostered Milholland's well-publicized popular image. Newspapers achieved their peak influence in the 1910s, with daily circulation of the biggest of some 2,500 dailies occasionally surpassing a million copies.[81] Journalists had deemed the "beauty" as a worthy subject, and the pictorial Sunday supplements were fat with photographs of lovely women from heiresses to chorus girls. The sensational yellow newspapers vied to sate readers' growing hunger for celebrity. Milholland appeared on the suffrage scene as the movement began to pitch its message using the mass culture tools of the rising consumer society. The beautiful yet forceful Milholland was perfect for selling the image of the modern suffragist through the expanding mass media.[82] Perhaps equally important to Milholland's rising media star was her fortuitous resemblance to the fictional "Gibson girl" created by artist Charles Dana Gibson in the 1890s. His ubiquitous lithographs of the tall and casually elegant Gibson girl, a "major exemplar of the new woman," set the dominant ideal of female beauty for a generation.[83]

Like Milholland, the Gibson girl wore her dark hair swept up in a loose bun and dressed in a modern shirtwaist blouse tucked into a skirt short enough to allow her to swing a golf club or pose in myriad other athletic pursuits. Never was the Gibson girl portrayed at home. Her outdoorsy athleticism and air of insouciance symbolized the modern young woman's rebellion against Victorian constraints. Yet her image was so feminine and clean cut that she assuaged fears about the New Woman. The Gibson girl was a hot commodity at the turn of the century, when her likeness appeared on magazine covers, calendars, china, wallpaper, and innumerable other objects.[84] Milholland seemed the embodiment of this coveted creature, which accounts for much of why the mass media latched onto her. The Gibson girl, however, had been an apolitical and unemployed figure slightly on the wane when Milholland entered college. Milholland added a political, socially responsible, career-minded facet to the Gibson type that revivified the aging icon. She also was sexier, although the press accentuated her wholesome idealism while downplaying her sexual radicalism. The smitten press seemed to work overtime to make her palatable to the public. Paradoxically, the unfailingly positive media coverage of Milholland legitimized the new ideas she represented even as it diluted their radical potential. Newspapers approvingly, if hyperbolically, credited Milholland with single-handedly transforming old-fashioned Vassar into a citadel of both suffrage and socialism; one scholar labeled her the *New York Times'* "poster girl of radicalism."[85]

Suffrage leaders such as the media-savvy Blatch and soon the even more exploitative Alice Paul were quick to latch onto Milholland as a headline-making machine. An appearance by Milholland at a suffrage event guaranteed coverage and often a photograph; her likeness associated the recently laughable suffrage movement with modernity, idealism, and femininity. Milholland's rise coincided with the mass media's switch from suffrage foe to advocate of votes for women—and Milholland can fairly be credited with playing a major role in accomplishing that transition by demonstrating that a woman could play politics and keep her sex appeal. However, although Milholland's prominence in the public eye served the votes-for-women movement well by transforming the image of the suffragist from nineteenth-century biddy to an attractive, vibrant, and reassuringly feminine young woman, the image also conspired against feminism.

Milholland's picture was in the newspaper primarily because of the way she looked, and beauty was a key component of her public persona. The effect was complex. On one level, her popularity reified the belief that a woman's power lay with her beauty rather than her intelligence or accomplishments, in direct contradiction to the feminist agenda. Even more nefarious, the mass media's glorification of the patrician Milholland as ideal New Woman reflected American racism and classism.[86] Milholland's

Inez giving the Class Day speech at Vassar at her graduation in May 1909.
Courtesy of Archives & Special Collections, Vassar College Library.

media image also performed a positive function. Her name or photograph invariably appeared in conjunction with a progressive notion, be it votes for women or redistributing wealth. She never appeared as just a pretty face. Always, she appeared in opposition to authority, set on accomplishing what patriarchal culture told her women could not do. Milholland's image suggested a world of possibilities to all nascent female rebels, a perfect example of the media process described by Martha Banta "that altered social perceptions and formed new conceptions of what it was possible for females to do and to be."[87] As she exited the Vassar stage, she was about to test whether the promise of those possibilities matched reality, even for the ideal New Woman.

A week after graduation, Milholland sailed to London with her father. The ease with which she hopped back and forth across the Atlantic symbolized the freedom she expected in all aspects of life. Once ashore, Milholland expanded her horizons in important ways. She plunked down two pounds and change to officially join the Pankhursts' WSPU.[88] Police nearly arrested her for soap-boxing about suffrage, but the crowd protected her. "The men just surged around the policeman in a big wave and swallowed him up," she said.[89] Henry Lynch, a smitten Liberal member of Parliament, got tickets for the three Milholland women to sit in on the House of Commons.[90] Milholland brought her father to a rally to hear Emmeline Pankhurst. When that same night father and daughter attended a reception for suffragette nemesis Prime Minister Henry Asquith, Milholland refused to remove her WSPU purple, white, and green "Votes for Women" badge.[91]

Milholland also sneaked off to attend the summer school of the Fabian Society, a socialism-inclined group of middle-class English intellectuals that sought to influence politicians to enact their progressive social policies. The nonpartisan Fabians were idealists rather than agitators who, lacking faith in the proletariat's ability to rise up against the establishment, believed it was up to a benevolent elite to create a new world order.[92] The call to the elite to offer salvation to the poor held the key to the Fabians' appeal for Milholland, as well as their vocal support for votes for women; more than twenty members were jailed for participating in suffragette demonstrations.[93]

Milholland signed herself in as a "would-be lawyer" in the guest book at "Pen-Yr-Allt" in northern Wales on August 20, 1909.[94] College students, journalists, teachers, suffragettes, and even a sanitary inspector joined her in the sprawling stone manor house perched on a hill overlooking Cardigan Bay. Their days began with an invigorating Swedish gymnastics drill followed by a daily lecture on topics as abstract as "Greek Political Theory and Socialism" or as practical as "The Prevention of Infantile Mortality." Outdoor activities filled the rest of the guests' day before they regrouped around the fireplace at night to talk more about improving society.[95]

Milholland sold some jewelry to raise the train fare to Wales to satisfy her "intellectual curiosity" about the summer school. Her parents reacted to their twenty-three-year-old daughter's plans as if she were running off with pirates. The day after she arrived at Pen-Yr-Allt, Inez wrote her father: "I am sorry you don't consider my judgement of what is good for me of any value, but good or bad my own judgement is what I must live my life by, or else be a hanger on, and it seems to me now that I am old enough to begin exercising it. Don't you agree?" Her father sent a family maid to fetch her.[96] The next month, Milholland sailed back to New York, a revolutionary who needed a maid to pour her bath, eager to change the world.

Strike

"Our cause is your cause"

4

Unlike Vassar star Inez Milholland, Theresa Malkiel rose at dawn during her teenaged years before trudging off to stitch baby clothes until dusk in a Lower East Side sweatshop. Like the college girl twelve years her junior, however, the Russian Jewish émigré also challenged male authority. At age twenty, Malkiel helped found the Infant Cloak Makers' Union of New York. When bosses set out to break the union, Malkiel helped stage a walk out.[1] From there she rose to top levels of socialist leadership. Fifteen years later, the rich socialist and the poor socialist found themselves together on the barricades of the most important women's strike in American history.

Milholland's small but significant role in the "Uprising of 20,000" shirt-waist strike in winter 1909–10 tested her commitment to social reform. She had first heard about shirtwaist makers' travails when speakers from the New York Women's Trade Union League asked Vassar students to buy only clothes bearing the union label.[2] Milholland joined the league, the main meeting ground between socialist working-class women and upper-class supporters. Even if they never got their hands dirty, these wealthy leaguers championed financial independence for women. And they had the time and money to help organize female factory workers, shunned by male labor organizations.[3] The uprising was remarkable partly because of the unprecedented sisterhood temporarily achieved by women of different classes, religions, and ethnic groups. The strike defied the stereotype of women as too submissive, emotional, and physically weak to scrap for their workplace rights. Strikers virtually shut down the sprawling garment industry, which by 1909 employed more than thirty-five thousand workers. Those numbers made a bitter joke of anti-suffragists' claim that the vote threatened women's place in the home, as shirtwaist workers were among millions of women who toiled as factory workers or in other low-paying jobs in the early 1900s.[4] More than five hundred shirtwaist shops employed mostly female Jewish immigrants between the ages of sixteen and twenty-four who labored ten hours a day stitching shirtwaists.[5]

Ironically, the shirtwaist more than any other apparel symbolized American women's expanding freedom. The simple blouse of sheer, translucent cotton or muslin usually worn tucked into a long skirt became the favored fashion of New Women, Milholland among them. The Gibson girl usually wore a shirtwaist. Its buttoned collar opened wide across the bosom and then narrowed with a series of darts and tucks or pleats that showed off the feminine waistline. At $16.50 to $18.00 a dozen wholesale, the affordable shirtwaist required mass sales to turn a profit.[6] Profit required cheap labor. For every dollar earned, shirtwaist workers sewed ten dozen pair of sleeves, five dozen bodices, or eight hundred yards of tucks—with needles and thread they bought themselves.[7] They stitched seven days a week from about 7:30 a.m. until 6:30 p.m. for roughly five dollars a week in cramped loft buildings converted into garment factories.[8] The tiny International Ladies Garment Workers Union had struggled for years to sign up disgruntled workers. Then in October 1909, the owners of the Triangle Shirtwaist Co. locked out its workers because they dared discuss a union.[9] The workers went on strike.

Milholland literally found herself in the middle of the strike. The Triangle Shirtwaist factory occupied the eighth and ninth floors of the Asch Building on Washington Place, on the eastern edge of Washington Square. Behind it, dingy tenements bulging with immigrants carpeted the Lower East Side. Three blocks north of the square in more comfortable quarters, Jean Milholland was settling the family into a three-story brownstone at 9 East Ninth Street while her husband remained behind in London to try to sell his mail tubes business.[10] In November ILGWU Local 25 expanded the Triangle strike to more shops. The standoff turned nasty: Police manhandled and arrested the pickets; factory owners hired thugs and prostitutes to infiltrate their line. Socialist women picketed with workers and signed workers with the union, while WTUL headquarters at 43 East 22nd Street became the strike's epicenter. The league raised bail money, volunteered legal and secretarial services, fed strikers, provided witnesses for arrested strikers, and explained the strikers' cause at meetings across the city.[11] Milholland volunteered for the most dangerous duty, watching picket lines to make sure police did not violate pickets' rights. Standing guard in the slushy streets educated her about the rougher side of reform. The upper-class women's presence made police seethe. One plainclothes officer growled to Vassar alumna Elsie Cole, "You uptown scrum, keep out of this, or you'll find yourself in jail."

Police went too far when they arrested WTUL president Mary Dreier. Even though an embarrassed judge immediately released her, the arrest of an upper-class woman splashed sympathetic strike coverage across the front pages of city newspapers.[12] The incident spurred the angry WTUL to formally vote to picket the factories three times a week and, more importantly, "take an active part in preventing police interference in all strikes in which women were concerned."[13] Meanwhile, thirty-thousand shirtwaist makers massed at four sites on November 22. Inside Cooper Union, a young woman in the back of the hall interrupted the parade of male speakers. Clara Lemlich had fled a Russian pogrom as a child and spent what little free time she had educating herself among the shelves of the East Broadway branch of the New York Public Library. She helped form one of the original ILGWU locals when she was only thirteen. Thugs on the Triangle picket line already had cracked six of her ribs. Several men hoisted Lemlich to the stage. She declared she was tired of talk. "I move," she shouted in Yiddish, "that we go on a general strike."[14] A roar of approval followed.

Lemlich's brash interruption of the hall's male discourse signaled women workers' determination to speak for themselves. The teenaged workers fashioned a new kind of public figure. They also were New Women, truly financially self-supporting and infused with agency. A giddy, celebratory atmosphere pervaded the garment district the morning that tens of thousands of them, dressed in their best clothes, walked away from their machines and spilled into the streets. Feeling feisty and happily self-conscious they would be on public display, some showed off hats sporting expensive ostrich feathers, while others warmed their hands in fur muffs. Union leaders could not convince their gleeful minions to dress plainer and act more decorously to convey the image of the rational, downtrodden working girl they believed played better in the press. Many pickets could not resist catcalling the scabs brought in to replace them. They threw rotten eggs at their harassers. Occasionally, a teenaged girl could be seen throwing a punch at an officer who collared her.[15]

Besides lifting an invisible class before the eyes of the nation, the strike lay the foundation for stable, successful women's unions. The strike marked a "moment of crystallization" for twentieth-century feminism because women recognized their gender as a bond that transcended class.[16] The most extreme example of the cross-class alliance was an elegantly dressed bulldog of a woman who became the strikers' most prominent supporter. Millionaire socialite Alva Belmont had shocked Gilded Age society when the former southern belle divorced William K. Vanderbilt on grounds of adultery. "Society was by turns stunned, horrified, and then savage in its opposition and criticism," she recalled. She persevered as a matter of social justice for high society's many abandoned wives who lived "half lives rather than divorce."[17] After the sudden death in 1908 of her second husband, millionaire Oliver H. P. Belmont, she discovered kindred spirits among the fiery British suffragettes while mourning in London. As she said, "I was a born rebel!"[18] Now a plump, wattled matron whose henna-colored hair matched her rouged cheeks, she threw her determination and money into the suffrage movement. Despite a twenty-year age gap, she and Milholland became close.

Belmont got involved in the shirtwaist strike after she shared a dais with WTUL president Dreier at a farewell rally for Emmeline Pankhurst at Cooper Union only days after the hall had reverberated with calls for the shirtwaist makers' gargantuan walkout. Just the week before, Milholland had passed the hat at Carnegie Hall during a speech by her London acquaintance to raise two thousand dollars for the strikers.[19] At the farewell rally, the notorious Pankhurst broke the hush awaiting her first words: "I am what you call a hooligan."[20] Outside, a harried police officer threatened to arrest Milholland and other soapboxers addressing the overflow crowd of hundreds that blocked Fourth Avenue. But they stood firm, part of an increasingly vocal chorus of Progressive Era dissidents asserting their right to free speech.[21] Inside the hall, Pankhurst choked backed tears as the crowd cheered and stamped its feet in tribute. All knew she faced imprisonment in England, but only a handful knew that her only son, Harry, had been crippled by polio. The regal fugitive undertook the American lecture tour to raise money to secure him the best medical care. Blatch closed the meeting by offering a resolution calling for the State Department to demand that the British free Alice Paul, a young American on a hunger strike in a London jail where she was serving thirty days for sneaking into a political banquet, shouting "Votes for Women," and hurling a shoe through a stained-glass window.[22] Perhaps in the midst of the emotional Cooper Union farewell, suffrage leader Blatch and WTUL leader Dreier persuaded Belmont that helping strikers could enlist thousands of them as suffragists.[23]

The next day, Belmont announced her suffrage club would host a fundraiser in the city's cavernous Hippodrome. The strikers needed the boost: Although many small shops had capitulated, the largest factories declared war on the remaining strikers. Their opposition bode for a long, cold winter for the ten thousand women still out.[24] Pickets continued to endure clubbings, fines, and arrests. Socialists and suffragists urged them to hang on. Socialist and ex-seamstress Rose Pastor Stokes, a hero in the strikers' eyes for realizing the dime-novel dream of marrying a millionaire, exhorted them, "Starve to win, or you'll starve anyway."[25] At the Hippodrome, Anna Howard Shaw, president of NAWSA, the nation's largest suffrage organization, told the cheering standing-room-only crowd, "Our cause is your cause, and your cause is our cause."[26]

This intoxicating swirl of protest, socialism, and suffrage swept Milholland off her feet. Her speeches on the strike demonstrate she clearly understood how gender figured into the conflict. She charged the pickets were fined only because they were women.[27] "[L]et no man think he may exhaust the working capacity of his women and then fling them, worn out and disordered, upon the community," she told one audience. She blamed prostitution on the factories' unlivable low wages. "I think there is a point where submission to unfair treatment becomes abject and slavish," she lectured middle-class listeners, "and retaliation in one form or another is indicative of self respect." But the poised rabble rouser revealed her uptown roots when she assured audiences that better conditions sought by the strikers would help spell an end to the "unsocial classes."[28]

The two arrests Milholland experienced while monitoring the picket line further illustrate the chasm between her and the proletariat, despite her good intentions. The socialist daily the *Call* recorded more than two hundred arrests in the first two weeks of the general strike.[29] Magistrates who heard the charges against the strikers refused to recognize their right to picket, a right the Supreme Court had yet to uphold.[30] When one picket demanded a warrant for the arrest of a man who attacked her, the magistrate replied, "You had no right to be picketing. . . . [Y]ou only got what was coming to you."[31] Another upbraided a group of battered young women: "You are on strike against God and nature, whose prime law is that man shall earn his bread in the sweat of his brow." Most of the teenaged pickets received fines after spending a few hours in jail cells alongside prostitutes and criminals, but some endured weeks of hard labor at infamous Blackwell's Island workhouse.[32]

On December 15, Milholland donned an evening gown before walking down to the Beerman & Frank factory at 84 Fifth Avenue. She was headed for the opera after picket observation duty. When she saw an officer arrest three women, Milholland protested and followed the group to the police station, where she was arrested at the door. Once inside, police released her, but she accompanied the women to night court. The magistrate brushed aside Milholland's objections and fined Lottie Gold five dollars, dismissing charges against the other two pickets.[33] Presumably, Gold went back to the line and Milholland went off to the opera. Only Milholland's name, however, appeared in a page-three headline of a *New York Times* story recounting her experience.[34]

Publicity lavished upon upper-class supporters such as Milholland rankled many strikers and their unglamorous socialist supporters.[35] The strikers resented uptowners appropriating the role they were working so hard and proudly to fashion for themselves. Shirtwaist strikers disliked being patronized by some bourgeois suffragists who viewed them as victims; they viewed themselves as heroic and powerful, agents of change in their lives.[36] They prided themselves in their independence, which they flaunted by indulging in public pleasures such as dance halls, movie houses, vaudeville shows, and amusement parks.[37] These working-class New Women bristled when the socialites tried to take over.[38]

Many socialists also opposed twinning labor strikes with suffrage because they feared female members would divert their energies from the broader workers' struggle to suffragists' middle-class agenda.[39] They distrusted their elite benefactors. "The papers say that Mrs. Belmont is worth millions; that each of her hats and suits is worth hundreds of dollars," said the protagonist in the fictionalized "The Diary of a Shirtwaist Striker" serialized in the *Call*. "If this be true and if she is affected by the girls' sufferings, why doesn't she try to do something more for us[?]"[40] The author was Theresa Malkiel. Her "Diary" coupled an idealized vision of the strikers with an acerbic view of their middle-class allies. One of Malkiel's targets was Milholland.

Perhaps more than any other participant, Milholland bridged the gap between socialites and socialists. Participating in the British suffragette movement had graced her with a confidence in public confrontation perfected by those scrappy aristocrats. As a member of Branch One of the city's socialist local, she spun as lithely in its convivial social circle as she did in a London ballroom.[41] She shone at a socialist reception for pickets just released from Blackwell's Island. Laughter and songs punctuated the gathering of more than two thousand workers at St. Mark's Place. Renowned labor organizer Leonora O'Reilly, herself a veteran of ten-hour days bent over sewing machines, awarded medals to each of the young inmates.[42] Milholland admired O'Reilly, saying once, "The story of her suffering is told by the trouble in her eyes, the lines about her mouth, the fluttering nervousness of her hands, and the tears in her voice."[43] Milholland joined the roar that greeted O'Reilly's comment, "I think I speak for all when I say that there is not a soul among us who will not go to prison if that be necessary." Milholland's friend, radical lawyer Crystal East-man, led a chorus of "The Marseillaise." Milholland convulsed the crowd with her performance of several humorous one-woman skits. The crowd clamored for encore after encore. Everyone danced until near dawn.[44]

Milholland lent her car for another gleeful shirtwaist outing, careening along Fifth Avenue in an auto rally organized by the WTUL's Harriet Laidlaw, a banker's wife and suffrage leader. Belmont lent her French-imported vehicle for the rally while WTUL colleague Anne Morgan, daughter of mega-financier J. P. Morgan, leased seven taxis to carry more strikers. Milholland chauffeured nineteen-year-old striker Bertha Elkin, who served four days for throwing an egg at a police officer, in her own car, a royal blue, 28-horsepower automobile her father gave her as a college gradua-tion present. These rambunctious women at the wheel presented a vivid picture of why driving so powerfully symbolized New Women's indepen-dence: their mobility seemed synonymous with freedom. The women merrily honked their horns as they roared past the shirtwaist factories. The *Call* observed: "It was amusing to see rich women carrying cards on which was proclaimed the need for organization for labor and which de-manded shorter hours and increased pay." When police showed up at the WTUL's headquarters to investigate whether the signs met the legal test for incitement, attorney Ida Rauh lectured them on the First Amend-ment.[45] Rauh's challenge to male officialdom, in addition to suffragists' protest on behalf of the Pankhurst soap boxers, provided Milholland with role models for her own confrontations with the law as well as the power of a legal education.

By the time of Milholland's second arrest on January 17, 1910, the strik-ers' glee had disappeared. Over seven hundred pickets had been arrested, and the big factories still held out.[46] Milholland was monitoring a demon-stration in front of a factory at 21 Waverly Place when police accosted her. At her side stood the latest in a merry-go-round of male companions, army lieutenant Henry W. Torney. When several spoke with Milholland, police captain Dominick Henry ordered the protest stopped. Milholland stepped up. "Magistrate Barlow told us we were within our rights so long as we kept moving."

"You must stop this at once," the captain growled back.

The pickets continued, and Henry yelled for his officers to arrest them. When he grabbed a girl, several strikers rushed him. More police rushed in and began grabbing pickets by their necks. They hauled off fourteen pickets on charges of disorderly conduct. Milholland and Torney steamed after them. When Milholland challenged the desk lieutenant about the arrests' validity, Henry ordered the pair arrested. A matron ushered Milholland off to a cell in the notorious Tombs jail. She telephoned her father, who put Meadowmount up as bail for Milholland and Torney.[47] In night court, the magistrate threw out the disorderly conduct charges against all sixteen defendants, hastily replaced with charges of unlawful assembly. The fourteen shirtwaist workers trudged back to their cells in lieu of three hundred dollars bail apiece until the general court session began later that night. Free on bail, Milholland asked to be tried immediately. "If Miss Milholland wishes to give herself up now she may surrender and I will put her with the others in the pen," the magistrate replied. She declined, but he agreed to delay the trial until morning. As a result, the fourteen pickets she ostensibly championed spent the night in the dank Tombs.[48]

At the next morning's hearing, Milholland estimated the number of pickets at about fifty, along with some two dozen supporters; police put the crowd at eight hundred to a thousand people. A doctor who had been passing by testified he was struck by Milholland's "gallant conduct and wise advice to the girls."[49] Captain Henry testified he originally arrested her because he thought she was a shirtwaist worker. She claimed he hurled obscenities at her and never warned her of any legal offense during the melee. The charge was dropped—but not before Milholland's name again appeared in big type atop the front page of the next morning's *Times*.[50] Malkiel read the news with less than admiration. Malkiel placed the fictional heroine of her "Diary of a Shirt Waist Maker" among the pickets netted with Milholland in one of the series' installments in the *Call*. Her tale offers an insight into how the largely anonymous pickets felt about interlopers such as Milholland. Malkiel's imprisoned striker writes from the Tombs that she is madder at "that fluffy thing who was the cause of our arrest than I am at the cops." She goes on:

> She didn't lose anything by it—had all the excitement she was looking for, posed as a martyr, had a dozen or more pictures taken free of charge and was then taken home by her rich pa. It's on account of her that we'll have to stay here over night, for she had the trial postponed until tomorrow. I think it's a shame; it was she that started it all. I'm pretty sure none of the Jew girls would be that mean. And when I come to think of it, what did she do for us girls all these weeks, and yet the papers were full of her.[51]

Malkiel's acid portrait of Milholland reflected increasing strains between the socialist and suffragist supporters competing for the strikers' hearts and minds. Strikers who showed up at Belmont's Madison Avenue mansion, for instance, were offended when she declared she was too busy to meet with them.[52] In fairness, Belmont not only donated one hundred thousand dollars to the strikers but also once showed up at night court at 2:30 a.m. blanketed in furs to bail out four strikers.[53] Another fund-raising rally she sponsored at Carnegie Hall sparked more friction. After the WTUL's Morgan blasted socialist Leonora O'Reilly's speech as too radical, Malkiel countered that strikers should shun "bourgeois" reformers. She charged the strikers' cause was endangered by the "pretended friendship of the Miss Morgans, who came down from the height of their pedestals to preach identity of interest to the little daughters of the people."[54] Malkiel's antipathy reeks of a self-reliant woman offended by the assumption she could not take care of herself; Malkiel's assertion of her agency was the stamp of the quintessential New Woman. Other gestures by the banker's daughter also grated on proud strikers. For instance, Morgan invited workers to relate their stories at the exclusive Colony Club, the city's first dining and sports club for women. Pathetic tales such as that of a fifteen-year-old girl who supported her disabled mother and three siblings on $3.50 a week jarred the club women to pass a hat they stuffed with $1,300. Then all took tea together. Some strikers and socialists found this charitable voyeurism humiliating.[55]

Socialist socialite Milholland was sensitive to such charges, which echoed in uptown circles. But she dismissed them as nonsense and blamed the press for sowing unfair criticism. The recent graduate said college women simply "have felt it worthwhile to contribute what they might to this heroic effort on the part of working women to better the conditions of their lives." She said volunteers shrugged off criticism with the "satisfaction of knowing that they have prevented many wrongful arrests and brought many abuses to light."[56] She was most bothered by charges she and others were motivated by sentimentality, a trait she and her peers despised as an odious vestige of Victorianism. When a colleague called her sentimental, she recoiled: "Do you suppose she's right? Horrors!"[57]

When the strike ended in February 1910, ILGWU Local 25 had signed contracts with 354 firms. Although the new union won a fifty-two-hour work week and 12 to 15 percent wage increases among other concessions, many of the larger firms never settled. They included the Triangle Shirtwaist Co., an omission with tragic consequences. On March 25, 1911, 146 workers burned or leaped to their deaths after fire broke out on the eighth floor of the building where the shirtwaist strike had started so ebulliently fifteen months earlier. Among the ignored demands had been the installation of fire escapes and an end to the practice of locking exterior doors.[58]

Many obstacles remained along the miles of picket lines ahead, but the underdog, teenaged strikers had established women as a force in labor.

And the strike helped establish a feminist consciousness among women work-ers.[59] However mercurial, working-class and upper-class women achieved an unprecedented degree of sisterhood. A shard of the strikers' glory reflected on the WTUL, whatever its shortcomings. The strikers could not have weathered the hurricane of protests for six months without the help of the league and members such as Milholland.

The experience revealed some of Milholland's strengths and weaknesses. Her luminous idealism lit up the public imagination. She drew the press like moths to a flame; her presence guaranteed publicity for a cause. Her abilities as a speaker rose with her prestige. She showed courage in con-fronting authority, even seeming to revel in it. Yet she was unwilling to abandon the privilege that accompanied her status as a wealthy, educated, beautiful, white, Protestant woman, traits that explained much of her pub-lic fascination. Given the choice, she could not bring herself to endure jail with the strikers. For all of Milholland's empathy with the factory workers, she was not one of them. Her experience encapsulated the thorny issues that class and other differences would pose for women's rights activ-ists as they tried to sustain solidarity among the diverse groups that com-prised their sex. Milholland also discovered the downside of the power of celebrity when critics slammed her for playing at radicalism. The charge held some truth. The life-quaffing Milholland excelled at play. In fact, during the tumultuous strike she plunged into one of the first real love affairs of her life.

Villager

*"Simple but magical words
<u>new</u> and <u>free</u>"*

Inez Milholland caroused with the boisterous young radicals who jammed the Greenwich Village apartment Max Eastman shared with his older sister Crystal like turtles on a sunny log in a pond. The Village, the bohemian pond on which 118 Waverly Place floated, was the epicenter of change that rippled across the nation in the decade before World War I. Villagers rejected conventions in business, labor, art, culture, and sex. As Milholland herself observed, "The quality of the age is a flat refusal to submit to anything on faith, but to insist on testing and examining life at every point."[1] New Women played a leading role in its cultural revolution. Crystal Eastman could have been discussing her good friend Milholland when she rejoiced that the most exciting people lived in New York, "who are working hard at something all the time; and especially the radicals, the reformers, the students,—who really live to help, and yet get so much fun out of it,—because they are open-minded, and eager over every new movement."[2]

Striding from her parents' brownstone three blocks northeast of Washington Square Park, Milholland could pass under Stanford White's soaring marble Washington Arch that marked the foot of Fifth Avenue and within minutes join the revelry at Polly Holladay's convivial Macdougal Street restaurant. Upstairs in the Liberal Club, Villagers collected around two large, open fireplaces to talk passionately about any idea that signified the "simple but magical words <u>new</u> and <u>free</u>": socialism, anarchism, feminism, modern art, free love, free speech, free verse, new theatre, new psychotherapy, new morality, New Women. If not talking they were playing, most outrageously when they dressed as pagans and fairies and flitted about at bacchanalian "pagan routs."[3] As Floyd Dell recalled, "Life seemed extraordinarily simple and happy in Greenwich Village."[4] The raffish Village remained as inspirational for free spirits in 1910 as when Tom Paine penned the *Crisis* there.[5] Diverse residents shared an affinity for personal freedom: settlement workers, socialists, artists, suffragists, writers, and New York University students. Not yet tethered by subway to the rest of the city, its streets groped like twisted fingers on old footpaths south and west of Washington Square. Its quaintness belied its cultural importance. "Where the Village led," observed William O'Neill, "millions would soon follow."[6]

One direction in which the Village led was the sexual revolution. Perhaps the New Woman's most revolutionary demand was for validation of female sexual pleasure.[7] It marked the biggest difference between the first and second generation of New Women, and the sexual revolution plumbed deeper than physical satisfaction: Sexual autonomy came to signify freedom for women in all spheres.[8] New Women envisioned no less than a new relationship between men and women, the so-called Human Sex, in which the socially constructed artifices of gender could be replaced by what Village intellectual Randolph Bourne characterized as "genuine comradeship and healthy frank regard and understanding."[9] The requisite for a sexual relationship no longer was marriage but "the ability to have open, deep, and honest communication."[10]

Milholland's beliefs about sexual love mirrored those sentiments. She was well versed in the decade's calls for sexual freedom by Emma Goldman, Margaret Sanger, Ellen Key, and Havelock Ellis.[11] Sigmund Freud had recently toured the nation, and the new science of psychology—some would call it the new religion—propelled individuals to obey rather than suppress their desires.[12] Milholland caught this enthusiasm and later took classes in abnormal psychology at Columbia University with Professor Frank Hollingsworth, whose wife, psychologist Leta Hollingsworth, authored a pioneering study that found women are not mentally debilitated during menstruation.[13] Strongly influenced by the liberating ideas about sex floating about them, couplings among Village radicals were purposefully unconventional. Many, including Milholland, discovered sexual freedom deceptively complicated, even an oxymoron. "Sexual experience became as much of an imperative for the practitioners of the new paganism as abstinence had been for the puritans who had preceded them," observed historian Leslie Fishbein.[14] Couples, such as the writers Neith Boyce and Hutchins Hapgood, tried open marriage.[15]

Women's call for sexual freedom threatened society much more than their call for votes. Most Americans remained prudishly Victorian. The vice squad, for instance, banned George Bernard Shaw's play about prostitution, *Mrs. Warren's Profession*, from Broadway in 1907; the same year, the Metropolitan Opera was forced to shut down its production of *Salome*.

Futile dancehall bans tried to stamp out feral dance crazes such as the kangaroo dip, grizzly bear, and turkey trot, one of Milholland's favorite steps. In this nervous atmosphere, the New Woman's revolutionary claim that women could and should enjoy sex outside of marriage unleashed middle-class fears that uncontrolled sex would render marriage obsolete and shatter the foundation of society. Milholland, in contrast, slipped into the Village's amoral ambiance as comfortably as if it were the sable stole she favored. Even in this neighborhood of remarkable women, she stood out—"so darkly beautiful and spirited," as Inez Haynes Irwin described her.[16] Villagers recognized Milholland as an activist, but they mainly remembered her as one of its great beauties. Dreamy intellectual Max Eastman was among the decade's modern young romantics who imagined an Amazon lover. He believed he found her in Milholland, the first important love of his eventful life in an affair immortalized in a chapter of his memoirs called, "My Amazon Comes True." He wrote, "Her eyes were a deep hue of the jewel called aquamarine, bright mischievous lakes of eyes, her skin's crimson and ivory was as vivid as though it had just been rubbed with snow, and her hair was a deep lustrous brown like Juno's."[17]

Milholland knew his sister Crystal, a 1907 graduate of New York University Law School, from socialist and suffrage rallies. Crystal Eastman worked her way though the law school by managing an East Side recreation center and lived for a while in a settlement house. After graduating, she studied more than a thousand industrial accidents as part of the groundbreaking "Pittsburgh Survey." Eastman also found time for a merry-go-round of suitors and socializing. "She was for thousands," wrote another New Woman, *Nation* editor Freda Kirchwey, "a symbol of what the free woman might be."[18] Eastman and Milholland enjoyed a close friendship that besides suffrage rallies included raucous wine-fueled dinners that lasted past midnight. Madeleine Doty, another radical lawyer, also roomed at the Eastmans, where a frequent visitor was Ida Rauh, an actress, poet, and attorney. Crystal's lanky brother Max was a doctoral student in philosophy at Columbia University. His prematurely white hair and chiseled profile made him resemble a diplomat more than a mischief-loving iconoclast.[19] By fall 1909, Inez and Max were rising radical stars, celebrated for their handsome looks and soaring oratory. "He looked Beauty and spoke Justice," a male friend said of Eastman. Another called him "the sleepy Adonis."[20] She invited him along on picket duty, and he accompanied her to court a couple of times when she testified for arrested pickets. When the pair shared a podium at a suffrage rally in Cleveland, Ohio, they also shared a sleeping porch that night where their hostess, a Vassar classmate of Milholland's, put them up in two beds. Max Eastman promptly fell asleep. His dispassion worked like an elixir on Milholland. She soon declared to him that she loved him.

He was taken aback. Despite her looks, he had found her humorless, insensitive, and overly intense. Gradually, however, he began fantasizing that she was the Amazon he had conjured in his dreams and poems. "Her faults of harshness and slow sympathy, or headstrong selfhood—even the swamp-flower coarseness of her beauty—were just what would trouble a poet in a gorgeous female warrior if she came to life," he rationalized.[21] When finally kissing her goodnight at her parents' door, Eastman discovered he had mistaken as intellectual fervor Milholland's well of sexual passion. Her transformation in his arms from Amazon to adoring lover made his knees quake. Still, for two weeks he resisted her demand that he declare his passion, finally blurting on December 3, "I love you." When she implored him to elope, he explained soberly why they should not. But she beguiled him. His sister sent him fifty dollars to woo her friend, tickled that her brother had fallen "gloriously in love after all these lean years."[22] Eastman invited Milholland to meet his parents in southwestern New York. He spent the week before she was due in Elmira enraptured—hero worship, he tellingly called it. He recalled, "I walked about in a perpetual joyful surprise at the constancy of my emotion."[23]

The shirtwaist strike was consuming Milholland's passion by mid-December, however, and she failed to show up in Elmira. The morning after her first arrest, Eastman left a note for his parents: "Excuse me, I've gone to New York to get my girl." Milholland scribbled a note for her parents and slipped away with him. She got along famously with his mother, Annis Eastman, the nation's first female Congregational minister and a fellow suffragist, who felt overwhelmed by this "strange great bird from another world."[24] Milholland and Eastman skated on the Chemung River, where he received a taste of his beloved's bruising frankness when with a brusque shake of her head she dismissed his ebullient attempts to impress her with his prowess on blades. The couple suffered another jolt of reality when they sleighed to an abandoned house to consummate their affair. In the middle of a caress, Milholland informed Eastman he was not inspiring her to make love. That chilly encounter was the most intimate moment the mismatched couple could muster. They returned to the city that Sunday, and Eastman joined the Milhollands for tea. Her father railed against the many manifestations of Satan, of which he believed Eastman to be but one. Eastman wrote his mother, "I would go mad in two months in that house."[25]

The affair wound down torturously slowly, as Milholland and Eastman could not admit that despite their best efforts, neither loved the other. He was as emotionally conservative as he was politically radical. "My devotion to you is above anything that I thought I could feel," he wrote. "But I can not make in my mind or heart the conventional connection between that and our plunging headlong into an enterprise [marriage] that a glance at either of our characters would show to be tremendous and of doubtful outcome." He signed it, "Your foolishly deliberate lover."[26]

In contrast, she fired off a string of smoldering letters that demonstrated the pattern of future love affairs. She reveled in confessing unfaithfulness, begging forgiveness as she spilled details of dalliances with other men. She called Eastman in the middle of one night and begged him to rush to her side. "Something tragic and terrible has happened," she dramatically intoned. He raced to her house. A mutual male friend, she told him, had kissed her—and she had kissed him back. She cried, however, that she had thought of Eastman throughout the sordid encounter. "[S]he spoke as though those kisses were the sin against the Holy Ghost," he recalled. They parted in tears near dawn. Then she went home, turned on the gas, and halfheartedly tried to kill herself.[27] Although only Eastman's suspiciously self-serving account survives, Milholland's histrionics are another indication of her underlying emotional instability and battle with depression. Theirs would not be her last operatic romance.

Soon after they split up, Eastman became editor of *The Masses*, a scrappy mélange of art and politics. Lack of money created constant crisis for the anti-capitalist magazine, on the verge of collapse when he bumped into Milholland in the lobby of the Hotel Manhattan in December 1912. When he told her *The Masses'* fate, Milholland arranged for him to dine at Alva Belmont's mansion. She brought along her new beau, novelist John Fox Jr. After a jovial meal, Belmont offered Eastman two thousand dollars to keep the magazine rolling off the press. After a pregnant pause, the conservative Fox pledged another thousand.[28] The donations kept the revolutionary periodical alive until government censors killed it in World War I.[29] Milholland and Eastman remained lifelong friends, an admirable trait of most of her romances. He later married and had a son with her friend Ida Rauh.

Milholland tried to begin law school in January 1910, but the combination of her studies and strike duties proved too taxing. She grew ill. Despite her athleticism, Milholland could be physically frail. On March 15, 1910, she entered Roosevelt Hospital to have her appendix removed after faith healers called in by her parents failed to cure her. Despite her protests, her father knelt at her bedside to pray for her recovery. Her own attitude toward the operation was stoic. Her recovery appears to have been slow, and she found herself hospitalized again in May. Stormy encounters with her father did not speed her recuperation. Besides her agnosticism and socialism, he raged, he feared she now was becoming a "slave of sense," his synonym for sex.[30]

John Milholland found an outlet for his own passions in his crusade against racism. Aghast at rampant lynching and legalistic terror of African Americans, the tiny circle of nascent civil rights crusaders to which he belonged was finally moved to action when in 1909 white mobs killed six blacks and drove two thousand others from Springfield, Illinois. One of Milholland's colleagues was the African American journalist Ida Wells-Barnett, whose newspaper *Free Speech* was torched in Memphis a decade earlier when she wrote an editorial blasting the lynching of three black grocers. Barnett represented another type of New Woman; born to abject poverty and considered a pariah by most Americans because of her race, she shared the determination to live a full, meaningful life that character-ized New Women.[31] At the group's unprecedented civil rights conference that May, Barnett meticulously detailed the horrors of 3,284 lynchings over the past quarter century, and Atlanta University professor W. E. B. Du Bois assailed Booker T. Washington.[32] Attendees separated with a com-mitment to create an organization that would use the U.S. Constitution to fight racial discrimination.[33] John Milholland lobbied for his Constitu-tion League to serve as that organization, but when the group reconvened the next May, they created the National Association for the Advancement of Colored People.[34] Milholland promptly raised five thousand dollars as NAACP treasurer but provided a better service by recruiting Du Bois to edit a new periodical suggested by Milholland called *The Crisis*.[35] The following year, Milholland was instrumental in organizing in London an unprecedented Universal Congress of Races that brought together a thou-sand people representing fifty races and ethnic groups to discuss how to improve global racial and cross-cultural relations.[36]

Inez Milholland did not get involved with her father's cause that spring, possibly because she remained weakened by her surgery, but she later joined the NAACP.[37] Several years later, she spoke at the landmark Amenia Conference that marked the ascendance of the NAACP's aggressive con-stitutional approach to civil rights. She suggested Negroes create their own political party, an idea Du Bois liked so much he propounded it in *The Crisis*. The editor joined the chorus of men taken by the "glory of her young womanhood."[38] But during the historic first meeting of the NAACP, Mil-holland was still recuperating from her appendectomy at Alva Belmont's 140-room seafront castle on Long Island, the model for Gatsby's mansion in F. Scott Fitzgerald's *The Great Gatsby*. Weekends, they received guests such as English suffragette Ray Costelloe and American suffrage leader

Anna Howard Shaw. "Life is very pleasant and luxurious, but I couldn't live like this always and be content," Milholland wrote her parents, who worried about the millionaire's hold on her daughter.[39]

Their fears were not ungrounded; the status-hungry Belmont had even locked her teenaged daughter Consuelo into her bedroom until she agreed to marry the stuffy, aging Duke of Marlborough, and her shabby treatment of Doris Stevens, another promising young New Woman whom she later employed as a sort of publicist, became a feminist scandal.[40] Belmont admired Milholland's "gallant fiery spirit," in stark contrast to her own beauteous but pliant daughter, perhaps seeing in Milholland a youthful version of herself.[41] Milholland reciprocated her affection but was too independent—and independently wealthy, unlike Consuelo and Stevens—to become victimized. Other suffragists probably did not recognize Belmont in a tribute Milholland once paid the officious millionaire: "Her most striking characteristic is a complete absence of egotism."[42] The pair sailed to London in Belmont's flower-filled, first-class cabin on the *Lusitania*.[43] Although they told reporters the purpose of their trip was to study British suffragette methods, they seemed to be cramming for an exam on society's latest fashions, menus, and dance steps.[44] The London social season glittered with parties and the ostentatious display of wealth. Belmont's daughter, the Duchess of Marlborough, described it as "a pageant in which beautiful women and distinguished men performed a stately ritual."[45]

Milholland shook off the toll of the long, cold winter observing picket lines by submerging herself in the social scene as if it were a hot bubble bath, finally surfacing as a speaker at the suffragettes' "monster demonstration" at Hyde Park on July 23. Milholland joined twenty thousand women in a two-mile parade to the park.[46] Inside, a quarter million people darkened the park grounds as they jockeyed to hear more than 150 speakers on forty platforms.[47] Although her platform stood on the outskirts, Milholland attracted a responsive crowd. "I thought her the most beautiful thing in all the world," an American woman in the audience recalled.[48] She spoke among heady company, notably Emmeline and Christabel Pankhurst. Lady Constance Lytton, still weak from force feeding by tubes during a prison hunger strike, held forth atop another platform that she shared with Emily Wilding Davison. The intense Davison would achieve suffrage martyr status in 1913 when she died after throwing herself in front of the king's horse on Derby Day.[49] After a bugle blast cut off the speeches, Milholland joined the multitude's booming call for votes for women as it thundered above the park and rumbled across the Atlantic.

Although Milholland shed her suffrage badge for a silk gown a few days later for more balls in Paris, the Hyde Park rally had stirred her sense of political commitment. That did not stop her from shopping for couture gowns or enjoying the Folies Bergere with Belmont and another refugee from the shirtwaist strike, Anne Morgan.[50] But the New Woman's creed of leading a meaningful life and working to improve society was deeply ingrained in her, and she was chafing at the formalism of Parisian society. As the European coastline disappeared behind the friends sailing home in September, Milholland felt rested and ready to acquire the serious tools she would need to effect social change. The high life was seductive, but professional success remained the most important goal for this New Woman. Reporters at the pier peppered her with questions about suffrage, which was beginning to heat up the 1910 elections. What did she think about a politician's crack that suffragists were "frumps"? Would she ride in the chariot reserved for the most beautiful suffragist in the October parade? What did she do in London? France? What exactly would she do in New York? Milholland laughed, a Turkish turban trailing rakishly from around her neck. When they persisted, she allowed it might be wise to send the prettiest suffragists to legislators; it seemed impossible to move the press's focus from physical appearances to more substantive issues. As for her own plans, she stated, illness had pushed behind her studies. She planned to return to Greenwich Village to study law.[51]

Lawyer

*"To discharge my own individual
debt to society"*

Milholland bent over her typewriter and pecked out, "I am intending to practice law." When she finished her three-page, single-spaced letter, she slipped it into an envelope addressed to the dean and faculty of the School of Law at Harvard University.[1] Milholland was determined to smash Harvard's ban on women although the British law schools at Oxford and Cambridge universities already had rejected her because of her sex.[2] After returning from London in autumn 1909, she visited several Boston lawyers seeking recommendations that she be admitted as the first female student in the ninety-two-year history of the nation's oldest law school.[3] In October, on the eve of the shirtwaist strike, she mailed off her missive explaining why Harvard should break the sex barrier. "I realize that such a step would be attended with changes of various kinds, and that changes are often disconcerting, and usually unwelcome," she wrote, "but if one is once convinced of the desirability of the end which the changes are supposed to bring about, then even the small annoyances of the first stages are accepted with equanimity." Men and women must learn to work together. She challenged the faculty: "Why should not Harvard help to inculcate this new spirit of 'camaraderie' in the younger generation, instead of following, as it must sooner or later, where others point the way?"[4]

Precious few law schools had offered to lead. New Yorker Lemma Barkaloo in 1869 had to travel to Washington University in St. Louis before she could find a law school willing to enroll her as the nation's first female law student.[5] In 1872 the U.S. Supreme Court upheld the denial of Myra Bradwell's admission to the Illinois bar. Justices concurred with the state court: "The natural and proper timidity and delicacy which belongs to the female sex evidently unfits it for many of the occupations of civil life. The constitution of the family organization, which is founded in the divine ordinance, as well as in the nature of things, indicates the domestic sphere as that which properly belongs to the domain and functions of womanhood."[6] The invocation of God's will points to how deeply inscribed was the concept of separate spheres. Milholland's argument to Harvard that men and women must learn to study and work together chipped at this wall between gender roles, already etched by cracks by the time she applied to law school. The year she was born, for instance, the New York state legislature passed a special bill allowing Kate Stoneman to enter the bar.[7]

In 1910 a mere 558 of 114,704 lawyers and judges were female, in contrast to more than 9,000 women among 151,132 physicians.[8] No Wall Street firm would hire Alice Dillingham, NYU's Class of 1905 valedictorian, for instance, so she took a job with the Legal Aid Society.[9] Vassar alumna Mabel Witte despaired of the "vast amount of prejudice and sentimentality" she had to overcome in the field. The profession considered it inappropriate for women to handle criminal law, divorce cases, and sensational jury trials; clients were skeptical about a woman lawyer's competence, eliminating them from many cases. Firms did not want to even hire female clerks because they worried about sending them to serve subpoenas at night.[10]

Milholland, nonetheless, had wanted to study law even before she entered Vassar. "I see that almost everyone that has done anything in a literary way, unless born with a natural genius, has been trained by the study of this profession," she noted in 1905. "So law for me!"[11] By her senior year, she had refined her goals to becoming a lawyer for women's rights.[12] Law, despite its chilly climate, was the career of choice for many New Women because they recognized its power to reform. The number of women lawyers more than tripled to 1,738 during the decade.[13] Milholland concluded her plea to the Harvard faculty with a New Woman argument for "self realization": "[E]ven if only one woman wanted to realize all her possibilities in the best way, should she not have a right to[?]"[14]

Milholland brought the Harvard trustees a bouquet in the suffragette colors of purple, white, and green, but they rejected her appeal even though the faculty was willing to admit her.[15] She was angry and hurt. "I told them that I felt it was time to get rid of that old idea of only sentiment between men and women, and that they should begin to work together on a business basis as they will have to meet in the world."[16] Milholland's encounter with sex discrimination in the male-dominated professional world mirrored that of thousands of women college graduates who discovered they had been exotic plants in an academic greenhouse. Milholland's conclusion to her letter indicated the self-negation that patriarchy could instill even in talented, ambitious women who internalized negative stereotypes.

"I apoligize [*sic*] for having talked so much," Milholland concluded. "It is one of womens [*sic*] faults which we hope a liberal training will eliminate."[17]

Milholland's insistence upon a career illustrates a key trait of New Women. "[I] want to be self-supporting," she explained. "I don't have to, of course, but for my own self-respect I feel I must be."[18] New heroines of popular fiction in the 1910s reflected women's new dreams beyond marriage, formerly the Holy Grail of female protagonists. In the new stories, marriage threatened their ambitions. In "Shelter," for instance, the retort of Dorothy Eades, happily treading her way as an automobile saleswoman when her beau offers to marry her, shows work symbolized more than paying bills: "I've been taken care of and taken care of til I'm half smothered! I've just got out of my box and—you'd put me back in it, and feed me through a hole, and let a few chosen people come near enough to speak. No, George! No!"[19] In conjunction with their strong sense of self, many New Women possessed an intense sense of social responsibility. Milholland's senses were especially well-honed because both her parents and her high school had instilled in her a sense of social obligation. "I am trying to discharge my own individual debt to society," Milholland explained, "by improving the conditions of life for women and children."[20]

Career options remained limited, however, for Vassar's Class of 1909. Many parents who sent their daughters to college did not want them to hold a job; they expected them to return to the family fold better read but basically unchanged. The middle-class aversion to working women created a cruel irony for the new wave of female degree holders eager to apply their skills.[21] Of 2,363 Vassar alumnae responding to a 1915 survey, nearly two-thirds of those who had ever held a job had only worked in the low-paying, sex-segregated ghetto of teaching. "It never occurred to me," said a woman who graduated a year behind Milholland, "that I could be anything but a school teacher." Only four Vassar alumnae were lawyers in 1911.[22] One was Crystal Eastman, who served as a powerful role model for Milholland's ambitions. Eastman earned her degree from the School of Law at NYU in 1903. NYU encouraged legal education for women as early as 1890, when it sponsored a women's law class that evolved out of a free legal aid program for poor women.[23] By the 1910s, however, NYU's law school graduated more women than any other. Besides Eastman, Milholland's colleagues Ida Rauh, Madeline Doty, and Jessie Ashley were NYU law graduates. The university's welcoming atmosphere "attracted a remarkable number of spirited, adventurous women eager to topple any obstacle that stood between them and full equality," Phyllis Eckhaus observed.[24]

Eastman, for example, published the groundbreaking *Work-Accidents and the Law* and served on the state Employers' Liability Commission—a rare and prestigious appointment for a woman in 1910—where she helped write the nation's first workmen's compensation law.[25] Journalist Doty went undercover to investigate prison conditions after she was named New York state's first woman prison commissioner in 1912. Rauh chaired the legislative committee of the WTUL. Ashley and Rauh were arrested when they passed out birth control pamphlets in Union Square. All helped jumpstart the climactic suffrage campaign of the 1910s. Ashley and fellow NYU law school alumna Elinor Byrns helped Harriot Stanton Blatch organize the first Fifth Avenue suffrage parade; Eastman became a founding executive of NAWSA's Congressional Union.[26] These were the women who offered Milholland a blueprint of how to pay back "the debt that we owe society."[27] They helped shape Milholland's quintessentially New Woman philosophy that "one is here in the world to develop—to expand one's personality—to become broadgazed and courageous and happy."[28]

Within days after arriving home from London, Milholland began classes in contract law, torts, agency law, common law pleading, personal property law, criminal law, and the New York Code of Civil Procedures. She hated the minutiae of civil procedure but excelled in pleading cases. Her grades that year included one B, two Cs, three Ds, and an F in the Code of Civil Procedures. She received the sole A of her law-school career in common law pleading, a reflection of her affinity for arguing for the underdog as well as her flair for the dramatic and acting experience gained at Vassar.[29]

Abundant diversions help account for her lackluster performance. The suffrage movement was snowballing, and Milholland was involved with two of the city's liveliest suffrage clubs—Women's Political Union, successor to Blatch's ELSSW, and Belmont's Political Equality Association. In 1910 the two groups joined forces against anti-suffrage candidates. Evenings, Milholland could be found riding in noisy auto caravans that honked across the Twenty-fifth assembly district decrying anti-suffrage Assemblyman Artemus Ward Jr.[30] The WPU systematically called upon every Republican in the district, pointing out blemishes in Ward's voting record methodically uncovered by Blatch. One night Milholland and Belmont barged into the local Republican club meeting, and on another they joined a torchlight parade to Union Square.[31] Other nights Milholland soapboxed against anti-suffrage legislators outside the Hotel Normandie.[32] Blatch boasted no one could walk a block in the district without bumping into a suffragist slamming Ward. He hired a horse and cart that toted the slogan, "Every Girl Likes Artemus Ward Except the Suffragettes," but a sharp-eyed suffragist noticed the animal's limp and called the humane society, which ordered it back to the stable.[33] On Election Day, Milholland joined some fifty WPU members who arose early to watch the polls.[34] When the tally came in, Ward barely squeaked back into office and the district's anti-suffrage senator was defeated.[35] Statewide, fifty-nine legislators who opposed votes for women lost their seats.[36]

That same year, suffragists celebrated a suffrage victory in Washington state, where voters broke the movement's fourteen-year drought. Milholland received the honor of pinning a fifth star on the suffrage flag at a Cooper Union rally. "We have found that protestation did no good," she told the crowd, "and we have had to revolt. Friends, we have revolted in the spirit of the men of '76." The applause drowned out the band playing "My Country 'Tis of Thee" as the big blue flag dropped and she pinned the fifth star in its center. Milholland concluded the evening by proposing that everyone give up something for Thanksgiving and send the money to Arizona suffragists, in the throes of a rough campaign.[37] In 1911 Milholland occasionally could be seen chalking suffrage announcements on the sidewalk in front of the Hotel Normandie, her sable stole brushing the pavement. She had witnessed how London suffragettes used this inexpensive advertising medium. She told onlookers why women should vote and invited them inside to browse through the suffrage literature.[38] Milholland also rode up to a bar in Harlem with Blatch to soap-box against another anti-suffrage politician.[39]

Milholland stole off that October to Louisville, Kentucky, for NAWSA's annual convention. The kinetic energy that charged the convention must have been fresh air for the law student swimming in legal minutiae. On a single panel, Milholland heard Emmeline Pankhurst, Anna Howard Shaw, and Jane Addams.[40] Milholland contributed to the sorority that infused these annual gatherings by performing her humorous one-woman skit "If Women Voted."[41] The four-page script showed her sentiments clearly lay with the working class, even if the Vassar alumna could only caricature its speech: Barney Shea returns to his East Side tenement tipsy on Election Day after voting for "Big Bill," the local political boss. His wife, Nora, indignantly puts on her hat and prepares to cast her vote against Big Bill — a skill she learned from "dthe wimmins political classes" of the WTUL.[42] Milholland lent working-class women more sober support when she called for criminal punishment of the owners of the Triangle factory at a mass meeting of the WTUL after authorities dropped some charges stemming from the fatal fire.[43] Another lively diversion from memorizing legal codes was the WPU's 1912 suffrage ball, where laundry workers danced along-side millionaires. Milholland refused to dance with a man during the grand march. "Oh," she cried as the music struck up, "I must begin the grand march with a woman suffragist." She grabbed a friend's hand and waltzed her into the line.[44] The next year, Blatch had to rent an armory to squeeze in more than eight thousand revelers.[45] Belmont's PEA also sponsored Saturday night dances.[46] The festivities reflected suffragists' ability to cut across class lines and mesh politics with pleasure as well as New Women's desire to nurture their playful instincts in addition to their social consciences.

Inez found more diversion from law with her brother and sister. Jack, who entered Harvard in fall 1910 after graduating from St. Paul's School in Concord, New Hampshire, now towered over the older sister that he idolized. The dreamy, book-loving boy who reveled in quiet communion with nature had sprouted into a handsome six-foot, 170-pound athlete. In London, he was a scholastic boxing champion; at Harvard he played first base for the Crimson's baseball team and was a drop kicker for its football team.[47] Brother and sister spent a September weekend together at Meadowmount, rousing themselves from the Big House's comfortable big porch to indulge in one of their favorite pastimes, baseball.[48] Inez was also close to Vida, a softer, shorter version of herself. After she left Vassar, Vida had studied voice, harmony, piano, and languages in New York.[49] Inez was proud of her sister, who enjoyed a successful singing debut that June, but could not resist occasionally hectoring her.[50] Sibling rivalry perhaps colored the relationship between the sisters. Although Inez was close to her mother, Vida and Jean were practically inseparable. Her mother stayed with her during her singing studies at home and abroad. Although her father once described the accommodating Vida as "an angel in human form," he devoted more attention to routing the devil in Inez.[51] Inez, as the eldest child, and Jack, as the only son, found themselves frequently at odds with John. Vida played the stereotypical role of the middle child who declined to rock the boat and enjoyed the smoothest relationship with their father. Vida found herself forever in the shadow of her more dramatic sister not only in public but also at home.

Despite all these diversions, Milholland managed to pass her final examinations that May. She mustered a C in her second try at Codes of Civil Procedure, along with another C, three Ds, and a B, in insurance law.[52] That gave her the requisite twenty-four credit hours for an LL.B. She opted to clerk for a law firm instead of attending a third year of law school, an alternative for admittance to the New York bar.[53] Before graduating, she stretched gender boundaries at the law school a bit by joining

Vida Milholland with pet dogs. *Courtesy of Meadowmount School of Music.*

the senior men for one of their previously all-male smokers.[54] Earlier she had been elected class vice president, running on a strictly suffrage platform.[55] On June 5, 1912, she was one of 10 women and 128 men handed diplomas during the school's eightieth commencement ceremony.[56] After graduation she immediately sailed to England even though the sinking of the *Titanic* on April 12 made transatlantic travel seem less casual. The disaster claimed her father's close friend *Review of Reviews* publisher William T. Stead, and John had thanked God none of his ocean-hopping family had been aboard.[57] The summer after her graduation, Inez wallowed less in ballrooms. She fattened her suffragette credentials by delivering a speech at Albert Hall and soap-boxing again in Hyde Park.[58] She did attend a dinner honoring Marconi, still a close family friend, and on another evening scandalized other proper British guests by dancing the turkey trot with a female friend.[59] She cut her sojourn abroad short, however, and returned to New York at the end of July with her maid, Florence, to finally begin her career.[60]

Given Milholland's lackluster grades, it seems surprising she landed a job as a clerk for the well-known firm of Osborne, Lamb, & Garvan at 115 Broadway. James W. Osborne was a former district attorney with twenty-five years of experience as a criminal lawyer.[61] Milholland's sympathy toward the underdog inclined her to the defense side of the courtroom. Milholland served as stenographer in the Tombs during Osborne's interview with an accused murderer, and she interviewed witnesses for his defense. When not clerking for Osborne, she spent hours observing trials and even had herself handcuffed to an inmate "just to see how it felt."[62] "Miss Milholland is always able to find some excuse for the prisoner," observed the *New York World*. "She feels that they are all 'defectives' to be cured or treated rather than enemies of society to be punished for their crimes."[63] She added prison reform to her lengthening list of causes.

Suffrage colleagues worried Milholland's demanding new career would absorb all of her energy. She already had offended Barnum & Bailey Circus suffragists when in the middle of law exams she failed to show up at Madison Square Garden to name a baby giraffe "Miss Suffrage."[64] When NAWSA president Anna Howard Shaw congratulated her after her graduation from law school, the octogenarian admonished her not to stop working for votes for women.[65] Shaw needn't have worried. Milholland had no intention of exiting center stage of New York City's increasingly spectacular suffrage campaign.

Spectacle

"One of the high priestesses of the woman suffrage cause"

7

A bugle blared and banners snapped. Inez Milholland stepped into her first American suffrage parade on May 7, 1911. The semester's law exams loomed, but she had no intention of missing the biggest demonstration of the suffrage campaign, witnessed by 150,000 spectators jammed along forty-three blocks of Fifth Avenue. The march of three thousand women was one of a series of escalating spectacles that lit up the final decade of the suffrage campaign like fireworks on the Fourth of July. Milholland and another young woman each grasped a tether that held aloft the corners of a huge yellow banner carried by a third marcher. The refrain from a nineteenth-century English hymn embroidered in black letters on the banner remained forever associated with Milholland:

> Forward, out of error,
> Leave behind the night,
> Forward through the darkness,
> Forward into light.[1]

The press lapped up the medieval spectacle of banners, floats, and bands. Parades brought suffrage the mass media exposure that transformed the cause into a mass movement. They challenged the notion of female spectacle as purely passive and forced society to accept women's presence in the public sphere.[2] The physically imposing Milholland proved the perfect woman to wed spectacle with agency. The Fifth Avenue parades she led in 1911, 1912, and 1913 snared suffrage more positive publicity than it had received in the past half century, thanks in no small part to media fascination with her Gibson girl good looks.[3] "No suffrage parade was complete without Inez Milholland," the *New York Sun* contended, "for with her tall figure and free step, her rich brown hair, blue eyes, fair

Inez as marshal of the 1913 Fifth Avenue parade. *Courtesy of Archives & Special Collections, Vassar College Library.*

skin and well cut features, she was an ideal figure of the typical American woman."[4]

Milholland saddled up a fractious bay in Washington Square as part of the cavalry leading ten thousand marchers in May 1912.[5] That fall Milholland traded her saddle for a seat in a gold chariot representing Wyoming in a torchlight parade celebrating the admission of Arizona, Kansas, and Oregon into the suffrage column.[6] The herald of Newark's suffrage parade was dubbed the "Inez Milholland" of New Jersey.[7] Her fame extended across the Atlantic. An enterprising *London Daily Mail* reporter sent her a fan letter in a blue envelope addressed only with her photograph and the words, "New York, USA." She received his message, which read, "Madam, wishing you every success for the quiet way you are going about things. Yours, England."[8]

The ubiquitous Milholland attracted even more attention when she starred in suffrage pageants, in which players posed motionless and mute in historical and allegorical scenes. These earnest extravaganzas briefly flourished before millions of Americans made a weekly pilgrimage of going to the movies, another proliferating segment of mass media. Milholland portrayed Cornelia, an ideal image of classic motherhood, in the nation's first suffrage pageant in 1911 and materialized the following spring as "Woman Enfranchised" in the finale of a WPU suffrage pageant, *A Vision of Brave*

Women, and portrayed New York state at the Metropolitan Opera House in *A Dream of Freedom.*[9] Idealistic pageants helped suffragists gain a sense of themselves as powerful beings with a proud past capable of changing the male-dominated world. They even achieved an edginess in *The American Woman: Six Periods of American Life,* sponsored by the New York City Men's League for Equal Suffrage, headed by Max Eastman.[10] In the finale, Justice summons man and woman of the future, the latter portrayed by no other than Milholland.[11]

Milholland was more down to earth in her appearances on the suffrage podium, where discourse followed the male model of an appeal to logic. Her arguments for why women should vote offer a window into contemporary feminist thought, an amalgam of radical and conservative views on the nature of womanhood. Milholland argued women voters would be the metaphorical "house-cleaners of the nation," suffragists' most common and conservative argument.[12] It softened their demand for the vote because it linked the female domestic sphere with the male public sphere. Conservative *Good Housekeeping* magazine, for instance, in an article that lauded "militant" suffrage leaders' "feminine charms," said Harriet Laidlaw joined the movement when she realized "how much the safety of the home depends upon politics."[13] Women's votes would sweep away social ills such as sweatshops, tenements, prostitution, hunger, poverty, and child mortality, suffragists maintained. Milholland characterized such issues as "essentially womanly questions" and frequently used domestic metaphors to further soften her demand to vote.[14] She told Dartmouth alumni, "Our absurd party system makes politics sound like the prize ring. In reality politics has more to do with the nursery."[15] She was repeating conservative suffragists' basic theme when she comforted her male audience about the breach of the separate spheres: "[Y]our dear and familiar ideas concerning woman: her sphere, her sacred rights and duties, are not being demolished, but enlarged, extended and ennobled."[16]

Milholland sounded as conservative when she cited the vote as an antidote to "race suicide," the widespread, Anglo-Saxon fear that poor, ill-educated immigrants flooding the cities were reproducing faster than superior Yankee stock and sullying the American genetic pool. "The source of a race is in its mothers," she maintained. "No race rises higher than its source."[17] The reformer nonetheless believed that environment also played a major role in shaping human beings: "If you want a nation of strong, vigorous, happy and well educated citizens, you must see to it that the mothers of those citizens are well born, well bred, well educated and well developed."[18] But an analogy she drew between feminism and horse breeding was thoroughly grounded in eugenics, a popular idea that society could improve the human being through human engineering: "Hitherto it was considered any broken down clumsy mare would serve the purpose provided the stallion was satisfactory. To-day the mare must be clean of wind and blood and limb."[19] So entrenched were the purportedly scientific principles of eugenics in popular thought that even an alleged egalitarian such as Milholland could nonchalantly contrast the "haphazard" mating habits of "savages" to unions between members of the "higher races."[20]

Milholland also invoked the popular suffrage argument that women's maternal instincts made them better citizens. Suffragists sought to reclaim motherhood from the anti-suffragists, who shrieked that the vote would wreck the family. "Women excel in the care of all living things," she told the legislature in 1910. "We want the mothers [*sic*] point of view, we want her humanity and her zeal for the conservation and the upbuilding of life incorporated in our laws and our administration."[21] This sentimental appeal also was shrewd, part of what Mary Ryan called suffragists' "arsenal of expedient devices to achieve their goal."[22] Milholland, in fact, could as easily muster a feisty natural rights argument that the vote was an inherent right of women, and she often did.[23] On the other hand, her statements about such "essentially womanly qualities" as affection, tenderness, and intuition appear so frequently and passionately in Milholland's writing that they indicate she truly shared the prevailing cultural view that more than biology accounted for differences between the sexes.[24] The prewar feminists' essentialist argument that women possessed inherent female qualities (a debate that continues in the twenty-first century) even as they pursued the same treatment as men under the law and the same opportunities in the work world eventually would undermine their campaign for equal rights.[25] Whatever arguments suffragists made, the very act of women speaking out in public remained radical. Milholland helped make the act acceptable. She talked about suffrage at smokers, churches, theatres, in the chamber of the New York State Assembly, before the Pilgrim Mothers, the Albany Women's Legislative League, Plattsburgh voters, and even in the rain at the 1912 Illinois State Fair.[26] Contemporary accounts indicate she was a universal success.

"She has held scores of audiences by the hour," claimed *McClure's*, which called her the suffrage movement's most effective spokesman. Once again, her looks were integral to her success, a harbinger of how image would dominate messages in twentieth-century mass media. "Young, of immediately attractive appearance, and self-possessed, she instantly centers attention."[27] The phenomenon of women talking in public just like men carried an inescapable erotic charge that seemed to crackle when Milholland took the stage. She did not recoil. Outfits such as the one Milholland wore to the Dartmouth Club in Manhattan, a "tight-fitting white satin gown, which clung to her with the same tenacity with which she clings to the suffrage cause," as duly noted by a *New York Press* scribe, may help explain her popularity with university men.[28] Yale men vowed to create a suffrage club after Milholland dropped by the student newspaper office.[29] Milholland seemed astute about how to play her male audiences to make palatable her radical message for sexual equality. *McClure's*, for instance, attributed her success to her soothing approach: "no demands, no denunciations, no ranting—a quiet, even statement, the more effective because her gestures and phrases continue to convey a flattering sense of appreciation for the attention of her auditors."[30]

Milholland's suffrage spiels gave her entrée into worlds generally open only to men; she sometimes addressed rows of hundreds if not thousands of men. She was the only woman present at a Society of the Genessee dinner at the Ritz Carlton, for instance, where she educated diners about the arrest of Susan B. Anthony for trying to vote in Rochester in 1872.[31] When Dartmouth alumni cheered her, "Da-di-di-, Dartmouth! Wah, hoo, wah! Votes for women!" she jumped up from her seat. "To test your sincerity, I want every man who favors woman suffrage to raise his hand." Nearly half raised their hands. "How many of those who oppose woman suffrage will raise their hands?" Only five dared.[32] She was a hit with women, too. Belmont appreciated Milholland's ability to charm audiences at big rallies held at Marble House before passing her trademark wide-brim hat.[33] She exhorted another all-female audience to emulate the spirit if not the violence of the British suffragettes. "Until we learn here to make sacrifices," a skill at which she was not especially adept, she said, "we are not going to make a fight worthy of the cause."[34]

Public speaking made her nervous, though, and she worried she sounded too tough.[35] "[H]ow valuable a sense of humor is nobody knows better than a would-be propagandist," she said. "It oils the wheels of the persuasive machinery as does nothing else." This sense of humor did not come naturally to Milholland. "It is something to be devoutly hoped for, prayed for, and laboriously acquired if possible, no matter how severe the pain of acquirement may be."[36] The soapbox was a graduate school in public speaking, as suffragists had to field cracks from drunks and loudmouths. In St. Louis, for instance, when a man heckled Milholland that woman's place is in the kitchen, she shot back, "There are 9 million women who can't stay in the kitchen because they must go out and work."[37] She relished debate. Her favorite part of speeches was taking questions from the audience. She even invited written questions from anti-suffragists in Brooklyn too shy to speak up. "I can understand that feeling, even though you may not believe it," she quipped, drawing a laugh. When the chair started to silence a teacher who stood up and challenged some of Milholland's assertions, she waved her off. "It is all right. We are getting on well together."[38]

A sense of glamorous Milholland as democratic everywoman added to her popularity. The *Woman's Journal* said: "She is a beauty, but she doesn't care; she is rich but she means to 'earn her living'; she is a student, but she does everything rather than be a bluestocking. She is frank and democratic, and ready to lend a hand everywhere."[39] *Good Housekeeping* chimed in that Milholland "remained quite unspoiled by all the admiration and attention which she has commanded."[40] NAWSA courted this adulatory mass media image, a welcome relief from decades of ridicule suffragists endured at the hands of cartoonists and editorialists who lampooned them as unsexed and ineffectual. Even taking into account her good looks and winning manner, it is difficult to account for her hold on the mass media imagination; she seemed to feed the public need for heroes. As one member of the press admitted, "One unconsciously drops into superlative encomium when speaking or writing about Inez Milholland, one of the high priestesses of the woman suffrage cause in this country."[41]

Milholland was capable of kind and grand gestures that actually lived up to this superhuman image. A woman journalism student at Columbia University never forgot a 1912 interview with Milholland. When she heard that Sarah Addington was the only female member of the School of Journalism's inaugural graduating class, Milholland offered to help her find a job. Milholland fired off a letter accompanied by a photograph of herself to an editor friend at Times Square. Addington got the job. Years later, the journalist remembered Milholland's kindness toward a cub reporter at a time when "every woman needed a leg up."[42] A grander example of her kindness occurred while she was in college: Milholland had stood up at the midnight feast of a New Year's Eve celebration and called for donations to help earthquake victims in Italy. Revelers handed over three hundred dollars.[43]

She thrived in the idealistic suffrage community. The movement crystallized New Women's call for sweeping freedoms; women never could be agents of their lives without casting ballots. Votes for women united a wide range of women of different races, religions, and economic classes who found their participation in a mass movement transcendent. "It is so worthwhile to be part and parcel of a movement that makes for efficiency and concentrated and purposeful endeavor that requires audacity, good humor and kindliness that develops imagination, generosity and a zest for life," Milholland once said.[44] Contact with fellow suffragists invigorated Milholland when she covered the 1912 NAWSA convention in Philadelphia for *McClure's*. "When she spoke," she said of Jane Addams, "it was like a cooling breeze going through the heated chamber of the assembly."[45] The fledgling journalist's flowery appraisal of the proceedings, which shared a byline with Wallace Irwin, characterized the gathering as "feminine": "[T]here was a tendency to quibble on small matters and to rise splendidly to large ones."[46] She left the convention feeling as if a "great, new compelling force for good had already come into American life."[47]

Another feminist wellspring for Milholland was Heterodoxy. The only rule of this New York City club of New Women was that members hold unorthodox opinions—the more unusual, the merrier. Founder Marie Jenny Howe was a former minister married to People's Institute director Frederic C. Howe. Milholland met the effervescent Howe through their mutual friend Crystal Eastman. Besides Milholland and Eastman, the list of members who paid the annual two dollar dues read like a who's who of New Women: labor agitator Elizabeth Gurley Flynn; author Inez Haynes Irwin; radical teacher Henrietta Rodman; actress Fola LaFollette; playwright Susan Glaspell; lawyer Ida Rauh; socialist Rose Pastor Stokes; salon hostess Mabel Dodge; actress Agnes deMille; birth control activist Mary Ware Dennett; author Charlotte Perkins Gilman; and journalists Bessie Beatty, Zona Gale, and Rheta Childe Dorr, author of the popular suffrage tract *What Eight Million Women Want*. Some were married; others were gay. Some were socialists, and at least one was a stockbroker.[48] Their distinguishing characteristic was their agency, as all had carved satisfying careers and lifestyles for themselves that usually went against the grain of mainstream culture.

The club exemplified New Women's openness to new ideas to achieve self-realization. Every other Saturday, they met for off-the-record lunches featuring provocative speakers, often other New Women such as anarchist Emma Goldman who shared members' perspective that freedom lay with difference.[49] Heterodoxy has been described as the first consciousraising group.[50] Margaret Sanger's stories about tenement mothers broken by pregnancy could counter a husband's disapproval of birth control; a successful female writer's revelation about her long, solitary hours at her desk could steel an aspiring author's resolve. The gatherings gave these New Women, different in so many ways save for their individuality, an opportunity to replenish their independent spirits.[51] It was a rowdy sanctuary from the world men ruled. As much as she reveled in the company of men, all her life Milholland enjoyed close friendships with women. Most of her female friends were like her: independent, suffragist, activist, sexually liberated, fun-loving nonconformists. Milholland's relations with Heterodoxy's accomplished female activists sustained her and helped put her celebrity in perspective.

Another celebrity suffragist captured the American imagination at about the same time as Milholland. "Silvia Holland" was the only child of steel magnate John J. Holland. Attorney Silvia also was a socialist arrested in England with the suffragettes and for picketing with the shirtwaist strikers in New York. She had even sponsored an illicit suffrage rally at college. Silvia was the heroine of Isaac N. Stevens's popular novel *An American Suffragette*. The author sent Milholland a copy hot off the press.[52] The novel begins when Silvia catches the eye of handsome Dr. Jack Earl as she leads a suffrage parade down Fifth Avenue, like "Amazons conquering Asia."[53] They become romantically involved when they save the life of an injured tenement child. The doctor abandons his frivolous, anti-suffrage fiancée for a stimulating, committed life with Silvia. The ending is significant because Jack changes instead of Silvia, of whom Stevens wrote, "She showed grace and energy in every movement and intellect and force in every glance."[54] Intellect and force in a woman were aphrodisiacs concocted for the new century and not the old, when the cult of true womanhood eroticized female submission and piety.[55] Milholland epitomized this new ideal in female sex appeal.

The flesh-and-blood "Silvia" similarly held the upper hand in romantic relationships, a fact that made Milholland unusual even among New Women. She easily adopted the male model of open sexuality that many women found difficult to follow no matter how intellectually committed to free love. She initiated liaisons—she once called herself a "hunting leopard"—and did not seem to lose herself in trying to meet her lovers' needs, a hazard for New Women charting the new sexual politics.[56] Milholland was courted by a string of men. Her perfumed love letters made suitors drunk with desire.[57] One claimed that just the thought of her rendered him "utterly faint, and a divine trembling runs through my every limb."[58] John Black, an aspiring playwright and *Chicago Tribune* reporter, wrote her, "Dear beast you are the wonder woman, you free wild dancing thing and I love you." Her independence also vexed these admirers, and it wasn't long before a disenchanted Black destroyed her letters. "I got you all wrong," Black wrote her. "Unless that you're deliberately going to experiment, because men always have, and you're as good as men—is that it?"[59]

Hapless Upton Sinclair, mired in a bad marriage, came courting Milholland in spring 1911. Sinclair's radical politics and writing appealed to

Milholland. The thread that wove through all of his muckraking fiction was his "idealistic opposition to an unjust society," a calling card for Milholland. The author of the phenomenally successful *The Jungle* had also founded the Intercollegiate Socialist Society to which she had belonged.[60] Sinclair told her she embodied "all that is noble and beautiful in womanhood."[61] Unfortunately, Milholland labeled him a sentimentalist—the kiss of death for romance as far as she was concerned.[62] Her cool replies chilled him.[63] "What do you do when you read my letters—smile, because now he's learning to be human?" Sinclair wrote.[64] He wrote to her all summer, when she stayed in New York to focus on her law studies rather than take her annual vacation to London.[65] Milholland deemed Sinclair incapable of spontaneous emotion. This shattered him. "No man ever felt a more genuinely true emotion because of a woman than I do because of you." Sinclair begged her to understand his "frightfully tormented" sex life. Sinclair kept up his pursuit and continued to conjure her as a "vision of loveliness," even though he correctly surmised she would find the phrase "loathsomely sentimental."[66] He announced he would seek a divorce, but Milholland remained unmoved.[67] He grew bitter when she failed to respond and demanded the return of his letters. If she refused, he threatened, he would write her father. Milholland ignored him.[68]

It did not take long for her to find a new boyfriend, this one also in the interminable death throes of a bad marriage. Kentucky-born John Fox Jr.'s sentimental tales about plucky mountaineers made him one of the world's first blockbuster authors. His 1903 novel, *The Little Shepherd of Kingdom Come*, reputedly was the first book printed in the United States to sell a million copies. Fox was only a couple of years younger than Milholland's father, and the two men may have crossed paths when both worked as journalists in New York City in the 1880s. Fox stuck with journalism, covering the Spanish-American War for *Harper's Weekly* and the Russo-Japanese War for *Scribner's*. In 1908 he married opera star Fritzi Scheff, to whom he dedicated his next blockbuster, *The Trail of the Lonesome Pine*.[69] Like the hero of *Lonesome Pine*, Fox was torn between the mountains and modernity. The Harvard graduate lived in Big Stone Gap, Virginia, but reveled in big city sophistication. Milholland's combination of nonconformity and sophistication fascinated him. He enjoyed hearing this lively young woman a generation his junior expound on socialism, suffrage, and the new morality, especially in light of his rocky marriage. Milholland engrossed him in abstract conversation about the meaning of life. She in turn enjoyed sparring about votes for women with the charming but conservative Virginian. "The Southerner, you know, believes women should have everything they want," he once said, "but that there are some things they should not want."[70] Although socialism appalled Fox, Milholland even persuaded him to subscribe to *The Masses*.[71] In fact, Fox was the date she dunned for a contribution at the dinner she had arranged at which Alva Belmont bailed out Max Eastman's *Masses* magazine.

As she had with Eastman, Milholland kept Fox well apprised of her other suitors.[72] Fox, like Eastman, declined to profess love as swiftly as she did. He rebuked her that the words "I love you" spilled too easily from her lips. "[T]hey have come so often, to so many, in so short a space of time," he wrote.[73] Yet only thoughts of Milholland gave him strength to finish his latest novel at Big Stone Gap. "Forgive me, Inez," he wrote, "—and be patient with me."[74] He spent Thanksgiving 1912 at Meadowmount.[75] The holiday season was tough for the Milhollands. A mysterious malady that made Vida's joints ache had hospitalized her for months in Plattsburgh, about an hour north of Meadowmount.[76] John's finances once again were so shaky he feared losing his beloved farm.[77] Fox's visit proved a pleasant relief from these woes for Jean and John, who surely enjoyed Fox's mountain tales. Full of local color such as corn shucking parties and one-room cabins, his stories must have reminded John of his Adirondack childhood. Fox later sent a thoughtful thank-you note to Jean along with wishes for improved health for Vida, who remained hospitalized on Christmas Day. The family gathered in her hospital room and ate a subdued holiday dinner at a nearby restaurant.[78] But Milholland harbored no plans to marry the well-mannered author. No sooner had Fox finally uttered "I love you" than Milholland's attraction evaporated.[79] Although she spent a weekend with him early in December, by Christmas she wanted to end the affair.[80] The wounded Fox possibly struck a nerve when he tore into her:

> You howl about following yourself and your joy and so far you've done nothing but follow other people and their ideas of joy—people, too, by the way, whom I more than half believe are in more than half the cases either impotent, or anaemic or intermediate.
>
> Suppose you get busy thinking just a trifle less about <u>yourself</u>? Do this and you'll remember this as the best Christmas present that has come to you for many a year.[81]

Milholland undoubtedly was self-centered, but this angry reaction shows the kind of criticism New Women like her faced when they insisted on independence. It took a strong woman to withstand such verbal assaults. Milholland, although always receptive to male attentions and a quite capable coquette, never seemed to succumb to putting a lover's interests ahead of her own, a pitfall for a number of her peers. The drive that initially attracted Fox to Milholland eventually irked the basically apolitical novelist. Milholland's only persevering passion was for suffrage. No sooner had she disentangled herself from Fox than she headed for Washington, D.C., for the most significant suffrage spectacle yet, the first national suffrage parade and pageant.

Riot

"Every inch the herald of a great movement"

Milholland shivered as the bracing March breeze sliced through the folds of her white parade herald's cape. The ivory horse she rode trotted off so quickly at the start of the first national suffrage parade that its five thousand women in costumes and on floats lagged several blocks behind her on Pennsylvania Avenue. Another kind of chill coursed down Milholland's spine when she rounded a corner past the Capitol and saw a drunken, howling mob that blocked the avenue as far as she could see.

Parade mastermind Alice Paul had chosen a woman suffrage march up the nation's most politically charged avenue in America in spring 1913 to make a publicity splash as newly installed chair of NAWSA's narcoleptic Congressional Committee.[1] Only a year older than Milholland, Paul wrestled with none of the social distractions that kept Milholland from a nun-like dedication to women's rights. The Philadelphia Quaker with a master's degree in sociology from the University of Pennsylvania was married to the cause. Slender and pale, the doe-eyed Paul usually wore a lavender dress to symbolize her allegiance to suffrage militants, parting her dark hair in the middle and pulling it back from her face in a severe bun. The feisty spectacle of the British militant suffragettes had first drawn her into the fight for equal rights while she pursued a doctoral degree in economics in London. Paul had endured hunger strikes with other suffragette inmates in London's infamous Holloway Jail. Her resistance when jailers forced tubes of milk and raw eggs down her throat foreshadowed the tenacity with which she refused a demand by District of Columbia police that the suffragists delay their march until after Wilson's inauguration. Paul's masterful use of spectacle and imagery marks her as a pioneer of public relations before the term was coined. Her insistence that the parade occur on the eve of the inauguration is one example of her savvy manipulation of the mass media. Another example is that Paul recruited the glamorous Milholland to lead the parade.[2]

Paul's political vision was unique because it wed feminism with femininity. She wielded beauty as a political tool through public spectacle and aimed to prove that women could be citizens without losing respectability and dignity. The emphasis on femininity was radical on one level because it offered a highly visible alternative to the male model citizen. Yet on another level, the emphasis on female beauty risked subsuming the parade's political message. Paul's national suffrage demonstration, however, won the cause unprecedented national publicity, as even the Fifth Avenue suffrage parades had been viewed as a New York phenomenon. To ensure the Washington spectacle made a powerful impression, Paul had the parade culminate with another first, a lavish allegorical pageant on the U.S. Treasury building portico. Female occupation of this male space coupled with the parade's setting sandwiched amid the patriotic monuments along Pennsylvania Avenue made it an especially powerful statement for women's rights. "In this space," observed Lucy Barber in her study of protests in the nation's capital, "participants and organizers carefully arranged themselves to communicate that they were national citizens."[3]

In the weeks leading up to the parade, Milholland was helping Osborne prepare for a big murder trial as well as cramming for the New York state bar exam. She received word she passed the bar on February 28. The next day, Milholland and her mother sped on the night train to Washington, where they met her father, in town for another round of badgering Congress to buy his million-dollar mail tube system. On the eve of the parade, she helped raise more than five thousand dollars at the Columbia Theatre alongside suffrage big guns Carrie Chapman Catt, Anna Howard Shaw, and Harriot Stanton Blatch. Watching from the audience, her father surely was the only man in the capital to assert over the next few days that she carried her audiences "by brains rather than beauty."[4] Physical appearances dominated press coverage even before the parade started. The *New York Tribune* alerted residents that its "beautifulest" suffragist had left the city early to get acquainted with her horse "Grey Dawn." The *Washington Post* conceded Milholland lent "complete support to claims of suffragists' beauty." The rival *Evening Star* concurred, "Miss Milholland has been hailed as one of the most beautiful women in all the land, and today she deserved the title." Besides quashing rumors she was engaged to Fox, Milholland was busy answering insipid press queries about the connection between beauty and the ballot. She finally blurted she wished NAWSA press releases would emphasize her mind instead of her

Inez astride the white horse she rode as herald of the 1913 parade in Washington, D.C.
Courtesy of Schlesinger Library, Radcliffe Institute, Harvard University.

looks "as that is much more essential."[5] In her own bylined dispatches to the *New York American*, Milholland had emphasized cross-class unity: "[W]omen of all classes are standing shoulder to shoulder for a high principle."[6] Milholland's egalitarian vision became a reality for at least that afternoon, embodied in the color-coordinated brigades of lawyers, college students, factory workers, doctors, businesswomen, social workers, teachers, librarians, actresses, women from other countries, the Woman's Christian Temperance Union, and other organizations that marched to the tempo of ten all-female bands.[7]

Milholland nonetheless was very conscious of how she would look at the head of the parade. "It has occurred to me that it is much more fitting to have the woman's parade heralded by a symbol of the future rather than a relic of the middle ages—a medieval herald," she told organizers. Milholland grandiloquently opted for "something suggesting the free woman of the future, crowned with the star of hope, armed with the cross of mercy, circled with the blue mantle of freedom, breasted with the torch of knowledge, and carrying the trumpet which is to herald the dawn of a new day of heroic endeavor for womanhood." Milholland's desire to have her outfit conjure freedom illustrates the concept's primacy to her. They agreed as long as the costume was yellow, matching the other heralds along the route. Milholland wore white, determined as always to stand out from the crowd.[8]

Milholland literally portrayed the suffrage movement's white knight, a striking appropriation of male imagery. The inauguration of the first Democratic president in twenty years had attracted a boisterous crowd, which fortified itself against the cold with alcohol. Within minutes after setting off from the Capitol, marchers found themselves blocked by a sea of human heads bobbing without a break all the way to the Treasury. At one point, Milholland found herself alone in the belly of the howling mob. It looked as if some of the drunks might pull her down. She spurred her horse and charged into the horde. Milholland was an adept rider who often rode at Meadowmount. In the saddle, Milholland was taller, faster, and more powerful than the somewhat awed men looking up at her. Even the anti-suffrage *New York Times* described her as imposing on Grey Dawn.[9] In her Joan of Arc costume, she personified suffragists' version of idealized woman.[10] "You men ought to be ashamed of yourselves," she shouted into the crowd, "standing there idly and permitting this sort of thing to continue. If you have a particle of backbone you will come out here and help us to continue our parade." The crowd fell back. Some cheered her. She kept moving. Soon after, U.S. cavalry troops galloped in from Fort Myer just across the Potomac River. People screamed as soldiers and horses charged up the avenue to clear the way for the suffragists, who struggled for hours to reach the Treasury Building while the mob kicked, grabbed, cursed, howled, and spat at them. Ambulances carted hundreds of spectators to hospitals, but the women kept marching.[11]

At the Treasury, spectators who paid five dollars for covered bleacher seats waited patiently for hours for the marchers to arrive and signal the start of *The Allegory*.[12] A particularly anxious observer was pageant author Hazel MacKaye, who watched the proceedings from an upstairs window of a building overlooking Pennsylvania Avenue. She finally spied the banners and heard the bands in the distance. "Now there appeared a gallant figure out of the pressing throngs," she recalled, "a girl in white upon a white horse, dressed in flowing Crusader's cloak—Inez Milholland, 'the most beautiful suffragette'—and the most courageous." The crowd erupted in cheers when it spotted her. With a tilt of her head, Milholland acknowledged the acclaim and turned to raise her hand in solemn greeting to the pageant players. "Then she passed," MacKaye recalled, "and soon the radiant young crusader was swallowed up in the surging crowds beyond."[13] None of the twenty thousand *Allegory* spectators cheered Milholland louder than her parents. John recorded in his diary that night: "It was a great day for Nan. Bless her big heart she certainly did triumph. She looked and laughed at all she saw, the crowd, the cheers, the tableaux. . . . The sunset never fell on a girl more fair in all the pageants that this old capital has ever witnessed. On this point an almost perfect consensus of opinion prevails."[14]

Another consensus was that the parade violence was a national disgrace. Furious marchers that night demanded an investigation at their "indignation meeting" at Continental Hall. The next morning, newspaper readers across the continent awoke to read about beauty and the beasts in Washington. The banner headline of the *Los Angeles Times* was typical, "U.S. CAVALRY ROUTS MOBS IN WASHINGTON, D.C." Spurred by NAWSA's protest, the Senate launched an investigation that gave suffragists a forum to criticize patriarchal politics for two more weeks.[15] Milholland declined Paul's request that she testify at the hearings. She doubted her comments would be helpful, she claimed, as the police she saw tried hard to control the crowd, although there weren't enough of them. She also declined to characterize the crowd as hostile. "They were eager and unmanageable and out for a good time—but nothing worse," she wrote. She also was busy working.[16] When she helped James W. Osborne finalize the defense for a man charged with killing one of four men who died in a spray of bullets in Chinatown, spectators crowded the courtroom just to see her, and her minor role in the trial received national publicity.[17]

Despite her disclaimer to Paul, however, Milholland told a Greenwich Village rally on the afternoon the hearings began in Washington that she witnessed marchers slapped in the face and barraged by obscene taunts. "Most of them were directed at the young women," she said. "The older ones were told to go to the old ladies home. The police were almost as bad."[18] More than 150 witnesses, in fact, related chilling accounts of abuse over five days of exhaustively covered parade hearings that mushroomed into a national forum on women's role in society. A man grabbed Verna Hatfield's foot as she sat on the "Old Liberty Bell" float. Others rubbed the women's arms or plucked the flowers from their coats. Men spat at the suffrage flags and threw lighted cigarettes and matches onto them. A marcher charged, "They would have taken better care of a drove of pigs being driven through the streets by some farmer than they did of us." One woman testified she saw a police officer spit on a woman, and another testified that a drunkard spat tobacco juice in a woman's face. An officer had snarled at one victim, "There would have been nothing like this happen if you women would stay at home."[19]

The testimony proved a boon for suffragists because it prompted the mass media to champion women's right to public space. Basically conservative, the mainstream press tends to respect traditional avenues for working for change, especially the venerable right to assemble peaceably, so it was sympathetic to the female marchers' plight.[20] Even the New York Times conceded the women had a right to parade unmolested. "Like other Americans," it stated, "they were entitled to protection." Thanks in part to the capital thugs, the national suffrage parade made mainstream America acknowledge that women had a right to participate publicly in politics.[21] The mayhem spawned immediate tangible progress for suffragists: President Wilson met with Paul on March 17, and the Senate reactivated its moribund Woman Suffrage Committee, adding four pro-suffrage members, and for the first time in more than twenty years, that June the committee issued a favorable report.[22] The 745-page Senate report echoed editorials: "It is unfortunate that a quiet, dignified parade, composed mostly of women, could not be held upon the best known avenue in the nation's capital without interference or insult."[23] The publicity boom probably helped inspire two other politically charged pageants in 1913, also considered cultural landmarks, the "Paterson Strike Pageant" and W. E. B. Du Bois's "The Star of Ethiopia," a graphic depiction of black history.[24] The parade aftermath convinced Paul—who needed little convincing— that publicity held the key to the suffrage amendment, a policy that would profoundly affect Milholland's life.[25]

As the parade's white knight, Milholland played a key role in asserting public space for American women. Her romantic image was captured by the ever-obliging media in a headline, "Fair Inez Milholland on her White Charger Dashed into the Mob." Newspapers nationwide splashed across their front pages a wire story that described her charge through the mob; many ran photographs of her astride Grey Dawn. Milholland was the "real heroine of the procession," claimed the *Los Angeles Times*.[26] Literally taking the reins into her own hands, Milholland tangibly displayed female agency. Her aura of independence and invincibility intensified when the press reported toward the end of the hearings that the heralded parade herald had just helped win an acquittal in her first case, for the accused Chinatown murderer. By then, she was a national celebrity. This New Woman offered an inspiring role model to women seeking greater control over their destinies, although none knew she remained wholly financially dependent upon her father. Almost everything about the bicontinental Milholland conjured freedom. Reporters noticed how her long hair fell loosely over her shoulders, a style associated with fallen women in the not-so-distant Victorian past but celebrated on Milholland. The *Evening Star* applauded her unconventional costume: "Riding astride her handsome horse, the loose folds of her costume hanging gracefully, she looked every inch the herald of a great movement." The association with looseness appears in Milholland's case to have held a positive connotation. Her flowing robes certainly offered more freedom than did the organ-crushing corsets that New Women had shed.[27]

An unacknowledged aspect of women's increasing physical freedom was the parade's sexually charged atmosphere. Anti-suffragists decried the barefoot young women in Grecian gowns, evidence of modern dance pioneer Isadora Duncan's influence.[28] The *Star's* allusion to the parade as a "battlefield captured by Amazons" illustrated the simultaneous power and sensuality conveyed by marching women.[29] Milholland's big, white horse contributed not only to her mobility but also to her mystique in part because of the eroticism associated with women on horseback. The parade's sexual undercurrent also underscored the risks women took in wielding beauty as a political weapon.[30] The sensuality and carnival of suffrage spectacles always teetered on the brink of sheer frivolity. Worse, the Washington riot showed how their transgression of parading themselves in public physically endangered women.[31]

Yet voteless women somehow had to engage the male gaze, which rendered them passive objects, to spur men to action.[32] As Martha Banta observed, "Somehow the feminist had to *dress* her ideas and her inner convictions in order to let them be expressed, however inadequately by the surface she presented."[33] The fact that by winter 1915 the all-male New York legislature agreed to put suffrage—a joke before women started marching in 1910—on the ballot the following November indicates parades played an important part in changing the political climate. Although NAWSA president Carrie Chapman Catt later said she believed parades turned off as many voters as they converted, it is difficult to imagine how suffragists could have gained so much support so fast without packaging their unpopular message as entertainment on the streets.[34] Although the referendum failed, it did win more than a half million men's votes, and a second referendum in 1917 succeeded. Suffrage marchers' manipulation of the male gaze demonstrated their creativity in transforming a form of oppression into a political tool.

Parading themselves before the male gaze, however, inevitably reduced female marchers to sexual objects. Categorizing citizens by their appearance was inherently degrading, and using beauty as a barometer of political entitlement reduced women's civil rights to a beauty contest. "Granny! Granny!" young men yelled at gray-haired marchers. "We came to see chickens, not hens."[35] Just as beauty attracted attention to the parade, it could divert attention from its political purpose. As a *San Francisco Examiner* reporter commented after he beheld Milholland, "It is likely that not a single man among the thousands of spectators thought of votes for women."[36] Milholland embodied women's contradictory attitudes about flaunting their sex appeal. On the one hand, she resented how NAWSA exploited her good looks; on the other hand, she insisted upon leading the parade in a unique and sensual outfit designed to command attention. Sexuality remained a quandary for New Women. Their celebratory attitude of female sexuality was revolutionary, but flaunting their sexuality not only opened them to criticism in a society that still held to a double standard about sex for men and women but also diminished women's agency. It demonstrated how externally and internally even radical New Women such as Milholland remained dependent upon men's approval. As Linda Gordon noted, "[T]heir survival and success still largely depended upon pleasing men."[37]

Anti-suffragists latched onto the indignity of parades using "sex appeal" to win favor. The flashy Milholland especially offended because she personified the spectacle that repulsed anti-suffragists, who argued women worked more effectively for reform quietly behind the scenes. For her part, Milholland dismissed anti-suffragists' argument that women's beauty and charm gave them enough power over men. "The idea is especially dear, no doubt, to women who need to assure themselves that they have charm and attractiveness," she shrewdly observed. "But it is also dear to many men to enjoy the feeling that it gives them to offer their chair to a woman and enjoy it so well that they are inclined to think the female world in general ought to be more than satisfied."[38]

The darkest aspect of the primacy of physical appearance in the suffrage movement related to race. NAWSA leaders did not want black suffragists to march in Washington. Paul pointedly ignored requests to participate by the head of Howard University's Delta Sigma Theta sorority.[39] Paul and other white suffrage leaders were notoriously hostile to black suffragists largely because they needed southern support.[40] In 1903, for instance, NAWSA established a states-rights policy that implicitly endorsed white supremacy in the South, and in 1914 the *Suffragist* newspaper assured southern readers that poll taxes and literacy tests would continue to keep undesirable voters out of the ballot booth after women won the vote.[41] Even NAACP member Milholland was not above slipping into the decade's ubiquitous racist vernacular, referring at least once in private to a young Negro client as a "nigger." Neither is there evidence that she protested Alva Belmont's decision to exclude Negro members from the 1912 suffrage ball.[42]

But Milholland spoke out when she got word of NAWSA's snub of black women. She demanded the Howard students be allowed to march in the college section, according to civil rights activist Mary Church Terrell, who marched with the Howard women. Emmett J. Scott, Howard's secretary and treasurer, said later, "[Milholland] was unwilling to participate in a parade symbolizing a movement which was not big enough or broad enough to live up to the principles for which it was contending."[43] In the end, two dozen Howard sorority sisters chaperoned by a male professor marched together in the "Education" section.[44] Ironically, however, Milholland's unofficial anointment by the press and suffragists as suffragists' ideal woman symbolized the movement's exclusionary nature. It would be decades before feminists would address racism in the women's movement and the dangers of imaging the ideal woman as white, well educated, beautiful, heterosexual, and wealthy.[45] The pedestal upon which suffrage leaders and the press had placed Milholland rested upon her many privileges, even as she challenged those privileges. In fact, she was tiring of her perch upon the "absurd pedestal."[46]

Milholland finally received attention for her intellectual feats a month after the parade, when she was sworn in to the New York bar. Friends swarmed around her to congratulate her when the swearing-in ended. Milholland had worked hard for this day and felt much more deserving of her friends' congratulations than she did of the adulation heaped upon her after the spectacle in Washington, D.C. She hoped the occasion marked the beginning of a career in which she could fight for women's rights in the dignity of the courtroom rather than have to parade herself for them. The fact that she was one of only three women among 107 new attorneys provided glaring evidence that the courtroom remained very much male territory.[47]

Two weeks later, Milholland saddled up for her final suffrage parade. By this time, the *New York World* joked, it seemed impossible to get any suffrage event underway without her. Save for the cavalry in black cutaways and black straw hats, every woman in line, including Milholland, wore white. Mindful of the black eye D.C. police had suffered, New York City posted ten officers along every block of Fifth Avenue. When Milholland raised the American flag she grasped in her left hand and shouted "March!" ten thousand marchers obeyed. Purple, green, and white WPU streamers twirled behind "the official beauty of the parade" as her horse trotted under Washington Arch and north toward 59th Street. Milholland's command of New York's most vibrant public space symbolized women's strides in all segments of the public sphere. Exhausted but triumphant, she noted of the 150,000 spectators after she dismounted near the Plaza Hotel, "I didn't hear a hiss or a single disrespectful remark from one end of the march to the other." The *New York Sun* also observed: "[Y]esterday instead of the jeers and jokes of other years, there was applause, an accompaniment of hand clapping, a ripple of cheers from the start to the finish."[48]

Milholland's career as parade herald ended on that high note. She redirected her energy to law. She received a plum assignment when Osborne was designated a special deputy attorney general to help oversee a Westchester County grand jury investigation into charges of graft and inhuman conditions at notorious Sing Sing state prison in Ossining. A far cry from her role as suffrage glamour girl, the appointment afforded attorney Milholland an opportunity rarely offered a woman. She not only pored over records but interviewed guards and inmates. According to one account, she was the first woman allowed to meet alone with prisoners: "She talked with the men; she unearthed appalling conditions; but she did not flinch."[49] She wrote much of the damning document that resulted in the indictment of Sing Sing's warden and other officials by the grand jury at the beginning of summer. The investigation resulted in a revamping of the prison administration based on the then-radical notion that rehabilitation rather than punishment should be prison's goal. The appalling facts

Milholland uncovered bolstered her belief that "[c]rime is merely misdirected energy." The study helped usher in a new era of prison reform.[50]

No sooner had she completed this landmark assignment, however, than Milholland took a break from the working world she had inhabited less than a year. The habits of Milholland's privileged youth held fast, and London beckoned. Milholland sailed with her former fiancé, wireless inventor "Billy" Marconi, and his wife, Beatrice. The Marconis brought along his pal and second cousin, a strapping Dutch businessman with a bacchanalian laugh and a poet's soul. Eugen Boissevain booked his passage as soon as he learned Milholland would be aboard.

Love

*"The most completely vital force
in the world"*

9

Eugen Boissevain was walking on water with Jesus. "Now look!" he told the son of God. "You're not doing it right—just watch the way I put my foot down!"[1] The strapping, dark-haired, blue-eyed Dutch adventurer burst into laughter at his own hubris as he related his dream to friends. "Handsome, reckless, mettlesome as a stallion breathing the first morning air," wrote one of his many friends, "he would laugh at himself, indeed laugh at everything, with a laugh that scattered melancholy as the wind scatters the petals of the fading poppy."[2]

Born in Amsterdam on May 20, 1880, he stood just below five feet, eleven inches tall.[3] His grandfather made a fortune in shipping between the Dutch Indies and Amsterdam. His father, Charles, published *Algemeen Handelsblad*, the Netherlands' leading newspaper, and his Irish-born mother, Emily Heloise MacDonnell, was the daughter of the provost of Trinity College in Dublin. The couple raised eleven children. Boissevain matched Milholland in his unconventional views and lust for life. Like Milholland, Boissevain was impulsive and blunt. His strong will and ego were made palatable by his self-deprecating charm, irreverence toward all pomposity, and sheer delight in life. He hunted big game in Africa, rowed in the Henley Regatta, and was psychoanalyzed by Carl Jung.[4]

He first set eyes on Milholland two days after he and his older brother Jan arrived in the United States in early June 1913 to visit another brother, Robert, forty-one and rebounding from a recent messy divorce, who worked for United Fruit Company. They planned to spend the summer touring America. Those plans changed abruptly on June 12 after Milholland walked into the dining room at the Holland House, where the Boissevain brothers were eating. She was accompanied by their close friend and distant cousin Guglielmo "Billy" Marconi, with whom she had remained close, and his wife, Beatrice. Eugen was thunderstruck. During dinner, she mentioned she might sail to London. The Marconis exclaimed they were departing for England on July 2 and invited her to join them. Eugen dropped his vacation plans.[5]

When John Milholland arrived at the *Mauretania* late on the eve of its early-morning departure to wish his daughter bon voyage, white-jacketed stewards were delivering bouquets of fresh flowers and bottles of champagne to the Marconis' luxury suite. John settled into a deck chair to await Inez's arrival. Beatrice introduced him to Eugen, who shocked John when he jumped up and kissed the keel of the lifeboat after Beatrice announced Inez was sharing their suite. "Emotionalism in pantaloons," John sniffed. In no time, the two men were embroiled in an argument over whether prostitutes could be rehabilitated. When Inez arrived, she was pleasantly surprised to find Eugen aboard. John and other friends reveled with the travelers until after midnight.[6] At dawn, the ship's horn sounded. Tooting tugs nudged the luxury liner's four enormous, rakishly angled black red-topped funnels toward the rising sun.

Few settings are more romantic than an ocean liner, none more so than Cunard's sleek 790-foot *Mauretania*, whose 31,000-horsepower turbine engine was shaving the Atlantic crossing closer and closer to an even four days.[7] It accommodated 2,335 passengers, including 560 first-class passengers who feasted on entrees such as lobster amid hand-carved panels of Latvian oak that lined its three first-class dining rooms.[8] "Every ship has a soul," reminisced Franklin D. Roosevelt, one of her passengers, "but the Mauretania had one you could talk to."[9]

Before the cruise ended, Milholland had proposed to Boissevain—three times by one account.[10] After landing, they traveled with the Marconis to his fabulous family estate, Eaglehurst, on the coast in Surrey. After they made love in its tower, Boissevain whispered to her, "Oh, we're going to be happy together."[11] She was intoxicated by his smell, the pucker in his brow, the curls in his hair, the way he held a cigarette in bed after sex.[12] The next day, they decided to marry immediately in London. The Kensington registry office, however, informed the couple they had to wait until the next week. Milholland already had wired her mother at 4 Prince of Wales Terrace: "Married Eugene [*sic*] Boissevain today home for dinner at 7:30 leave for Holland 8:30 very happy please wish me luck tell no one yet all my love Nan."[13] Jean collapsed into bed (John was in Philadelphia).[14] Vida fended off reporters. "Oh, that is too silly," she scoffed at the *New York American* reporter who broke the story. "[M]y sister amuses herself with a good many men," she parried. "Perhaps it's just one of those."[15]

Inez and Eugen, still single, spent the weekend in Amsterdam with his large and doting family. When they returned to London on Monday, July 14, they headed straight for the Kensington registry office. The only witnesses were Jan Boissevain and Inez's brother and sister. Marconi served as best man.[16] Then, the newlyweds finally made their way to 4 Prince of Wales Terrace, where a recovering Jean pronounced her new son-in-law "most likeable."[17] With disarming honesty, Eugen explained to a reporter why the couple was reluctant to tell the Milhollands about their marriage: "You see, I am something of a loafer."[18] Even if his accomplishments seemed slim at thirty-three, the centered Boissevain was a New Woman's dream: He had a strong sense of self and no need to prove himself or justify his life to anyone. His sensibilities were totally modern. His mind was open to everything new, and he questioned conventions. Self-realization was his religion. He seemed remarkably free of stereotypical masculine traits, such as a need to dominate women or chase a high-powered career that sidetracked many men who gave lip service to the sexual revolution. Boissevain truly believed in the new sexual politics that called for intense communication and equality between the sexes. Like Milholland, he believed in free love.

Back in the United States, John Milholland's secretary met him at the train station and thrust a stack of newspapers in his arms. Screaming headlines reflected Milholland's public persona: "Inez Milholland Surrenders to a 'Mere Man,'" and "Inez Milholland, Prettiest Militant Suffraget [sic], Succumbs to Dan Cupid."[19] The wedding was reported prominently in dozens of newspapers on two continents. Stunned, John cabled Jean. So many rumors had floated about Inez's romances in the past few years that he hoped the report was a mistake. "Great God!" he wrote in his diary. "How terrible it all seems, so incredible that I fear the worst."[20] Confirmation of the marriage crushed him, even though Marconi cabled him attesting to the groom's character. Milholland recoiled at his memory of the excitable young man he'd met on the *Mauretania*. "Think of being father-in-law to such a creature! Oh the horror of it all. And Inez his—wife! Marble to mud . . . enamored by an ass!"[21] He wired a brutal cable chastising Inez, but the seasoned newspaperman masked his hurt as he cajoled reporters who trailed him to his Wall Street office.

"It came like a bolt from the blue," he admitted. "That's just Inez's way of doing things. I always had faith in Inez's judgment. She acted on impulse from her youth up, but I did not fail to notice that she was right just about all the time."[22] He recalled that he and Jean had married impulsively but couldn't resist adding that his daughter would remarry in a church after he arrived in London. This announcement set off a transatlantic father-daughter feud that unfolded on the front page of the *New York Times*. "There will be nothing of the sort," she was quoted about the proposed church ceremony. She blamed her father for leaking the news. "We certainly would have married either with the approval or the disapproval of our parents," she said. "We were not marrying each other's families."[23]

Meanwhile, Jean began to warm to her charming new son-in-law and his devotion to her glowing daughter. John retreated to Meadowmount and climbed Mt. Jacob to pray before booking passage to England.[24] Eugen had fallen ill with blood poisoning, however, and was recuperating at Eaglehurst when John arrived. Father and daughter enjoyed a brief, testy reunion before Marconi fetched her to visit Eugen.[25] Two days later, Inez returned with her groom. "I won't describe him accurately perhaps," John recorded in his diary, "so I'll only say to myself that he is one of Life's bitterest disappointments."[26] Eugen did his best to get along with his sulking father-in-law and invited the Milhollands to meet his family in the Netherlands.[27] The septuagenarian Boissevains proved gracious and stately hosts at their country estate, Drafna, a three-story wooden chalet on forty acres along the Zuider Zee. The Boissevains impressed the Milhollands not only with their business accomplishments but also with their closely knit large family, including twenty-eight grandchildren. The younger generation was charmed if slightly shocked by their uncle's stunning new wife. Inez smoked cigarettes and smooched with Eugen at the dinner table. "They were both splendid physical specimens, they were a match for each other," one of Eugen's nephews recalled. The Boissevain brothers predictably fell under Inez's spell, but her sisters-in-law were not unhappy to see her go.[28]

After dinner the next evening, the Boissevains sang for the Milhollands, a common entertainment in the pre-electronic age. The next morning, a softening John huddled with Eugen for two hours, inviting him to learn the pneumatic tubes business. The next day it was the Milhollands' turn to entertain their hosts at a luncheon at the Hotel Amsterdam. Then everyone clambered into the Boissevains' motorboat for a tour along the Amstel River. The convivial day ended with John giving the couple his blessing before he and Jean sailed back to London late that night.[29]

Inez and Eugen stayed in Holland the rest of the summer. In mid-September, Eugen crossed the English Channel to discuss joining the tube business with John, who promised Eugen and Inez one hundred thousand dollars in common stock. Given the enterprise's precarious finances, the gift was considerably less substantial than it may have sounded. Before Boissevain returned to Holland, he accepted John's job offer.[30] Inez lingered in Holland another month with her husband. Her father was pressuring her to return to New York alone to pursue her law career, and when they returned to London, he delivered another long lecture to the newlyweds. This sparked a fight about the couple's radical views on morality. Inez nonetheless bowed to her father's wishes and sailed for New York in mid-October.[31]

Letters during their frequent separations offer an intimate peek into the erotic life of a married New Woman. One of New Women's accomplishments was that they insisted upon moving the sex act into daylight. Silence had been the rule about sex during the Victorian era, the pinnacle of two centuries of increasing sexual repression.[32] Shortly before sailing for London, Milholland had proclaimed the New Woman's "assertion of sex rights" in her column on women for *McClure's*.[33] "The mating or ripening period is a natural, a beautiful thing," she wrote. "It imperatively demands fulfillment in its own time. It exists in and out of law—in the light and in the dark. It is the most completely vital force in the world. It is everywhere."[34] She believed sexual frankness marked the first step toward women's liberation. Several readers cancelled their subscriptions after she wrote that a wife should find sexual pleasure elsewhere if it was missing from her marriage. Society mistakenly confined love to marriage, she informed readers, where economic burdens crushed it.

Milholland's Greenwich Village cohorts were equally wary of conventional marriage, to say the least. Villagers' distrust seemed borne out after Crystal Eastman, whose love life rivaled Milholland's, married an insurance salesman and moved to Milwaukee. She was back in New York and divorced within several years.[35] Although many Villagers proclaimed marriage "backward, and probably a capitalist plot to enslave women," it proved a hard habit to break.[36] Popular culture propagandized tirelessly for the institution; fiction, for instance, almost uniformly instructed women they would find true fulfillment in family rather than career.[37] Virtually all of the Villagers married.[38] Even Doris Stevens, another sexual radical who, like Milholland, conducted affairs with married men, wanted them to marry her.[39] As Ellen Trimberger put it, Milholland's boundlessly optimistic crowd believed wives could "combine satisfying sex, psychological intimacy, and motherhood, while also doing important work and maintaining an individual identity."[40] Radical New Women such as Milholland, so sure of their ability to change the world, simply decided to change the institution of marriage to fulfill their agenda for a freer culture.

Ignoring the contradiction between marriage's demand of lifelong commitment and their determination to act upon spontaneous emotion, they strove in their marriages for no less than a perfect fusion of mind, body, and soul. Free love contradictorily often remained their ideal. Mabel Dodge raised few Greenwich Villagers' eyebrows when she blithely divorced the second of her four husbands and moved in with journalist John Reed. But the pain Reed's subsequent infidelities (although they never married) caused Dodge was indicative of many New Women's discovery that sexual freedom could be as oppressive as sexual repression.[41] Female partners especially found themselves at a disadvantage in a culture where men had more power and privilege and benefited from a sexual double standard that was more accepting of male promiscuity. Hutchins Hapgood and Neith Boyce, for example, were intellectually committed to free love, but their open marriage pained both, especially Boyce. The prolific writers and parents of four children persevered for nearly a half-century, however, in what Trimberger called "their creative struggle for the possibility of a more fulfilling personal life."[42]

Boissevain and Milholland, who shared the radicals' view that traditional marriage was "sex-property enslavement," grandly vowed never to limit each other's freedom.[43] "No man who has ever known a free woman — a woman who shares with him his workaday life, his soul life, his intellectual life," Milholland once declared, "is ever again content with the woman who is an ornament only, a creature perhaps to protect and cherish but whom he must leave when he goes into the deeps of life."[44] The couple chose not to wear wedding rings, which she considered a "badge of slavery."[45] Another way a married New Woman could challenge the institution was to keep her own name, a practice that symbolized how integral maintaining a sense of one's self was to the New Woman. Besides Boyce, for instance, journalist Louise Bryant kept her name after marrying John Reed and playwright Susan Glaspell kept hers after she married George Cram "Jig" Cook, founder of the Provincetown Players.[46] When Max Eastman married Ida Rauh, she kept her name but added his after. The simple act of painting both surnames on their mailbox was radical enough to elicit a *New York World* article, "No 'Mrs.' Badge of Slavery Worn by This Miss Wife."[47] Milholland compromised by tacking Boissevain onto her last name. She nonetheless aspired for their union to be a role model for free spirits. When a friend teased that Boissevain might be flirting with other women back in Europe, Milholland retorted they were above such petty concerns. "People are such asses —," she wrote her husband, "baby we can teach them a lot."[48] Despite its hubris, the remark reflects Milholland's underlying courage in charting the rocky shoals of the new sexual politics.

One way Milholland displayed sexual independence was masturbation. If sex with someone other than one's spouse seemed radical in the 1910s, sex with one's self remained unspeakable. Masturbation was the

Victorians' biggest phobia, said to cause insanity or even death. Havelock Ellis, however, one of the influential modern sex theorists, wrote approvingly of masturbation.[49] The frank Milholland still did not use the word, instead employing the euphemism that she "made myself happy." When she masturbated in her *Mauretania* suite, she was not only breaking a cultural taboo but also defying her husband. Boissevain believed masturbation a poor substitute for intercourse and would chastise her for giving into her erotic impulses, but he admitted it excited him to think of her making love to herself.[50] Boissevain also believed in keeping marriage spicy. "Love dies out of marriage so soon because there is no imagination, no play brought to bear on this relation," he once said. "It is like an icebox with always some cold chicken in it."[51] On the ship to New York, Milholland came to orgasm fantasizing about being with him. "I thought of everything—of the fact that you had asked me not to—and deliberately did it—partly experimental, partly animal passion, partly defiance," she told him. ". . . I thought of nothing while I did it—I just <u>did</u> it. Afterward again I thought of you."[52]

Another assertion of her sexual independence was to flirt and share details with Boissevain. "I shall tell you of my successes with frank egotism—" she wrote him from New York, "so here's the apology for all!" She then proceeded to spell out in forty-three perfumed pages a string of shipboard flirtations. A lively squash game rendered a French businessman sleepless with longing. A "badly smitten" director of the White Star Line spilled out details of the *Titanic* disaster as they strolled the ship deck. Another conquest tagged after her like a puppy dog. "I never had such an immediate and overwhelming success before," she told her groom.[53]

Although one would not expect love letters between newlyweds to read like political tracts, the twenty-seven-year-old feminist's letters are remarkable for their obsession with seduction. It is as if her entire sense of self hinged upon unhinging every man she came into contact with. Ironically, her obsession portrays her as totally succumbing to the power of male gaze she so successfully defied in the Washington parade. Perhaps her obsession was a reaction to Victorian sexlessness or perhaps she so feared being subsumed by marriage that she needed to flaunt her sexual independence. Her compulsion to share all with her husband, however, seemed to exceed the New Woman creed of open communication between partners. Her detailed account of her seduction of a handsome Englishman named Beresford is revealing.

When they faced off against each other in the final match of a mixed doubles tennis tournament, she wrote Boissevain, "I was full of admiration for him—his skill—his coolness—his awareness—his conquered self consciousness, and I knew that, he was thinking of me all during the matches." The spectators that gathered stoked her exhibitionist streak; a skilled tennis player, she performed marvelously. "I knew the game displayed a vigorous figure to the best advantage," she wrote. When she and Beresford found themselves together again at dinner, Milholland determined to be the life of the party. They danced and played "Truth." At Beresford's turn, he asked Milholland whom she liked best. "I startled and delighted him, disgusted my other beaux by saying 'you.'" That night alone in her cabin, she informed Boissevain, "I thought long and excitably in bed—of him and of you." She tossed in bed for a long time wrestling with her lust. "[I]f he had come to my door at that moment I should have let him in and loved him. In times past, I should have gone to look for him—that was the only difference."[54] The next morning, she stayed in bed and read because she got her period, which often incapacitated her. When Beresford dropped by, Milholland took his hand. They kissed, and she began stroking his hair just as their boisterous companions piled into the room. After everyone left, Beresford returned. They kissed again and he stroked her breasts. "I loved being stroked and said so and restrained him not at all," she told Boissevain. "I thought of you and spoke of you and told him I should tell you all."[55]

Before Beresford disappeared from her life, he asked if Milholland would drop everything for love. "Of course," she replied. Even Eugen? "Certainly," she replied, if she loved another.[56] Although she told Boissevain not to worry, she added, "But if he had been in my room when I came home last night—I should have loved him. I don't explain dear—I just state facts." She admitted forbidden love made him more attractive. "Naughty naughty Nan!—but she adores being naughty. It's the most enticing thing in life."[57] She scribbled the truest words of her life, "Excitement is the breath of life to me."[58]

Although Boissevain was not immune to jealousy, much of his wife's appeal lay with her independence. Decades later, he said: "Unless you are a fool and so conceited as to think you are the greatest, the most wonderful man in the world, how can you expect a woman to love only you! And if you could know for a certainty that never, never would the personality of another appeal to her, you would be bored. You would be like the people who travel with a schedule. . . . Others—and they are the kind of people I like—go to Paris *hoping* to see everything but never even step inside the Louvre because, living in the mood of the moment, they were attracted to other pleasures. That, to me is the way to live."[59]

Husband and wife shared a ribald attitude toward sex. Their letters display the celebration of sexuality that the radical faction of New Women of the 1910s pursued as part of their break with Victorian silence and constraints. He liked to shock people by making jokes about oral sex, and the pair traded banter about "Simon," their nickname for his penis. "How's Simon?" she asked him when he was away on a business trip in California in 1916. "I kiss you and kiss you on that most kissable mouth in the world and on your breasts and down your back and Simon and his little companions."[60] He replied: "Simon gets naughtier, and Eugen has the devil of a time to keep control of Simon. . . . But I want you, and only you, and I will not waste Simon or my burning passion on empty hallucinations, or worse still, some second class female."[61] The couple reveled in sensual fantasies. Milholland asked, "Have you lots of wicked stories to tell me and have you thought of exciting situations for us to bring about?"[62] She suggested Boissevain read a book she enjoyed, *L'Amour Physique*.[63] Her scented letters aroused him: "I want to put my face between your legs."[64] He wanted to take her to Havana's erotic nightclubs.[65] She asked her "Greek God" to mail her a nude picture of himself.[66] Neither was she modest about her own charms. After comparing herself with other women at a Turkish bath, she exclaimed, "No wonder you love Nannie!"[67] When he wrote he loved her soul more than her body, she replied, "I don't. I love your body best."[68]

Newlywed Milholland compensated for her breathless accounts of her brushes with infidelity in fall 1913 by assuring Boissevain of how much she missed him. She ended one letter: "Sweet, sweet, sweet Nannie wishes she could put her head on your breast and nestle in your arms to-night, and smell your divine smell, and love you passionately."[69] He wrote that he disliked working on the tubes, and he could not shake a mysterious illness. These subjects became recurring themes in their marriage: illicit relationships, professional frustration, ill health. No matter their troubles, however, they always saw better times on the horizon. Milholland wrote Boissevain nearly every day that fall. They swore never to leave each other again.

Marriage

"Here's to our work—
yours and mine"

Milholland clutched a novel called *A Husband of No Importance* as she stepped off the ship clad in an ankle-length, fur-trimmed coat. She explained with a laugh to the posse of reporters staking out her arrival that a fellow passenger lent her the book. Reporters hungry for a look at the man who captured America's Amazon were disappointed that a friend who greeted her was not Boissevain.[1] She invited them to follow her to James Osborne's law office, where they peppered her with questions before she even could check her mail.

Alva Belmont called to wish her well, sending along congratulations from her guest, Emmeline Pankhurst.[2] Others were eager to meet the mystery groom. The wedding of the nation's most visible advocate for votes for women shocked Milholland's feminist friends almost as much as it did her family. Much of society still found marriage and a public life mutually exclusive for women. Even Harriot Stanton Blatch joked that Milholland had deserted suffragists.[3] One consolation for feminists was that Milholland had proposed to Boissevain—making good their claim that "women had the right to be equally as aggressive and forceful in love as men."[4] Reporters pressed her on whether she would continue her suffrage and law work. The question of whether a woman, even if childless, could combine a career with marriage weighed heavily on the public mind throughout the decade.[5] A few stellar, distant successes shone like beacons to young wives with aspirations; in France, Marie Curie and her husband even shared a Nobel Prize (she was the first woman to win one) in physics for their work with radioactivity.[6] Popular magazines, however, continued to advise that women stop working after marriage, even though many observers acknowledged the average middle-class wife had little to occupy her at home.[7] Some even blamed the spiraling divorce rate—increasing five times faster than the population, up to one in twelve marriages—on married women's idleness. New Women were suspected culprits in this assault on the family.[8]

Milholland's untraditional decision to keep working after marriage exemplified the goals of the New Woman. Marriage would not subsume her, and she would continue to contribute to society. An integral aspect of the "New Marriage" Milholland and her peers envisioned was that it leave room for a woman to develop her creative and professional self. Despite the barrage of discouraging advice from popular culture, the number of professional women jumped 226 percent during the New Woman's heyday between 1890 and 1920, almost triple the number for men.[9] Doing good work was essential to Milholland's self-esteem. She despised the "idle, parasitic woman."[10] "Here's to our work—" she toasted Boissevain, "yours and mine!"[11] He was exceptionally supportive of her professional aspirations, in contrast to many radical men who often viewed the strong New Women they married as mother figures.[12] Boissevain made no such demands of his wife, and in fact, played the role of nurturer throughout their marriage.

She once joked about a separation case she landed in which the wife charged cruelty against the husband. "Cunnilingus!" Milholland explained. "But she seemed to like it. She stayed several years. Rather a common person but nice."[13] Boissevain avoided the temptation to snicker and admonished her not to gossip about salacious cases: "If it came out that you talked about your case it would kill you."[14] He encouraged her in other ways. He was delighted she landed a case involving an African American teen in the Bronx and seconded a judge who predicted she would become a crackerjack trial lawyer. "It is a tedious, slow uphill work," Boissevain counseled, "but you'll succeed."[15] He did have total faith in his wife's talents and always would maintain Milholland "opened my mind to all the great questions of existence."[16] Boissevain claimed she gave him a soul. "Lead on, lead on my goddess," he told her. "I follow."[17] He tried to rudder the passions that inclined her to scatter her energies. Her mother recognized his positive influence on her daughter. "She is quite worthwhile," Jean told Eugen, "but needs all your good judgment and plain sense to keep her steady."[18] Inez also appreciated her unflappable husband. She wrote, "If ever Nannie does anything in the world she'll have Eugen to thank."[19]

Milholland purposely wore an old dress and hat to her first day back at work to emphasize to co-workers that she had not changed.[20] She reassured her feminist friends: "Tell them that I shall continue my law practice and will never, never give up my suffragette activities."[21] The only woman with a law degree in Osborne's firm, she returned to her clerk duties even though as a member of the bar she was certified to try cases. Because of sex discrimination, many female graduates of law school could not even find work as law clerks, like the young woman who wrote Milholland for advice on how to break into the profession. After nine fruitless months on the job market, Gertrude Smith disconsolately wrote, "People advise me to become a stenographer."[22] That, in fact, that is what many women lawyers did.[23] Milholland's duties included routine matters such as settling a foreclosure debt or refereeing a firm's financial dispute.[24] Milholland acknowledged, "People hesitate to entrust a serious legal business to a woman whom they have been trained to feel is not capable of dealing with seriousness."[25] She got a taste of sex discrimination when the rest of the lawyers traveled to Buffalo to prosecute a big libel trial. Osborne left her behind because he feared the opposition would drum up a scandal about a woman traveling with male co-workers.[26] Women were banned from the state and county bar associations, key venues for networking. Frustrated women lawyers formed their own association. Milholland co-edited its monthly, the *Women Lawyers' Journal*.[27]

Milholland's career was further threatened by another tentacle of patriarchal culture the moment she walked down the gangplank upon her return from London. The immigration inspector told her she could not land as an American because she was the wife of a Dutch citizen. His greeting acknowledged a 1907 federal law that formalized the long-held legal assumption that a woman assumed her husband's nationality.[28] Blatch, another victim of the law because her husband was English, had long campaigned against it.[29] Friends at WPU headquarters greeted Milholland, "Hello, Dutchy!"[30] It even appeared she might lose her license to practice law because the New York state bar required U.S. citizenship; however, no other woman lawyer had ever been in her position. An expert she consulted said an 1895 precedent might enable her keep her citizenship if Boissevain applied for citizenship.[31] Milholland asked Senator James O'Gorman to intercede during the next Congress. "Marriage is a purely personal affair, and should in no wise interfere with public capacity," she wrote him. She asked him to support a pending bill to change the law, enclosing an eight-page memorandum listing legal citations related to her case. Despite O'Gorman's support, the bill failed.[32] She was prepared to take the matter to court if anyone challenged her appearances as an attorney. Apparently, no one did, because she continued to practice. But the loss of her American citizenship rankled. Her American passport became invalid.[33] The law's "ignominy" exacerbated Milholland's anger about her lack of the ballot.[34] She wrote: "I do not believe that members of our national legislature any more than anyone else do things for nothing. They busy themselves, and quite rightly, with those of their constituents who have something to give them in return for their activities." The message hit home harder when a former Sing Sing inmate asked her to endorse his application to have the governor restore his citizenship. She bitterly remarked, "I am in a position to help this man, yet I am in no position to help myself."[35]

Besides returning to law, she also leaped back into reform activities. She advocated creation of a public relief fund to help widows at a city hall hearing and protested the fire department's refusal to hire women.[36] A full-page *World* feature on feminism was decorated with a portrait of Milholland surrounded by her law books.[37] She appeared in the Maxwell Motor Company's showroom to endorse its hiring of women to sell cars, while a fellow feminist in blue jeans disassembled a car motor.[38] Nearly every night found her out—at the Hippodrome, at the theater with the William Randolph Hearsts, dining at the Plaza or Delmonico's.[39] She even turkey trotted all night with New York's new pro-suffrage mayor at his victory party.[40]

She also began to set up her first home, a cheerful two-bedroom flat at 35 East 30th Street. Milholland disdained housework, although before her marriage, *Good Housekeeping*, in a glaring example of the mass media's limitless capacity for idealizing her, had speculated that "although she may not be familiar with formulas for desserts or salad dressings, there is no doubt that in any domestic crisis she would master all cooking difficulties by mixing brains with reliable recipes."[41] "I had no idea housekeeping meant getting so many things," she said after spending nearly a thousand dollars on linen, silver, plates, and other sundries to make the flat "gay and artistic."[42] Robert Boissevain moved in along with "Roger," a female friend. One of Eugen's sisters worried Robert would fall in love with Inez, but luckily, Robert held no physical charms for her.[43] Her maid, Florence, moved from the Milholland household to work for Inez for twenty-five dollars a month. Since her father was subsidizing the household, he was irked by the flat's annual rent of $2,200.[44] Neither did he appreciate the hairdresser who called to do Inez's hair and nails.[45]

Eugen cabled he would arrive in New York in mid-December. "But baby don't come unless you are well—I can't be controlled when I first see you—and I don't want to make you ill again," Inez warned him.[46] The couple celebrated Christmas with Jack. Eugen's kindness toward Inez's brother, now twenty-one, hastened his acceptance of the "elegant loafer" into the family circle.[47] The honeymoon was over, and it was time for the two free spirits to settle into their roles as husband and wife.

Invitations poured in from New Yorkers eager to meet the mortal who captured the Amazon. Newspaper magnate Medill McCormick wanted Boissevain to go big-game hunting with him. Newlywed Crystal Eastman and her husband came for dinner and made merry. They whiled away one rainy Sunday afternoon with friends debating the merits of modern art.[48]

Milholland's double duties as lawyer and homemaker were lightened considerably by Florence and a cook. Milholland prided herself on her humane relations with them. Reporters had once called upon Milholland for her views on a strike of waiters and chefs at the Hotel Vanderbilt. Milholland—still a student who lived with her parents—supported the idea. "If I were running a home I'd gladly give my servants union conditions, I dare say."[49] The married Milholland told the press minions fascinated with the minutest details of her life that she planned the menus and made sure her help rarely worked more than eight hours a day, crediting her smoothly running household to her scientific management. Milholland was parroting a new crop of experts when she declared homemaking a "fine art" that should be left to those with special training. The modern call for professional homemakers served to elevate the role of domestic help and helped justify the desire of mothers who wished to work outside the home.[50] As the modern Milholland claimed, "Were I to sweep a floor or wash dishes, as I have done at times, I would approach these things with the same sense of system as I would in making out a brief. But why should I do the cooking and sweeping when my present work is more pleasing and more suitable for me? A woman should do that which makes best use of her energies, and leave to others the work better suited to them."[51]

She preferred to devote her time to suffrage. This again surprised many observers, even suffragists, who assumed she would withdraw from feminist activities.[52] In fact, she hoped marriage would make her appear more serious in the public eye.[53] She held forth on votes for women at the Twilight Club on one night and enlightened her suffrage chums about the Dutch woman suffrage movement on another.[54] She narrated a suffrage pageant in April 1914.[55] When suffragists sponsored a frenetic "Suffrage Day" instead of the usual May parade, Milholland parried questions at a street meeting at Grant's Tomb. "Don't ask us what we are going to do with the vote when we get it," she shot back at a heckler. "We will answer that question when you men give us the vote."[56] The highlight of Alva Belmont's 1916 operetta, *Melinda and Her Sisters*, which featured a suffrage soapbox rally and parade, occurred when Milholland appeared at the end of the parade carrying the American flag. As the procession reached the stage of the Waldorf Astoria ballroom, "her tall figure dominated the scene."[57]

Boissevain basked in his wife's glow.[58] His enthusiasm, good humor, and openness to new ideas made him popular among the Greenwich Village set. In a skit at the Palace Theatre, he portrayed "Peter Jackson" opposite actress Fola LaFollette as his wife in a mock trial in which Milholland played the judge. Jurors Mabel Dodge and Jenny Marie Howe ruled in favor of Mrs. Jackson's claim that $395.17 in household savings belonged to her.[59] Boissevain vouched for the pleasure of marriage to a suffragist in a speech for votes for women. "I like it so much I am sorry for a man married to an anti," he said.[60] Her celebrity did not threaten him, although he joked about the injury to his "assonine [sic] male vanity" when people introduced him as Inez Milholland's husband.[61] Boissevain "really enjoyed being the husband of a gallant Feminist leader," according to Floyd Dell.[62] "I like to look up to and admire the people I love," Boissevain once said. "I love people who are great personalities."[63]

Milholland's most significant suffrage step was to get more involved with Alice Paul's Congressional Union, successor to the NAWSA Congressional Committee that organized the Washington parade. The CU had grown increasingly aggressive in its campaign for a federal amendment, which helped spur its split in 1914 from the more conservative NAWSA.[64] That May, Milholland and Crystal Eastman called upon a representative from Peekskill, and Milholland helped lead a CU delegation to Senator O'Gorman's Wall Street office.[65] Stockbrokers leaned out of their office windows to cheer them, a far cry from when they dumped trash on suffragists in 1908. The official delegation already comprised two hundred women, but Jessie Hardy Stubbs invited hundreds more spectators into the meeting with O'Gorman.[66] The rambunctious assembly spilled out of his office. "Aren't you women going too hastily?" the rotund, goateed senator blurted to the horde pressed around his desk. His visitors recoiled. "Too quickly!" one woman called out. "After forty years!"

"Can freedom come too quickly?" retorted Milholland, squaring off against him in front of his desk. O'Gorman refused to be moved from his opposition to tampering with the Constitution even after Milholland, well versed in constitutional law, rebutted his arguments at some length.[67] He was unmoved by her final statement, which succinctly summarized the CU's increasing alienation: "Those who are not with us are against us."[68]

Milholland addressed the state senate in February 1915 as part of a suffrage rally celebrating the legislature's momentous decision the previous week to hold a suffrage referendum in November. Milholland waved

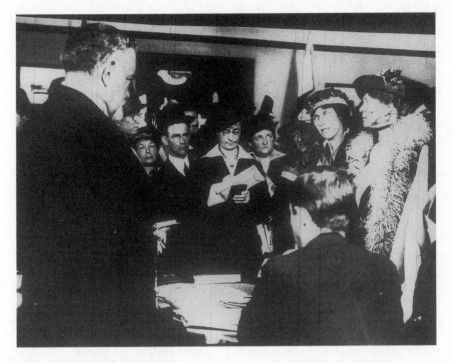

Inez leading a delegation of suffragists to New York senator James O'Gorman's office in 1914. *Courtesy of National Woman's Party.*

off charges women voters would give "demon rum a black eye," predicting they would split on Prohibition.[69] Constant speaking, however, drained her. Throughout her life she had to ration her energies, a task she found nearly impossible. When the Palace Theatre invited her to appear for a week in a vaudeville routine touting votes for women, she begged off, pleading exhaustion.[70]

The marriage also felt strains. One of the couple's biggest challenges was getting their careers off the ground. Boissevain started a Dutch Indies tobacco import business that floundered, and Milholland's law clerk salary came nowhere near supporting their lifestyle. Neither did the five hundred dollars annual income bestowed upon her by her father when she graduated from Vassar.[71] They remained dependent upon her father for even more money, a source of friction. The mail tubes' sole customer, the U.S. post office, was dragging its feet on buying the underground system. John Milholland's financial empire was built on the assumption the tubes would fetch at least a million dollars from the federal government. He began spending weeks at a time in Washington lobbying Congress to buy them. He began borrowing money again, and even stopped making cider and serving alcohol at Meadowmount to trim the farm's mounting deficit.[72]

Inez's relationship with her father remained complicated. "I don't want you to think Dad," she once wrote him, "that it's only when you give me things that I can be pleasant. I hate that just as much as when you ask things of me if you have done something for me. . . . [B]luntly, what I mean to do away with, is the idea of either 'working' the other."[73] John remained miffed by Inez's "self satisfaction" in a marriage he called mad. When Inez was away, her father cornered Eugen and lectured him about money and wrote savagely to both about finances.[74] The amiable Eugen continued to reach out. He respected his father-in-law's racial crusading. As time passed, the two outspoken men learned to get along. They occasionally met for dinner or a smoke. Eugen also tried to curry favor with Jean. Eugen reported to Inez two years after they eloped, "I believe she is beginning to understand how much I love you."[75]

Most disappointing to the couple, they were unable to conceive a child. They began fantasizing about children—Peter and Eugenie—almost as soon as they married.[76] "Soon I shall think of being in your arms—of love—and of Peter," Milholland wrote Boissevain soon after her Atlantic passage.[77] She adored children and they reciprocated; her sense of fun and freedom made her a great playmate. She won over her swarm of Dutch nieces by bringing them the wildly popular kewpie dolls. Even though Milholland supported birth control, she did not practice it, an indication she suffered reproductive health problems. When Milholland had her period, she took to her bed and canceled engagements and speeches, although that was the common practice among women at the time. She referred to the process as being ill, the common and telling term used for menstruation.[78] A mysterious discharge also began to plague her, and it frustrated her that running up hills and cold showers failed to stop it.[79] Her inability to conceive weighed heavily on her and hurt her pride. "I long for [children] more and more every day," she told Boissevain.[80] One night the couple cried together about her failure to get pregnant.[81] Her sense of failure, already heightened by frustrations in the career so central to her sense of self, deepened.

For all of Milholland's independence, she believed motherhood a sacred institution and important mission. Even this radical New Woman had internalized the pervasive cultural view that deified motherhood. Her apparent inability to perform this defining act of womanhood depressed her. Milholland believed maternal instinct was innate—in fact, the source of women's superior fitness for citizenship. Many married professional women of the time still believed reproduction rather than pleasure was the main reason for sexual intercourse, despite the expanding discourse on sexual pleasure.[82] In one speech, Milholland simply offered a modern twist on Victorian values when she declared motherhood no less than the best service a woman could provide to the state.[83] Of course, this view conflicted with the basic New Woman tenet that female potential should not be limited by biology, but its powerful hold was among contradictions that conflicted New Women. In another speech, Milholland couched her radical demand that the legislature create a mother's pension in the most conservative terms. Mothers should be wards of the state, she argued, "to be cherished, protected and nourished."[84] Milholland's arguments mirrored the message of the paradoxical Ellen Key. Perhaps the most widely read feminist of the decade after Charlotte Perkins Gilman, Key boldly validated female sexual desire couched in the language of eugenics: Free love fostered superior sexual unions that produced superior offspring. Radical because it was anti-patriarchal—Key argued there was no such thing as illegitimacy—her message was simultaneously Victorian. Milholland, among Key's many fans, perhaps also absorbed Key's anti-feminist message that women produce "a hundred thousand novels and works of art, which might better have been boys and girls!"[85]

Eager as Milholland was to have a child, she had plenty of other individuals and causes to nurture. She may have packed away her Joan of Arc parade costume, but over the next few years she crusaded like a knight in shining armor for the many causes and people who came knocking on her door.

Crusader

"I must have a value somewhere"

Soon after Milholland returned from London in fall 1913, she, Alva Belmont, and Emmeline Pankhurst stepped down from a chauffeured car and entered Gimbel Brothers at Broadway and Fifth Avenue. The trio's high heels clicked assuredly on the cavernous department store's marble floors as they strode past its shelves of linens, hats, and innumerable other goods. Just before the six o'clock closing time, they headed for the exits, where they were joined by a dozen other suffragists and labor organizers. By then, the well-scrubbed clerks sagged behind gleaming counters after being on their feet for practically ten hours. The visitors called out to the several thousand tired clerks streaming out of the building and handed them leaflets inviting them to join the embryonic Retail Clerks Union. The leaflets called for a fifty-four-hour week, double time on Sundays, one-week vacations, and equal pay for women. Comforts such as roof gardens and rest rooms failed to compensate for low pay, she told the young women tramping past her. The exhortations from the fur-clad woman standing in the back seat of a fancy car must have grated on the workers' ears. They spent almost all of their day obsequiously serving affluent women such as Milholland. "To get better pay you must help yourselves," she called out to them. "You have nothing to fear. Lose your position if necessary."[1]

Retail clerk was a relatively new position for young women, a white-collar job with more prestige than working in a factory even if pay and working conditions were little better, if not worse. Department stores' elaborate facades beckoned female customers inside, where ornate fixtures, grandiose architecture, and comfortable restaurants created a safe but exotic public space for women. Gender and class distinctions permeated the stores: Underpaid, overworked working-class women waited upon middle-class customers, their socioeconomic gulf assumed bridged by their sex. Clerks normally worked six days a week from eight in the morning until six at night. Sitting or talking was forbidden.[2] When sociologist Annie Marion MacLean went undercover to expose the shop girls' working conditions in 1899, she reported, "The cloak, toilet and lunch rooms were the gloomiest and filthiest it was ever my misfortune to enter." At the end of two weeks, she had earned $11.88 for 175 hours of work, but after the first week's expenses, she only had eleven cents left.[3] Labor organizers had abandoned hopes of organizing clerks, who in 1914 still earned less than nine dollars a week, the lowest livable wage.[4] Buoyed by the strides of the shirtwaist workers, however, the same middle-class clientele that the clerks served spearheaded renewed efforts to improve their lot in the 1910s.[5] Milholland was among New Women who adopted their cause as one of her crusades.

Retail clerks were a different breed of New Women from professionals and independently wealthy women such as Milholland and Belmont.[6] Although their life choices were more limited, like shirtwaist strikers they prided themselves on their agency. Self-realization may have meant something different to them than to a Greenwich Village poet living off a trust fund, but both made their own decisions about how to conduct their lives. Their job allowed them to get dressed up and offered greater opportunities to exercise initiative and autonomy than most jobs.[7] Clerks' appearance on store floors was another step into the public sphere, as was their presence at Coney Island or baseball games, venues that did not exist or were out of bounds to women a generation earlier. As Kathy Peiss points out, such public pursuit of pleasure was empowering for working women.[8] Even if most clerks did not see themselves as victims, most worried about paying bills. Although most were unmarried, many helped support their families. Those who lived on their own usually found a room in a boardinghouse. A cheaper alternative was working-girls homes, but the paternalistic attitude of their managers and endless rules chewed at residents, who sought independence. Women's hotels were cheerier alternatives. Although retail clerks may have been proud of holding a job and living independently, their lives looked dismal to the middle-class women who championed them. "It is the monotony and loneliness of their lives that is the most trying thing to the girl workers," wrote a journalist who investigated their lives.[9]

The inhumanity of a joyless life struck a nerve in Milholland. "[W]e know that only happy people are 100 percent efficient," she told the National Retail Dry Goods Association.[10] Her offer to mediate differences between management and counter clerks was unintentionally condescending in its assumption the clerks needed her to intervene. "The stupid girl, the servile girl, the sneak is satisfied with conditions pretty much as she finds them," she told storeowners. "But the high-spirited girl, the girl of intelligence and capacity who wants to get on . . . does care."[11] She criticized the New York stores in an article for influential *Harper's Weekly* magazine, another foray into journalism. She claimed she knew two clerks driven insane by the pressures of the Christmas shopping season. Her remedy was a union. Besides her pragmatic argument that treating employees well would increase business, she raised the specter of boycotts. It was not an empty threat; a number of social-minded middle-class women avoided stores that exploited employees. Rheta Childe Dorr stopped buying Christmas presents in department stores after a painful stint selling handkerchiefs ten hours a day as part of yet another undercover exposé. Rose Pastor Stokes, in fact, eventually renounced unionization in favor of boycotts.[12] Milholland wrote, "I know many people who refuse to deal in a shop where the faces of the employees express discontent, hurry, weariness, nervous, exhaustion, etc."[13] Like many social-feminist issues, her crusade for sales clerks was ahead of its time.[14] Many progressive demands for protecting workers would not be met until the 1930s, as part of the New Deal.

Among criticisms of the sales clerks' lot was that low wages forced them into prostitution. For decades, women reformers had waged war upon what they delicately referred to as the "social evil" or "white slavery." Unease about loosening sexual mores and morality fueled many reformers' fixation upon prostitution, which resulted in passage of the 1910 Mann Act. Milholland and other radical New Women, however, targeted prostitution as the most onerous example of women's economic dependence on men. "We can never solve the problems of prostitution," she said in a suffrage speech, "until woman has become the economic and political equal of man."[15] One of Milholland's first public talks while she was still at Vassar addressed prostitution, obscurely titled "The Social Problem and the College Girl." Before she married, she had testified before a legislative committee that poor wages drove women to prostitution. "I do not see how a girl can avoid it who is earning $3.50 a week for her sole support," Milholland said.[16] She pitched for training prostitutes versus punishment, "very patiently, for these women have lost all capacity for concentration."[17]

Milholland's reputation as an advocate for female underdogs drew women to her office at Osborne's firm on lower Broadway. Some of Milholland's crusades were as simple as firing off a letter to a well-placed person. For instance, she encouraged the blatantly elitist Alice Paul to open up the CU to working-class women.[18] She maintained ties at Sing Sing prison and sometimes helped released inmates find jobs.[19] In May 1914, the widow of an accused murderer sought her advice when she had to testify in the trial. Even though Milholland did not formally represent the woman, she attended the trial to give her moral support. "[S]he chose to give her wonderful vitality to the neediest claimants on her sympathy," reformer Frederick C. Howe recalled.[20] Such cases made headlines but little or no money.[21] Milholland, however, could not resist them. As one colleague said, "Whenever a woman came to me for advice I sent her to Mrs. Boissevain, for I knew she would help her without charging her anything."[22] Interestingly, virtually the only women's issue of the decade in which Milholland did not seem to play an active role was birth control. Birth control was key to the New Woman's sexual freedom, and a number of women were jailed in the mid-1910s for distributing birth control information, still illegal. Greenwich Villager Margaret Sanger fled to England to escape prosecution after the New York postmaster seized her *Woman Rebel*. Milholland supported birth control, although she did not practice it. "The necessity of birth control is so obvious," she wrote. Her disinterest may have stemmed from her own infertility or may simply have reflected a lack of time. By the time Sanger opened America's first birth control clinic in October 1916 — 464 clients visited before authorities shut it down nine days later — Milholland was deeply involved in campaigning for suffrage during the presidential election.[23]

Her crusading spirit helps explain her attraction to journalism. The field had emerged as an exciting and accessible profession for New Women.[24] Nearly six thousand women worked as reporters and editors by the end of the 1910s, although discrimination remained daunting.[25] Popular fiction romanticized female reporters, like the feisty heroine of a 1915 *Good Housekeeping* story, "The Sob-Lady," too busy racing around the city chronicling fires and murders to worry about her hair or clothes.[26] Milholland grew up amid journalists, and she was among the elite who helped the William Randolph Hearsts celebrate their tenth wedding anniversary at a posh party in April 1913.[27] She had been the subject of countless newspaper interviews and knew how the press worked. As a highly visible participant in the publicity-savvy suffrage campaign, she saw how much influence the press could wield over the public imagination. She also enjoyed an easy rapport with the profession's ragtag individualists, who invited her to address the New York Newspaper Association and New York Press Club.[28] Milholland had dated journalists, including Joseph Patterson and Max Eastman, and boasted numerous journalists as her friends, notably Sophie Loeb. Loeb was typical of Milholland's friends in that she worked hard and played hard. The *World's* sob sister wielded the journalist's pen and pad the way Milholland envisioned it should be: as a voice to empower the voiceless. Milholland's smattering of articles in *McClure's* and *Harper's* similarly aimed to reform society.

Given Milholland's respect for a free press and penchant for controversy, it is not surprising that she adopted free speech as another crusade. Fellow suffragist Inez Haynes Irwin caught the prewar radical spirit when she said that anyone with a megaphone could announce in the middle of Manhattan, "I am here to gather recruits for a movement to free . . ." and "even before he could state the object of his crusade, he would be in the center of a milling crowd of volunteers."[29] Americans spent much of the 1910s hashing out—in the streets as well as in the courtroom—the practical application of the noble ideal of free speech. One result was the American Civil Liberties Union. Draconian repression against dissent during World War I would intensify the debate, but it began earlier during labor struggles, demands for sex education and birth control, and the creation of powerful new media such as motion pictures. Officialdom's routine reaction to change was to forbid it, which during the cataclysmic 1910s led to bans on everything from the tango to red flags. Milholland tasted censorship when trustees barred her and socialist Rose Pastor Stokes from speaking at a Boston church.[30] She asserted, "The result of official suppression is revolution."[31]

She turned out in February 1914 to support publisher Mitchell Kennerley at his federal obscenity trial. Kennerley found himself a victim of the Puritanical "Comstock laws" enacted by Congress in 1873 in response to rigorous lobbying by Anthony Comstock. Milholland reviled "Comstockery," which forbade even the mildest references to sexuality as obscene and illegal. Censors cared not for the public good, she claimed, but for "the smug feeling of self-approval which condemning somebody else is able to bring."[32] She was eager to lend her name to the cause when Kennerley was charged with sending Daniel Carson Goodman's *Hagar Revelly* through the mail. Despite its racy sex scenes ("intoxicated by the cataclysmic enormity of her first real entrance in the secrets of sexual passion, [she] clung to him, returning throb for throb, pulsation for pulsation"), *Hagar's* tone was highly moralistic. The "good" sister who raises the illegitimate child of the other wins the decent man both love.[33] Kennerley chose to fight rather than pay a fine, marking the first time an American novel was defended in court by its publisher. On the trial's opening day, a federal district court judge refused to hear the testimony of literary experts his lawyers had assembled, including Norman Hapgood, editor of *Collier's* magazine. The next day, Milholland sat elbow to elbow with playwright Susan Glaspell, "Jig" Cook, and other writers who packed the courtroom, following along in their own copies of the novel as lawyers read passages to the jury. On the third day, the jury delivered a surprise acquittal in an important endorsement of freedom of expression.[34]

The new "moving pictures" faced even more severe censorship. The First Amendment was not yet deemed applicable to movies, to which twenty-six million Americans flocked weekly by 1910, and a National Board of Review weeded out immorality in the new mass medium. Films about prostitution were particularly problematic, as feminists who argued the public needed to be educated about the trade were frustrated when films on the subject were banned. The board condemned *The House of Bondage*, for example, even after the producers cut a brothel scene and kissing.[35] Milholland took on a similar case in 1914.[36] When police shut down a screening of *The Inside of White Slave Traffic* at the Park Theatre, Milholland protested that only frank discussion of the subject could remedy the social evil.[37] Other issues surrounding the case also appealed to her desire for open discussion of sex as a "subject full of deepest beauty and truth." Her stance drew a public rebuke from John Sumner of the New York Society for the Suppression of Vice, who charged she confused "freedom with the abuse of freedom."[38] Milholland attended several screenings of the film at other theatres, and persuaded prominent suffragists, including Belmont and Carrie Chapman Catt, to view it and attest to its social relevancy.

Milholland jeopardized her professional credibility, however, because she did not reveal she worked for the producers. When they refused to pay her, her lawsuit claimed that her services included enlisting the suffrage leaders and writing letters to editors. The *New York Times* chided her in an editorial for confusing disreputable press agentry with legal work. Failing to reveal that she had a financial interest in the film's fate "must tend to weaken her standing with the public as a disinterested reformer." It called her actions "pretty poor business for an avowed reformer and social uplifter."[39] The incident showed her guilty of poor judgment, at the least. She did not respond to the *Times* but continued to speak out against censorship.

The next year, Milholland was among a minority of liberals who opposed a call by the NAACP to ban *The Birth of a Nation*. D. W. Griffith's action-packed pioneering feature film not only introduced Americans to the image of the burning cross but also portrayed African Americans as buffoons and rapists. The film posed a dilemma for liberals who championed civil rights and free speech. Milholland's stand pitted her against her father, as the NAACP unsuccessfully asked the National Board of

Censorship in Moving Pictures to cut offensive scenes and forced hearings in several cities on banning or editing the film.[40] Milholland agreed *Birth* was abysmal. But she subscribed to the classic liberal belief in the marketplace of ideas. "Prohibition I have always believed is the lazy man's way of dealing with a problem."[41] She counseled *Birth* foes: "Your liberty lover must take pains . . . to point out the falsities and dangers of the evil thing, and its consequences." She staunchly believed the antidote to offensive speech was more speech.[42]

Milholland also pitched in to help former beau Max Eastman defend freedom of the press. *The Masses* had charged the Associated Press with conspiring to keep secret the workers' side of a long, violent coal miners strike in 1913 in Paint Creek, West Virginia. Eastman wrote a blistering editorial condemning the AP accompanied by a damning cartoon by the acidic cartoonist Art Young. It featured the head of the AP pouring "lies" out of a bottle marked "Poison" into a reservoir of "News" at the edge of a city with the American flag flying above it. Six months later, Eastman and Young were indicted on criminal libel charges. The AP chose an especially heavy-handed way to protest *The Masses'* insult, as libel cases usually were handled in civil court. Defenders of free speech lined up to champion the accused.[43] Milholland presided at a "Free Press Protest Meeting" sponsored by the Liberal Club at Cooper Union. Speakers represented the stars of American liberalism: wealthy reformer Amos Pinchot; muckraker Lincoln Steffens; writer Charlotte Perkins Gilman; editor Norman Hapgood; and William English Walling, a founder of the NAACP.[44] While some fifteen hundred supporters filed into the hall, outside in Rutgers Square police swiftly swooped down on a member of the International Workers of the World who tried to speak on unemployment. They dispersed the gathering crowd. Inside, Milholland announced the arrest to her audience. Hisses ricocheted throughout the hall. Milholland proclaimed dryly, "My country, 'tis of thee, Sweet land of liberty."[45] The dubious case festered in the courts two years before district attorneys quietly dropped it.

Eastman finally met his successor in Milholland's affections the next summer. Milholland and Boissevain had rented with her father's money a luxurious bungalow owned by the famous opera singer Lillian Nordica. It nestled on a wooded hill in Harmon, a pastoral parcel forty miles north of the city adopted by Villagers as a refreshing summer retreat. The nurturing Boissevain pitched into gardening, growing lettuce, radishes, spinach, parsley, and onions.[46] When Milholland bumped into her old flame in the city, she invited Eastman up to meet her husband. "[Y]ou'll love him," she predicted. The two philosophical soul mates became best friends. The trio stayed up all night dissecting the mystery of love, which, Eastman immodestly suggested later, rivaled "the most famous discussions of this subject."[47]

Milholland loved showing off her adoring husband. She got a chance to display him at Vassar's fiftieth reunion in 1915. Students were electrified at the sight of their legendary alumna, her husband at her side easily identified by the name badge he sported above a rose boutonnière. People who saw the couple noticed how pleased they seemed with each other.[48] Her return was marred, however, because newly installed President Henry MacCracken forbade a campus suffrage rally publicizing the next month's suffrage referendum that would have featured her during the reunion. "It could not be allowed any more than a lot of college boys would be allowed to paint fences red," MacCracken said. Nearly a decade after the illicit cemetery rally, Milholland's presence still ruffled feathers at her alma mater. MacCracken claimed Milholland's appearance would embarrass his predecessor and, most fantastically, sniffed she was only a second-rate speaker anyway. A more plausible reason is that the moderate MacCracken found Milholland too radical. MacCracken later refused two more requests by the Suffrage Club to have Milholland speak.[49] When she received word that the reunion rally was canceled, Milholland waved off the rejection. "Oh, never mind! I'd much rather play basketball again." The former holder of the school basketball toss record borrowed a bedraggled gym suit and charged into a game against students.[50]

Among students stirred by Milholland was junior Edna St. Vincent Millay. She had won a scholarship to Vassar based on the phenomenal success of a remarkable poem she wrote at age twenty, "Renascence." A willowy wisp whose cloud of copper hair lent her an ethereal look, Millay had filled Milholland's shoes as the school's resident rabble rouser and star thespian. Milholland may have caught a reflection of her youth when Millay materialized in the college's elaborate "Pageant of Athena" as the French poet Marie de France, wearing a white satin gown trailing a train so long it required two pages as wranglers. The Vassar junior was thrilled to meet the "great suffragist."[51] One of the poet's biographers claimed Milholland offered the young Millay her "most dramatic example of feminism in action."[52]

Another cause arose that Milholland and her fellow reformers felt compelled to address but were ill-prepared to remedy when on June 28, 1914, a Serb killed the archduke and duchess of Austria-Hungary. The Great War stunned Milholland's idealistic generation. Recalled pacifist Emily

Balch, future recipient of the Nobel Peace Prize, "[W]ar seemed as obsolete as chain armor."[53] Progressive Era activists had been so sure that achieving world peace was only a matter of organizing enough committees to educate the public and set politicians straight. It was incomprehensible for war to break out in cultured Europe. The Milhollands gave up their lovely home at 4 Prince of Wales Terrace. Her father mourned as he watched soldiers drill among the daisies in Kensington Gardens.[54] He and Jean took a sumptuous flat at 247 Fifth Avenue that would be home for the next decade. Opposition to the war was one cause both Inez and her father agreed upon. "The Devil rides in triumph," John sadly observed as he took stock of twentieth-century technology's deadly new toys: submarines, zeppelins, airplane fighters, gas, dynamite, shrapnel.[55] Inez lined up with other New Women who preached peace, many of whom joined the Woman's Peace Party founded by Jane Addams and others early in 1915.[56] Years before Wilson proposed the League of Nations, the pacifist-feminists advocated an international court of law to mediate disputes. Like other suffragists, she saw war as another argument why women clearly needed the vote. For Inez, the women and children who ended up as defenseless victims of war represented the ultimate underdogs.

She saw an opportunity to help end the war when Italy appointed Billy Marconi to oversee military wireless operations after declaring war on Austria in late May 1915. Although Milholland feared people would call her a "quitter," she decided on the eve of Marconi's departure to leave her job with Osborne and sail with her old friend to report on the war in Italy as a freelance correspondent. She bitterly opposed Italy going to war and hoped bearing witness to its toll could help bring peace.[57] Another motivation was she hoped that reporting from the battlefields of Europe would bring her the professional success that had eluded her while scrapping in New York courtrooms. The foreign correspondent's job promised the requisite glamour and danger Milholland needed to fit her self-image as a crusader. Her minor successes in the high-profile *McClure's* and *Harper's* boosted her confidence that she could succeed in this most dangerous avenue of journalism, one virtually uninhabited by women.

She pushed herself to go because she considered her career a failure. Milholland hid her self-doubt from the crowds that cheered her, but alone her shortcomings plagued her. The depression that had occasionally struck her over the years came over her again like a fog. "Shall I always be [a] parasite do you suppose? Shall I never earn? Have I no value?" she asked. "Eugen, I am so tortured and unhappy."[58] The New Woman credo of self-sufficiency seemed more like a burden than a boon to her, compounded by her demands upon herself to shine in a society structured to oppress women. Once again, however, she failed to succumb and stirred herself to action. Travel and movement always were for Milholland an antidote to doubt or disappointment. She wanted Boissevain to join her, but he decided to stay in New York and work to reduce their growing debts.[59] Money woes added to her sense of failure. The couple were about to lose their apartment, and Boissevain's financial prospects dimmed after he sold his coffee business for five hundred dollars that spring, and his tobacco import business never amounted to much. Now he was weighing an offer to help the U.S. government obtain overseas supplies.[60] Milholland hoped to land a couple of lucrative interviews in Italy; Eastman predicted an exclusive with the king or prime minister could fetch up to $2,500.[61] Boissevain supported the endeavor despite its danger, which bolstered her. "I keep saying," she wrote, "if Eugen finds something to love in me, I must have a value somewhere."[62]

Her boss wished her well, while her mother worried about her health, always more precarious than it seemed on the surface. Milholland dismissed her mother's fears and threw her clothes into her trunks. On May 22, 1915, when Boissevain delivered her to the *St. Paul*, her loyal mother showed up to see her off. "Please promise me that you will take no unnecessary risks," said a note Jean handed her. "You are very precious to all of us."[63] Inez told her mother to think of the trip as a holiday but burst into tears as she bade good-bye.[64] At the last minute, her disapproving father could not resist wiring her a hundred pounds. "Poor wild Nan!" he wrote in his diary. "God keep her on Sea and Land; from her baser self, from the great transgression."[65]

Italy

"The spirit of war hangs heavy"

The bulky life jacket she wore over her nightgown allowed Milholland little sleep the night before the *St. Paul* docked in Queenstown. Officers were so worried about a submarine attack that they ordered all six hundred passengers to sleep in life jackets the final night of the voyage and issued instructions on what to do if the ship was torpedoed. Just two weeks before Milholland crossed the Atlantic in May 1915, a German U-boat had torpedoed the *Lusitania* off the Irish coast, killing twelve hundred people on the liner on which she had delivered a suffrage speech in 1910. On the *St. Paul*'s previous crossing, corpses from the *Lusitania* had bobbed off its starboard bow, interrupting a memorial for the sunken ship. The *St. Paul* sailed through the macabre flotsam for the next hour, including a raft carrying the corpse of a half-clothed woman clutching a dead baby.[1] Marconi's presence made the *St. Paul* a tempting target for the U-boats, and the captain feared Germans might try to board the ship and remove him. Marconi's name did not appear on the passenger list (although newspapers printed front-page stories about his voyage), and he gave Milholland his personal papers. When the ship finally landed, the captain confided to Milholland and Marconi that a submarine had followed them. That tidbit became the foundation for Milholland's first cabled report, which the *Tribune* slapped onto page one under a two-column photograph of its new correspondent and the inflated headline, "Submarine Pursued St. Paul to Mersey."[2] Her editors were pleased with their celebrity cub reporter's enterprising debut, an adequate bit of journalism written in the first person.[3]

It required a tremendous amount of courage for a woman to travel alone to war in 1915. Milholland likely was inspired by the war dispatches from popular novelist and playwright Mary Roberts Rinehart, whose series of

Inez sailing to Italy with one-time fiancé, Guglielmo Marconi, to cover the war in 1915. *New York Tribune*, May 23, 1915.

special reports from the Belgium front began appearing in April in the nation's most widely read magazine, the *Saturday Evening Post*. Rinehart's most thrilling piece placed her in the middle of the action during a midnight foray into "No Man's Land" between German and Allied trenches. "My cape ballooned like a sail in the wind," Rinehart recorded. "I felt at least double my ordinary size, and that even a sniper with a squint could hardly miss me."[4] Such adventure surely appealed to Milholland, and Rinehart's spunky prose made war reporting sound deceptively casual. But virtually no other woman had written about combat. Before Rinehart, Milholland had to go back nearly seven decades to find a true role model, the extraordinary Margaret Fuller. Fuller also reported to *Tribune* readers from

Italy, on the fall of Rome to Napoleon III. Her account made her one of the world's first war correspondents of either sex, adding to her luster as one of the century's first feminists.[5] The *Tribune* retained its reputation for employing women reporters, most famously "front-page gal" Emma Bugbee, who more than once had called Milholland for a juicy quote. In December 1911, Bugbee marched for two weeks up the east bank of the Hudson River alongside a band of New York City suffragists delivering a petition to the governor in Albany, hitchhiking each evening to the nearest telegraph office to file her story with the *Tribune*.[6] The *Tribune*, like most U.S. newspapers, desperately needed to boost its European presence when Milholland offered her services. U.S. coverage of foreign affairs had reached a nadir by 1914.[7]

As the war spread, Milholland joined a wave of excited amateurs who hustled for credentials. "Sporting editors, baseball reporters, dramatic critics, book reviewers, gossip columnists, even cartoonists were being provided with passports, riding breeches, and American Express checks and rushed across the Atlantic to cover the impending conflict," recalled E. Alexander Powell.[8] Boissevain stayed on at the cottage that Milholland's father rented in Harmon, in the lower Hudson Valley. Boissevain and Milholland congratulated themselves for charting new conjugal territory. "Only Eugen and Nannie could leave each other because they love each other so much—Nothing can separate them," she wrote from the ship.[9] Although Boissevain missed her terribly, he rationalized he was helping modernize marriage. Theirs was proof, he told Milholland, that individuals "need not wait for society to change."[10] Letters again became the vital link in their relationship, and absence served as an aphrodisiac. "I have throbbed in the arms of many, many women, some young, astonished, afraid, seeking, with hard little bodies and a rose untouched," he wrote her, ". . . but of all roses, it is yours that I want." He sent a rose and instructed her to wear it. "Kiss it for me."[11] Boissevain picked up her expense checks at the *Tribune* and *Collier's* to forward to her and sifted through her papers at Osborne's office. He tried to keep himself busy. Mornings he rode Prince, his father-in-law's retired race horse, and he and Jack Milholland bought a scull.[12] He dined and danced with their entertaining neighbors, including Upton and Mary Sinclair, Isadora Duncan, and actor Edgar Selwyn, whose tennis court was the site of many spirited matches among the expatriate Villagers.[13] He half-heartedly tried to quit smoking cigarettes.[14] It depressed Boissevain when Crystal Eastman left her husband. "Is perfect love so difficult—so rare?" he asked his wife three thousand miles away. "Let us show the world what perfect love is."[15]

After lounging in London for three weeks while Marconi settled some business, Marconi and Milholland finally bade Bea Marconi good-bye at

Victoria Station. They ferried across a calm channel to Boulogne, where the French admitted Milholland as a *"correspondent de guerre pour divers journaux Americain."* They joined Will Irwin, who waited on the pier in his chauffeured car to drive them to Paris. Irwin was the first American reporter to reach Belgium after the German invasion. War still thrilled him, before the death and gore he wrote about over the next four years encased his heart like lead.[16] Milholland quickly sensed the excitement as the car steered into the herd of ambulances, military vehicles, and soldiers. "I loved the throb of it and I felt my blood mounting with excitement," she recorded. The sight of two broken bodies twisted on stretchers jolted her back to reality. "I realized I was letting myself get in the grip of a spirit whose present manifestation I detest—a spirit begotten by the joy of doing active and colorful things in crowds. An admirable spirit really turned to abominable use."[17]

Her account of her drive to Paris with Irwin reveals a reporter's eye for detail. She wondered why the Red Cross nurses were ordered to stand back until officers disembarked: Was it because "the one who destroys is considered of more importance than the one who reconstructs," or just another routine example of women's subordination? Once they hit the road, she nervously slipped a cigarette to appease the first of more than twenty sentries who stopped them. As they drove further from the coast, military traffic thinned and the villages seemed empty and lifeless. Milholland felt a kinship with the teenage girls who peeked from behind stone walls. She speculated how easy it would be for them to fall in love with German soldiers. "I know what I should have done, as a young girl, cheated of throbbing life, left behind to a dreary driven existence in a deserted town," she told readers. Darkened Paris was unrecognizable as the city where she had spent glittering evenings in the past. She felt ill and depressed. Everything she longed for—freedom, peace, passion, and children—seemed alien to the landscape. Even lunch with Jane Addams at the American embassy failed to lift her spirits.[18] She was on the verge of menstruation, which always sent her to bed. She had been diagnosed as anemic, which helped explain why she tired easily; Boissevain suggested she drink a glass of wine daily to thicken her blood.[19] Since she viewed signs of physical weakness in herself as a character flaw, she didn't treat the condition seriously: "[M]y anaemic little trouble seems so ridiculous in a world of wounded and naked suffering."[20]

She and Marconi bade Irwin farewell and boarded a train for Rome early the next morning.[21] At the border, Milholland was repelled by a line of drunken, singing volunteers bracketed by cheering civilians as they marched toward a train taking them to the front.[22] The army had massed in the mountainous eastern provinces on the 484-mile Austrian frontier running from the Swiss border to the Adriatic Sea. The Italians pushed back the Austrians during the first month, but the rugged nine-thousand-foot-high Dolomite Mountains formed a formidable obstacle in the quest to reach Trieste. Austrian bombs and Italian artillery fire pocked villages; corpses from both sides littered the slopes.[23] The Italian infantry inched ahead, bayoneting defenders and capturing terraces row by bloody row. By mid-July, however, the Italians were stuck along a seventy-five-mile front bordering the Osonzo River.[24] Milholland hoped to visit the front when she applied for press credentials from the Ministry of the Interior and sought permission to join a group of journalists scheduled to visit the war zone. She attached letters from the *Tribune* and *Collier's* magazine and letters of introduction from several Americans.[25] While she waited at the Grand Hotel for word from the ministry, she typed up articles never published about the volunteer efforts of the American ambassador's wife and a charity kitchen operated by an American woman who married an Italian prince.[26] She even met poet-soldier Gabriele D'Annunzio, but no story appeared.[27] The government denied her request for an interview with the queen.[28] Dozens of flea bites pocked her flesh, Rome's streets were dirty, and the dank castles where she called upon the aristocracy stank. She said, "I have come to look on Italy as a most slovenly and inefficient country."[29]

She left Rome to try to drum up stories. She hopped a train full of officers to Bologna, on the edge of the war zone, where she heard many wounded were housed. She toured a military hospital with the American countess who headed its nursing staff. She visited the wards, passing out cigarettes and joking with the men in French. Some showed her bits of shrapnel pulled out of their wounds thanks to a wondrous new bit of medical technology, the X-ray machine. Another patient awaited the amputation of his shattered arm. "What I would not give for the power to make any fellow creature happy to the point of forgetting pain by my mere presence."[30] But again, the article did not see the light of day. Italy's sexist customs further irritated the New Woman. She refused to budge when informed that no self-respecting Italian woman sits at a café without her husband.[31] In Vicenza, armed soldiers followed her when she left the railroad station to get some fresh air on the platform. When they ordered her back inside, she plopped herself on a chair just outside the station door with an expression of weariness. They left her alone. Another time, she commandeered a café table in the sunshine even though the flustered manager told her it was reserved. "I told him with equal excitement that I wanted to dine in God's sunlight and not in a dingy room, and that I could be through before the people arrived who had made the reservation." She kept the table.[32]

The war correspondent's role could daunt even the most seasoned journalist. Milholland tried to report on what she saw around her but was untrained in the craft of gathering and synthesizing facts. Her earlier pieces for *McClure's* and *Harper's* had been more like essays that involved no real reportage and dealt with subjects in which she was well versed. Her reformer's heart informed each of the half-dozen bylined, first-person articles that the *Tribune* published. Each was short on facts and long on indignation. They inevitably reverted to proselytizing against war and for feminism in the righteous language suffragettes spouted from the soapbox, the type of discourse in which Milholland excelled. It did not help her reportage that she was denied access to the battlefield. Her first scathing articles appeared about a month after she mailed them. Demonstrations that some touted as Italy's war readiness, she wrote, were merely drunken exhibitions. "It's exciting to kill with your mouth," she wrote. "To stay safe at home and shout for the other fellow who is going to do your fighting is easy."[33] Her copyrighted piece on the "stupidity of war" predicted Italian resources would be exhausted long before the fighting ended. The piece demonstrated her passion for peace but also her inexperience as a journalist. It contained no reporting save a secondhand anecdote about an Italian mother angry that her three disabled sons were excused from the army. Milholland asked, "What is the unholy power of this war sentiment that makes natural and maternal instincts sink into insignificance?"[34]

One of her strengths was a keen sensitivity toward women's involuntary role in war. It sickened her to see women left behind struggle to care for families alone, consumed with worry about loved ones sent to the front. She used her articles as a forum for an unlikely feminist manifesto, that men should bear the brunt of war since they voted for governments that plunged all citizens into war. "They are led to the slaughter like dumb sheep," she wrote. "For that slavish stupidity perhaps, they deserve to be massacred like dumb sheep."[35] Sarcasm dripped like blood from her justification of the sinking of the *Lusitania*. "To sink a shipload of non-combatants is no worse than to attempt to starve a nation—women and children included—into submission."[36]

She could not resist lecturing readers, as if she were still on the suffrage soapbox, as in this cryptic wish for peace: "When that day comes we shall have no longer a world of types but of individuals, no longer a world of monotony but of spontaneity, we shall have courageous people instead of cowards; liberty lovers, men and women of principle and faith and spirituality and joyousness. The world set free!"[37] That piece never saw the light of day; the *Tribune* also rejected a gushing report on the king and queen and an analysis of the Italian war that ended in perplexing purple prose: "We are delivered from a life of lies, and we feel for the first time in our natural existence, our life founded on a basis of truth, and ready to grasp the destiny of our dreams."[38] *Collier's Weekly* never published anything by Milholland.

Although Milholland did not know her articles' fate, she already felt she had failed again. She had magnified the journey into epic proportions, entangling its significance with her failure to produce a child. She told Boissevain (referring to herself in the third person): "She shall not bring into this world a child until she has gone forth to prove that she is herself equal to the world."[39] Significantly, she was quoting a mawkish poem called "Child of the Amazons" Eastman had written about her, an indication of how closely she identified with her idealized Amazonian image.[40] She vowed to get pregnant when she returned.[41] Yet she could not settle down until she had achieved her superhuman standards of success. She sought the "big thing" to set the couple free, an apparent reference to her career goals. Fear of failure stalked her like a tiger. "I'm after my chance," she had explained to her worried mother. "Maybe I won't get it. But I'll get it sometime. . . . Don't blame me if I fail."[42]

The restlessness that Vassar colleagues once romanticized in Milholland as impatience with inequity was beginning to resemble dilettantism. Even as an undergraduate, classmates noticed how her interests veered. "Her eager inconsequent spirit followed now this path and now that, shifting always to what promised the swiftest way to its goal," observed one.[43] Her breadth of causes—suffrage, labor, prison reform, free speech, law, pacifism—revealed not only the breadth of her interests but also a tendency to scatter her energies. Contributing to Milholland's inability to succeed were the conflicting values instilled by her parents. They inculcated in their daughter a deep sense of social responsibility and an intense desire to leave her mark on the world but simultaneously surrounded her with privileges that left her ill-prepared for the drudge work that professional success often entailed, especially for a woman in the 1910s. Things came easily to her—clothes, men, getting her photograph in the newspaper. Cajoling her father made money easy, although instead of interest she paid with her self-esteem.

The most significant obstacles to professional success, of course, were beyond her control: the institutional and cultural barriers preventing women from fully participating in public life. Not even Milholland and her perceptive New Woman peers were fully aware of how crippling were these strictures, as they had much emotional investment in the notion of the power of individual will. Unaware that sex discrimination in Italy would again stymie her quest for professional success, Milholland set off determined to follow the New Woman's credo of performing meaningful work. She set punishing standards for herself, evidenced by her ill-conceived venture into an overseas war, and criticized herself when she was unable to meet them. The frustrations she faced in Italy are an extreme example of similar frustrations experienced by many New Women venturing into less exotic but still foreign professional or personal terrain. The inner conflicts of the ideal New Woman hint at how stressful life must have been for the many less-privileged women who struggled to be as independent, confident, and successful as they imagined Milholland. The depth of her self-loathing spilled out of letters to the solicitous Boissevain. "If I can do something valuable and worthwhile, I think I shall find peace perhaps—and have failed again," she wrote. "Your poor Nannie. I don't think she has found herself. She's a very unhappy Nan tonight—and very homesick. She is in a luxurious room, in a luxurious hotel, making friends fast . . . but Nannie is sad and depressed—the spirit of war hangs heavy, and happiness seems sinful and dead in the world."[44] These tortured words spilled from her pen even before she left England.

Her new friends included a lover in London. Her heady public rhetoric about independence could not quell Milholland's need for validation from the opposite sex. After experiencing sex discrimination trying to get into law school and in Osborne's office, perhaps she deduced sex appeal rather than intellect held the key to any power she possessed. She found it easy to lapse into flaunting her sex appeal to get attention. Stuck in London while Marconi attended to business matters, she amused herself flirting. "Isn't Nannie naughty and lazy!" she wrote her husband. "Just flirting around, eating up admiration, and forgetting her job?"[45] In mid-June, she sent details of her tryst and proclaimed she would take another lover if she got lonely in Italy. Boissevain's façade of indifference crumbled by the hour. At first, he wrote, "For Christ's sake forget that we are married. Just think we are or were lovers. You are free. So am I—stray if you want."[46] He denied Milholland's affair made him jealous—"Only want to understand. . . . I feel utterly alone"—but worried about the child they dreamed of, "Is Peter safe? Will he be mine?"[47] Within days he was begging Milholland to come home. When Boissevain finally chastised her, it was not about her betrayal of him but of her professional goals. He chided her to be serious about her work: "Do it well and completely, but Inez, don't waste time talking when you ought to be on the job." His charge surely stung more sharply than that of adulterer: "Please don't be a dilettante at it."[48]

Milholland was among the most sexually radical New Women. Unlike many New Women who ultimately felt exploited by the new sexual freedom, including her British role model Christabel Pankhurst, Milholland never seemed to experience the pain of other theoretically sexually liberated New Women who struggled to reconcile themselves to their husbands' infidelities.[49] They included her friend Ida Rauh and fellow Greenwich Villagers Neith Boyce, Susan Glaspell, and Mabel Dodge. In contrast, Milholland flaunted her infidelities and justified them in modernist rhetoric about self-realization, much like their husbands. Milholland also had the advantage of being wed to possibly the most nurturing and faithful husband in the annals of feminism. A less effusive interpretation is that Milholland's love life highlights the complexities of celebrating female sexuality and balancing intimacy with independence. Milholland struggled with the meaning of sexual freedom, since as Leila Rupp put it, "the course of a New Woman who welcomed the sexual revolution was not always smooth."[50]

Boissevain tried to live up to their free-love creed but found himself sadly lacking as a philanderer. Although he tried to avenge Milholland's infidelities while in California on a business trip the following spring, the closest he got was when he plucked a pretty young woman out of the raging surf. "I put on my best sentimental movie hero look," he said, "and was going to carry her into the house." But he didn't.[51] As was typical of their crowd, he framed free love as an act of liberation. "I don't think it will be easy for him," Boissevain wrote of himself to his wife. "But he'll succeed some day!"[52] All his life, Boissevain exhibited a remarkable commitment to free love despite his own disinclination toward promiscuity.

Boissevain left for Naples within a few days after receiving Milholland's news. The reunited couple tried to repair the emotional wreckage by traversing Italy together as war correspondents, although Boissevain's sole credential was a stint in the Dutch army.[53] After unraveling two months of red tape, Milholland finally received permission to visit the *zona di guerra* in the Dolomites. The front by then had migrated further east and the trenches were deserted, but she traveled to Brescia to observe captured Austrian soldiers and watch fresh Italian recruits drill. Boissevain stayed in Rome to arrange for freelance press credentials for himself. In Brescia the charmed Italian officers went out of their way to make Milholland comfortable as she awaited her credentials. "You cannot imagine the fun and excitement of being the only woman," she wrote Boissevain, who probably could imagine only all too well. But when the male journalists visited the trenches, Milholland had to stay behind. Despite their attentiveness to Milholland, the American correspondents asked the Italians to forbid women reporters at the front.[54]

Milholland barely had settled in when she received the crushing news in mid-August that the government inexplicably had recalled her to Rome.[55] She persuaded the sympathetic press officers to grant her a twenty-four-hour extension, which gave her time to sleep with an Italian officer, possibly the escort assigned as her guide and censor. She had coyly typed in her copy that he inspected: "I must tell you (and him) how much I like the officer in charge of me—for I do. . . . He is young and very handsome, thoughtful and intelligent. . . . Altogether he is a very loveable person and perhaps it is just as well for me and my work that I am a thoroughly married woman. Otherwise I should certainly proceed to make love to him."[56] She left "Guido" *délicieusement* at the Hotel Milano in Verona in another assignation in late August.[57] He wrote her from Vicenza in bad French, "Thank you a thousand times, divine creature, for having wanted to meet me again, and for having given me this immense happiness, before our separation, in time and space."[58] She again felt compelled to tell Boissevain all.[59] His response this time was less sanguine. "God damn the stinking little Italian macaroni monkey!" he wrote months later, "La rose est ma rose!"[60]

Back in Rome, Milholland called upon the prime minister and demanded to know if the men's protests against women reporters prompted her expulsion. He denied it. He explained she had been booted out of the country because her anti-war articles displeased the government.[61] Irwin, in fact, blamed her pacifist articles for a ban Italy imposed on all correspondents from neutral countries.[62] Reporters fishing for quotable passengers at New York's West 34th Street pier in late September 1915 spied Milholland disembarking a ship. It is an intriguing comment on celebrity that her stature in the press remained so disproportionately high in contrast to her accomplishments. She was not above capitalizing on this phenomenon and recognized that being kicked out of Italy would be a "great ad" for her.[63] Reporters slavishly scribbled her meaningless boast: "Give me supreme command of the press of Italy [or] any of the warring countries, and I will guarantee to turn the sentiment of that country for peace inside of a month."[64] But it must have wounded the would-be war correspondent to know that the only way her name would appear on the front page was not in a byline above an article from the front but tacked onto her latest facile remark.

Although Milholland castigated herself for not coming home a brilliant success, she was tougher on herself than she deserved. Unlike Rinehart, who enjoyed the sponsorship of the Belgian queen, Milholland foraged for stories on her own under extremely discouraging conditions. She had accomplished what virtually no woman had done before, written and published articles about a foreign country at war. A person less demanding of her self would have found some satisfaction in that fact. Back in New York, Milholland again cast about for a sense of purpose to her life.

Pacifist

"I have worked well"

Milholland correctly predicted her eviction from the Italian front would be great publicity.[1] Back in New York, the trip became another romantic adventure that padded her credentials as a fearless crusader.[2] The epitome of the independent New Woman and her husband, however, were now totally dependent upon her parents for their keep as the young couple foundered professionally. They moved into the flat at 247 Fifth Avenue when they returned from Italy.[3]

Bouts of depression continued to haunt her. She blamed herself for failing in Italy and remained frustrated with law. Milholland was neither the first nor last public woman who privately doubted her self-worth. As biographers of other New Women have pointed out, breaking cultural convention exacted a psychic toll. Rules about women's behavior remained deeply inscribed on their psyches. It required tremendous willpower to reject cultural precepts, no matter how intense a woman's feminist sensibilities. Immersed in a culture that still expected selflessness in women, she could not help feeling guilty about her focus on herself. Surrounded by a society that valued sexuality above all in a woman, this intelligent and beautiful feminist could not help reverting to sex appeal when professional success foundered. As Charlotte Perkins Gilman's biographer noted of her subject, another New Woman who projected confidence but wallowed in feelings of worthlessness, "women often find it hard to respect themselves, much less to recognize, accept, and respect authenticity and purpose in their work."[4]

Milholland's suffrage colleagues were thrilled that she arrived home in time to campaign for New York state's 1915 referendum on votes for women. The respect she was accorded in feminist circles helped dust off the disappointment of her Italian venture. After a short rest at Meadowmount, she threw herself into the campaign, weaving her Italian experience into suffrage spiels.[5] In October the Boissevains talked jointly to the Woman's Peace Party about their trip.[6] On the eve of the referendum, she told parishioners at a Brooklyn church, "Only the forces of evil" opposed woman suffrage. She and Rose Schneiderman soap-boxed the post-theatre Broadway crowd until the wee hours of Election Day, trying to drum up every possible vote.[7] But more than a half-million "yes" votes were not enough to win. At midnight Carrie Chapman Catt addressed weary workers in the headquarters of the Empire State Campaign Committee she chaired. The loss by nearly two hundred thousand votes was not a defeat, Catt declared, but the opening of the decisive battle for the vote. Milholland and others immediately set off for the streets again to thank the public for its support.[8] The next day, suffragists massed at Cooper Union to launch their campaign for the 1917 referendum.[9]

Milholland was unaware that Henry Ford had launched another campaign that would send her back to Europe. The automobile magnate was one of those fabled self-made Americans whose ingenuity and hard work greased the nation's transformation into a twentieth-century world power.[10] By 1915 the Ford assembly plant churned out a new car every twenty-four seconds, raking in a five-million-dollar net profit for the year. Its proprietor, who liked publicity and abhorred war, announced to great fanfare that he would devote his life and fortune to end the war. The millionaire offered to finance any feasible plan to stop the fighting, aligning himself with socialists when he declared: "I hate war, because war is murder, desolation and destruction, causeless, unjustifiable, cruel and heartless to those of the human race who do not want it, the countless millions, the workers."[11]

About the same time the millionth Model T rolled off the assembly line, Hungarian pacifist feminist Rosika Schwimmer wangled lunch with Ford. A labor organizer in her country, Schwimmer had helped create the Woman's Peace Party with Jane Addams and Carrie Chapman Catt the previous January. Addams and Catt saw pacifism as an intrinsic facet of feminism; they opposed war as women's worst enemy and men's worst vice. So did pacifist Milholland, who pitched in with Crystal Eastman's radical New York branch of the party. The party manifesto calling for a conference of neutral nations to mediate the war was the latest in a series of peace plans proposed by suffragists. Suffrage and peace were twin aims of the International Council of Women founded in 1888 in London. The council became the International Woman Suffrage Alliance, which by

1914 comprised twenty-six nations and was headed by Catt, giving suffragists an unusually broad global perspective. Members well understood the connection between male global dominance and violence against women. Olive Schreiner, observing that men bear arms but women bear armies, articulated many feminists' belief in women's inherent pacifism. Suffragists clearly saw war as a woman's issue and viewed the ballot as their weapon for creating a peaceful world.[12] When the specter of world war devastated their vision, feminist pacifists on both sides of the Atlantic became prime movers behind calls for mediation.[13] Labor organizer Kate Richards O'Hare voiced their fears when she wrote, "It is the women of Europe who pay the price while war rages, and it will be the women who will pay again when war has run its bloody course and Europe sinks down into the slough of poverty like a harried beast too spent to wage the fight."[14]

Milholland toted anti-war signs alongside colleagues Madeleine Doty, Ida Rauh, and others in anti-war protests. She believed Eastman made a mistake, however, when her friend totally abandoned suffrage for pacifist work.[15] Doty was one of some forty Americans among 1,136 delegates at a remarkable International Congress of Women at The Hague who braved ridicule and danger to attend the world's first assembly of women to stop

Inez participating in a pacifism demonstration in New York in 1914. She is fourth from right; her sister, Vida, is second from right. *Courtesy of Swarthmore College.*

Inez's husband, Eugen Boissevain, seeing her off on the Ford peace expedition, December 1915. *Courtesy of Wisconsin Historical Society.*

war in spring 1915.[16] Only the trust created by their suffrage networks enabled women from warring nations to sit down together to try to hammer out a program to stop the war. Significantly, alongside their call for mediation was a demand for global woman suffrage.[17] Schwimmer was a key player. The previous fall, she and Catt had even visited President Wilson, who rebuffed their entreaty that he call for mediation. After The Hague congress, Schwimmer, Addams, and other pacifist feminists again futilely rapped on his door. Ford's wife, Clara, even contributed eight thousand dollars to the Woman's Peace Party for telegrams urging Wilson to call a conference of neutral nations.[18]

Schwimmer pressed Ford for funds for the conference at their New York luncheon. By evening the talks had expanded into a flamboyant scheme for Ford to sponsor an unofficial American delegation to mediate the spiraling European conflict: a peace ship of notable concerned citizens. Ford raced back to the Biltmore Hotel and reserved all first- and second-class space on the Scandinavian liner *Oscar II*, departing December 4. As the door shut on 1915, feminist pacifists latched onto Ford's unofficial mission as their last chance to save the world. Those hopes dimmed, however, as soon as Ford made the ill-considered boast that he would bring ten million men home from Europe's trenches by Christmas.[19] An already skeptical press leaped on this hubris as more evidence of the foolishness of Ford's quixotic-like quest.[20] Thomas Edison, John Wanamaker, William Jennings Bryan, and Walter Lippmann declined Ford's invitation, as did Anna Howard Shaw, Helen Keller, Crystal Eastman, and an ailing Addams. Even Clara Ford refused to go.[21]

Milholland accepted with the remark, "The expedition may fail, but the world has been the better for gallant failures."[22] Milholland had seen for herself the misery inflicted by the European war and felt obligated to do anything she could to end it. "Woman has nothing to gain by aggressive warfare; she has everything to lose," she once said. "[M]en call the tune and the women pay the piper."[23] So, although annoyed that she had to travel under a Dutch passport, Milholland added her name to the passenger list of some 160 Americans on the *Oscar II*. A third of the voyagers belonged to a restive press corps of more than fifty reporters, cartoonists, photographers, feature writers, and newsreel makers, all traveling at Ford's expense.[24] The overwhelming presence of these cynical news hounds ravenous for conflict did not make sailing smoother. Milholland was the most glamorous of the relatively undistinguished peace delegation.[25] The passengers' mission was to develop a mediation plan to be considered at a Ford-financed Conference for Continuous Mediation of neutral countries set to begin in Stockholm on February 8, 1916.[26]

A brass band blared the popular tune "I Didn't Raise My Boy to Be a Soldier" amid speeches galore at the sendoff from Hoboken where twelve thousand well-wishers waved "Peace" flags and sang "America." Milholland chatted animatedly with the press before bidding her husband another tearful farewell.[27] When she discovered she was sharing a cabin with two other women, Milholland pleaded for a single inside cabin because, she said, ocean travel made her so sick. During their one night as roommates, University of Wisconsin professor Julia Grace Wales found Milholland smart, frank, and congenial but was taken aback by her sensational dress and the gifts of extravagant bouquets of flowers and bottles of champagne that filled their cabin. Wales deemed her roommate a publicity hound and felt relieved when Milholland moved out. Ford's opulent approach to peacemaking became apparent when delegates sat down to a six-course dinner on the first night of their voyage. While most of the green-faced travelers relied on Mothersill's Seasick Remedy, Milholland settled her stomach with champagne.[28] The voyagers settled into a routine of morning lectures, tête-à-têtes on how to make world peace, and evening entertainment. The convivial press corps elected her vice president and general counsel of the "Viking Press Club."[29] The first few days at sea were nirvana for Milholland—lots of laughs amid constant conversation about how to save the world. She stuck with the students and younger party-going delegates and avoided the "Sunday schoolish" members. "It really is a wonderful party aside from its purpose," she told Boissevain. She added she was behaving unbelievably chaste. She had learned from Italy.[30]

Rougher seas lay ahead for the *Oscar II* as the shipload of strong-willed individuals entered the minefield of shaping a workable peace plan to unveil in Stockholm. Grizzled reporters geared to constant city room deadlines churned out dispatches making fools' fodder of the idealists who talked much but seemed to do little. The mission's purpose remained fuzzy, and Milholland agitated for greater organization. The autocratic Schwimmer antagonized delegates by flaunting a big black bag she falsely claimed contained secret documents about their mission. Somewhat paranoid about her grasp on power, she enlisted spies and concocted an atmosphere of suspicion and friction. The bored press fed on the dissent like sharks smelling blood.[31] Milholland clung to faith in Schwimmer despite her disastrous way of dealing with people and the press. In perhaps her only direct conversation with the aloof Schwimmer, Milholland urged democratic methods to achieve unity of purpose, a statement Milholland repeated to every influential person she could buttonhole. She never even met Ford, who retreated to his cabin. She nonetheless idealized the home-spun carmaker, as did millions of Americans. "He is a wonder—a saint, a great man with an angel's countenance," she said. "Everybody loves and worships him."[32]

Five days out to sea, the resolutions committee sent out a resolution oppos-ing Wilson's newly announced and highly controversial war-preparedness policy. Failure to sign, the committee declared, meant dismissal from the peace mission. When word of the resolution reached the lounge, Samuel McClure, founder of the eponymous magazine, loudly criticized it. Oth-ers shouted he was a militarist.[33] Milholland defended him. "If we are to mediate in Europe's troubles we must first learn to mediate among our-selves," she said. The quarrel escalated as delegates clamored to speak, and the meeting broke up with delegates badly divided.[34] At the press corps' mock trial of McClure, a reporter testified that the months it took McClure to pay for articles was evidence of the publisher's unprepared-ness. The mock trial so lifted the mood that reporters staged another two nights later, in which Milholland defended a delegate charged with being a German spy.[35] Milholland's stand with McClure, however, alienated her from the ship's leaders. Milholland attempted unsuccessfully to medi-ate between factions. She took her appointment seriously and steeled her-self to finish her job. "I work, I sleep, I am honest, I behave courageously," she told Boissevain. "I only flirt moderately."[36]

Milholland clung to the hope that some good would come of the trip when the ship pulled into its first neutral port at Christiana (now Oslo), Norway, on December 20, 1915. Norway's bright, snowy hills and its citi-zens' ruddy faces spelled welcome relief from the dreary north Atlantic. Although delegates talked too much about idealism and too little about a practical program for peace, she maintained, they were on the right track. The party enjoyed a jubilant dinner its first night ashore at the Grand Hotel before splitting up for meetings. Milholland found her room at the Victoria Hotel cold but comfortable.[37] She received the welcome news that Boissevain had a new job. Life seemed to be gelling for the couple as Milholland approached her thirtieth birthday. Boissevain's job meant they would not have to move to the Boissevain plantation in Java, an option he had been weighing. Once again, she proclaimed that when she returned the couple would have children. She exhibited a seriousness and concen-tration on the peace ship that bolstered her self-esteem and bode well for her return to law after she returned to New York. She was proudest of her newfound resistance to romance. "Oh, I am happy and confident and eager to get home and begin," she wrote from Christiana. "I have learned so much."[38]

Unfortunately, the Ford expedition began to implode. In the midst of the gala captain's dinner at Christiana, reporters discovered Schwimmer was pressing Ford to send the press home. They exploded like the bottles of champagne uncorked for the dinner toasts. Ford rejected the ouster, but bickering escalated. Milholland continued to try to smooth over the differences, noting, "We cannot attempt to pacify Europe until we have pacified ourselves."[39] The death of the ship's social director from pneumonia, however, seemed a macabre omen for the mission.[40] Milholland was hurt when she began to be frozen out of discussions. Schwimmer did not appreciate her attempts to democratize the mission and later complained to Ford that she had spent the entire voyage trying to "stir up all the trouble she could."[41] Milholland acknowledged, "I am very much persona non grata." The lack of a formal forum for voicing diverse views frustrated her. Robust discussion was a given among New York's New Women. As she once said, using one of her analogies linking the domestic and political spheres, "If there is anything in this world that looks like a complete failure it is a successful kindergarten, and much the same thing is true of any successful experiment in self government."[42] As an adroit practitioner of the art of public relations, Schwimmer's block-headed inability to court the press appalled Milholland. "Individually folks are nice enough (who could help being nice to your Nannie?)," she wrote home, "but officially I might as well not exist." Yet she persevered.[43]

Disappointed she would miss spending Christmas with her in-laws in Holland because the ship left Christiana late, she rationalized that the high stakes were worth it. "We have no right to despair of democracy until we have tried much harder than we have and by means that are not undemocratic to cure its evils. So my place is with the group and with my shoulder to the wheel so long there is the slightest chance."[44] Her dedication waned when she and the rest of the entourage spent two hours in the icy Christiania railroad station waiting for the train's engine to thaw before it could carry the group to Stockholm. Deep snows forced the train repeatedly to stop and back up as it chugged across Scandinavia in sub-zero temperatures. Twelve hours late, the frozen, hungry party finally arrived in Stockholm on the morning before Christmas, only to discover Ford had deserted his peace ship in the middle of the night as Milholland and the rest of his recruits shivered at the Christiana railroad station. The Swedes went out of their way to welcome delegates, serving a lavish Christmas Eve dinner and staging a traditional yule ceremony the next morning. At a meeting on Christmas afternoon, Milholland protested Ford's appointment of a Committee of Seven to command the mission. The scheme was undemocratic, she charged. No one backed her up. Feeling isolated and ill, Milholland did the sole thing she had resolved not to do: She quit.[45]

Milholland outlined her reasons in a ten-page letter. "The undemocratic method employed by the managers of the expedition is repugnant to my principles," she stated. "The result has been ill-feeling, suspicion, condemnation and dissension."[46] Her criticisms appeared prominently in newspapers across the United States, which irked the committee.[47] Members informed her that the mission was not a democracy. "We feel that we came as guests of Mr. Ford, with no more right . . . to organize and legislate than we should have if you personally did us the honor to invite us to your home for a week-end visit."[48] Milholland tried to salvage at least a byline from the trip when she traveled with McClure and others to Berlin. Although she wrote an article based on her meeting with German Foreign Minister Arthur Zimmerman, who "admired her extremely," the interview never was published.[49]

She hungered for Boissevain, who spent Christmas at Meadowmount with her family.[50] Once again, she promised better times ahead. "If that desire is ready to flower when I come home—my wanderings spiritual, mental and bodily, will be forever over," she told him. "If not, then we'll keep gaily and lovingly and laughingly to work until the time is ready— just as we have done in the past—only with deeper knowledge from me." Although Milholland was worn out, unlike in Italy she felt sure she had done the best job she could. She had stuck to her principles and treated her mission seriously. "I have worked well," she said. "I have left undone nothing to further the work I came for that I could do."[51]

Yet the disastrous Ford expedition failed to provide her with the success she so craved. It was one more task she had been unable to complete. She sailed home with less faith in the power of well-intended talk to solve problems and more resolve to concentrate on her own work. The debacle did not quash Milholland's feminist pacifist beliefs. The following spring, she joined the American Union against Militarism chaired by suffragist– social worker Lillian Wald. She did, however, resign from the Woman's Peace Party, ostensibly because afternoon board meetings conflicted with her law practice.[52] Of course, the efforts of those pacifist organizations also failed to halt the war, which would snuff out much of the reform spirit personified by women like Milholland and Wald.

Even if unsuccessful, the pacifist feminists' international efforts had symbolic value because they showed that women's ties could transcend nationalistic militarism. The 1915 International Congress of Women, for instance, set the precedent for creation of the United Nations. Feminist pacifist organizations seeded two other important social-justice organizations: The Woman's Peace Party became a branch of the Women's International Committee for Permanent Peace, which became the Women's International League for Peace and Freedom, and the American Union against Militarism's Liberties Bureau evolved into the American Civil Liberties Union.[53] As for Ford, in March he pulled the plug on the ineffectual neutral Conference for Continuous Mediation at The Hague. The voyage cost him a mere four hundred thousand dollars. Louis Lochner, youthful co-architect of the peace ship, figured the industrialist regained the sum in interest on his pile of capital just sixteen days after sailing. Back in Detroit, Ford converted his factories to war production. After the war, he boasted that free advertising generated by the peace ship helped him crack the European auto market for a fraction of its projected cost. Years later Lochner bitterly recalled, "The hopes which [Ford] raised in millions of breasts were rudely shattered. The idol they set up for themselves proved possessed of feet of clay."[54]

Boissevain's new job did not last long, an anticipated appointment by the Dutch government failed to materialize, and the couple took out a loan.[55] He was under increasing pressure from his in-laws to become self-supporting.[56] Jean scored her son-in-law when he thanked her for being a gracious hostess the past seven months. "I cannot bear Inez being poor," she told him. "[I]f you only develop concentration along with your quantities of energy."[57] Nearly thirty, Inez was eager to be in her own home. She told her husband, "I want to have a love-nest."[58] The stress took its toll on the Boissevains: Eugen's health seemed to falter, and their sex life appeared to suffer. Acknowledging he was a "rotten provider," Eugen headed to California in April 1916 to launch a coffee import business from the Dutch Indies with his older brother, Jan, the best business decision he ever made in his life.[59] Jan and Eugen made a solid team: The quieter elder brother excelled at the technical end of importing, the boisterous younger brother at closing deals.[60] Jan boasted to Inez, "[A]s soon as Eugen shows his great big formless and sunburnt nose, all Frisco magnates stumble over themselves in their eagerness to help us along."[61] After they signed their first contract, for three hundred dollars, Eugen promised to send fifty dollars to his financially strapped wife, but she blithely told him to use it to buy himself something "wasteful and amusing."[62] Inez again rationalized separation was good for them. "I love to separate!" she declared, "—because every exchange that we make then becomes driven into consciousness and intensified."[63] Absence also made their disputes seem smaller. "What a happy pair we are anyhow. Teeny troubles to the contrary notwithstanding."[64] He assured her better days lay ahead.[65] She was glad to hear "Simon" was recuperating. "I saw tragedy ahead of us— for I knew I could love no one but you, and yet could not love you the way I want."[66]

Milholland almost went west herself in April for Alice Paul's increasingly militant Congressional Union. Member Mabel Vernon, for instance, disrupted a Wilson address to the Senate by unfurling a suffrage banner from the gallery in the middle of his speech.[67] Paul's next plan was to send a "Suffrage Special" railroad car of CU speakers west to recruit women from the western suffrage states where women voted to attend a June convention in Chicago, where Paul planned to create the nation's first women's political party. Milholland's mentor Harriot Stanton Blatch would lead the hard-working coach load of twenty-three suffragists. Although Milholland endorsed the CU's plan to flex women's newfound political muscle, she still smarted from the Ford peace ship debacle. She was reluctant to accept the invitation to sign on for another political tour in cramped quarters. Paul also had misgivings about her making the trip: She worried Milholland was too frivolous. When the CU's New York branch offered to sponsor Milholland, Paul countered that historian Mary Beard or publicist Florence Brewer would be better choices. Milholland's close identification with the abortive Ford mission could embarrass the Woman's Party, Paul worried.[68] "We are very anxious, of course, to have the party composed of women of the highest dignity, with a reputation for solidity and general strength," she wrote. "It seems to me that Mrs. Boissevain (as far as her reputation goes—which may be quite unearned, for all I know) would not add to the weight of the expedition as a serious undertaking."[69] Paul softened when Beard replied her own reservations about Milholland dissolved when they appeared together in Syracuse. "I have quite come under her spell," she told Paul. "The women loved her and every man seems eager to do what she asks."[70]

Milholland was no more eager to make the trip than Paul was to sign her on. Her father was pushing her to go because he was convinced the national exposure could open the door to a political career. Her husband agreed.[71] But she told him, "I lock up against this tour so." She felt ill again, despite religiously exercising and sleeping a lot. She wanted to focus on her law career and find a house. Besides, a tour required a new wardrobe, and she had been chagrined to discover she no longer could buy clothes on credit.[72] At the last minute, Milholland backed out of the "Suffrage Special." "I couldn't be happy going higgledy piggledy with everything in disorder, believe me," she explained. "And I couldn't go back to bills, bills, bills with nothing to show for my labors."[73] She told Paul somewhat disingenuously, "I have nothing to fall back on, since I earn my own living. . . . Don't be disappointed at me. Just be sorry for me."[74]

Boissevain urged her to reconsider. "I hate and loathe the idea of you not doing what you want on account of money." When she reported her father was furious—"Thought I missed the chance of a lifetime"—Boissevain ricocheted to her side. His faith in her was her husband's greatest gift to her. "Your father talks nonsense!" he consoled her. "A personality like yours cannot be forgotten, and it wants but a little to make it burst out, nation-wide." Even if she had wanted to go, Milholland confessed, she did not feel up to it. "Isn't it funny?" she wrote. "I sleep and sleep and walk and, up to the last two days, have been doing exercises, yet I feel punk."[75]

Work remained a tonic for Milholland. As she told suffrage audiences, "When one is on the job one hasn't time to think of physical ailments. When one is on the job, one hasn't time for pettiness and meanness of vision."[76] On the cusp of her thirties, Milholland was frantic to make her professional mark as 1916 began. She downplayed the frustrations of the professional world when she encouraged other women to enter it in speeches: "I'm happy. And I want other women to know the content that I feel. And to do that they must develop! Work! Share the honors and ills of life with men. It all means a great deal to me."[77] Attorney Milholland sometimes worked late into the night struggling to keep clients out of jail. "A failure to make good after his first chance at parole is no proof that a man's character is hopelessly bad," she cajoled a judge in favor of an errant client.[78] Satisfaction coursed through her after she engineered a compromise with seven lawyers and a district attorney to reduce another client's bail.[79] Frustration engulfed her when she defended four boys for stealing pigeons; although she won suspended sentences for three, one went to the penitentiary.[80] Her experiences revived her interest in prison reform, which stretched back to her work on the 1913 Sing Sing investigation. Like other radicals, she especially opposed capital punishment. Soon, it would become the focus of another of her crusades.

Execution

*"You are your
brother's keeper"*

Just before midnight on July 28, 1916, Milholland and Boissevain leapt into their car at Harmon and raced toward New York City. Inez clutched a briefcase under her arm containing papers that could save a man's life. As the couple sped through the dark villages, Charles Stielow, an illiterate apple picker convicted of killing two people, sat in the Death House in Sing Sing awaiting the dawn in which he would become the 136th man to die in its electric chair.

The state of New York implemented the electric chair after experiments with "westinghousing" dogs, cattle, and horses in the late 1880s determined it killed more quickly and kindly than hanging. Opponents challenged the new method of execution all the way to the Supreme Court, but the Court ruled electrocution did not violate the constitutional prohibition of cruel and unusual punishment. On Milholland's fourth birthday, alcoholic ax murderer William Kemmler became the first person in the world to die in an electric chair.[1] The controversy over capital punishment lived on. New York remained the leader in executions, electrocuting seventeen men at Sing Sing in 1915.[2] The state's zeal spurred renewed calls to outlaw capital punishment by the time Stielow entered Sing Sing.[3]

Milholland belonged to the Humanitarian Cult, one of several liberal groups that protested execution as barbarous by any means.[4] She rallied alongside Connecticut suffragists who rescued from the gallows a mother of two children convicted of helping her lover murder her husband in 1913. They argued Bessie Wakefield was convicted under laws that, as a disfranchised woman, she had no say in enacting. "She has been sentenced to die by man-made laws," Milholland said.[5] She sent letters to dozens of state representatives beseeching them to support a bill abolishing capital punishment. She wrote, "State murder is not human, is not Christian, is not scientific, and does not protect society."[6]

Her opposition to capital punishment grew out of her legal reform work. Long an advocate of revamping legal attitudes toward prostitutes, just a few weeks before joining the Stielow legal team, Milholland presided at a program at the Plaza Hotel that called for abolishing the women's night court, whose magistrates sent thousands of streetwalkers to the workhouse each year for as long as six months.[7] While Milholland was in Italy, a group of women lawyers organized to take turns volunteering to represent prostitutes in night court. Milholland helped pressure the city to create the public defender's office, an important step toward establishing a more enlightened rehabilitative approach to criminal justice.[8] She had seen brutal conditions inside Sing Sing when she had helped James Osborne during the 1913 grand jury investigation. She not only spoke out for prison reform but also befriended inmates. While her husband was in California, for instance, she took the train upstate to attend the Passover feast at Sing Sing.[9] A friend recalled her standing by the telephone for hours appealing to the governor, judges, or other influential people trying to free someone she believed innocent.[10] It was not unusual for a released Sing Sing inmate to find his way to her office, where she could be counted on to help him find a job. She helped the inmates' Mutual Welfare League obtain a typewriter to help train inmates for jobs.[11] She and her sister Vida once serenaded eleven hundred inmates in an unprecedented concert inside the prison chapel.[12]

Convinced human nature was innately good, she argued crime was the result of poverty or poor education. More than half of Sing Sing's inmates were products of reformatories, she once said. "Take these children off our streets, keep them in schools and playgrounds, control their misplaced energy and you abolish 50 percent of crime." She also subscribed to the popular belief in social Darwinism, blaming "defective heredity" for creating criminals.[13] A more cerebral reason for her identification with criminals was her estrangement from the American middle class. Radicals of her generation who rejected mainstream American values often related to the viewpoint of society's outcasts and saw criminals as victims of capitalism. Generally, Milholland and her peers blamed virtually all crime on society rather than individual behavior. She somehow even scientifically quantified at 4 percent the segment of habitual criminals whose crimes could not be attributed to environmental factors. She was unequivocal that "[t]he others are victims of circumstance."[14]

The Stielow case probably attracted Milholland for reasons beyond simple justice. Saving the life of a single man seemed infinitely more manageable than her previous crusades to stop world war. Unlike her foray as a war correspondent in Italy, the Stielow case employed skills she possessed. Unlike the Dolomites, the courtroom was familiar territory. And unlike the Ford peace expedition, she could conduct this crusade at home, enveloping herself in Boissevain's welcoming arms practically every night in Harmon. Another powerful motivation for Milholland was the specter of the suffering Stielow's widow and three children would endure if he died. Protecting women and children was the reason she got into law in the first place. Although Milholland's faith in Stielow's innocence wavered, she remained steadfast in her belief that the execution of a mentally retarded man exemplified the immorality of capital punishment. A handful of like-minded, mostly female lawyers, journalists, and activists adopted the case and threw themselves into trying to win him a reprieve. The day of Milholland's midnight dash to Manhattan, the governor twice declined to stop the execution despite new evidence Stielow's supporters believed would clear him. The governor's refusals spurred Milholland to carry that evidence to Supreme Court Justice Charles L. Guy of Manhattan in a desperate flight to save Stielow's life.

The Boissevains had settled for the summer into the Harmon section of pastoral Croton-on-Hudson after he returned from California. They rented a weathered bungalow nestled on a hilly copse of trees from opera diva Lillian Nordica, with whom Milholland had shared the stage in the 1913 suffrage pageant "A Dream of Freedom." The bungalow was just a few miles from steep Mt. Airy Road, populated by Villagers including Mabel Dodge, John Reed, Louise Bryant, *Masses* artist Boardman Robinson, Max Eastman, Crystal Eastman, lawyer Dudley Field Malone, cartoonist Robert Minor, and writer Floyd Dell.[15] Boissevain looked forward to a quiet, romantic summer among like-minded friends in the country. His coffee import business was taking off, and Milholland's criminal law practice finally was getting off the ground. He beseeched his wife not to leave him again—"not for suffrage, nor for peace, nor for criminals."

Suffrage beckoned first. The "Suffrage Special" had enlisted fifteen hundred delegates for the inaugural convention of the Woman's Party of Western Voters held in Chicago June 5–7, 1916. The suffrage states they represented contained four million women, representing a third of the votes necessary to elect a president.[16] Creation of a woman's party was the logical culmination of New Women's campaign to incorporate women in political life. Voting would be a tangible symbol of their agency. Paul and her followers hoped the convention would mark a milestone in women's political history and would herald women as a real political power. Paul placed her faith on her untested theory that gender bonded women be-yond differences of race, class, and religion. Inside the Blackstone The-ater, Woman's Party delegates cheered claims they held the key to the White House. Belmont got so carried away she pledged a half million dollars for a suffrage campaign in conjunction with the fall presidential election.[17] The specter of a female political party spooked the *New York Times* into charging the Woman's Party with using the "influence of sex for political blackmail."[18] Much of the male political establishment was, in fact, in the Windy City the first week of June, as the publicity-savvy Paul scheduled her convention to fall on the eve of the Republican and Progressive national conventions. The Woman's Party invited a represen-tative from each of the five parties fielding presidential candidates to ap-pear before it. "We do not ask you here to tell us what we can do for your party," chair Anne Martin of Nevada informed them, "but what your par-ties can do for us." Her tone marked an assertive departure from the tradi-tional suffrage strategy of persuading men that women were worthy of the vote. Journalist Ida Tarbell observed, "These women know how to play the political game—like men."[19]

Milholland was in the speakers' lineup on the third and final day of the convention, addressing the convention's "Suffrage First!" luncheon. The phrase referred to the party's refusal to let their cause take second place to war. Milholland shared the dais with Rheta Childe Dorr; Crystal East-man; and Helen Keller, the blind, deaf graduate cum laude of Radcliffe College who also was an ardent suffragist. When Milholland rose to speak, she threw her trademark picture hat on the table and playfully declared she was tossing her hat in the ring. Then she leaned over the table toward her audience, her eyes kindling like blue flame. Her speech continued on the assembly's bold note. "Suffrage for women is a gift of no one to con-fer," she cried. "It is a right!" The Woman's Party's strategy of challenging the established male parties appealed to Milholland's fighting spirit. She went on: "I believe, and every woman of spirit and independence be-lieves, that women are human beings with a definite part to play in the shaping of human events, and that any attempt at reconstruction of the world after this war is ended is inadequate and abortive without their help. We must make the rulers of the actions feel that to attempt a reconstruc-tion without the cooperation of women is not to be tolerated. We must say, 'Women first.'"[20] The crowd responded generously when she cried, "Let's have a dollar shower!" More than a half century later, activist Mabel Vernon vividly remembered Milholland's charisma. "Not just beautiful," she recalled, "but brilliant."[21]

Criminals beckoned next. The case of Inmate No. 66335 intrigued Deputy Warden Spencer Miller, who convinced Warden Thomas Mott Osborne, also an opponent of capital punishment, that Stielow was innocent.[22] Miller then approached lawyer Grace Humiston, a volunteer for the inmates' Mutual Welfare League. Humiston's most famous case won a pardon for a woman condemned to death for the murder of her husband. Admirers called her a "feminine 'Sherlock Holmes.'"[23] After Humiston won Stielow a temporary stay, she recruited Milholland and journalist Sophie Irene Loeb to the case.[24] Milholland was close to the Russian-born Loeb, ten years her senior. She admired Loeb's crusading reportage about slum children in the *New York Evening World.* Those articles spurred several legislative reforms, and her reports on the plight of working-class widows led to the creation of the New York Commission for the Relief of Widowed Mothers, to which she was appointed. Loeb went on to win more state aid for housing, maternity care, and schools as president of the New York Board of Child Welfare and wrote a book on the subject, *Everybody's Child.* Loeb's varied campaigns made her a familiar face to Albany legislators. As it did Milholland, the Stielow case struck a chord against injustice in Loeb.[25]

The women spent much of summer 1916 chasing after appeals and searching for clues to the real murderer among the placid apple orchards south of Lake Ontario. "No modern drama has ever been written that contains all elements of tragedy, coupled with such conflicting evidence as has made up this case," Loeb wrote in her sob-sister account.[26] Stielow's lawyers invited the detective who had wrung the confession out of him to New York on the pretense of helping untangle a big blackmail case. Believing the lawyers were clients interviewing him for the job, George Newton regaled them with an account of the strong-arm tactics he had used to induce Stielow to confess. The "clients" actually were other detectives who switched on a dictograph machine while the detective rattled on. After Stielow won another stay of execution, his lawyers had a week to prove he deserved a new trial.[27] Six days later, however, the New York Supreme Court rejected their motion and re-sentenced him to die at sunrise on Saturday, July 29.[28] Governor Whitman agreed to review any new evidence produced through that Friday. The lawyers intensified their efforts. In Buffalo, Humiston pursued a mysterious peddler said to be near the murder scene the night of the murder. But once located in an upstate jail, Erwin King denied any connection to the case.[29]

Back at Sing Sing, the prison psychiatrist estimated Stielow's mental age at less than eight years old.[30] Milholland spent hours dissecting Stielow's dubious confession, by now part of a two-thousand-page court record. "Impossible planning for an imbecile mind," she scrawled on a section that detailed a convoluted scheme Stielow allegedly had described for covering his tracks.[31] An exhausted Milholland collapsed into bed in Harmon that Tuesday. Before dawn she was awakened by a call from Loeb, bedridden by her exertions but unable to forget the case. They agreed that a rally in support of Stielow in Medina, the commercial center of Orleans County, could help their cause. Milholland was dead tired, but she hopped a train that day for Medina, drafting her speech as it chugged west.[32] Loeb convinced Misha Appelbaum, head of the Humanitarian Cult, and Stuart Kohn, Stielow's attorney of record, to hurry to the rally to circulate petitions to the governor. They invited the jurors who convicted Stielow and sent horseback riders to pass out handbills summoning residents across the county to the mass meeting that night at the downtown theatre.[33]

Stielow's wife, Laura; daughter Ethel, thirteen; and son Roy, eleven, remained poker-faced in their box to the right of the stage as lawyer Kohn gave a graphic description of electrocution. Milholland followed his unnerving spiel: "My friends, you are your brother's keeper." Others circulated petitions asking the governor to commute Stielow's sentence to life imprisonment. Milholland did not claim to know whether Stielow was guilty, but she was sure it was wrong to kill an imbecile. "I want you all to protest and protest in a hurry so you may feel that you have rid your souls of a stain of having put to death a man with a crippled mind." Cheers trailed her as she left the podium. Appelbaum was more emotional: "For the sake of Mrs. Stielow and the children. For the sake of our own children, for the sake of humanity. For the sake of the flag of our country and the spirit of 1776 I beg of you to sign these cards and save a child-man from death." Then young Ethel mounted the stage and told the crowd her father never left the house the night of the murders. About 550 listeners signed the petition.[34] Milholland called Loeb at midnight to report on the evening's success, collapsed into bed in a local hotel, and left for Harmon the next morning, the eve of the execution.[35] Mrs. Stielow and the children went to Sing Sing compliments of the Death House's other fifteen inmates, who collected $41.20 so the Stielows either could rejoice with Charles or bid him good-bye.[36]

The rest of Stielow's legal team took the train to Albany to present the petition to Governor Whitman. Humiston showed the governor intriguing new evidence she believed proved Stielow's innocence. She had shown Erwin King a letter from Ethel to her condemned father that ended, "We all know you was not out of the house that night, and God knows it as well as we do, and may answer our prayers of that which we ask of Him." King blurted out. "I'm the one that killed Phelps and Mrs. Walcott [sic]—not Charles Stielow."[37] He repeated his confession to the judge and sheriff.

Other revelations included the damning dictograph records. But Whitman declined to interfere. Appelbaum called Loeb with the bad news; she called Milholland and begged her to go to Albany to make a final plea on Stielow's behalf. Milholland boarded the train headed north. She reached the capital at seven o'clock that night and picked up the materials from Humiston but failed to win the reprieve. Before returning home, she telegraphed Loeb and disconsolately telephoned Sing Sing. The prison operator made a suggestion: The lawyers could seek a stay of execution from a state supreme court justice. Milholland immediately dialed Loeb's number. She got a busy signal. Milholland's train was about to pull out. She boarded and arrived in Harmon at eleven o'clock. Soon after she finally reached Loeb, who excitedly agreed to notify Judge Guy.

So hours before Stielow's third scheduled execution, Loeb was on the telephone explaining to Judge Guy that Milholland would be knocking on his door before dawn. Loeb was so ill a nurse held the telephone for her. She insisted on making the call because she knew the judge personally. Kohn also was on his way to the city from his home on Long Island. Both lawyers pulled up to Guy's house at half-past three o'clock. Appelbaum awaited them on the sidewalk. A police officer attracted by the commotion guided them to a twenty-four-hour Western Union office. Milholland dictated the final lines of her brief to a clerk at a typewriter. They bolted back to Guy's home, where the judge awaited them in his library. The clock read a quarter-past four, about ninety minutes before Stielow's scheduled execution. Fifteen minutes later, he issued the stay of execution until eleven o'clock the next night and scheduled a meeting with the lawyers later that morning to discuss a longer stay.[38] But when Guy called Sing Sing, he learned that the stay had to be in the hands of its chief guard at the prison twenty-seven miles away before officials could stop the execution. The group in Guy's library groaned. Kohn, however, tucked the stay in his pocket and sped away in his car at 4:38 a.m.

At Sing Sing, the thirteen execution witnesses assembled in the warden's office. Laura Stielow awaited sunrise on the verandah of the nearby warden's house while her children slept inside. The executioner tinkered with the wires on the squat black chair. Keepers shaved Stielow's head and slit his clothes so the electrodes would work quickly. Stielow proclaimed his innocence to the minister summoned to counsel him in his final hours. The only person aware a stay was en route was the head guard, who paced back and forth outside the prison gate. At 5:23 a.m., a car horn honked in the distance and grew louder. Kohn pulled up and handed the stay to the guard as he ran alongside the car. With only minutes to spare,

Stielow was saved.[39] An exhausted Milholland collapsed into bed at 247 Fifth Avenue. She was back at her desk in Osborne's office less than three hours later. That afternoon Guy ordered the court in Rochester to show cause why Stielow should not be granted a new trial. The case returned to the court of appeals, which would hand down its ruling in October. By then Milholland would be on the other side of the country, decrying Woodrow Wilson.

Initially, Milholland rebuffed Paul's invitation to become the Congressional Union's "special flying envoy" in the West to campaign against Wilson and other Democrats in the fall election. The CU had employed a similar strategy in 1914 based on British politics, helping to defeat twenty-three of forty-three Democrats they opposed.[40] Stakes were higher in 1916, however, with the White House hanging in the balance and the nation on the brink of world war. John Milholland again pushed his daughter to go, but she protested she could not leave Stielow and had more cases pending. Nor did she savor the prospect of more travel. The entire anti-Democrat campaign was jeopardized when Belmont broke the funding pledge she made at the Chicago convention; however, John Milholland salvaged it when he gave Paul five thousand dollars, cognizant of the campaign's potential to provide a national platform for his daughter.[41] With Milholland's father footing the bill, Paul expressed none of the doubts about her abilities she had expressed in April. She sweetened the offer by inviting Milholland to be the Chicago rally's keynote speaker. Her talk would culminate in the technological marvel of simultaneously telephoning her appeal to Woman's Party headquarters in each of the suffrage states.[42] Geared to generate maximum headlines for the party, the Western campaign certainly would place Milholland in the national media spotlight.

The Stielow drama had further drained Milholland's vitality, but instead of admitting that her heart sometimes beat oddly or that she felt exhausted, Milholland voiced to Paul concerns about accommodations. "I am a very poor traveler and unless I can mitigate my internal discomfort by external comfort, I am worse than useless," she informed CU headquarters. "[P]ity a woman who never gets any pity because she looks big and husky but who gets sick on a steamer or train or swing or even waltzing in a ballroom!"[43] Boissevain, whose blossoming coffee import business was making more demands on his time, would support whatever decision Milholland made, but her reservations lingered. "I cannot seem to get up enthusiasm or zeal for an anti-Wilson, pro-Hughes campaign," she wrote, a reference to Republican candidate Charles Evans Hughes. "I think Hughes is a stuffed shirt."[44]

To make the journey more palatable, her father offered to pay for Vida to accompany her. An ardent if less visible suffragist than her sister, Vida's true passion was singing. Now twenty-eight, the lyric soprano had trained for years for an opera career. Dark-haired with beautifully expressive eyes, she had sung in the Metropolitan Opera chorus and studied in England with stars of the Met and the Grand Opera in Paris. She had performed in London and debuted on the New York concert stage that March. Critics were encouraging.[45] She also was recovering from a love affair the previous year with middle-aged Frederic Howe, husband of Heterodoxy founder Jenny Marie Howe.[46] Vida agreed to interrupt her music studies to follow the sister she idolized. But she made a point of serving as more than Inez's companion. She planned to sing at each stop as well as report on the campaign for the CU's weekly newspaper, the *Suffragist*.[47] John Milholland had reasons beyond nurturing his daughter's career for encouraging her to campaign against Wilson. Postmaster General Albert Sidney Burleson was pushing Congress to dump the multi-million-dollar pneumatic mail tubes system in which Milholland had invested more than twenty years. Dixie Democrat Burleson was loath to enrich a Republican, much less an outspoken gadfly like Milholland.[48] John was desperate for a Republican victory so that his life's work would not disintegrate. He erased his daughter's final objection to making the trip by promising to use his political connections to ensure Stielow stayed alive while she was away.[49] Inez reluctantly headed west.

Campaign

"Women will stand by women"

15

The sisters left New York on October 4. Compounding the guilt she felt about Stielow, Milholland felt sick throughout the eighteen-hour train ride to Chicago. It was an onerous omen for the campaign's jam-packed four-week itinerary of street meetings, luncheons, railroad station rallies, press interviews, teas, auto parades, dinners, receptions, and speeches in the West's grandest theatres. She would whistle through Wyoming, Idaho, Oregon, Washington, Montana, Utah, Nevada, California, Colorado, Arizona, and Kansas before winding up at the big Chicago rally on election eve.[1] The killing schedule helps account for why Crystal Eastman, Rheta Childe Dorr, and Charlotte Perkins Gilman declined to go. Milholland canceled her first scheduled appearance at a street meeting and went straight to bed at the Blackstone Hotel. In the afternoon, she met with reporters and checked in at Woman's Party headquarters. That evening, she and Vida dined at the hotel with their father, in town on business. Inez announced her determination to succeed on the western tour. She told him, "I can do my best when I realize it is all upon me the success or the failure of it."[2]

Yet Milholland felt so wretched she visited a doctor. Her head, neck, and shoulders ached. She felt dizzy, and her heart palpitated. Inexplicable black and blue bruises belted her body.[3] A stiff, dizzying pain at the back of her neck caused her the most misery. She felt reassured when the doctor announced, "A more perfect specimen of physical womanhood I never examined."[4] He diagnosed infected tonsils that had been draining into her system for more than a year.[5] The doctor thought she looked anemic but drew no blood. She felt encouraged when he pronounced her fit to complete her tour before getting her tonsils removed. When she asked him for medicine to help her get through the month, he prescribed arsenic and strychnine.[6]

Sheets of rain soaked Inez and Vida when at midnight they stepped onto the station platform at the official start of the campaign, Cheyenne, Wyoming. The Congressional Union's "special flying envoy" carried an appeal to western women from eastern women asking for their help winning the vote by punishing the party that withheld it.[7] The appeal was revolutionary because it asked the enfranchised women to align themselves politically with their sex instead of the male political parties.[8] "Politically speaking, the women of America have been a weak and helpless class without the political pressure to push their demands," Milholland told western women voters in her standard spiel. "Now, for the first time in our history women have the power to enforce their demands, and the weapon with which to fight for women's liberation."[9]

Harriot Stanton Blatch joined Milholland for a joint appearance in Cheyenne before they split to follow their separate itineraries. A drooping Milholland stayed in bed all the next day until the final minutes before her speech that night at the Plains Hotel. Vida pleased the formally dressed audience by singing a few songs, and a revived Inez wowed them, although she thought her speech terrible. Wyoming's Republicans also disappointed. "They are so dead and sleepy they deserve to lose the state," she said.[10] In fact, just about everyone she met bored her. Perhaps because she was tired, depressed, and ill, privately she did not reciprocate the adulation that western audiences heaped on her. "I think American people so unadventurous and stale," she wrote Boissevain on the train from Wyoming to Idaho. "There's not a one I want to speak to. . . . I am frank to say that unless I was as busy as I am every minute I could not stand such a trip without a love adventure."[11] The private railroad car in which she and Vida rode the first few days of the trip further illustrated the gap between the Milhollands and the average American. Although the sisters' chaotic schedule made it a short-lived luxury, reporters pestered the Woman's Party about this extravagance throughout the campaign.[12] The private car permitted Inez the luxury of breakfast in bed the next morning, her last relaxed interlude on the trip. Even brief station stops became performances because people rode miles to remote outposts to catch a glimpse of the famous suffrage Amazon. Inez wondered why a great crowd had gathered at the Montpelier, Idaho, station platform. "They're looking for you," the brakeman told her. Her heart sank when someone cried, "There she is." But she made her way to the train's rear platform and mustered a solid speech.[13] However, Vida recalled, "After each meeting, she wilted and looked like a ghost."[14]

Sara Bard Field joined Milholland at Pocatello the next morning. Another Woman's Party barnstormer, the thirty-four-year-old poet garnered headlines the previous year when she drove a car advertising suffrage from San Francisco to Washington, D.C., a bone-rattling adventure when few paved roads linked the route. Field conducted open-air rallies and collected petitions along the way, spooled into an 18,333-foot document that the CU in its inimitable manner delivered in a colorful parade to the Capitol building.[15] So many people turned out to hear Milholland and Field at the Yellowstone Hotel that three hundred gallant men gave up their seats for women, then clustered outside the theatre to listen.[16] Later, when Milholland launched an impromptu suffrage rally on the mail train to Boise, passengers congregated around her as arguments flew.[17] Milholland was beginning to enjoy the journey despite her illness. She felt she was speaking better and the growing crowds' excitement gratified her. When their train steamed into Boise that evening, they discovered they had a rare night off because everyone was at a revival. They dropped by. The agnostic Milholland declared it dreadful. "Worse than Billy Sunday. Made me despair of Americans' spirituality. These people are desexualized."[18] Milholland felt so sapped she delegated her sister to fill in for her at the obligatory local press interview.

The next night, a band preceded the speakers to Boise's Pinney Theatre, where Milholland rallied to deliver her pitch for women to support women. The local newspaper declared her personality "magnetic" and "as beautiful as her pictures promised." The praise anticipated the rave reviews heaped upon her throughout her entire trip. The newspaper likened the petite Field to her as "a pretty little wind anemone, compared with a splendid rose."[19] Milholland's fire awed Field, who vouched that Milholland was so beautiful and sincere she didn't need to say a word to impress the crowd. In her speech, Milholland dramatically intoned, "I don't like this world as it is, do you?" She dropped her voice to a near whisper. "There are too many little sad-eyed children in it; too many unfulfilled hopes; too many weary minds and bodies; too many souls that die before the body dies. Don't you think women want to make these things different just as much as men do?"[20]

"Nannie was good," Milholland bragged in a letter to Boissevain, for once pleased with her speaking, "wonderfully good."[21] Boissevain remained her anchor during the disorienting tour. She received a supportive telegram from him at every stop, which helped her summon the energy to dazzle the crowds.[22] Few people realized the emotional toll speech-making took on the woman they viewed as a goddess at the podium. Part of her loved the exchange with people, but speaking in public always made her nervous. She struggled to tone down the aggressiveness she sometimes used to hide her fear and worked hard to improve her delivery.[23] She strived for color. "Don't be like the hound dog, that turns and licks the hand that beat it," she said in one speech.[24] Not so naive as to believe the scattered Woman's Party speakers could swing the election, she was optimistic the campaign would scare Democrats enough to force the next Congress to pass the suffrage amendment.[25]

Asking women to reject Democratic candidates even if they supported suffrage, however, remained a tough sell. The CU's narrow distinction between campaigning against Wilson but not for Republican Hughes eluded many observers. Further confusing the CU campaign was the appearance of the "Hughes Special," a trainload of eastern women whose western tour for the GOP candidate was just one step ahead of the CU's anti-Democrat speakers. The "Hughesettes" routinely were derided in the Eastern press as wealthy political meddlers. They attracted vexing counterdemonstrations, such as local Democratic women who greeted the Hughesettes' train with suffrage yellow banners supporting Wilson.[26] Milholland was spared similar annoyances but struggled to make her mission distinct. The Hughes women, for instance, spoke in the same theatre in Spokane the night before Milholland. She tried to explain: "We are not pro-Hughes, pro-Republican, pro-Socialist or pro-Prohibition. . . . We are simply pro-Woman."[27] The theme of women standing together wove through her speeches as she hopscotched across the plains. "This is the time to demonstrate our sisterhood, our spirit, our blithe courage, and our will," she entreated listeners. "It is women for women now, and shall be till the fight is won."[28] She told them to let their male representatives know they were angry about the suffrage impasse: "Let them know that women stand by women. Show them that no party may deal lightly with the needs of women, and hope to enlist your support." She was conscious of the historical import of the campaign. "Our mission is of almost sacred importance," she said. "We come to do what has never been done in the world before."[29]

In Boise, the crowd so warmed her she lingered onstage until half-past ten, answering dozens of questions. The three women celebrated their success in New Woman style with a cocktail and a smoke at the hotel before racing off to catch the 2:00 a.m. train to Portland. The evening's glow dimmed when Milholland discovered all upper sleeping berths were taken; a sleepless night yawned ahead of her. The next day in the coach, she sat next to Field wan and silent, chin propped on her hand. She conceded only a sore throat and feeling tired.[30] The next day, the train stopped at several small towns where her brief appearances were exciting diversions. In The Dalles, both cowboys and Indians were among the enormous crowd that swarmed the train with gifts of flowers and fruit. She loved the commotion.[31] Every woman in the region seemed to be there and cheered in one voice when she told them eastern women looked to them to win the fight for votes for women. When a lone voice piped up, "Vote for Wilson!" the crowd drowned him out with a resounding, "No!"[32]

That afternoon Milholland conducted a meeting at the crowded library in Medford, and an enthusiastic demonstration greeted her in Grants Pass.[33] Reporters and photographers who met Inez and Vida at the Portland station in the early evening of October 10 stuck to them like glue. Some five hundred residents packed the banquet room of the Multnomah Hotel, where she addressed Wilson's powerful slogan, "He kept us out of war." Better, Milholland said, for women to vote on such grave matters than to rely upon one man to decide for them. She shook hands with guests after dinner and huddled one-on-one with journalists until after midnight.[34] "We travel every night, get up early and keep on the go all day," she told one. "I cannot see how I am able to keep going, but I just have to." She leaned against a wall, clutching a bouquet of roses someone handed her, while Vida gathered their trunks for the next leg of their journey. "I am just too tired to go up to my room and change my dress," Inez sighed. "Oh," Vida encouraged her, "you'll feel alright in the morning."[35] Vida hid her own disappointment that the pace had become so rushed there was no time for her to sing at most stops.[36]

Another frustration was the arrival of Woman's Party national press chair Abby Scott Baker. Although John Milholland pressured Alice Paul to send Baker after Vida cabled him they needed better publicity, Baker's presence increased rather than relieved their stress.[37] She infuriated Inez by insisting on speaking with her in Portland, and her aggressiveness grated on both sisters.[38] Neither would talk to her, and they tried to persuade her to travel a day ahead of them. Local organizer Ida Finney Mackrille also antagonized her charges when she spoke at a reception in Spokane for Inez. Mackrille claimed "Lady Milholland" sulked and refused to speak well if anyone else was on the program. She complained Milholland failed to publicize the Woman's Party. She sniffed, "Much publicity for Inez herself, her dogs, her husband, her hobbies."[39]

Vida sent Paul a note requesting she honor her sister's request that she be the sole speaker at their dates. A second speaker made Inez too self-conscious, she said, and she performed best when she assumed sole responsibility for a successful event.[40] Local organizers eager to share the spotlight with Inez, however, resented her terms. In Arizona, Vivian Pierce carped, "Snobbery is much worse to me than stealing."[41] Paul, however, backed Inez. She instructed Baker to go to Montana, citing an "apparent lack of team work" between the two women, although Baker continued to travel with the sisters.[42] In addition to John Milholland's cash contributions, glowing press and staff reports Paul received about Inez's appearances had made her a fan. Woman's Party press releases churned out accounts about the overflow crowds attracted by the "beautiful flying envoy of the Woman's Party."[43] Decades later, Paul recalled Milholland as a "<u>superb</u>" speaker. "She was <u>extremely</u> beautiful and so radiant and lovely."[44]

Milholland wafted into fog-swathed Seattle at the crack of dawn. Although cheered by the exquisite accommodations at the Sunset Club, her voice was cracking. She visited another doctor. Her throat so shocked him he recommended operating immediately to stop the poison dripping from her tonsils into her glands. He attributed her huge bruises to a calcium deficiency. The simple, curable diagnosis relieved her, but she replied she must finish her tour. He gave her more drugs.[45] Milholland's almost masochistic insistence upon completing the tour can be explained by her past failures. The ideal New Woman's self-respect was on the line. After Italy and the Ford debacle, she could not absorb another public failure. She liked her Amazonian image and viewed physical weakness as a trait of ineffectual Victorian women, the antithesis of how she viewed herself. Milholland had confronted police officers, senators, and strikebreakers and had made a career of tackling overwhelming obstacles. Her pesky illness seemed minor in comparison. Doing meaningful work remained at the heart of her self-image despite all her distractions. Suffrage was the dearest of all her causes, and the applause and big headlines she received at each stop acted as a tonic. Above all, Milholland could not stand the thought of herself as a quitter.

She spoke that afternoon at the Northwest Land Products Exposition and then dined with about a hundred elite citizens at the Sunset Club before moving to the Moore Theater. Rumors flew that Democrats planned to heckle her. Milholland relished the challenge, deciding not to worry "a hoot in hell" about them.[46] Nervous at first, she soon hit her stride and held the entire audience. "[S]he was more like a blazing spirit of freedom, than a beautiful girl with a boyish stride," one newspaper reported.[47] Listeners liked her crack about Wilson's counsel that women be patient: "The only thing the Bible calls patient is an ass."[48] Observers called her the "finest political speaker" ever to visit the city and the *Post-Intelligencer* editor believed she could sway the state for Hughes if she stayed longer.[49] Even Milholland was pleased. "I am getting to be a real speaker," she crowed to Boissevain.[50] Vida finally had to drag her away from answering questions after most of the lights had been switched off.[51] Milholland sank into a deep sleep in the luxury of a real bed and stayed there until nearly noon, when she scarfed up an enormous breakfast.

Bad news later that day jolted her out of her good mood. A telegram informed her Charles Stielow's motion for a new trial had been denied.[52] She considered returning to New York but got word from James Osborne that Stielow supporters had the situation under control. Boissevain consoled her not to beat herself up and advised her that her father was organizing a committee to send another appeal.[53] Her husband predicted John Milholland would jump both Hughes and Governor Whitman if they refused to "help him to help his adored Inez to help the poor devil. . . . [Y]ou don't realize the slave you have in your father. My devotion is reasonable, for I get fair returns."[54] She continued west on another sleepless all-night train ride to Spokane.

The ubiquitous news cameras flashed in her face when she arrived at the Davenport Hotel. A pleasant but taxing afternoon reception at which she shook the hands of five hundred clubwomen drained her. She collapsed into bed to rest before her evening speech but was unable to sleep because she was so worried about Stielow. At a reception preceding the speech, women clung to her words, peppering her with questions while she sank into an armchair.[55] Word that the city Democrats planned to "eat her up" at that night's speech roused her. "Let 'em come," she said.[56] But no foes surfaced amid the standing-room-only crowd of eighteen hundred people. Somehow she summoned the energy to command Spokane women to "rise up, stand on your rights and smother the party that has opposed you." During questions, a man asked who was funding the Woman's Party campaign. "Throw him out!" shouted a woman, but Milholland replied, somewhat disingenuously, that western audiences were footing the bill — prelude to a squad of young women in purple, white, and gold appearing with collection baskets.[57] Then she tossed a question back: "Now tell me, you men, if you think we're on the right track?" Bass voices echoed from all corners, "Yes, you're all right!"[58]

Unfortunately, she was not all right. Despite her pluck, she nearly collapsed onstage. Her whole body aching, she barely managed to stagger onto the 10:00 p.m. train for the long ride across Montana. Vida got their luggage to the station despite an attack of sciatica. Soon after friends waved them off, however, the sisters discovered they were on the wrong train, headed back to Seattle. They got off at a railroad agent's house and caught the correct train to Montana. Dust covered Inez's white dress and shoes, and Vida's back ached. Inez burst into tears. She took more drugs to stoke herself for a street rally on Saturday afternoon during a brief layover at tiny Shelby. Great Falls turned out to be a delightful surprise. A brass band met them when they finally pulled into the town shortly after dark. A gaily decorated auto caravan followed, including a car full of Blackfeet Indians in war paint. The parade delivered them to the opera house, where Milholland spoke with conviction and energy, pleased with her success in the Democratic stronghold. She felt so good after dinner she went dancing.

Poor health, however, was catching up with her. Milholland paid for her partying in Great Falls when she awoke early Sunday with a sore throat and fever in addition to her aching body. Two meetings lay ahead of her in Helena. By the time she got to Butte, "My head had on a tight iron cup of pain, my throat was jumping like a sore tooth, and I was so weak I could not stand." For the first time, she considered quitting.[59] She summoned another doctor who pronounced her "utterly anemic." But he neither tested her blood nor gave her iron. Instead, he prescribed more strychnine and strong coffee. "Lo and behold, I got out of my bed—and worked," she told Boissevain. "Oh, I could swing any state if only we had time." Milholland spoke at the Silver Bow Club and charmed her hosts in Butte.[60] She tried to get out of a date the next day in Ogden, Utah, but the luncheon was scheduled and the theatre reserved. "Disaster to our work if change made situation critical," a field worker wired Paul.[61] Paul wired this information to Milholland, who agreed to go but revealed she had tonsillitis and needed a day off to recuperate, an admission that must have pained her as much as her burning throat.[62]

Paul was scrambling to salvage the disintegrating western campaign.[63] Ailing labor organizer Rose Winslow quit in Phoenix.[64] A week of catching trains crisscrossing Wyoming in the middle of the night and staying at hotels without food service had exhausted Blatch. "Younger women must do the work," the sixty-year-old grandmother griped.[65] She quit in mid-October.[66] The campaign had been conceived in haste, and the indefatigable Paul had grossly underestimated the emotional and physical limits of her followers and the hellish logistics of scheduling such a trip across the West. Paul, the ultimate one-issue politician, was so focused on winning a federal suffrage amendment that she was blind or indifferent to campaigners' discomfort. The envoys perhaps could have handled the travel if arrangements had been more humane, but Paul and her staff cranked out a schedule guaranteed to knock the most robust person to her knees. For someone as run down as Milholland, it was a killing schedule.

Milholland stuck to it because she so desperately wanted to succeed. Her record of quitting shamed her, and she was determined to finish the job. She was loath to acknowledge physical infirmity, viewing it as a reflection of weak character. Despite her illness, Milholland was thriving on the tour. She felt she was doing her best work ever, and her letters conveyed a seriousness and confidence in stark contrast to the obsessive flirtations that she chronicled for Boissevain during their first separation as newlyweds just three years earlier. Newspaper accounts show she was greeted like royalty and packing halls with cheering crowds wherever she touched down, surely balm to the bruising her ego had taken on her past two disastrous journeys. She also was aware that Paul was counting on her and of her father's high expectations for the tour. Her own expectations for herself were similarly grand; perhaps the western tour would be the "big thing" that would establish her as a success. As the doctors poured drugs into her and she delivered one winning speech on top of another, she may have deluded herself she was invincible, like an Amazon.

When Milholland arrived at dawn in Ogden, however, after traveling all night by train, she could barely stand. She shivered one minute, shuddered the next. She doubled over in pain and tripled her dosage of painkiller.[67] After surviving the gauntlet of more than a hundred women in a receiving line before lunch, she pulled herself together to repeat the party mantra, "Women will stand by women." Vida, she claimed, was moved to tears.[68] Back in Salt Lake City that evening, as many people were turned away as entered its biggest theatre. Milholland tried to skip her speech and jump into fielding questions. "We want to hear from you," called out a voice. "Oh dear," she replied, before obliging with a few of her standard remarks.[69] She rated her speech "rotten."[70] Milholland left for Nevada at midnight. Nearly twenty-four hours later, Woman's Party chair Anne Martin met her at a station tucked high in the Sierra Nevadas and drove her to remote Winnemucca.[71] No sooner did Milholland fall asleep than she was awakened and delivered to the cold train station to await the 3:00 a.m. train for Reno. The seven-thousand-foot altitude exacerbated Milholland's illness, but she hid it well. An eager committee of women greeted them in Reno at 8:30 a.m. with speeches and flowers. She was permitted a few hours of rest, but after lunch the women were back on the road to Virginia City. A shrill of mine whistles, fire whistles, and school bells summoned its five hundred residents into the street. It was a tribute to Milholland's charm that her audience was unaware that the ghost town depressed her; instead, she so fired up the women that many rushed to town hall to register to vote. The Wild West spirit beckoned Milholland, who wished she had time to go horseback riding in the desert.[72]

As much as Milholland reveled in this kind of campaigning, her headache and sore throat hung on as the women motored off to yet another rally in the picturesque mining town of Silver City. When they honked the horn in front of the telephone office, men, women, and children poured onto the empty, dusty street. As the town's folk settled themselves attentively on benches set up in front of the speakers, the sunset behind the speakers dyed the mountains that sandwiched Silver City a dramatic Woman's Party purple. After dark the trio pulled into the state capital, Carson City, and did not begin their bitterly cold drive back down the mountain until 1:00 a.m. Milholland spent most of the next day in bed, rising to attend a reception in her honor at a private home. She sat in an armchair to chat with people who approached her. Yet again she revived herself for her big speech to two thousand people that night in Reno's Majestic Theatre.[73] Then Milholland was off to yet another frigid train station to await the 3:00 a.m. train to San Francisco.

"And all the time I am saying, 'One day nearer my beloved,'" she wrote Boissevain. Milholland's respite from the rigors of making history was writing him nearly every day. A suckling calf in Idaho reminded her of him, and watching mothers holding babies on the trains increased her longing for a child.[74] "I want to have a baby born out of a moment of intensest desire," she wrote Boissevain, who was spending a pleasant fall in Manhattan at his in-laws', taking in the occasional show with *Masses* pals Max Eastman and Art Young.[75] Now that Boissevain's business was showing some signs of success, his relations with Milholland's parents also improved.[76]

She was excited by his proposal they visit Holland after the election. Sailing abroad on a luxurious ocean liner where she would be waited on hand and foot sounded delicious to the frazzled barnstormer. She would have her tonsils removed in Holland. She wrote Boissevain, "I was hoping to get well and yet not be away from you. . . . I am going to concentrate these next months on getting a baby."[77]

No sooner did Milholland deliver her speech in Reno than she and her sister sped to California on a train that deposited them in Sacramento on Saturday, October 21, at 5:55 a.m. The rapid descent from the Sierra Nevadas coupled with the all-night train ride depleted Inez, scheduled for another auto parade through the capital. Although by then she could barely raise her head, as if in a dream she mustered the energy to deliver a rousing speech at a luncheon for wealthy club women at the Sacramento Hotel, not even minding that Maud Younger shared the podium.[78] She tottered onto a crowded day coach to San Francisco that afternoon. Vida feared her ashen sister would collapse as she stumbled off the train. She panted and shivered despite her fur coat. As they entered the Palace Hotel, a reporter cornered Inez in the elevator. When she finally got to her room, she was unable to eat. A steady stream of reporters and photographers knocked at the door all afternoon and into the evening. When Woman's Party organizer Doris Stevens arrived to escort her to the ballroom, Inez barely had time to climb into her white dress.[79] Unbelievably, she rallied again.

"Men and women of San Francisco, how do you do?" she addressed fifteen hundred people crammed into the cavernous ballroom. It trembled with cheers and clapping. After her speech, she remained on her feet another three hours, fielding questions and shaking hands with hundreds of listeners who flocked to the podium. She looked ghostly by the time Vida and others dragged her upstairs but told her sister, "It was worth it." Too keyed up to sleep, she tossed and turned all night.[80] On Sunday afternoon, her hosts drove her and Vida forty miles to Pleasanton for tea at the estate of Phoebe Hearst, an executive of the Woman's Party and mother of the newspaper magnate.[81] Her older sister's deathly pallor terrified Vida, still coping with her own painful sciatica. Fatigue fell upon Inez like a blanket after the tea, but they had to drive back to the city that night to catch yet another train. She had already left the hotel by the time a bouquet of flowers arrived from her husband.[82] He had the schedule worked out for their reunion at the Blackstone on November 4: They would make love that evening, wake up with the sun streaming into the hotel window, eat breakfast in bed, make love again, smoke a cigarette, and then discuss the trip to Holland. Just thinking about their reunion made her quiver. She coaxed him to bring her "everything naughty," like a negligee or erotic books.[83] Boissevain declared this trip their final separation.[84] "We must not leave each other any more," he wrote. "It's rotten."[85]

Car trouble delayed the travelers in San Francisco, so Milholland's handlers half carried her at a run into the railroad station. A freight car wreck, however, made the train to Los Angeles six hours late. Vida and a porter worked feverishly to revive Inez as she lay limp and panting. The train finally pulled out of San Francisco at 3:00 a.m. Organizers in Los Angeles were forced to cancel lunch at the California Club, the city's "social holy of holies," which they had figured would garner them priceless publicity in the society pages.[86] Young Beulah Amidon, harried organizer of the Los Angeles events, frantically jumped into Mrs. Berthold

Baruch's limousine in the afternoon to substitute for Milholland before some six hundred disappointed Pasadena clubwomen.[87] No one was more relieved than Amidon when Milholland's train finally arrived in the late afternoon. At least she would be able to appear at the widely publicized mass meeting at 8:00 p.m. at Blanchard Hall.[88] The sisters summoned a doctor as soon as they arrived at their hotel. Milholland instructed him to "fix her up" so she could speak. He complied.[89]

A thousand people crowded Blanchard Hall on the evening of October 23. They flattened themselves against the walls and crowded the doorways. A hundred were turned away. California Club president Shelley Tolhurst, who was supposed to introduce Milholland at the luncheon, did the honors instead that evening. Whatever the doctor gave Milholland seemed to work. She spoke with her usual fire and conviction, although later she did not remember a word she said. "President Wilson, how long must this go on?" she asked. By then, her head was swimming. "Let me repeat—we are not putting our faith in any man or in any party but in the women voters of the West." She raised her arm to make a point in the middle of a particularly impassioned plea. But the effort was too much. Milholland crumpled on stage like a wilted rose.[90]

Martyr

*"Like depriving the desert
of some oasis"*

16

The audience gasped as America's Amazon collapsed in front of them. Several people rushed over to aid her. While they carried her off to a dressing room, Beulah Amidon stepped up to the podium and stalled for time. Fifteen minutes later, Milholland returned to the stage. The crowd erupted. Pale and disheveled, she occasionally swayed in the chair she sat in to finish her speech. She worried the audience would attribute her collapse to female frailty. Not so, she claimed. She simply suffered from a severe case of tonsillitis that could fell anyone. Then she carried on with her damning indictment of Wilson and the Democrats. She even stuck around to answer questions.[1] "Mrs. Inez Boissevain is not less of a suffragette for being more of a woman," the *Los Angeles Times* editorialized. "It is feminine to faint under a severe strain, but it is also feminine to come back and finish the work at hand."[2]

The moment Milholland left the stage, Vida and friends whisked her to their room at the Alexandria Hotel. Dr. Catherine Lynch was summoned to the hotel room the next morning. Alarmed by her patient's bleeding gums and weakness, Lynch called in throat specialists who determined the illness had affected her heart. They warned she could die if she did not cancel the tour and have her tonsils and several infected teeth removed as soon as possible. Devastated, Milholland protested she needed only to rest a few days, even though she could barely sit up. The doctors absolved themselves if she did not enter the hospital immediately.[3]

Alice Paul failed to grasp the severity of the situation when Milholland wired her the news. Telegrams ricocheted between the women over the next forty-eight hours. At least show up at the Arizona dates, Paul suggested, but don't speak. She wired California organizer Doris Stevens to persuade Milholland to soldier on and was irked that Milholland failed to

Good Samaritan Hospital in Los Angeles, ca. 1912. *Courtesy of Archives of Good Samaritan Hospital.*

respond to three messages.[4] "Calamity for you abandon tour," she wired.[5] So deaf was Paul to Milholland's needs that she still counted on her to deliver the final dramatic telephone appeal from Chicago on November 5.[6] Paul finally faced reality and asked Crystal Eastman to speak in Chicago.[7] She declined, but Blatch agreed to take over Milholland's schedule through Colorado and Kansas and deliver the keynote speech in Chicago.[8]

The news from Los Angeles grew graver. After Inez keeled over when trying to stand, Vida insisted she enter the hospital. Unused to taking charge in Inez's presence, Vida rose to the occasion. She stayed by her older sister's side and wired her parents and Eugen. As Paul and her lieutenants continued to pressure Inez, Vida announced the tour was cancelled. She would not let the Woman's Party jeopardize her sister's life.[9] Inez entered Good Samaritan Hospital later that day. A doctor who examined her said she would have dropped dead in her next speech. A blood test—the first since she began weakening months ago—revealed Inez's red blood cell count had dropped to half the normal figure. Doctors diagnosed aplastic anemia, a serious disease in which the body cannot make red blood cells. They gave her liquids and food to raise her hemoglobin levels, and she rallied briefly before her pallor returned. Great dark circles ringed her eyes, and fatigue swamped her. No matter how many blankets nurses heaped upon her, she could not get warm.[10] At first, doctors hoped they could strengthen her enough so that she could return to New York for her operation. When she failed to respond, however, doctors operated on her infected teeth. She would need three weeks to recuperate before the more serious throat operation.[11] Milholland was distraught that she had to quit the tour and sent word to Paul how much she regretted bowing out.[12]

The nation responded with disbelief and sympathy for the felled Amazon. She received about forty telegrams a day as well as several long-distance telephone calls.[13] Newspapers in cities where she spoke posted frequent updates on her condition.[14] A news photographer sent her a photograph he took of her at Portland along with his get-well wishes. A female physician who heard her speak in San Francisco invited her to recuperate at her home. From New York, four thousand fellow members of the Humanitarian Cult sent her wishes for a speedy recovery. One of the most moving messages came from Sing Sing inmate No. 66224, who fondly recalled the Milholland sisters singing in the prison chapel. He signed off as someone "who has known what it is to suffer and not have a friend in the world so I will close by saying a prayer for you this night."[15] Other fans sent suspect advice on how to regain her health: Christian Science, Swedish massage, juice fresh from a cut of upper round steak, blood transfusions from vegetarians, ground raisins in warm water, King of Beasts Liniment, tea from the Kalahari Desert.[16] Residents of a homeless shelter prayed for her, as did a Presbyterian congregation in Seattle.[17] "Mrs. Boissevain Very Ill," the New York Times reported October 26, followed five days later by "Mrs. Boissevain Better."[18] But she did not get better.

On November 6, as Blatch bellowed the final appeal that Milholland was supposed to have delivered in Chicago, doctors decided her only hope was a blood transfusion.[19] Vida's blood matched, so she was positioned in a chair beside her sister's hospital bed. In the primitive manner of early transfusions, one end of a tube was inserted into a vein in her arm and the other in Inez's arm.[20] She rallied slightly and was further cheered when told South Dakota women had won the vote.[21] That was the only good election news for the Woman's Party. The strategy of campaigning against the party in power sorely disappointed as Wilson won handily, taking all suffrage states except Illinois and Oregon.[22]

The transfusion results also disappointed. Vida called Meadowmount on election night to deliver the sad news her sister was dying. Her parents departed the next morning for Los Angeles. As Inez deteriorated, all visitors were forbidden except Vida and Eugen, who virtually never left her bedside after his arrival in early November.[23] Vida and Katherine Stimson, a friend with whom she had been staying, met the Milhollands at the station. Eugen met them outside the hospital and advised them against entering the building, as doctors would not let them see their daughter; they feared she would realize their presence meant death loomed. Distraught, her family took tea at Stimson's before checking into a hotel. Jean and Vida withdrew to deal with their grief together. John conducted a brief press conference, where he blamed her collapse on impassioned speechmaking. "Inez feels enthusiasm for her subject," he said, "and she puts into her addresses an intensity which robs her of her vitality."[24] Inez needed more blood, but Vida was too weakened by previous transfusions to give more. Neither her parents nor Eugen matched her blood type. Other offers to give her blood poured in, including one from a woman who felt guilty because she asked Milholland a question at the end of her speech the night she collapsed.[25] Inez finally received a fourth transfusion that day from a childhood friend, who fainted. Although her temperature dropped, she remained critically ill.[26] Her teary-eyed, weary parents, still forbidden from seeing their daughter, kept vigil outside her room.[27] "We have shot our last ball," a doctor told John. He retorted, "Well, I am more confident than ever that she will get well."[28]

The Milhollands finally were allowed to visit Inez November 17, when Inez appeared on the verge of death. Pleurisy, the potentially lethal inflammation of the chest lining that made each breath hurt, had set in. Inez was burning up at 106 degrees and her pulse raced at 150 beats per minute.[29] John and Jean tried to hide their shock at the sight of their Nan, robust and laughing the last time they had seen her. She had not lost much weight but her color was ashen. Her face perspired, while her hands were like ice. "The dew of death seemed on her lips but her mind was clear," her father recorded. She faintly inquired where her parents were staying. She sank into her bed in relief when informed there would be no more transfusions or dreaded ice baths, which had failed to drop her fever below 103 degrees. "Then I do not have to fight any more today, doctor?" she whispered. She worried about her parents. "I'm going to get well," she assured them.[30] But her doctors began to allow her visitors to bid their final good-byes. Amidon came calling. "It's not going to be so hard now," Inez said of the suffrage fight to the young campaigner, who was shocked by the weak voice she recalled as so vibrant. "Women have shown their power."[31] When Inez did summon the strength to speak, it was to try to save the life of another. Charles Stielow had been re-sentenced to die the week of December 11. Via Eugen, she continued to communicate with

Sophie Loeb. Eugen and John assured her they would let no harm come to Stielow.[32]

As always when life seemed bleak, John Milholland turned to God. He spewed out his grief to the pastor of a church for the homeless; he prayed alone in his hotel room and on his knees at Inez's bedside.[33] He fasted.[34] Christ was watching Inez, he consoled himself after a religious epiphany. "Oh," he wrote, "what a joy came to my heavy soul!"[35] None of his family shared his religious fervor, least of all his logical, agnostic daughter. John, in her hospital room when Inez begged Eugen not to leave her side, could not resist chiming in that God would watch over her. Inez turned her head away.[36] He infuriated the rest of the family when a front-page *Los Angeles Examiner* headline proclaimed, "Miracle Is Claimed for Suffragist." It was based on an interview in which John proclaimed Inez was getting better thanks to the prayers of millions across the country. He said, "I believe my daughter's escape from seemingly inevitable death last Friday was a miracle as surely as the dealings at the hands of Peter and John." Vida and Jean raged at him in tears; they may even have moved out of the hotel and back in with Stimson. Eugen and the doctors also were furious. John congratulated himself for spreading the word about the "Great Physician's" work in the face of such wrath. He wrote, "May I never again fail to stand up for Him on Earth!"[37]

The next day, Saturday, November 25, Inez was even worse. Early in the afternoon, her temperature plummeted and she shook with cold; then it skyrocketed to above 106 degrees.[38] Jean summoned John to the hospital. "Inez is dying!" she blurted, sobbing, when he arrived.[39] Inez moved in and out of consciousness as her family huddled solemnly at her bedside. The strange, deep black and blue bruises that blotted her body grew darker. There was no escaping the reality of her imminent death as Eugen, Jean, Vida, and John helplessly watched her writhe in agony, heaving her chest in desperate gasps for breath. Yet her mind remained clear. As her parents leaned over her bed, she murmured, "Inez is dying. Inez must die."[40] In her last conversation with her husband, Eugen asked, "Shall I come with you?" "No," she replied. "You go ahead and live another life."[41] Late that evening, she awoke and asked her father for the latest news about Stielow. John lied and told her the governor had promised to grant him clemency.[42]

Fifteen minutes later, at 10:55 p.m., Inez Milholland Boissevain died.[43]

Her family's grief exploded in uncontrolled sobs. "I can never sing again!" Vida cried, over and over. Inez's widower and father literally began to fight over her body. John vowed to return her soul to God in a church funeral; Eugen countered he would fulfill Inez's wish that her body be unceremoniously cremated. The two men railed at each other over the body of the woman both loved. Her father won. "Satan's mouthpiece," he called his son-in-law. An attendant led the distraught Eugen, Vida, and Jean out of the room. John lingered until midnight, finally rousing himself when the undertakers gathered outside the door. He carried her body to the hearse, kissed her brow, and knelt by her side. The undertakers closed the wagon door and drove away. Back at the hotel, he could not sleep. "Oh what a dawn!" he cried. "Inez no longer on Earth to see the sunshine she loved!"[44]

The Milhollands declined offers to hold a service in Los Angeles, although they accepted a resident's gift of an American flag to drape the casket of the woman the anonymous donor hailed as a modern Joan of Arc.[45] They wanted to take their daughter home. John went alone to the undertakers to select a glass-topped coffin, and he made arrangements to transport her body. Vida and Eugen left almost immediately on the order of doctors who believed the pair on the verge of collapse. Friction between the two men may also have hastened Eugen's departure. John and Jean left Los Angeles three days after Inez died. Onboard the train, John stuck close to Inez's casket, draped in an American flag and dozens of bouquets. "How she came, saw and conquered," he reflected on her triumphal reception in the West as they rolled across the desert. "Poor dear big Heart and Brain. How you must have suffered in silence—too brave to complain too noble to find fault."[46] The Milhollands originally had planned a funeral at the family's old place of worship, Madison Square Presbyterian Church, but were appalled when Alva Belmont requested their permission to stage a large, public memorial service. Their loss would not be turned into a suffrage publicity stunt. The Milhollands decided to hold the funeral at Meadowmount.[47]

It was still dark when the Twentieth Century steamed into Albany early Saturday. Jean headed alone for Manhattan, where she met Jack, Vida, and Eugen at 247 Fifth Avenue. In contrast to Vida and Eugen's hysterics, Jack was heartbreakingly silent. The younger generation was so paralyzed by grief that the stricken Jean tended to most of the details. She scheduled a small, private memorial service for Sunday in Inez's childhood church, presided over by long-time family friend Dr. Charles Parkhurst. The altar flowers were red instead of the traditional white mourning flowers. "In life she was brilliant and beautiful" explained the *Tribune*, "in death her friends thought only of American beauty roses."[48] Among the small circle of guests was Loeb. Later that evening, Loeb again beseeched the governor to spare

This 1924 purple, gold, and white poster advertising the "Forward into Light" pageant transformed Inez into a blonde, bob-haired woman in fashion with the Roaring Twenties. *Courtesy of National Woman's Party.*

Stielow's life. "The most beautiful and beneficent thing you can ever do is to heed her dying wish." Loeb wired him: "It will partly alleviate the distress of her family, as well as the minds of many good people." The next day, the governor commuted Stielow's sentence to life in prison.[49]

Back in Albany, John watched railroad workers transfer Inez's casket to the train headed north. A small crowd of mourners met the train under a mackerel sky at the Westport station, where the flower-laden casket was loaded onto a wagon pulled by Meadowmount's aging team of black horses. Then John drove Inez's body home to the Lewis farm. Over the next two days, hundreds of neighbors paid their respects at Meadowmount, a place they associated with joyous events such as harvest barn dances and Fourth of July fireworks.[50] Although Inez had spent little time at Meadowmount, Essex County was among entities proud to claim her as one of its own. The local paper wrote, "The strength of these hills and their largeness was in her crusader soul."[51] When the mourners left, her father kissed her brow and held her hands a long time as tears streamed down his face.[52] The rest of the family arrived Monday. John chose a gravesite at the cemetery next to the white clapboard Congregational church, walking past his parents' tombstones and up the knoll overlooking the cemetery, settling upon a plot at the top. The Adirondacks' Great Range loomed behind the grave in the west; toward the east, the grave overlooked Mt. Discovery, the small, rounded peak in the center of Meadowmount that John had renamed Mt. Inez.[53]

At two o'clock the next day, the family assembled at the church for the funeral. Hundreds of neighbors, friends, and kin joined them, although it does not appear that Boissevain attended. Floral arrangements from across the nation smothered the casket. One of the smallest nestled conspicuously at its head. The wreath of autumn leaves filled with white chrysanthemums bore the initials, "M. W. L.," the inmates' Mutual Welfare League at Sing Sing. Inside the casket, three mementos lay alongside Inez: the flag, the small Bible her mother gave her as a child, and a crimson rose from her father, who called her favorite flower her "red badge of courage." The service was simple. The minister succinctly summarized Inez's creed as "I want to make everybody happy and I want everybody to love me." Her father mustered a few words before a choir sang hymns. After prayer, the mourners filed out of the church and followed several long-time Meadowmount employees who carried the coffin up the hill to the gravesite. After the minister's sermon, the loved ones she left behind walked slowly down the hill.[54] Jack Milholland came last, alone. Within the year, Jack would wed an Italian countess in a short-lived marriage that his father was convinced was a misguided attempt to compensate for the loss of his beloved sister. Eugen and Vida attended the couple, who sailed to Java where Jack joined Eugen's export business.[55]

While the Milhollands quietly mourned the intimate loss of a daughter, sister, and wife, suffrage leaders displayed their grief much more publicly. Belmont ordered the flag flown at half-mast at the New York Congressional Union office, where tearful members huddled inside.[56] For feminists, the significance of Milholland's death transcended a mere presidential election. Perhaps not even the war in Europe so shattered these idealistic, life-quaffing New Women. Prior to her death, they believed they could change the world; afterward, they were not so sure. "I am still too dazed and stunned over the cruel rapaciousness of Death in taking all this youth and beauty and ability from us," said Sara Bard Field. "It is like depriving the desert of some oasis."[57] Military metaphors abounded in suffrage tributes: "She had the heart of a soldier," said Abby Scott Baker.[58] Woman's Party chair Martin declared America's "Joan of Arc" died on the field of honor as truly as soldiers in France.[59] Even NAWSA president Carrie Chapman Catt, an adamant foe of the CU's western campaign, offered, "She was a very devoted suffragist, and its cause cannot afford to lose so good a soldier."[60] Paul sent the words Milholland probably would have appreciated most: "Inez Milholland has this day finished a work for her sisters that will not be forgotten."[61]

Crystal Eastman organized a memorial on December 21 in Cooper Union that focused on the future instead of the past, which Inez's family had insisted upon before sanctioning it. "I am sure she does not want us to mourn her now, but to hurry up and do something to make the world better," Vida had explained.[62] Besides Crystal, speakers included her brother, Max; lawyer James Osborne; reformer Frederic Howe; labor organizer Rose Schneiderman; and the Woman's Party's Martin.[63] Crystal noted the range of groups that claimed Inez. "How can it be? How can her spirit at once express for socialist-trade unionist-prison-reformer-feminist-suffragist-pacifist the hope that sustains us[?]" she asked. "Because, my friends—all our great movements at which the dull world laughs—are one at heart—they are phases of the struggle for liberty."[64]

The speeches confirmed what the Milhollands already knew about the broad swathe of Inez's influence from the flood of condolence telegrams.[65] Editorial writers mourned Inez; some even declared her a martyr.[66] The *Women Lawyers' Journal* Inez once edited captured the feelings of many when it said, "Inez Milholland Boissevain was indeed a superwoman, a rare and radiant creature."[67] Numerous reform organizations expressed sorrow.[68] Strangers wrote poems about her. So did Carl Sandburg, possibly an acquaintance. He wrote:

> They are crying salt tears
> Over the beautiful beloved body
> Of Inez Milholland,
> Because they are glad she lived,
> Because she loved open-armed,
> Throwing love for a cheap thing
> Belonging to everybody—
> Cheap as sunlight,
> And morning air.[69]

Militant suffragists found a perfect martyr in Milholland. "She represented ideals that these women cherished," observed Marjory Nelson.[70] Her suffrage colleagues were determined that she did not die in vain. When it had briefly appeared that her sister would win her fight for life in Good Samaritan Hospital, Vida had written a long letter to Paul detailing the horrors of their journey. She also made a proposal: Since Inez was incapable of continuing her tour, the party should capitalize on her illness by publicizing her sacrifice for women's rights. Vida pointed to the example of the hunger-striking English suffragettes, who won worldwide sympathy by publicizing the horror of force-feeding imprisoned suffragettes. The Woman's Party, she suggested, could use her ailing sister as an example of how far American women would go to vote. Vida wrote, "It sounds cold-blooded but you understand the situation."[71]

Indeed Paul did. Milholland's death ushered in the final, most militant phase of the suffrage movement.

Icon

"How long must women wait for liberty?"

17

Casting about for something meaningful for her Cooper Union speech, Anne Martin wired Amidon to discover Milholland's last words before she collapsed.[1] "PRESIDENT WILSON HOW LONG MUST THIS GO ON NO LIBERTY," Amidon wired back in terse telegraphic fashion.[2] In Martin's speech, this became, "President Wilson how long must women go on fighting for liberty?"[3] Militant suffragists adopted the line as their battle cry.

Although Sara Bard Field read poetry at CU memorials in San Francisco and Manhattan, the most salient feature of both was passage of resolutions calling for President Wilson to honor Milholland's sacrifice by coming out for the federal suffrage amendment.[4] The resolutions played into Alice Paul's grander scheme to capitalize on Milholland's death. She hustled to find a venue in Washington, D.C., suitable for a national memorial service to a martyr for women's rights, finally persuading Speaker of the House Champ Clark, a Missouri Democrat with no love lost for Wilson, to help her obtain the National Statuary Hall of the Capitol Building for an ambitious Christmas Day ceremony.[5] The service marked the first time the building had housed a memorial for anyone, male or female, who was not a member of Congress or the subject of one of the statues of prominent Americans that ringed the space.[6]

The Woman's Party transformed this citadel of American patriarchal power into a temple to feminism. The Capitol Building was a sea of purple, white, and gold from its dome, where tri-color banners flapped in the December breeze, to the statuary hall deep within the building. Massive tri-colored Woman's Party banners dangled from the domed hall's marble pillars and balcony. More flags stood behind every chair. Laurel and cedar banking the dais perfumed the space. Although many complained Christmas Day was a poor choice of date, nearly a thousand people revised or abandoned their holiday plans to attend the four o'clock service, including Boissevain and the Milhollands.[7] Vida represented the CU's New York chapter. On Christmas Eve, she, Jack, and their mother joined John in the capital; he had returned within days after burying his daughter to resume lobbying Congress to buy the pneumatic mail tubes.[8] The next afternoon, John and Jean were escorted to the front row of the hall, so packed that police had to turn people away. Eugen, Vida, and Jack sat in the balcony, opened for the first time in years to accommodate the crowd.

After the final seats filled, the organ struck up "Ave Maria." Next came the chanting of a boys' choir, which led a procession across the plaza from the House Office Building into the first floor of the Capitol, and up through the marble hallways and stairways that wound to the statuary hall on the second floor, adjacent to the massive rotunda where Abraham Lincoln had laid in state. The youths carried more purple, white, and gold flags past a row of oversized marble and brass statues of more than a dozen American heroes, including the hall's sole female figure, prohibitionist Frances Willard. One of four golden inscribed banners flanking the dais bore Milholland's revised last line, "Mr. President, how long must women wait for liberty?" As the boys took their places among the lilies and palms, they continued to chant the verse on the banner Milholland helped carry in her first American suffrage parade in May 1911. When a teenaged girl in white marched in behind them carrying a replica of the banner, many observers burst into tears as they read its familiar refrain:

> Forward, out of error,
> Leave behind the night,
> Forward through the darkness,
> Forward into light.[9]

The dignified spectacle was reminiscent of the funeral British suffragettes had orchestrated in 1913 for their martyr Emily Davison, who threw herself in front of King George's horse on Derby Day. After several hymns and tributes, keynote speaker Maud Younger took the podium.[10] When the Californian had protested to Paul that she felt unequal to the task, Paul brushed aside her doubts. Nonsense, she told Younger. "Just write something like Lincoln's Gettysburg Address."[11] If less eloquent than Lincoln, Younger still moved her listeners with her description of Milholland: "She went into battle, a laugh on her lips. Obstacles inspired her, discouragement urged her on. She loved work and she loved battle. She loved life and laughter and light, and above all else, she loved liberty."[12]

"It was unique," a pleased John Milholland recorded of the service, "absolutely unique."[13]

White House pickets in 1917 carrying banners bearing Inez's alleged last public words before she died, "How Long Must Women Wait For Liberty?"
Courtesy of National Woman's Party.

Before they left, the guests also heard two resolutions. The first was an expression of sorrow by Milholland's friend journalist Zona Gale, who wrote, "Inez Milholland stood for woman. She lived for woman. She died for woman. She is in the heart of every woman whose heart beats for to-morrow."[14] The second was blatantly political. It called upon Wilson to end "such waste of human life and effort" by coming out for the federal suffrage amendment.[15] Paul had wanted to make the ceremony even more political, but other CU members talked her out of it. Still, one account claimed some suffragists refused to attend because they feared CU propaganda would blemish the memorial.[16] Rheta Childe Dorr's coverage for the *New York Evening Mail* strayed from her profession's ideal of objectivity when she insisted the president surely would respond to the resolutions.[17] The seriousness of the resolutions' intent was reinforced at the end of the service, when the organ and strings struck up the militant chords of "The Marseillaise." Field had set the lyrics of her poem, "Song of the Free Women," to the universal anthem against oppression. First a few voices, then more and more, began to sing until the rotunda resounded with the words.[18] It was no coincidence that the solemn, tightly choreographed ceremony ended on a combative note.

In 1917 militant suffragists under Paul initiated two years of public protests, a number in Milholland's name, which elevated her in death from suffrage celebrity to women's rights icon. Imagery associated with Milholland figured prominently in these protests, among the twentieth century's first organized acts of civil disobedience.[19] On New Year's Day, Paul asked Wilson to receive an Inez Milholland Memorial Deputation.[20] A parade of suffrage delegations had passed through the White House since Paul arrived in town four years earlier, and both Wilson and the CU were tiring of the fruitless ritual. Neither was Wilson particularly broken up by the death of a young woman who had campaigned so intensely against him nor sympathetic to the nettlesome group that sent her west. The White House tried to ignore Paul, but as the *Suffragist* put it, Milholland's death fanned suffragists' resentment into a "burning flame" not so easily extinguished.[21] The publicity attending Milholland's death and memorials ultimately made it impossible, as Paul knew, for Wilson to snub them. The president agreed to meet the deputation on January 9, 1917, the eve of the opening of Congress.

Wilson was unaware they planned to demand that he call for a suffrage bill in honor of America's only suffrage martyr. The Milholland memorial deputation of three hundred women marched from CU headquarters on F Street around the corner to the White House on the appointed afternoon.

Once inside the East Room, speaker after speaker demanded Wilson stop the waste of women's lives personified by Milholland's death. His face grew stormy as Younger lectured him on his responsibility to "decide whether the life of this brilliant, dearly-loved woman whose glorious death we commemorate to-day, shall be the *last* sacrifice of life demanded of American women in their struggle for self-government."[22] By the time Field wrapped up the appeal, she faced a "very black thundercloud." She sallied on, asking Wilson to lead the charge for votes for women "in the name of this gallant girl who died with the word 'liberty' on her lips."[23] A furious Wilson spit out that he never would have received the women had he known their intent. Silence hung like a noose in the seconds before he stood, abruptly turned on his heel, and stalked out of the room.

The women trooped back to CU headquarters, where Paul and other officers capitalized on their black mood by putting forth a proposal to picket the White House. Dozens of hands shot up when Blatch called for volunteers to sign up as "silent sentinels of liberty and self government." They settled on the details, drummed up a few thousand dollars, and dispersed until morning.[24] Field shared the plan that night at dinner with John Milholland. It gratified him that the organization kept his daughter's name alive.[25] The CU's uncompromising ideals struck a chord with the aging crusader, who lent them moral support throughout the escalating confrontation.

The next morning dawned bright and cold. A dozen women bundled up at CU headquarters before picking up their banners and heading outside. Half of them marched to the east gates of the White House and the other half to its west gates. Once there, each group of pickets split again so that three women stood on either side of the gates. The center member of each trio carried a big, inscribed banner, flanked on each side by purple, gold, and white flags carried by the other two women. One big banner read, "Mr. President, what will you do for liberty?" The other bore Milholland's legendary final words on the suffrage trail, "How long must women wait for liberty?"[26]

The protests continued civilly for weeks, with Wilson tipping his hat to the silent pickets as his chauffeured limousine rolled through the gates. The encounters were too civil for Paul; without confrontation, the pickets soon lost news value. Paul capitalized on the memory of Milholland again when, on the eve of Wilson's inauguration, she girdled the White House with a parade of pickets. Plenty of militant suffragists would be in town for the March 4 protest, since it would be the culmination of a convention merging the CU and Woman's Party into the National Woman's Party.

Paul hoped the demonstration would make as big a splash as the inaugural-eve parade Inez led only four years earlier. Paul tapped Vida Milholland to lead the procession in her first major appearance with the NWP. Vida may have had second thoughts as icy rain pelted her for two hours as she marched at the head of a thousand women that four times circled the White House. She carried a golden banner bearing her sister's now-famous question for Wilson. Beulah Amidon followed with the revered "Forward into Light" banner. The size of this protest worried the White House more than did the small band of silent sentinels: Gates to the grounds were locked, and guards refused to announce the women's presence or deliver their resolutions. Late that afternoon, one of the gates opened and the president's car rolled onto Pennsylvania Avenue. The women won no tip of the presidential hat that day, as he and Mrs. Wilson stared straight ahead as the vehicle parted the marchers bunched at the gate.[27]

Relations with the White House deteriorated after the United States entered World War I on April 6. The silent sentinels irritated and embarrassed Wilson as they hung on throughout the spring. Sly new slogans that arose on protesters' banners alongside the Inez Milholland quote particularly irked Wilson, since they quoted him on the importance of fighting for democracy. War fever provoked crowds to attack the pickets, and Washington police reacted by arresting the women. The arrests marked a dangerous new step in the NWP's civil disobedience, as bail was not an option. The pickets' ideals and political strategy required they go to jail to stand up for their beliefs. After a judge sent the first NWP pickets to jail for three days at the end of June, Paul enlisted Vida to lead the Fourth of July delegation.

The mettle of the gentle soprano was sorely tested as the hostile crowd of some two thousand people pressed against her and another dozen women backed up to the White House iron gate. Sailors attacked them and ripped their banners out of their hands. "Send them over to the Kaiser," onlookers jeered. Smirking police arrested the suffragists.[28] Vida was among eleven women convicted of obstructing the sidewalk and sentenced to three days in nearby Occoquan workhouse in Virginia.[29] Most Americans supported the arrests, but not Alva Belmont. She wrote to the *New York Times*, "I ask you, Mr. President, and gentlemen of the Congress in the words of our valiant and beloved leader, Inez Milholland Boissevain, 'How long must women wait for liberty?'"[30] Vida probably was asking herself the same question inside the workhouse, where she was dodging cockroaches and rats alongside prostitutes and junkies. She called her worried mother from the workhouse, however, to report she was happy and comfortable.[31]

Once again, Vida's strong character, obscured by the glow cast by her golden sister, shone under duress. She had at least temporarily abandoned her music career, replacing her dreams of performing in the world's great opera halls with singing inside a jail cell. She led many of the suffrage songs the inmates sang to keep their spirits up.[32]

Their spirit demonstrated that hardball tactics to quash the militant suffragists were doomed to fail. Evidence indicates the Wilson administration approved the arrests and jailing to silence the Woman's Party protesters, a policy that eventually boomeranged as some segments of the public and press became appalled by the mushrooming repression. Although Wilson unsuccessfully tried to persuade the press to censor news of the pickets, the stories were too juicy for even sympathetic editors to bury in the police roundup.[33] Paul reveled in the new headline-producing, strong-arm techniques, and the NWP's pioneering press bureau blitzed the media with stories and photos of capital police harassing the harmless-looking, middle-class, peaceful pickets.

Sentences grew harsher. After discussing the matter with her father during a walk in the woods at Meadowmount, Vida declined Paul's request she picket again and risk another arrest. But Vida returned to Washington in November, after Paul received a draconian seven-month sentence in a District jail where she promptly led a handful of fellow suffrage inmates on a hunger strike. After several days, frustrated officials fearful of creating another martyr began to force feed them. The brutal process involved funneling a mixture of eggs and milk into tubes shoved down the victim's throat. This hard line played into Paul's hand; in 1909, it had taken five burly British prison guards to hold down the ninety-five-pound Paul while a doctor snaked a feeding tube into her stomach.[34] For Paul, force-feeding was like winning the lottery. She smuggled out a note to her NWP cohorts flagging them to fire this "excellent ammunition" at the public via the mainstream press as well as in the party's feisty weekly, the *Suffragist*.[35]

Vida remained close to the action. One night, she climbed the jailhouse wall and sang the suffrage "Marseillaise" to Paul and other suffrage prisoners. "Miss Milholland's voice is a clear high soprano, of great strength and sweetness," Philadelphia's *North American* reported, "and every note carried distinctly to the prisoners in their cells."[36] Her father also spoke up for Paul, whom he described as a "mere network of steel nerves about a cast-iron spinal column." He called her long sentence a "disgrace to democracy."[37] Authorities spirited Paul into the jail's psychiatric wing and tried to have her declared insane. They failed, but it looked as if the Wilson administration had won its battle against the depleted NWP when the organization summoned only a scant forty-one women for its final picket line on November 10. Most were jailed. They also stopped eating. Miraculously, the nightmare ended two weeks later when a federal district court ordered all suffragists released, ruling they had suffered unconstitutional cruel and unusual treatment.[38]

Vida was among former inmates honored at an NWP dinner in Washington in December. John and Jean Milholland watched from their seats in the packed Belasco Theater as Vida filed in line across the stage to be decorated with a tiny silver replica of an Occoquan cell door. It was a bittersweet night for her parents. Vida sang, her soprano voice by now an expected feature at NWP gatherings.[39] The party received more than $86,000 in pledges, more than a few in memory of Inez.[40] John was so taken with the Woman's Party that he invited several members to tea at his flat on New Year's Day. He said, "A braver, clearer-visioned body of American women does not exist."[41] The party got a belated Christmas present when Wilson came out for the vote on the eve of the new session of Congress. The next day, January 10, 1918, exactly a year after the picketing began, the House passed the suffrage amendment.

Milholland's image played a role in the NWP's next round of creative protests to pressure the Senate to approve the amendment. The biggest and liveliest demonstration celebrated her birthday on August 6, 1918, when a hundred women swarmed the Lafayette Monument and clambered up the statue to speak. Stationed at the base of the statue stood a woman bearing the banner carrying Milholland's last public words. Police arrested nearly half of the protesters.[42] Next, the NWP lighted "watch fires of freedom" in kettles in front of the White House and burned copies of Wilson's speeches on democracy. Vida returned to the Lafayette Monument with three hundred other protesters that December. She again sang the suffrage "Marseillaise" before the others burned copies of Wilson's speeches in a cauldron. There were no arrests.[43] The Senate still stalled, however, so in 1919 Paul organized a "Prison Special" railroad trip to further publicize the NWP campaign. Despite the bitter memories of her last trip west, Vida signed on. Twenty-six formerly imprisoned suffrage pickets crisscrossed the nation wearing copies of the gingham dresses and blue aprons they were issued at Occoquan, discussing their experiences and demand for the vote. Vida sang songs about their jailhouse sojourn.[44]

While the NWP pursued its embarrassing antics, the much larger and more conservative NAWSA had been persistently lobbying Wilson and Congress. NAWSA's more pragmatic and less confrontational strategy pledged its two million members to volunteer war work. The unintentional good cop–bad cop chemistry of NAWSA good citizenship versus NWP theatrics proved good politics. After the Senate approved the suffrage amendment on June 4, 1919, the well-organized NAWSA leaped into recruiting the thirty-six states needed to ratify the amendment. Finally, on August 26, 1920, more than seventy years after women first made the request, the Nineteenth Amendment granting women the vote was added to the Constitution.[45] By then, Inez Milholland was an icon.

The image of Milholland on her white horse remains an eternal symbol of feminist idealism. A more nuanced look at her life shows that the contradictory Milholland personified New Women's many contributions and conflicts in the 1910s. She possessed their best qualities: idealism, passion, courage, conscience, camaraderie, individuality, inquisitiveness, originality, and playfulness. Her insistence upon being the agent of her own life is emblematic of the New Woman's historical significance: New Women's quest for self-realization—no matter what direction it took them—is a seminal link between the pioneer woman's rights activists of the mid-nineteenth century and the women's liberationists of the late 1960s. Part of the reason Milholland appeals today is her pursuit of success both personally and professionally even when she herself felt keenly inadequate to the task. Even the strains in the Milholland-Boissevain marriage, for instance, reflect the couple's gameness to engage such eternally knotty issues as the meaning of love, the role of sex, the relevance of marriage, and how to negotiate an intimate long-term relationship without killing individuality.

Milholland's greatest legacy is her call for full freedom for women. Her quest for performing meaningful work and reinventing marriage resonates in the twenty-first century. Her imperfect attempts to stake her claim in the public sphere show how difficult it was for even the most privileged New Women to find their place in a man's world. Patriarchal culture conspired against female professional success, and Milholland's checkered record reflects the reality of thousands of unsung female professionals stymied by the patriarchal codes of the 1910s. Prejudice against women factored significantly into Milholland's Italian debacle and mediocre legal career. Yet she threw herself into the punishing atmosphere of the political and professional worlds dominated by men. The energy she had summoned in her failed bid for Harvard, for instance, would have sidelined a less determined individual. As June Sochen said of another talented New Woman who had trouble focusing her energies, "Perhaps her restlessness symbolized not only personal unhappiness but the failure of society to prepare women for significant roles."[46]

Just as Milholland's enthusiasm for a broad range of social causes reflected the New Woman's energetic embrace of life, however, her scattered approach to her career and causes lessened her impact. Interestingly, Sochen attributes these shortcomings to the entire generation of New Women in the 1910s, another indication of how Milholland embodied the type.[47] It would be denying Milholland's agency to blame all of her frustrations on American patriarchy or mass media image-mongers. Her perpetual perch on the edge of so many cultural movements smacks of an inability to focus and a pair of antennae trained to social trends. Perseverance was not her strength. Milholland seemed better suited for splashy appearances on the reform front instead of the less glamorous organizational work that ground on unheralded behind the scenes. The privileges that eased Milholland's life conversely made professional success more elusive. She moved in circles where summer-long vacations were viewed as a necessity. Although her parents inspired her desire to improve the world, the pampered existence they created for her unwittingly left her ill-prepared for the backbreaking work required of women who sought professional success in the 1910s. She never was able to shake off the constraints of class, as when she avoided a night in the Tombs during the shirtwaist strike, which prevented her from ever truly embracing the cross-class female solidarity she championed.

Sexuality also proved problematic. While Milholland's celebration of sexuality was liberating, her self-conscious seductions simultaneously risked reducing her to a sex object, an inevitable conundrum of patriarchal culture. The privilege of personal beauty posed another double-edged sword. Beauty remained the main source of Milholland's power, no matter how hard she struggled to transcend that ancient standard of a woman's worth. Her looks made it tempting for Milholland to fall back on the role of femme fatale and difficult for the press and public to absorb the substance of the radical messages beneath her pleasing surface. Yet minus her beauty, sadly, it is doubtful anyone would have paid attention to her in the first place.

Perhaps the true substance of her message paradoxically was her image. Her Amazonian image told women they could do anything. She was more than just a pretty face; her image was not simply that of a beauty but of a brave and bold woman who used her brains to right wrongs and champion the unfortunate. It is important to recognize Milholland's glamorous superwoman image was not merely the product of a voracious press or zealous suffrage publicists: She helped construct it. She defined herself as an Amazon and courted celebrity. The salutary effect of the image Milholland so assiduously helped shape, and that the mass media so affably advanced, encouraged women to take risks and make unconventional choices in the early twentieth century. This New Woman's life even if less than ideal mattered because of what she aspired to for herself and inspired in others. Her death just as she seemed to be approaching her prime (interestingly, at the same age the Gibson girl is said to have expired) left intriguing questions: Would she have succeeded as a lawyer? Been elected to Congress? Protested World War I and gone to jail? Resumed the bohemian life among expatriates in postwar Paris? Remained married to Eugen? Given birth to Peter and Eugenie?[48]

Milholland, ahead of Middle America in so many ways, aptly predicted the twentieth century would be characterized by the emancipation of women. She helped make it happen. The *Philadelphia Ledger* put it best back in 1916: "Beautiful and courageous, she embodied more than any other American woman the ideals of that part of womankind whose eyes are on the future. She *meant* the determination of modern woman to live a full, free life unhampered by tradition."[49]

The NWP clung to its idealized image of Milholland throughout the 1920s. It created an Inez Milholland Memorial Committee at Seneca Falls on July 21, 1923, in honor of the seventy-fifth anniversary of the first woman's rights convention. Planned college branches that would promote the NWP's new campaign for an Equal Rights Amendment, however, never materialized.[50] The new New Woman preferred dancing the Charleston to marching in parades; female agency became commodified by a commercial culture that reduced the liberating concept of choice to selecting a brand of soap. In the 1920s, self-indulgence emerged triumphant from the prewar-generation tension between individualism and collectivism, and the image of the hedonistic flapper elbowed aside the idealistic suffragist as the epitome of New Womanhood.[51] The triumph of fashion over feminism symbolized by the first Miss America pageant in Atlantic City in 1921 confirmed that beauty and not brains remained the measure of the ideal woman.[52] Women who remained politically active differed on the post-suffrage agenda, splintering their power. The Palmer raids and other manifestations of the "Red Scare" silenced radicals not already stunned into apathy by World War I. Very few young women of the Roaring Twenties responded to the NWP's call for the Equal Rights Amendment.[53]

In 1924 the NWP mustered a final burst of pageantry coupled with the memory of Milholland. More than a thousand players assembled on Meadowmount's fields in mid-August to perform "Forward into Light," a lavish pageant depicting the life and spirit of Inez Milholland.[54] The poster advertising the pageant depicted Milholland on a white horse as a blonde, bob-haired Joan of Arc in keeping with the Roaring Twenties' revised ideal image of the modern woman.[55] Ten thousand people filled ten acres of parking to see the pageant, which itself remained an anachronistic blend of pomp and bathos. Choirs sang, a band boomed; banner bearers paraded the purple, white, and gold standard; famous players froze in historical tableaus. Suddenly, Vida trotted up on a white horse, portraying her sister in the 1913 parade. She accepted the "torch of freedom" from one of the players and placed it on the "altar of humanity."[56] Then Vida, as Inez, passed out smaller torches to thirty young women. Instead of riding white horses, they roared off in automobiles to congressional districts where they hoped to elect women representatives.[57] The achingly sentimental "Forward into Light" was the last, large feminist demonstration until the 1960s.

Epilogue

"Take up the song"

John Milholland added a new route to his Adirondack rambles, walking or snowshoeing to the top of the cemetery hill where Inez lay buried. He covered her grave with a coffin-sized granite slab inscribed only "INEZ." Over time, her name faded under lichen amid the pine cones that dropped from the trees he ordered planted around what became the family burial plot, surrounded by lilacs and a low stone wall.[1] For several years, towns-people and suffragists returned to the cemetery on Inez's birthday, when village children scattered wildflowers on her grave after services in the little white church.[2] Plans for popular feminist author Mary Austin to write a biography of Inez, however, fell through when John quarreled with her.[3]

John spent most of his time trying to unload the mail tubes. His flimsy house of financial cards began collapsing as loans caught up with him and the value of his inflated tube stocks plummeted.[4] The spring before the mail tubes contract with the post office was due to expire, the Senate Committee on Post Offices recommended buying the tubes in five cities for $4.4 million, a purchase endorsed by city leaders.[5] Postmaster General Albert Sidney Burleson then penned an extraordinary letter opposing the purchase that he sent to every senator. Nonetheless, the Senate approved the purchase 31 to 19.[6] Soon afterward Burleson played golf with Wilson. The next day, Wilson vetoed the purchase.[7] At midnight June 30, 1918, the pneumatic mail tubes stopped.[8]

John Milholland scrambled for the rest of his life to reinstate the tubes. His health broke, and his mind wandered. The closest John came to de-voting the farm to helping humanity was to make it headquarters of the Essex County Sunday School Association.[9] Angry and ailing, in his final years he fancied himself "Noah" in a corrupt and collapsing world, which he planned to girdle with radio stations to preach the gospel. "Pretty tall order you will say," he scratched in his journal, "but God delights in big things."[10] His big heart finally broke. After he died alone on June 29, 1925, at 247 Fifth Avenue, he was widely memorialized for his humanitarianism. W. E. B. Du Bois wrote, "Milholland was less a man of deed than a poet of inspiration; his handsome head, and hearty voice, his thrill of belief, his whirlwind of big, joyful enthusiasm, and hot, scathing anger, made men move against their will and do things that could not be done."[11]

The family buried him next to Inez, cradled by his beloved mountains. Broke after paying John's debts, Jean and Vida were forced to move into the apartment of Jack, now a banker; his second wife, Mary Dorion, and their son, John Angus Jr.[12] The Milhollands continued to summer at Meadowmount but struggled to pay property taxes. During the Depression, Jack quit banking and moved to a house he built there. Before Jean Milholland died in 1939, she sold off parts of the farm.[13] Her children were relieved to finally sell the "Big House" and fifty acres in 1945 to a violin maestro, who converted it into a summer music camp for children.[14] After Jack died of lung cancer in 1949, the burden of managing the property fell solely upon Vida.[15] Vida sacrificed her career to work for liberal causes after Inez died.[16] She never married and devoted much of her life to caring for her parents.[17] Although she eventually performed as a soloist at the Metropolitan Opera House and Carnegie Hall, she mostly sang to benefit liberal causes, notably the peace movement. She once said, "[M]y one aim is to use my voice to give . . . the messages of liberty, justice, and true democracy."[18] She became a devout Christian Scientist and for years shared Meadowmount's small "Chimney Corners" cottage with her close friend, Westport native Margaret Hamilton.[19] Although friends treasured Vida for her optimism and ideals, shouldering Meadowmount's debts, waging legal battles over Jack's estate, and the loss of her family drained her. She wrote a friend in 1952, "[M]y nerves have given out and I have what they call an anxiety, depressive neuroses, and it is awful."[20] Two weeks later, she stepped into the bathtub at Chimney Corners and killed herself.[21]

The day after the Christmas memorial, Eugen Boissevain answered the door at his new apartment at 12 East Eighth Street and beheld Max Eastman with suitcase in hand. Eastman had just left his wife and son, and the friends shared quarters the next few years.[22] Eastman seldom saw his roommate, since Boissevain threw himself into work. He made a small fortune during the war importing coffee from the Dutch Indies, working out of an office at 24 Broad Street in a sixteen-story building that Eastman claimed had Boissevain's name carved in granite on the lintel. Although after the war the pair occasionally entertained Isadora Duncan's dancers, who lived near Eastman's summer home in Croton-on-Hudson, Boissevain avoided serious romance. That changed one April evening at a party in 1923 hosted by Doris Stevens and Dudley Field Malone at their oversized stucco bungalow in Croton. Boissevain was paired in a skit with the ethereal poet Edna St. Vincent Millay. They had met uneventfully a couple of years earlier, and although she had seen him with Milholland at Vassar's fiftieth anniversary, undergraduate Millay had been much more overwhelmed by his famous feminist wife. Something magical happened, however, as the couple acted out their party-game role as a city couple corrupted by a country couple, and the other guests watched them fall in love.[23]

Millay differed from Milholland in that she was petite and soft spoken. While not a classic beauty like Milholland, Millay radiated sensuality. Her red hair cascaded like flames down her back. She also was gifted. Twelve years younger than Boissevain, now forty-three, she had just received that year's Pulitzer Prize for poetry. Like Milholland, she also was seriously ill. When doctors announced she needed a serious intestinal operation, Boissevain insisted they marry immediately. The wedding took place in *Masses* staffer Boardman Robinson's yard in Croton on the morning of July 18, 1923; that afternoon, she entered the hospital for a bowel resection.[24] Boissevain nursed her to recovery as he could not nurse Milholland. He happily gave up his business to manage the couple's business affairs and household so Millay could write. The marriage, as might be expected of the widower of Inez Milholland, was unconventional. Until his death following complications from lung cancer in 1949, Boissevain dedicated his life to caring for his sensual and talented wife.[25]

Early in their marriage, the couple traveled to Washington, D.C., where Millay spoke at an NWP ceremony honoring suffragists. Milholland's presence must have seemed palpable to Boissevain as the stream of banner bearers followed a girls' chorus into the Capitol Building crypt, where politicians had relegated a seven-ton marble statue of the three suffrage pioneers, Susan B. Anthony, Lucretia Mott, and Elizabeth Cady Stanton.[26] Besides Millay, Milholland's suffrage colleagues Alva Belmont, Doris Stevens, and Inez Haynes Irwin spoke. The graying women's activists and the busts of the dead suffragists intensified the feeling inside the crypt that their era was history. The event inspired Millay to write a sonnet she later dedicated "To Inez Milholland." It ends:

> Only my standard on a taken hill
> Can cheat the mildew and the red-brown rust
> And make immortal my adventurous will.
> Even now the silk is tugging at the staff:
> Take up the song; forget the epitaph.[27]

NOTES

Abbreviations and Location of Sources

APP   Alice Paul Papers, Arthur and Elizabeth Schlesinger Library on the History of Women in America, Radcliffe Institute for Advanced Study, Harvard University, Cambridge, Mass.

CP   Cullen Papers, Sophia Smith Collection, Smith College, Northampton, Mass.

ECCH   Essex County Court House, Elizabethtown, N.Y.

ECHS   Essex Country Historical Society, Elizabethtown, N.Y.

FFP   Fox Family Papers, Special Collections, M.I. King Library, University of Kentucky, Lexington, Ky.

FPP   The Papers of the Ford Peace Plan, Library of Congress, Washington, D.C.

FSA   Fabian Society Archives, Archives Division of British Library of Political & Economic Science, London School of Economics and Political Science, London, England

HSB   The Papers of Harriot Stanton Blatch, Manuscripts Division, Library of Congress, Washington, D.C. (microfilm edition)

HSP   Historical Society of Pennsylvania, Philadelphia, Penn.

HF   Henry Ford Peace Expedition, Swarthmore College Peace Collection, Swarthmore, Pa.

HM   The MacKaye Family Papers. Special Collections, Dartmouth College Library, Hanover, N.H.

HUA   Harvard University Archives, Cambridge, Mass.

IMP   Inez Milholland Papers, microfilm edition, Arthur and Elizabeth Schlesinger Library on the History of Women in America, Radcliffe Institute for Advanced Study, Harvard University, Cambridge, Mass.

JAM   John A. Milholland Papers, private collection

JEM Diaries   John Elmer Milholland Diaries, Milholland Family Papers, Ticonderoga Historical Society, Ticonderoga, N.Y.

LTH   Records of the Lewis Town Historian, Lewis, N.Y.

MFP   Milholland Family Papers, Ticonderoga Historical Society, Ticonderoga, N.Y.

NAACP   National Association for the Advancement of Colored People Papers, Library of Congress, Washington, D.C.

NAWSA   National American Woman Suffrage Association Papers, Library of Congress. Microfilm ed. Sanford, N.C.: Microfilm Corp. of America, 1979

NWP   National Woman's Party Papers, 1913–1974, Library of Congress. Microfilm ed. Glen Rock, N.J.: Microfilm Corp. of America, 1977–78

NWP: SY   National Woman's Party Papers: The Suffrage Years, 1913–1920, Library of Congress. Microfilm ed. Glen Rock, N.J.: Microfilm Corp. of America, 1979

NYHS   New-York Historical Society, New York City, N.Y.

NYPL   New York Public Library, New York City, N.Y.

NYPL-LGH	New York Public Library, Local and Genealogical History, New York City, N.Y.
NYU	Bobst Library, New York University, N.Y.
NYSA	New York State Archives, Albany, N.Y.
PLHD	Paterson Local History Department, Paterson Public Library, Paterson, N.J.
PRONI	Public Records Office of Northern Ireland, Belfast, N.I.
RBKCL	Local Studies Collection, Royal Borough of Kensington & Chelsea Libraries and Art Service, London, England
RPS	Rose Pastor Stokes Papers, Tamiment Labor History Collection, Bobst Library, New York University, N.Y.
SFC	Suffragette Fellowship Collection of Museum of London, England
SL	Arthur and Elizabeth Schlesinger Library on the History of Women in America, Radcliffe Institute for Advanced Study, Harvard University, Cambridge, Mass.
SOC	Socialist Collections in the Tamiment Library, 1872–1956, New York University, New York, New York, microfilm ed.
SOHC	Suffragists Oral History Collection, University of California, Berkeley. Microfiche edition, Sanford, N.C. Microfilming Corp. of American, 1980
USP	Upton Sinclair Papers, Manuscripts Department, Lilly Library, Indiana University, Bloomington, Ind.
VC	Vassar College Archives, Vassar College, Poughkeepsie, N.Y.
VMP	Vida Milholland Folders, Swarthmore College Peace Collection, Swarthmore College, Swarthmore, Pa.
WEBD	W. E. B. Du Bois Papers, Special Collections and Archives, W. E. B. Du Bois Library, University of Massachusetts, Amherst, Mass.
WPP	Collected Records of Woman's Peace Party 1914–1920, Swarthmore College Peace Collection, Swarthmore, Pa.
WSC	Woman Suffrage Collection, Fawcett Library, London, England
WSC-VC	Woman Suffrage Collection, Vassar College, Poughkeepsie, N.Y.
WTUL	New York Women's Trade Union League Papers, Tamiment Labor History Collection, Bobst Library, New York University, N.Y.

Abbreviations of Individual Names

AP	Alice Paul
EB	Eugen Boissevain
IM	Inez Milholland
JEM	John Elmer Milholland
JTM	Jean Torry Milholland
VM	Vida Milholland

Introduction

1. "Miss Milholland Won't Surrender," *New York Times*, 9 October 1909, 19.

2. "Father Upset Plans of Inez Milholland," *New York Times*, 18 July 1913, 1.

3. Mary A. Hill, *Charlotte Perkins Gilman: The Making of a Radical Feminist 1860–1896* (Philadelphia: Temple University Press, 1980), 3. See Charlotte Perkins Gilman,

Women and Economics: A Study of the Economic Relation Between Men and Women as a Factor in Social Evolution (Boston, 1898).

4. See Equality League of Self-Supporting Women, *Report for Year, 1908–1909* (New York: 1909), 2, HSB; Harriot Stanton Blatch and Alma Lutz, *Challenging Years: The Memoirs of Harriot Stanton Blatch* (New York: G. P. Putnam's Sons, 1940), 107–109; Ellen Carol DuBois, "Working Women, Class Relations, and Suffrage Militance: Harriot Stanton Blatch and the New York Woman Suffrage Movement, 1894–1909," *Journal of American History* 74 (January–February 1987): 54–55; *Woman's Journal*, 14 June 1908, and Dorothy Smith Gruening (Recollections, sound recording), SL. The Poughkeepsie Equal Suffrage League did not organize until 1910. Elizabeth A. Daniels, *Bridges to the World: Henry Noble MacCracken and Vassar College* (Clifton Corner, N.Y.: College Avenue Press, 1994), 66.

5. See Barbara Goldsmith, *Other Powers: The Age of Suffrage, Spiritualism, and the Scandalous Victoria Woodhull* (New York: Alfred A. Knopf, 1998).

6. For more on the nineteenth-century suffrage movement, see Ellen Carol DuBois, *Feminism and Suffrage: The Emergence of an Independent Women's Movement in America, 1848–1869* (Ithaca, N.Y.: Cornell University Press, 1978); Eleanor Flexner, *Century of Struggle: The Woman's Rights Movement in the United States* (Cambridge, Mass.: Belknap Press, Harvard University Press, 1959; rev. ed., New York: Atheneum, 1971); and Aileen Kraditor, *The Ideas of the Woman Suffrage Movement, 1890–1920* (New York: Columbia University Press, 1965).

7. Equality League of Self-Supporting Women, *Report for Year 1908–1909*, 2; Blatch and Lutz, *Challenging Years*, 107–109.

8. For more on cultural constraints on American women in the nineteenth century, see Jean Beth Elshtain, "Aristotle, the Public-Private Split, and the Case of the Suffragists," in Elshtain, ed., *The Family in Political Thought* (Amherst: University of Massachusetts Press, 1982), 51–65; Elizabeth Janeway, *Man's World, Woman's Place: A Study in Social Mythology* (New York: William Morrow and Co., 1971); Linda Kerber, *Women of the Republic: Intellect and Ideology in Revolutionary America* (Chapel Hill: University of North Carolina Press, 1980); Glenna Matthews, *The Rise of Public Woman: Woman's Power and Woman's Place in the United States, 1630–1970* (New York: Oxford University Press, 1992); Carroll Smith-Rosenberg and Charles Rosenberg, "The Female Animal: Medical and Biological Views of Woman and Her Role in Nineteenth-Century America," *Journal of American History* 60 (1973–74): 332–56; Carroll Smith-Rosenberg, *Disorderly Conduct: Visions of Gender in Victorian America* (New York: Alfred A. Knopf, 1985); and Barbara Welter, *Dimity Convictions: The American Woman in the Nineteenth Century* (Athens: Ohio University Press, 1976).

9. See Paula Baker, "The Domestication of Politics: Women and American Political Society, 1780–1920," *American Historical Review* 89 (June 1984): 620–47.

10. For more on male gender roles in the 1910s, see "Men and Manliness," in Peter Filene, *Him/Her/Self: Gender Identities in Modern America*, 3rd ed. (Baltimore: Johns Hopkins University Press, 1998), 74–99.

11. John Demos, "The American Family in Past Time," *American Scholar* 43 (Summer 1974): 433.

12. See Nan Enstad, *Ladies of Labor, Girls of Adventure: Working Women, Popular Culture, and Labor Politics at the Turn of the Twentieth Century* (New York: Columbia University Press, 1999); Margaret Finnegan, *Selling Suffrage: Consumer Culture and Votes for Women* (New York: Columbia University Press, 1999); Susan Porter Benson,

Counter Cultures: Saleswomen, Managers, and Customers in American Department Stores, 1890–1940 (Urbana: University of Illinois Press, 1986); Nancy Schrom Dye, *As Equals and as Sisters: Feminism, the Labor Movement, and the Women's Trade Union League of New York* (Columbia: University of Missouri Press, 1980); Noralee Frankel and Nancy S. Dye, eds., *Gender, Class, Race, and Reform in the Progressive Era* (Lexington: University Press of Kentucky, 1991); James McGovern, "The American Woman's Pre–World War I Freedom in Manners and Morals," *Journal of American History* 55 (September 1968): 315–33; Kathy Peiss, *Cheap Amusements: Working Women and Leisure in Turn-of-the-Century New York* (Philadelphia: Temple University Press, 1986); and Barbara Miller Solomon, *In the Company of Educated Women* (New Haven, Conn.: Yale University Press, 1985).

13. Welter, *Dimity Convictions*, 41.

14. Allen Churchill, *The Improper Bohemians: A Recreation of Greenwich Village In Its Heyday* (New York: E.P. Dutton & Co., 1959), 28.

15. Unidentified newspaper clipping, JAM.

16. "M" to IM, n.d., Folder 16, IMP.

17. Oswald Garrison Villard to EB, 6 December 1916, Folder 18, IMP.

18. "Wasn't Mrs. Boissevain's Secret a Corking One?" *San Francisco Chronicle*, 19 December 1915, 5.

19. Demos, "The American Family in Past Time," 434. See also "The Cult of True Womanhood," in Welter, *Dimity Convictions*, 21–41.

20. Lois Rudnick, "The New Woman," in Adele Heller and Lois Rudnick, eds., *1915, the Cultural Moment: The New Politics, the New Woman, the New Psychology, the New Art, and the New Theatre in America* (New Brunswick, N.J.: Rutgers University Press, 1991), 71. See an early discussion on New Women in Sarah Grand, "The New Aspect of the Woman Question," *North American Review* 158 (March 1894): 270–76.

21. See Estelle Freedman, "Separatism as Strategy: Female Institution Building and American Feminism, 1870–1930," *Feminist Studies* 5 (Fall 1979): 512–49.

22. See Robyn Muncy, *Creating a Female Dominion in American Reform, 1890–1935* (New York: Oxford University Press, 1991).

23. LeeAnne Giannone Kryder, "Self-Assertion and Social Commitment: The Significance of Work to the Progressive Era's New Woman," *Journal of American Culture* 6 (1983): 26.

24. Eric Sandeen, ed., *The Letters of Randolph Bourne: A Comprehensive Edition* (Troy, N.Y.: Whitston Publishing Co., 1981), 82.

25. Rudnick, "The New Woman," in Heller and Rudnick, *1915, the Cultural Moment*, 74–77; Martha Banta, "American Girls and the New Woman," in *Imaging American Women: Idea and Ideals in Cultural History* (New York: Columbia University Press, 1987), 45–91; Leila Rupp, "Feminism and the Sexual Revolution in the Early Twentieth Century: The Case of Doris Stevens," *Feminist Studies* 15, no. 2 (Summer 1989): 289; Martha Patterson, "'Survival of the Best Fitted': Selling the American New Woman as Gibson Girl, 1895–1910," *ATQ* 9 (March 1995): 82–83; Elizabeth Ammons, "The New Woman as Cultural Symbol and Social Reality," in Heller and Rudnick, *1915, the Cultural Moment*, 83–97; Kathy Peiss, *Cheap Amusements*, 6; Marjorie Spruill Wheeler, *New Women of the New South: The Leaders of the Woman Suffrage Movement in the Southern States* (New York: Oxford University Press, 1993). The label later was applied to Second Wave feminists, as in a March 20, 1972, *Time* magazine cover story featuring "The New Woman," indicative of how their feminist foremothers had been swept from cultural memory.

26. Nancy Cott, *The Grounding of Modern Feminism* (New Haven, Conn.: Yale University Press, 1987), 13–16. The term *feminism* originated in French in the 1880s, migrated to England in the 1890s, and became common in the United States by 1913. Ibid.

27. Christine Stansell, *American Moderns: Bohemia New York and the Creation of a New Century* (New York: Henry Holt and Co., 2000), 231.

28. Lois Banner, *American Beauty* (Chicago: University of Chicago Press, 1984), 187.

29. Margaret Deland, "The Change in the Feminine Ideal," *Atlantic Monthly* 105 (March 1910): 292, 289 (emphasis in original). Deland is echoing Nora in the influential "A Doll's House" when she announces to her husband she is leaving him. "I have duties equally sacred. . . . My duties to myself." Quoted in Carolyn Forrey, "The New Woman Revisited," *Women's Studies* 2 (1974): 50.

30. Rudnick, *1915, the Cultural Moment,* 69.

31. For more on New Women, see Sandra Adickes, *To Be Young Was Very Heaven: Women in New York before the First World War* (New York: St. Martin's Press, 1997); Filene, *Him/Her/Self,* 20–24; "The New Woman," in Leslie Fishbein, *Rebels in Bohemia: The Radicals of the Masses, 1911–1917* (Chapel Hill: University of North Carolina Press, 1982), 136–43; Forrey, "The New Woman Revisited," 37–56; Patricia Marks, *Bicycles, Bangs, and Bloomers: The New Woman in the Popular Press* (Frankfort: University Press of Kentucky, 1990); "The New Woman as Androgyne: Social Disorder and Gender Crisis, 1870–1936," in Carroll Smith-Rosenberg, *Disorderly Conduct,* 245–96; and June Sochen, *The New Woman in Greenwich Village, 1910–1920* (New York: Quadrangle Books, 1972).

32. Phyllis Eckhaus, "Vita: Inez Milholland," *Harvard Magazine* (November–December 1994): 50; Elinor Byrns, "I Resolve to Be Restless," *Independent,* 10 January 1916, 50, 51.

33. See Lois Palken Rudnick, "The New Woman," in *Mabel Dodge: New Woman, New Worlds* (Albuquerque: University of New Mexico Press, 1984), 88–91.

34. Forrey, "The New Woman Revisited," 47; Alma J. Bennett, "A Critic's Response to Stage Representations of the 'New Woman' during the Progressive Era," *American Transcendental Quarterly* 10 (September 1996): 219.

35. Lynn D. Gordon, "The Gibson Girl Goes to College: Popular Culture and Women's Higher Education in the Progressive Era, 1890–1920," *American Quarterly* 39 (Summer 1987): 226; Martha Patterson, "'Survival of the Best Fitted,'" 73.

1. Childhood

1. "Suffrage Martyr's Life," unidentified newspaper clipping, 17 December 1916, MFP.

2. Tombstone, Congregational Church cemetery, Lewis, N.Y.; Census of Ireland for the Year 1831, County Londonderry, PRONI; *Primary Valuation of Ireland: Union of Magherafelt* (Dublin: Alexander Thom and Sons, 1859), 166, PRONI.

3. *Primary Valuation of Ireland,* 166.

4. *Ordnance Survey Memoirs,* 33, 34, PRONI.

5. James G. Leyburn, *The Scotch-Irish: A Social History* (Chapel Hill: University of North Carolina Press, 1962), 164; Kerby A. Miller, *Emigrants and Exiles: Ireland and the Irish Exodus to North America* (New York: Oxford University Press, 1985), 180, 183, 185, 194.

6. Census of Ireland Year of 1864, vol. 3, 239, PRONI.

7. Peter Quinn, "The Tragedy of Bridget Such-a-One," *American Heritage* 48 (December 1997): 47.

8. "Lewis Road District 1847," George Smith Papers, LTH.

9. George Smith Papers, LTH; Book of Deeds, M: 473, ECCH.

10. 19 May 1914, JEM Diaries; Book of Deeds, WW: 591, ECCH.

11. Winslow Watson, *General View and Agricultural Survey of the County of Essex* (The New York State Agricultural Society, n.d., Ticonderoga Historical Society), 889.

12. 1860 Essex County Census, Town of Lewis, ECCH. At least one other child died in infancy, according to the tombstones in the family cemetery plot in Lewis.

13. 21 December 1913, 29 May 1910, 31 May 1905, and 21 December 1913, JEM Diaries; *Elizabethtown Post & Gazette*, 1 March 1894, 3; and "Milholland Funeral Largely Attended," *Elizabethtown (N.Y.) Record-Post*, 9 July 1975, n.p., JAM.

14. 30 May 1914, 24 December 1917, 22 December 1914, 6 December 1908, 30 May 1914, and 1 July 1920, JEM Diaries.

15. Book of Deeds, vol. 64:8–11, ECCH; *Elizabethtown Post*, 31 August 1914, n.p., ECHS.

16. 1870 Essex County Census, Town of Lewis, ECCH.

17. 14 August 1919, 8 September 1910, 26 August 1909, 4 July 1913, 20 March 1905, 26 August 1920, and 13 May 1921, JEM Diaries.

18. Paterson, N.J., city directories, 1872–73, 1873–74, 1874–75, 1875–76, PLHD.

19. 27 June 1920 and 4 July 1913, JEM Diaries.

20. Hugh M. Herrick, ed., *William Walter Phelps: His Life and Public Services* (New York: Knickerbocker Press, 1904), 29, 41, 68; Bingham Duncan, *Whitelaw Reid: Journalist, Politician, Diplomat* (Athens: University of Georgia Press, 1975), 77; and *Owego (N.Y.) Times*, 12 April 1894, n.p., MFP.

21. 21 January 1909, JEM Diaries; *Elizabethtown Post & Gazette*, 1 March 1894, 3.

22. Herrick, *William Walter Phelps*, 65, 68.

23. "Parting Words," *Ticonderoga (N.Y.) Sentinel*, 10 August 1883, 4.

24. "Salutatory," *Ticonderoga (N.Y.) Sentinel*, 10 August 1883, 4.

25. "Some Progress Made," *Ticonderoga (N.Y.) Sentinel*, 10 December 1883, 4; "The Adirondacks," *Ticonderoga (N.Y.) Sentinel*, 12 December 1884, 4; and "The Preservation of Fort Ticonderoga by Town Ownership," NYPL-LHG.

26. 23 June 1913, JEM Diaries; JEM to JTM, 22 February 1883, JAM.

27. 6 March 1904, 8 March 1904, 8 March 1910, 12 March 1904, 11 March 1909, JEM Diaries; *Elizabethtown Post & Gazette*, 1 March 1894, 3; and "Valedictory," *Ticonderoga (N.Y.) Sentinel*, 6 March 1885, 4.

28. James G. Smart, "Information Control, Thought Control: Whitelaw Reid and the Nation's News Services," *Public Historian* 3 (Spring 1981): 35.

29. 12 July 1913, JEM Diaries.

30. 29 December 1915, JEM Diaries.

31. See "The Fly-Eye of New York," in Kate Simon, *Fifth Avenue: A Very Social History* (New York: Harcourt Brace Jovanovich, 1978), 53–72.

32. "Mrs. Boissevain Felt No Fear," *Los Angeles Examiner*, 27 November 1916, 3.

33. Duncan, *Whitelaw Reid*, 111; H. Wayne Morgan, *From Hayes to McKinley: National Party Politics, 1877–1896* (Syracuse, N.Y.: Syracuse University Press, 1969), 164, 317; Homer Socolofsky and Allan B. Spetter, *The Presidency of Benjamin Harrison* (Lawrence: University Press of Kansas, 1987), 9; 3 September 1915, JEM Diaries.

34. George A. Stevens, *New York Typographical Union Number Six* (Albany: New York State Department of Labor, 1912), 386–96.

35. Smart, "Information Control, Thought Control," 37.

36. Duncan, *Whitelaw Reid*, 152–54.

37. 3 September 1915, JEM Diaries.

38. "Milholland's Blood Is Up," *New York Times*, 24 March 1892, 5.

39. See "The Eleventh District Row," *New York Times*, 26 March 1892, 3; "Politicians from New York," *New York Times*, 26 March 1892, 4; "Platt Visits Washington," *New York Times*, 30 March 1892, 4; "Weary of George Bliss," *New York Times*, 1 April 1892, 1; "Likely to Treat for Peace," *New York Times*, 6 April 1892, 8; "Will Battle at the Polls," *New York Times*, 15 April 1892, 1; and "Thomas C. Platt," *New York Times*, 23 April 1892, 5. The Knights of Labor presented a petition to the White House bearing eighty thousand signatures protesting Milholland's removal. See "A Plea for Milholland," *New York Times*, 20 April 1892, 5.

40. "Milholland Successful," *New York Times*, 17 May 1892, 2; "The Bliss-Milholland Fight," *New York Times*, 8 August 1892, 8; and *New York Advertiser*, 1 October 1894, n.p., MFP.

41. "Milholland's Men Convene," *New York Sun*, 10 February 1894, 1.

42. *New York Sun*, 14 February 1895, n.p., MFP.

43. *New York Sun*, 12 March 1894, n.p., MFP.

44. Edmund Morris, *The Rise of Theodore Roosevelt* (New York: Random House, 2001), 584–86.

45. 18 June 1910, JEM Diaries.

46. Mrs. John E. Milholland, "Talks about Women," *Crisis* 2 (March 1911): 29.

47. "Boissevain, Inez Milholland," *The National Cyclopaedia of American Biography*, vol. 16 (New York: James T. White & Co., 1945), 216.

48. Sally Roesch Wagner, *A Time of Protest: Suffragists Challenge the Republic, 1870–1877* (Carmichael, Calif.: Sky Carrier Press, 1988), 104.

49. "Suffrage Martyr's Life," unidentified newspaper clipping, MFP.

50. Waldon Fawcett, "The United States Postal Service in the Twentieth Century," *Harper's Weekly* 45 (February 1901): 131.

51. John Wanamaker Papers, Box 65, Folder 17, HSP; Joseph H. Appel, *The Business Biography of John Wanamaker: Founder and Builder* (New York: Macmillan Co., 1930), 104.

52. Robert Hendrickson, *The Grand Emporiums: The Illustrated History of America's Great Department Stores* (New York: Stein and Day, 1979), 57.

53. See *Annual Report of the Postmaster-General for the Fiscal Year Ending June 30, 1893* (Washington, D.C.: GPO, 1893), 45–49, and B. Batcheller, *The Pneumatic Despatch Tube System of the Batcheller Pneumatic Tube Co.* (Philadelphia: J. B. Lippincott Co., 1897), 37, 10.

54. "Pneumatic Tube System," *New York Times*, 6 April 1897, 6; "Mail Tube System Begun," *New York Times*, 3 August 1897, 8.

55. "Opening of the Pneumatic Tube Service in New York City," *Scientific American* 77 (16 October 1897): 243.

56. "Sending Dogs, Chickens, Goldfish and Hot Tea by Mail," *North American* 4 (March 1906), JAM.

57. Albert Rossdale, "The Problem of the Mails," *Forum* 68 (20 July 1922): 627; "Pneumatic Pains," *Time* 31 (10 January 1938): 45–46.

58. 8 June 1905 and 24 September 1909, JEM Diaries.

59. Book of Deeds, vol. 116: 36; vol. 118: 172, 512, 598; vol. 202: 162–65, ECCH.

60. Sales Prospectus, JAM; 18 September 1908 and 10 May 1903, JEM Diaries; and VM to John Deming, 9 December 1950, JAM.

61. 19 June 1905, JEM Diaries.

62. 27 December 1912 and 23 December 1914, JEM Diaries.

63. 4 December 1920, JEM Diaries.

64. 12 August 1905, JEM Diaries.

65. 26 November 1909, JEM Diaries.

2. London

1. "Inez Milholland," *Suffragist*, 23 December 1916, 9. The man probably was family friend Arthur Lynch, a fiery Irish nationalist and member of Parliament later convicted of treason.

2. Ibid.

3. "Kensington Draft Valuation List, 1905–6," RBKCL; Frederic Whyte, *The Life of W.T. Stead*, vol. 2 (London: Jonathan Cape Ltd., 1925), 173. See also William Gaunt, *Kensington and Chelsea* (London: B.T. Batsford, 1975), and Annabel Walker, with Peter Jackson, *Kensington and Chelsea: A Social and Architectural History* (London: John Murray, 1987).

4. "Milholland Refused to Drink to Queen," *New York World*, 5 March 1900, 5.

5. 12 March 1904, JEM Diaries; Whyte, *Stead*, 173.

6. 14 and 15 September 1909, JEM Diaries.

7. 12 November 1917 and 27 March 1905, JEM Diaries.

8. 31 December 1903 and 1 January 1904, JEM Diaries.

9. Josephine Kamm, *Indicative Past: A Hundred Years of the Girls' Public Day School Trust* (London: George Allen and Unwin, 1971), 37, 47–48.

10. IM to JEM, 23 November 1900, 10 November 1901, 24 December 1902, and 24 October 1903, JAM.

11. IM to JEM, 24 October 1903, JAM.

12. *The Girls' Public Day School Trust 1872–1972: A Centenary Review* (London: Girls' Public Day School Trust, 1972), 14; IM to JEM, 16 May 1900, JAM.

13. "My Conversion to Woman Suffrage," *Woman Voter*, January 1917, 13.

14. 12 August 1905, JEM Diaries; unidentified clipping, JAM; scrapbook, MFP.

15. "Inez Milholland," *Suffragist*, 23 December 1916, 9.

16. John Demos, "The American Family in Past Time," *American Scholar* 43 (Summer 1974): 442, 440.

17. Mrs. John E. Milholland, "Talks about Women," *Crisis* 1 (December 1910): 28.

18. "Suffrage Martyr's Life," unidentified newspaper clipping, JAM.

19. "Inez Milholland," *Suffragist*, 23 December 1916, 9.

20. Mary Church Terrell, *A Colored Woman in a White World* (reprint, New York: G.K. Hall, 1996), 212.

21. 29 May 1910 and 27 November 1910, JEM Diaries.

22. JTM to JEM, 10 November [1903], JAM.

23. 7 June 1905, JEM Diaries.

24. 1 June 1904, JEM Diaries.

25. 28 February 1904, JEM Diaries.

26. Richard Collier, *The General Next to God: The Story of William Booth and the Salvation Army* (New York: E. P. Dutton & Co., 1965), 26, 66–67, 196–97; Harold Begbie, *The Life of General William Booth, the Founder of the Salvation Army* (New York: Macmillan Co., 1920), 94, 188–90.

27. 28 February 1904, JEM Diaries.

28. 8 January 1904, JEM Diaries.

29. JEM to JTM, 20 November 1909, JAM.

30. 5 September 1909, JEM Diaries; IM to JEM, 30 May 1903, JAM.

31. IM to JTM, n.d., JAM.

32. Max Eastman, *The Enjoyment of Living* (New York: Harper & Brothers, 1948), 36.

33. John A. Milholland, "Autobiography," ed. John Tepper Marlin, in author's possession.

34. IM to JEM, n.d., 15 November [1903?], 24 January 1903, and 24 December 1902, JAM.

35. 23 August 1915, JEM Diaries.

36. 25 August 1905, 22 March 1909, JEM Diaries.

37. 28 January 1909, 30 May 1915, and 23 September 1908, JEM Diaries.

38. JEM to [?], 14 October 1914, JAM.

39. 3 and 4 November 1905, JEM Diaries.

40. Mary White Ovington, "The National Association for the Advancement of Colored People," *Journal of Negro History* 9 (April 1924): 107; Daniel W. Crofts, "The Warner-Foraker Amendment to the Hepburn Bill: Friend or Foe of Jim Crow," *Journal of Southern History* 39 (1973): 345.

41. Oswald Garrison Villard to Booker T. Washington, 26 May 1909, in Louis R. Harlan and Raymond W. Smock, eds., *The Booker T. Washington Papers*, 13 vols. (Urbana: University of Illinois Press, 1981), 117.

42. Ann J. Lane, *The Brownsville Affair: National Crisis and Black Reaction* (Port Washington, N.Y.: Kennikat Press, 1971), 5, 23; 2 December 1906, JEM Diaries.

43. Lane, *Brownsville Affair*, 164–65; Terrell, *Colored Woman in a White World*, 269–73. The army exonerated the soldiers in 1972. See John D. Weaver, *The Senator and the Sharecropper's Son: Exoneration of the Brownsville Soldiers* (College Station: Texas A&M University Press, 1997).

44. Carolyn Wedin, *Inheritors of the Spirit: Mary White Ovington and the Founding of the NAACP* (New York: John Wiley & Sons, 1997), 66.

45. 29 May 1905 and 20 September 1906, JEM Diaries; Wedin, *Inheritors of the Spirit*, 69–70.

46. 30 May 1905, JEM Diaries.

47. 19 June 1905, JEM Diaries.

48. Quoted in Barbara Page, unpublished ms, in author's possession.

49. 10 and 11 August 1905, JEM Diaries.

50. Giancarlo Masini, *Marconi* (New York: Marsilio Publishers, 1976), 145–46; "The Time for Thinkers Has Come," pamphlet, VMP; 18 October 1903, JEM Diaries; and IM to JEM, 24 October 1903, JAM.

51. IM to JEM, 6 December 1903, JAM.

52. Degna Marconi, *My Father, Marconi* (London: Frederick Muller, 1962), 144, 149, 156; IM to JTM, [January 1905?], JAM; [IM to VM, February 1905], JAM; and 14 July 1917, JEM Diaries.

53. Gordon Campbell to IM, Folder 16, IMP; 5 September 1909, JEM Diaries; Irving Robertson to IM, n.d., Folder 12, IMP; and 23 December 1921, JEM Diaries.

54. 14–15 March 1903, JEM Diaries.

55. IM to JEM, 15 November 1903 and 10 January 1904, JAM (emphasis in original).

56. JTM to JEM, 28 August 1904[?], JAM.

57. IM to JTM, November 1904[?], JAM.

58. IM to JTM, January 1905[?], JAM.

59. IM to JTM, October 1904[?], JAM.

60. IM to JTM, January 1905[?], JAM.

61. IM to JTM, January 1905[?], 5 and 19 February 1905, JAM; IM to JEM, [December 1904], JAM.

62. IM to JTM, January 1905[?], JAM.

63. IM to JEM, 2 February 1905, and IM to JTM, 5 February 1905, JAM.

64. IM to JEM, 25 June 1905, JAM.

65. IM to JEM, 10 July 1905, JAM.

66. IM to JEM, 18 July 1905, JAM.

67. June Sochen, *Movers and Shakers: American Women Thinkers and Activists 1900–1970* (New York: Quadrangle, 1973), 90.

68. JTM to JEM, [September 1905], JAM.

69. IM to JEM, 24 October 1903, JAM.

70. JTM to JEM, [September 1905], JAM; 1905 Vassar College Catalogue.

3. Vassar

1. Dorothy A. Plum and George B. Dowell, *The Great Experiment: A Chronicle of Vassar* (Poughkeepsie, N.Y.: Vassar College, 1961), 4–5.

2. See Carroll Smith-Rosenberg and Charles Rosenberg, "The Female Animal: Medical and Biological Views of Woman and Her Role in 19th-Century America," *Journal of American History* 60 (1973–74): 332–56, and "Women's Higher Education Opposed as Injurious to Health," *New York Times*, 12 August 1886, 4.

3. Plum and Dowell, *Great Experiment*, 6–7.

4. Ibid., 9; Debra Herman, "College and After: The Vassar Experiment in Women's Education, 1861–1924" (master's thesis, Stanford University, 1979), 44, 46.

5. See "The New Psychology and the New Woman" in Rosalind Rosenberg, *Beyond Separate Spheres: Intellectual Roots of Modern Feminism* (New Haven, Conn.: Yale University Press, 1982), 54–83.

6. Barbara Solomon, *In the Company of Educated Women* (New Haven, Conn.: Yale University Press, 1985), 63; Nancy Woloch, *Women and the American Experience* (New York: Alfred A. Knopf, 1984), 276. See also Mary E. Cookingham, "Bluestockings, Spinsters and Pedagogues: Women College Graduates, 1865–1910," *Population Studies* 39 (November 1984): 349–64.

7. See Anna de Koven, "The Athletic Woman," *Good Housekeeping* 55 (August 1912): 148–57.

8. Letter to author from Office of the Registrar, Vassar College, 6 May 1998.

9. Plum and Dowell, *Great Experiment*, 27; unidentified clipping, VC.

10. "Philalethean Society," *Vassar Miscellany* 35 (June 1906): 527.

11. 1907 *Vassarion*, Vassar College.

12. Unidentified clipping, Box 5, Folder 23, WSC-VC.

13. IM to JTM, 9 May 1906, JAM.

14. *Vassarion*; Plum and Dowell, *Great Experiment*, 28, 29; Herman, "College and After," 162; and letter to author from Office of the Registrar, Vassar College, 6 May 1998.

15. 1908 *Vassarian*; "Philalethean Society," *Vassar Miscellany* 36 (June 1907): 504.

16. Margaret Deland, "The Change in the Feminine Ideal," *Atlantic Monthly* 105 (March 1910): 293 (emphasis in original).

17. IM to JEM, n.d., JAM.

18. E. Sylvia Pankhurst, *The Suffragette: The History of the Women's Militant Suffrage Movement, 1905–1910* (Boston: Woman's Journal, 1911), 26; Christabel Pankhurst, *Un-*

shackled: The Story of How We Won the Vote (London: Hutchinson, 1959), 49–52; Midge MacKenzie, *Shoulder to Shoulder: A Documentary* (New York: Alfred A. Knopf, 1975), 332; and Diane Atkinson, *Suffragettes in the Purple, White and Green: London 1906–14* (London: Museum of London, 1992), 9.

19. "Miss Milholland Won't Surrender," *New York Times*, 24 October 1909, 19.

20. "Inez Milholland," *Suffragist*, 23 December 1916, 9. Although Jean is quoted as saying the Milhollands hosted the WSPU's first London parlor meeting, that would have put their meeting in 1903; given Inez's ignorance about suffrage in 1905, it is more likely the meeting occurred in 1906 or 1907, when WSPU operations were in full swing in London.

21. NWSPU Second Annual Report through 29 February 1908, WSC.

22. Inez Milholland, "The Suffrage Question in England," *Vassar Miscellany* 37 (October 1907): 27–30.

23. "Vassar Students Are Now Radicals," *New York Times*, 9 May 1909, 8.

24. "Vassar Girls' First Field Day," *New York Times*, 9 May 1909, 8; 1908 Yearbook, VC; and "Editorial Tribute to Inez Milholland," *Adirondack Record-Elizabethtown Post*, 14 August 1924, 1.

25. "Philalethean Society," *Vassar Miscellany* 37 (June 1908): 517.

26. IM to family, [May 1905], JAM; "Suffrage Martyr's Life Described," unidentified newspaper clipping, JAM.

27. 15 August 1905, JEM Diaries.

28. *Vassar Miscellany Weekly* 45 (1 December 1916): 1.

29. Elizabeth A. Daniels, *Bridges to the World: Henry Noble MacCracken and Vassar College* (Clifton Corner, N.Y.: College Avenue Press, 1994), 67–68. The debate between Taylor and his faculty continued after Milholland left. Thirteen faculty members criticized Taylor's autocratic leadership and demanded to make decisions about campus life in a protest to the Board of Trustees in December 1912. The president announced he would retire the following year. Ibid., 68. Only after Taylor stepped down in 1914 did faculty establish a formal chapter of the College Women's Equal Suffrage League that had operated clandestinely during Milholland's day. Dale Mezzacappa, "Vassar College and the Suffrage Movement," *Vassar Quarterly* 69 (Spring 1973): 4. See also Elizabeth Daniels and Barbara Page, "Suffrage as a Lever for Change at Vassar College," *Vassar Quarterly* 79 (1982): 31–35.

30. Daniels, *Bridges to the World*, 68; "Vassar Students Are Now Radicals," *New York Times*, 9 May 1909, 8.

31. James Taylor, speech, "The Conservatism of Vassar," 1909, Box 5, Folder 23, WSC-VC.

32. Herman, "College and After," 201.

33. Daniels, *Bridges to the World*, 66–68.

34. Unidentified newspaper clipping, Folder 44, IMP.

35. Harriot Stanton Blatch and Alma Lutz, *Challenging Years: The Memoirs of Harriot Stanton Blatch* (New York: G. P. Putnam's Sons, 1940), 108. A brief account even reached London. "Suffragette Students," *Votes for Women*, 18 June 1908, 247.

36. James Taylor to *Rochester Democrat and Chronicle*, n.d., Box 8, Folder 40, WSC-VC.

37. "Editorial Notes," *Woman's Journal*, 20 June 1908, 97.

38. Sherna Gluck, ed., *From Parlor to Prison: Five American Suffragists Talk about Their Lives—An Oral History* (New York: Vintage Books, 1976), 147.

39. Ellen DuBois, "Working Women, Class Relations, and Suffrage Militance: Harriot Stanton Blatch and the New York Woman Suffrage Movement, 1894–1909," *Journal of American History* 74 (1987): 47–48.

40. "Inez Milholland Wedded in Secret," *New York Times*, 16 July 1913, 1, 2.

41. "The Woman Suffrage Demonstration," *Times of London*, 23 June 1908, 11.

42. E. Sylvia Pankhurst, *The Suffragette Movement* (London: Longmans, Green and Co., 1932), 285.

43. Unidentified newspaper clipping, Folder 44, IMP.

44. "Women Who Want the Ballot Give Their Reasons," *New York Times*, 8 November 1908, pt. 5, 6.

45. 9 September 1909, JEM Diaries.

46. Equality League of Self-Supporting Women, Report for Year 1908–1909, 3, Reel 1, HSB; "Vassar Students Are Now Radicals," *New York Times*, 9 May 1909, 8; "Suffrage Marching On," *New York Sun*, 3 January 1909, pt. 2, 2; and Blatch and Lutz, *Challenging Years*, 109. Blatch claimed she sent the men away.

47. "Women Who Want the Ballot Give Their Reasons," *New York Times*, 8 November 1908, pt. 5, 6.

48. "Suffrage Marching On," *New York Sun*, 3 January 1909, pt. 2, 2; "Miss Arnold Pleads for Woman Suffrage," *New York Times*, 19 December 1908, 3; and "Things the Ballot Can't Do," *New York Sun*, 19 December 1908, 9.

49. "Suffrage Marching On," *New York Sun*, 3 January 1909, pt. 2, 2.

50. "Suffragists at a Mass Meeting," *Poughkeepsie Daily Eagle*, 1 March 1909, 8; "Vassar Girl Suffragette," *New York Times*, 1 March 1909, 14; unidentified newspaper clipping, JEM Diaries; and "From a Speech Delivered at Columbia, Theatre, Poughkeepsie, 1909," Folder 28, IMP.

51. 1 March 1909, JEM Diaries.

52. "Miss Inez Milholland," *New York Times*, 2 March 1909, 8.

53. IM to JTM, n.d., JAM.

54. Max Horn, *The Intercollegiate Socialist Society, 1905–1921: Origins of the Modern American Student Movement* (Boulder, Colo.: Westview Press, 1979), 232, 1.

55. 25 December 1916, JEM Diaries.

56. 15 January 1909, JEM Diaries.

57. Lorraine Glennon, ed., *Our Times: The Illustrated History of the 20th Century* (Atlanta: Turner Publishing, 1995), 52, 18; Peter Jennings and Todd Brewster, *The Century* (New York: Doubleday, 1998), 16.

58. Nell Irvin Painter, *Standing at Armageddon: The United States 1877–1919* (New York: W.W. Norton Co., 1987), 264; Irving Howe, *Socialism and America* (San Diego: Harcourt Brace Jovanovich, 1985), 3.

59. Meredith Tax, *The Rising of the Women: Feminist Solidarity and Class Conflict, 1880–1917* (New York: Monthly Review Press, 1980), 19.

60. "Let Something Good Be Said," *Progressive Woman*, November 1909, 16.

61. "Hail! Highbrow Socialists!" unidentified newspaper clipping, MFP.

62. Deland, "Change in the Feminine Ideal," 294.

63. "Hail, Highbrow Socialists!" unidentified newspaper clipping, MFP.

64. Ibid. and 15 January 1909, JEM Diaries.

65. Max Eastman, *The Enjoyment of Living* (New York: Harper and Brothers, 1948), 298–99.

66. 15 January 1909, JEM Diaries.

67. IM to JEM, 21 February 19[03?], JAM.

68. IM to JEM and IM to JTM, n.d., JAM.

69. 25 December 1903, JEM Diaries; Jeff Hirsh, *Manhattan Hotels 1880–1920* (Dover, N.H.: Arcadia Publishing, 1997), 27.

70. IM to JTM, n.d., JAM.

71. IM to JTM, 19 February 1905, JAM.

72. JEM to JTM, n.d., JAM.

73. IM to JTM, n.d., JAM.

74. IM to JTM, [1911], JAM.

75. JEM to JTM, n.d., JAM.

76. 10 May 1908, JEM Diaries.

77. 11 July 1909, JEM Diaries.

78. "Class Day," *Vassar Miscellany* 38 (June 1909): 526.

79. "Vassar College Commencement Program," VC; 8 and 9 June 1909, JEM Diaries.

80. 1909 *Vassarion*, Vassar College.

81. Jean Folkerts and Dwight Teeter, *Voices of a Nation: A History of Mass Media in the United States*, 3rd ed. (Boston: Allyn and Bacon, 1998), 314–15; Edwin Emery and Michael Emery, *The Press and America: An Interpretive History of the Mass Media*, 8th ed. (Boston: Allyn and Bacon, 1996), 200, 212.

82. See also Margaret Finnegan, "'So Much Color and Dash': Fighting for Woman Suffrage in the Age of Consumer Capitalism" (Ph.D. diss., University of California at Los Angeles, 1995).

83. Lois Banner, *American Beauty* (Chicago: University of Chicago Press, 1984), 167, 200, 164, 163, 8, 11. For an early discussion of the Gibson girl ideal, see Caroline Ticknor, "The Steel Engraving Lady and the Gibson Girl," *Atlantic Monthly* 88 (July 1901): 105–108.

84. Martha Patterson, "'Survival of the Best Fitted': Selling the American New Woman as Gibson Girl, 1895–1910," *ATQ* 9 (March 1995): 74. See also "The Gibson Girl," in Banner, *American Beauty*, 154–74; Edmund Vincent Gillon, ed., *The Gibson Girl and her America: The Best Drawings of Charles Dana Gibson* (New York: Dover, 1969); Lynn D. Gordon, "The Gibson Girl Goes to College: Popular Culture and Women's Higher Education in the Progressive Era, 1890–1920," *American Quarterly* 39 (Summer 1978): 211–30.

85. Sandra Adickes, *To Be Young Was Very Heaven: Women in New York before the First World War* (New York: St. Martin's Press, 1997), 9.

86. See Martha Banta, *Imaging American Women: Idea and Ideals in Cultural History* (New York: Columbia University Press, 1987), 91; Carolyn Kitch, *The Girl on the Magazine Cover: The Origins of Visual Stereotypes in American Mass Media* (Chapel Hill: University of North Carolina Press, 2001), 3; and Patterson, "'Survival of the Best Fitted,'" 74, 81.

87. Banta, *Imaging American Women*, 88.

88. WSPU Annual Report, "List of Subscribers, March 1, 1909, to February 28, 1910" and "List of Subscribers, March 1, 1910, to February 28, 1911," Reel 13, WSC.

89. "Miss Milholland Won't Surrender," *New York Times*, 24 October 1909, 19.

90. 5 August 1909, JEM Diaries.

91. 8 July 1909, JEM Diaries.

92. Norman MacKenzie and Jeanne MacKenzie, *The Fabians* (New York: Simon and Schuster, 1977), 43, 155; A. M. McBriar, *Fabian Socialism and English Politics, 1884–*

1918 (Cambridge: Cambridge University Press, 1966), 107; and Edward R. Pease, *The History of the Fabian Society* (London: Frank Cass and Co., 1963), 186.

93. Margaret Cole, *The Story of Fabian Socialism* (Stanford, Calif.: Stanford University Press, 1961), 128; Membership files, FSA; MacKenzie and MacKenzie, *The Fabians*, 326, 345, 347; Polly A. Beals, "Fabian Feminism: Gender, Politics, and Culture in London, 1880–1930" (Ph.D. diss., Rutgers, State University of New Jersey, New Brunswick, N.J., 1989), 172.

94. "Fabian Summer School Visitors Book, 1907–1912," FSA.

95. "Fabian Summer School," pamphlet, FSA.

96. IM to JEM, n.d., JAM; 22 August 1909, JEM Diaries.

4. Strike

1. Mari Jo Buhle, *Woman and American Socialism 1870–1920* (Urbana: University of Illinois Press, 1981), 176–77.

2. Minutes of Executive Meeting, 23 March 1909, Reel 1, WTUL.

3. See "Women's Labor" in Buhle, *Woman and American Socialism*, 176–213; Nancy Schrom Dye, *As Equals and as Sisters: Feminism, the Labor Movement and the Women's Trade Union League of New York* (Columbia: University of Missouri Press, 1980); "The Women's Trade Union League" and "The Waistmakers' Revolt" in Philip S. Foner, *Women and the American Labor Movement: From the First Trade Unions to the Present* (New York: Free Press, 1982), 120–54; Robin Miller Jacoby, "The Women's Trade Union League and American Feminism," *Feminist Studies* 3 (1975): 126–40; "Part Two" in Annelise Orleck, *Common Sense and a Little Fire: Women and Working-Class Politics in the United States, 1900–6* (Chapel Hill: University of North Carolina Press, 1995), 51–87; and "Leonora O'Reilly and the Women's Trade Union League," in Meredith Tax, *The Rising of the Women: Feminist Solidarity and Class Conflict, 1880–1917* (New York: Monthly Review Press, 1980), 95–124.

4. In 1910, nearly 90 percent of boardinghouse operators, dressmakers, laundresses, milliners, and servants were women. See Joseph Hill, *Women in Gainful Occupations 1870 to 1920: A Study of the Trend of Recent Changes in the Numbers, Occupational Distribution, and Family Relationship of Women reported in the Census as Following a Gainful Occupation*, Census Monograph 9 (Washington, D.C.: United States Printing Office, 1929), Table 43, 62.

5. Foner, *Women and the American Labor Movement*, 133; Buhle, *Women and American Socialism*, 191, 185.

6. Leon Stein, *The Triangle Fire* (Philadelphia: J. B. Lippincott Co., 1962), 159–60.

7. "The Jobless Girls," *Call*, 29 December 1909, 2.

8. Buhle, *Women and American Socialism*, 188.

9. Stein, *Triangle Fire*, 158, 163.

10. Joyce Gold, *From Trout Stream to Bohemia: Greenwich Village—A Walking Guide through History* (New York: Old Warren Road Press, 1996), 45; 9 October 1909, and 1, 10, 11, 21 November 1909, JEM Diaries.

11. Secretary's Report to Executive Board, 20 October 1909, and Minutes of WTUL meeting, 7 February 1910, Reel 1, WTUL.

12. Rheta Childe Dorr, *What Eight Million Women Want* (Boston: Small, Manard and Co., 1910), 171–74; Stein, *Triangle Fire*, 164–65; Orleck, *Common Sense and a Little Fire*, 59; Foner, *Women and the American Labor Movement*, 140; "Mary E. Dreier

Suffers Arrest," *Call*, 5 November 1909, 1–2; Buhle, *Women and American Socialism*, 191; and "Arrest Strikers for Being Assaulted," *New York Times*, 5 November 1909, 1.

13. Minutes of Special Meeting of the Executive of the League, 13 November 1909, Reel 1, WTUL.

14. "30,000 Waist Makers Declare Big Strike," *Call*, 23 November 1909, 1; Foner, *Women and the American Labor Movement*, 137. Strike estimates ranged from 15,000 to 40,000 workers. Ibid.

15. These characterizations draw on Nan Enstad, *Ladies of Labor, Girls of Adventure: Working Women, Popular Culture, and Labor Politics at the Turn of the Twentieth Century* (New York: Columbia University Press, 1999).

16. Orleck, *Common Sense and a Little Fire*, 53.

17. "Memoir of Alva Murray (Smith) Vanderbilt Belmont," Matilda Young Papers, Duke Special Collections, Perkins Library, Duke University, Durham, N.C.

18. Draft manuscript, Alva Belmont biography, Box 9, Folder 289, Doris Stevens Papers, SL. See also John Sledge, "Alva Smith Vanderbilt Belmont," *Alabama Heritage* (Spring 1997): 6–17.

19. "Mrs. Pankhurst Stirs Big Crowd, $2,000 Is Raised," *New York American*, 25 November 1909, n.p., Reel 3, HSB.

20. "Mrs. Pankhurst Bids US Farewell," *New York Times*, 1 December 1909, 6; "Mrs. Pankhurst at Farewell Meeting," *Call*, 1 December 1909, 1; "Mrs. Pankhurst at Cooper Union," 1, *Woman's Journal*, 11 December 1909, 199–200; and Midge Decter, *Shoulder to Shoulder: A Documentary* (New York: Alfred A. Knopf, 1975), 142.

21. "Suffragettes in Row with Police in Cooper Square," *New York World*, 1 December 1909, 1.

22. "Mrs. Pankhurst's Farewell Address," *Woman's Journal*, 11 December 1909, 199. Milholland went to the pier with Blatch the next day to see Pankhurst off. *New York Herald*, 1 December 1909, n.p., Reel 1, HSB.

23. "Mrs. Pankhurst Bids US Farewell," *New York Times*, 1 December 1909, 6; Anita Raeburn, *The Militant Suffragettes* (London: Michael Joseph, 1973), 131.

24. Foner, *Women and the American Labor Movement*, 138.

25. "Suffragists to Aid Girl Waist Strikers," "Mrs. Pankhurst Sails," and "Benefit for Suffragists," all in *New York Times*, 2 December 1909, 3; "Waist Makers Fined a Flimsy Charge," *Call*, 2 December 1909, 1.

26. "Throng Cheers on the Girl Strikers," *New York Times*, 6 December 1909, 1.

27. Untitled speeches, Folders 31 and 30, IMP.

28. Untitled speech, Folder 31, IMP; "Medals Given to Girl Strikers Just Out of Jail," *New York World*, 23 December 1909, 1.

29. "Record of Police Persecution," *Call*, 8 December 1909, 3.

30. See *Thornhill v. Alabama*, 310 U.S. 88 (140); "Picketing as Free Speech: Early Stages in the Growth of the New Law of Picketing," *University of Pittsburgh Law Review* 14 (1953): 397–418.

31. "Girl Strikers Protest against Magistrates," *Survey* 23 (8 January 1910): 489.

32. Foner, *Women and the American Labor Movement*, 138, 139.

33. "Girl Strikers, 2,000 in Number, Beat Off Thugs," *New York World*, 18 December 1909, 3; "Medals Given to Girl Strikers Just Out of Jail," *New York World*, 23 December 1909, 1; and "Waist Strike Story Told to Rich Women," *Call*, 16 December 1909, 2.

34. "Inez Milholland Helping," *New York Times*, 16 December 1909, 3.

35. Tax, *Rising of the Women*, 114; Buhle, *Women and American Socialism*, 225; and Orleck, *Common Sense and a Little Fire*, 62.

36. Enstad, *Ladies of Labor*, 135, 109.

37. Lois Banner, *American Beauty* (Chicago: University of Chicago Press, 1984), 187–88, 195–201.

38. Dye, *As Equals and as Sisters*, 92–93.

39. Mary S. Oppenheimer, "The Suffrage Movement and the Socialist Party," *New Review* 3 (December 1915): 359–60; Buhle, *Women and American Socialism*, 171.

40. Theresa Malkiel, *The Diary of a Shirtwaist Striker* (1910; reprint, Ithaca, N.Y.: ILR Press, School of Industrial and Labor Relations, Cornell University, 1990), 106.

41. IM to New York Socialist Party treasurer, n.d., Reel 7, Socialist Party, Local New York, Letter Books, 1907–14, SOC.

42. "Medals Given to Girl Strikers Just Out of Jail," *New York World*, 23 December 1909, 1.

43. "Report on the Philadelphia Convention," undated speech, Folder 29, IMP.

44. "Waistmakers Winning in New York and Philadelphia Despite Police Persecution," *Call*, 23 December 1909, 1–2.

45. "Waist Strike Pickets Parade through Shop District in Autos," *Call*, 22 December 1909, 1; "Society Women Ride in Parade with Strikers," *New York World*, 22 December 1909, 4; and Virginia Scharff, *Taking the Wheel: Women and the Coming of the Motor Age* (New York: Free Press, 1991), 81; and "Autos for Strikers in Shirtwaist War," *New York Times*, 21 December 1909, 1.

46. "Record of Police Persecution in the Waistmakers' Strike," *Call*, 23 December 1909, 1; Mary Brown Sumner, "The Spirit of the Strikers," *Survey* 23 (22 January 1910): 550–55.

47. 11 December 1909, JEM Diaries; "Inez Milholland Held in Strike Case," *New York Times*, 18 January 1910, 1; and "Philadelphia Strikers Answer Bosses; New York Waist Makers Firm," *Call*, 19 January 1910, 1–2.

48. "Inez Milholland Held in Strike Case," *New York Times*, 18 January 1910, 1. A posthumous newspaper profile has Milholland being bailed out by her father under protest. *Adirondack Record–Elizabethtown Post*, 14 August 1924, 1.

49. "Philadelphia Strikers Answer Bosses; New York Waist Makers Firm," *Call*, 19 January 1910, 1–2.

50. "Inez Milholland Held in Strike Case," *New York Times*, 18 January 1910, 1.

51. Malkiel, *Diary of a Shirtwaist Striker*, 175.

52. Foner, *Women and the American Labor Movement*, 146–47.

53. Stein, *Triangle Fire*, 166.

54. Quoted in Buhle, *Women and American Socialism*, 200.

55. "Girl Strikers Tell the Rich Their Woes," *New York Times*, 16 December 1909, 3; "Waist Strike Story Told to Rich Women," *Call*, 16 December 1909, 1.

56. Untitled speech, Folder 31, IMP.

57. IM to EB, 20 October 1913, Folder 2, IMP.

58. *Call*, 28 March 1911, 1.

59. Rose Schneiderman and Lucy Goldthwaite, *All for One* (New York: Paul S. Eriksson, 1967), 96; Stein, *The Triangle Fire*, 168; and Helen Marot, "A Woman's Strike: An Appreciation of the Shirtwaist Makers of New York," *Proceedings of the Academy of Political Science in the City of New York, 1910*, no. 1 (1910): 127.

5. Villager

1. Inez Milholland, "The Liberation of a Sex," *McClure's* 40 (February 1913): 181–88.

2. Quoted in Sylvia A. Law, "Crystal Eastman: NYU Law Graduate," *New York University Law Review* 66 (1963): 1975.

3. Keith Richwine, "The Liberal Club: Bohemia and the Resurgence in Greenwich Village, 1912–1918" (Ph.D. diss., University of Pennsylvania, 1968), 42, 195–99.

4. Floyd Dell, *Homecoming, An Autobiography* (Port Washington, N.Y.: Kennikat Press, 1969), 247.

5. Albert Parry, *Garrets and Pretenders: A History of Bohemianism in America* (New York: Covici-Friede, 1933; rev. ed., New York: Dover Publications, 1960), 255.

6. William O'Neill, *The Last Romantic: A Life of Max Eastman* (New York: Oxford University Press, 1978), 29.

7. Linda Gordon, *Woman's Body, Woman's Right: Birth Control in America* (New York: Penguin Books, 1990), 189; Carroll Smith-Rosenberg, *Disorderly Conduct: Visions of Gender in Victorian America* (New York: Alfred A. Knopf, 1985), 292. See also "Breaking with the Past," in John D'Emilio and Estelle Freedman, *Intimate Matters: A History of Sexuality in America* (New York: Harper & Row, 1988), 222–35.

8. Nancy Cott, *The Grounding of Modern Feminism* (New Haven, Conn.: Yale University Press, 1987), 45.

9. Eric Sandeen, ed., *The Letters of Randolph Bourne: A Comprehensive Edition* (Troy, N.Y.: Whitston Publishing Co., 1981), 82.

10. Ellen Kay Trimberger, "The New Woman and the New Sexuality," in Adele Heller and Lois Rudnick, *1915, the Cultural Moment: The New Politics, the New Woman, the New Psychology, the New Art, and the New Theatre in America* (New Brunswick, N.J.: Rutgers University Press, 1991), 105.

11. See Leslie Fishbein, *Rebels in Bohemia: The Radicals of the Masses, 1911–1917* (Chapel Hill: University of North Carolina Press, 1982), 77, 75; Ellen Chesler, *Woman of Valor: Margaret Sanger and the Birth Control Movement in America* (New York: Simon and Schuster, 1992), 65; Ellen Key, *Love and Marriage* (New York: G. P. Putnam's Sons, 1911); Havelock Ellis, *Man and Woman: A Study of Human Secondary Sexual Characteristics*, 5th ed. (New York: Charles Scribner's Sons, 1915); and "Birth Control and Social Revolution," in Gordon, *Woman's Body, Woman's Right*, 183–242.

12. D'Emilio and Freedman, *Intimate Matters*, 223–26. See also John C. Burnham, "The New Psychology," in Heller and Rudnick, *1915, the Cultural Moment*, 117–27; Sanford Gifford, "The American Reception of Psychoanalysis," in Heller and Rudnick, *1915, the Cultural Moment*, 128–45; Nathan Hale, *Freud and the Americans* (New York: Oxford University Press, 1971); and "Bohemianism and Freudianism," in Arthur Frank Wertheim, *The New York Little Renaissance: Iconoclasm, Modernism, and Nationalism in American Culture, 1980–1917* (New York: New York University Press, 1976), 61–77.

13. Notes in Folder 37, IMP. See also "Letta Anna Stetter Hollingsworth," in Edward James, Janet Wilson James, and Paul Boyer, eds., *Notable American Women, 1607–1950*, vol. 2 (Cambridge, Mass.: Belknap Press, Harvard University Press, 1973), 206–208.

14. Fishbein, *Rebels in Bohemia*, 96.

15. For more on Boyce and Hapgood, see Ellen Kay Trimberger, ed., *Intimate Warriors: Portraits of a Modern Marriage, 1899–1944* (New York: Feminist Press, 1991).

16. Inez Haynes Irwin, "The Adventures of Yesterday," 454, unpublished manuscript, Inez Haynes Irwin Papers in "The History of Women," Reel 974, SL.

17. Max Eastman, *The Enjoyment of Living* (New York: Harper and Brothers, 1948), 320.

18. "Crystal Eastman," *Nation* 127 (8 August 1928): 124.

19. Blanche Wiesen Cook, ed., *Crystal Eastman on Women and Revolution* (New York: Oxford University Press, 1978), 6; 16 June 1909, JEM Diaries.

20. Joseph Freeman, *An American Testament: A Narrative of Rebels and Romantics* (New York: Farrar and Rinehart, 1936), 103; Allen Churchill, *The Improper Bohemians: A Recreation of Greenwich Village in Its Heyday.* New York: E. P. Dutton and Co., 1959), 27.

21. Eastman, *Enjoyment of Living*, 321.

22. Crystal Eastman Papers, Box 6, Folder 189, SL.

23. Eastman, *Enjoyment of Living*, 322.

24. See Jill Kerr Conway, "Annis Bertha (Ford) Eastman," in Edward James, Janet Wilson James, and Paul Boyer, eds., *Notable American Women, 1607–1950*, vol. 1 (Cambridge, Mass.: Belknap Press, Harvard University Press, 1971), 542–43, and Max Eastman to IM, 25 December 1909, Folder 9, IMP.

25. 19 December 1909, JEM Diaries, and Eastman, *Enjoyment of Living*, 324.

26. Max Eastman to IM, 25 December 1909, Folder 9, IMP.

27. Eastman, *Enjoyment of Living*, 326, 327.

28. Ibid., 403–404.

29. Churchill, *Improper Bohemians*, 29.

30. Eastman, *Enjoyment of Living*, 325–26; 15 March 1910, 29 May 1910, JEM Diaries.

31. See Linda McMurry, *To Keep the Waters Troubled: The Life of Ida B. Wells* (New York: Oxford University Press, 1998), and Patricia Schechter, *Ida B. Wells-Barnett and American Reform, 1880–1930* (Chapel Hill: University of North Carolina Press, 2001).

32. 8 and 9 March 1909, JEM Diaries; Jacqueline L. Harris, *History and Achievement of the NAACP* (New York: Franklin Watts, 1992), 26; and W. E. B. Du Bois, "National Committee on the Negro," *Survey*, 12 June 1909, 408. See also Margaret White Ovington, "The National Association for the Advancement of Colored People," *Journal of Negro History* 9 (April 1924): 107–16.

33. Part 1, Reel 1, NAACP.

34. Minutes of Special Meeting of National Negro Committee, 7 April 1910, Reel 1, NAACP.

35. Proceedings of the National Negro Conference, Reel 8, NAACP; 23 June 1910, JEM Diaries; and W. E. B. Du Bois, *The Autobiography of W. E. B. Du Bois* (New York: International Publishers, 1968), 256. Du Bois reported in August 1910 to an office provided by Milholland at 20 Vesey Street. Jean Milholland wrote a women's column for the *Crisis* from December 1910 through June 1911.

36. "The Races Congress," *Crisis*, September 1911, 200–209.

37. 14 May 1910, JEM Diaries; *Suffragist*, 23 December 1916, 3; IM to W. E. B. Du Bois, n.d., and 18 September 1916, Reel 5, WEBD; and "Two Friends," *Crisis*, January 1917, 116.

38. David Levering Lewis, *W. E. B. Du Bois: The Biography of a Race, 1868–1919* (New York: Henry Holt Co., 1993), 520; "The Negro Party," *Crisis*, October 1916, 268; and W. E. B. Du Bois, *The Amenia Conference: An Historic Negro Gathering*, Troutbeck Leaflet no. 8 (Amenia, N.Y.: Privately printed at Troutbeck Press, 1925), 18, in Special Collections-URL, University of California at Los Angeles.

39. 26 May 1910, 9 June 1910, and 28 August 1910, JEM Diaries; IM to JTM, n.d., JAM.

40. John Sledge, "Alva Smith Vanderbilt Belmont." *Alabama Heritage*, Spring 1997, 14; Consuelo Vanderbilt Balsan, *The Glitter and the Gold* (New York: Harper and Brothers,

1952), 169; and Leila J. Rupp, "Feminism and the Sexual Revolution in the Early Twentieth Century: The Case of Doris Stevens," *Feminist Studies* 15 (Summer 1989): 300–301.

41. Alva Belmont biography, manuscript, 16, Box 9, Folder 290, Doris Stevens Papers, SL.

42. "Report on the Philadelphia Convention," Folder 29, IMP.

43. 29 June 1910, JEM Diaries.

44. "Mrs. Belmont Goes Abroad," *New York Times*, 30 June 1910, 3.

45. Balsan, *Glitter and the Gold*, 90.

46. "Saturday, July 23," *Votes for Women*, 22 July 1910, 704–705; "Faith and Works," *Votes for Women*, 29 July 1910, 729.

47. "International Women's Franchise Club," *Votes for Women*, 15 April 1910, 463; "The Will of the People," *Votes for Women*, 29 July 1910, 724; and "Saturday, July 23," *Votes for Women*, 22 July 1910, 704–705.

48. 5 December 1920, JEM Diaries.

49. E. Sylvia Pankhurst, *The Suffragette: The History of the Women's Militant Suffrage Movement, 1905–1910* (Boston: Woman's Journal, 1911), 26; Christabel Pankhurst, *Unshackled: The Story of How We Won the Vote* (London: Hutchinson, 1959), 49–52; Midge MacKenzie, *Shoulder to Shoulder: A Documentary* (New York: Alfred A. Knopf, 1975), 332; Diane Atkinson, *Suffragettes in the Purple, White, and Green: London 1906–14* (London: Museum of London, 1992), 9; and "The Will of the People," *Votes for Women*, 29 July 1910, 724–25.

50. 26 July, 3 and 4 September 1910, JEM Diaries.

51. "Mrs. Belmont Home for Suffrage War," *New York Times*, 16 September 1910, 9.

6. Lawyer

1. IM to Dean and Faculty of Harvard School of Law, n.d., Folder 25, IMP.

2. "Inez Milholland a Suffragette Bride," *New York Sun*, 16 July 1913, 3.

3. "Harvard Rejects Suffragette Plea," *New York Times*, 22 October 1909, 5; letters from H. L. Higginson and George Ernest to President A. Lawrence Lowell, both 8 October 1909, Folder 959, President A. Lawrence Lowell's Papers 1909–1914, HUA.

4. IM to Dean and Faculty of Harvard School of Law, n.d., Folder 25, IMP.

5. Virginia G. Drachman, *Women Lawyers and the Origins of Professional Identity in America: The Letters of the Equity Club, 1887 to 1890* (Ann Arbor: University of Michigan Press, 1993), 4, 3.

6. *Bradwell v. Illinois*, 83 U.S. (16 Wall.) 130, 141 (1872). See also *In re Bradwell*, 55 Ill. Sup. Ct. Rep. 535 (1869).

7. Barbara J. Harris, *Beyond Her Sphere: Women and the Professions in American History* (Westport, Conn.: Greenwood Press, 1978), 110.

8. *14th Census of the United States Taken in the Year 1920*, vol. 4: *Population, 1920 Occupations* (Washington, D.C.: U.S. Government Printing Office, 1921), 42.

9. Karen Berger Morello, *The Invisible Bar: The Woman Lawyer in America to the Present* (New York: Random House, 1986), 198.

10. Mabel E. Witte, "Women in Law," *Vassar Alumnae Monthly* 2 (January 1911): 43.

11. IM to family, [May 1905], JAM.

12. Unidentified newspaper clipping, Folder 44, IMP.

13. *14th Census*, 42.

14. IM to Dean and Faculty of Harvard School of Law, n.d., Folder 25, IMP.

15. Corporation Records, 19 (1907–1910): 363, HUA; President and Fellows of Harvard College from Dean James Barr Ames, 9 October 1909, Folder 967, President A. Lawrence Lowell's Papers 1909–1914, HUA.

16. "Miss Milholland Won't Surrender," *New York Times*, 24 October 1909, 19. Milholland was not the first woman to apply to the Harvard law school; the school also rejected Helen Sawyer in 1871 and rejected a plea from Radcliffe College seniors in 1915. The ban stuck until 1950. Morello, *Invisible Bar*, 90, 69, 100.

17. IM to Dean and Faculty of Harvard School of Law, n.d., Folder 25, IMP.

18. "Miss Milholland Won't Surrender," *New York Times*, 24 October 1909, 19.

19. Quoted in Maureen Honey, ed., *Breaking the Ties That Bind: Popular Stories of the New Woman, 1915–1930* (Norman: University Press of Oklahoma, 1992), 69.

20. "The Spokesman for Suffrage in America," *McClure's* 39 (July 1912): 337.

21. "The First Year out of College," *Vassar Alumnae Magazine* 2 (January 1911): 45 and (November 1910): 11. See also "After Vassar, What?" *Outlook*, 30 June 1915, 518–23.

22. Debra Herman, "College and After: The Vassar Experiment in Women's Education, 1861–1924" (Thesis, Stanford University, 1979), 234, 251, 240, 214, 235.

23. "History of New York University—Women in the Law School," folder, NYU; "100 Years of Women—1892–1992," publication, NYU Archives.

24. Phyllis Eckhaus, "Restless Women: The Pioneering Alumnae of New York University School of Law," *New York University Law Review* 66 (December 1991): 1997, 2013.

25. Sylvia A. Law, "Crystal Eastman: NYU Law Graduate," *New York University Law Review* 66 (1963): 1991.

26. Eckhaus, *Restless Women*, 2003, 2007, 2009, 2005, 2006. Doty wrote a book about her findings, *Society's Misfits* (New York: Century Co., 1916).

27. Undated speech, Folder 30, IMP.

28. Undated speech, Folder 29, IMP.

29. Transcript, Office of the Registrar, NYU Law School.

30. "Women Will Be Watchers at Polls," *New York Times*, 8 November 1910, 8.

31. "Women Turn Tables on Artemus Ward," unidentified newspaper clipping, Reel 5, HSB.

32. "Snare for Voters Is Set by Women; Who Can Escape?" *New York World*, 6 November 1911, 6.

33. "How the Suffrage Referendum Was Won in New York State," *Women's Political World*, 7 July 1914, 6.

34. "Women Will Be Watchers at Polls," *New York Times*, 8 November 1910, 8; "Miss Milholland Was Given Great Ovation," *New York Enterprise*, 11 November 1910, n.p., WSC-VC, Box 8, Folder 40.

35. "Next Legislature Safely Democratic," *New York Times*, 9 November 1910, 3.

36. "Women Celebrate Washington Victory," *New York Times*, 11 November 1910, 9.

37. Ibid.; *New York Enterprise* clipping, 11 November 1910, n.p., WSC-VC, Box 8, Folder 40.

38. *New York Sun*, 15 July 1911, n.p., and *New York Press*, 16 July 1913, n.p., both in JAM.

39. "Women's Political Union after 'Cold Storage Looie,'" unidentified newspaper clipping, 27 October 1911, Reel 5, HSB.

40. Program of forty-third annual NAWSA convention, Louisville, Ky., 1911, Reel 58, NAWSA.

41. "Rejoicing Suffragists Meet in National Convention," *Woman's Journal*, 21 October 1911, 330.

42. "If Women Voted," script, Folder 29, IMP.

43. "Women Urge Triangle Trial," *New York Times*, 2 February 1912, 18.

44. "Grand Ball Given by Suffragettes," *New York American*, n.d., and "Pledged the Dancers at Suffrage Ball," *Sun*, 2 February 1912, both in Reel 2, HSB.

45. "Vast Throng at Dance of Suffragists," *Brooklyn Standard Union*, 12 January 1913, n.p., Reel 2, HSB.

46. Alva Belmont biography, manuscript, Box 9, Folder 290, Doris Stevens Papers, SL.

47. 22 September 1908, 22 August 1913, 21 March 1904, 29 November 1910, 4 February 1912, JEM Diaries.

48. 21 September 1910, JEM Diaries.

49. Mabel Ward Cameron, ed., *The Biographical Cyclopaedia of American Women*, vol. 1 (New York: Halvord Publishing Co., 1924), 22.

50. 7 June 1910 and 31 December 1910, JEM Diaries.

51. 24 September 1909, JEM Diaries.

52. Transcript, Office of the Registrar, NYU Law School.

53. *New York University Bulletin* 11 (9 June 1911): 31.

54. Unidentified newspaper clipping, Folder 40, IMP.

55. "Miss Milholland Was Given Great Ovation," *New York Enterprise*, 11 November 1910, n.p., Box 8, Folder 40, WSC-VC.

56. Commencement program, NYU Archives.

57. 21 April 1912, JEM Diaries.

58. 15 June and 14 July 1912, JEM Diaries.

59. 12 June 1912 and 5 July 1912, JEM Diaries.

60. 27 July 1912, JEM Diaries.

61. "Miss Milholland Gets Up Slayer's Defense," *New York World*, 19 October 1912, 16; 14 October 1912, JEM Diaries; "State Prisons Slave Pens, Osborne Says," *New York Sun*, 13 July 1913, 1; and "Facts about Sing Sing," Folder 32, IMP.

62. *New York Press*, 16 July 1913, n.p.

63. "Miss Milholland Gets Up Slayer's Defense," *New York World*, 19 October 1912, 16.

64. "Enlist Suffragists for a Circus Holiday," *New York Times*, 1 April 1912, 7.

65. Anna Howard Shaw to IM, 8 September 1912, Folder 27, IMP. Shaw also reminded Milholland about a hundred-dollar pledge she owed NAWSA. Ibid.

7. Spectacle

1. "Women Parade and Rejoice at the End," *New York Times*, 7 May 1911, 1; "Army in Skirts Has Day's March Toward Its Goal," *New York World*, 7 May 1911, 1–2; "Order of March of the Woman Suffrage Parade," *Woman's Journal*, 144; and "Great Parade," *Woman's Journal*, 13 May 1911, 145.

2. Shelley Stamp Lindsey, "'Eight Million Women Want—?': Women's Suffrage, Female Viewers and the Body Politic," *Quarterly Review of Film and Video* 16, no. 1 (1995): 3. See also Frances Diodato Bzowski, "Spectacular Suffrage; or, How Women Came Out of the Home and into the Streets and Theaters of New York City to Win the Vote," *New York History* 76 (1995): 71–74; "Parades: Shoulder to Shoulder, Women March," in Linda Lumsden, *Rampant Women: Suffragists and the Right of Assembly* (Knoxville: University of Tennessee Press, 1997), 70–95; and Michael McGerr, "Popular Style and Women's Power, 1830–1930," *Journal of American History* 77 (December 1990): 874.

3. See "View of Press Has Changed," *Woman's Journal*, 30 November 1912, 382. Inez missed the first Fifth Avenue parade in 1910 because she was recuperating from appendicitis.

4. "Inez Milholland Boissevain Dies in Los Angeles," *New York Sun*, 26 November 1916, 1.

5. "Suffrage Army on Parade," *New York Times*, 5 May 1912, 1.

6. "Half Million Cheer Parade," *Woman's Journal*, 16 November 1912, 361, 366.

7. "To Be 'Inez Milholland' for N.J. Suffrage Hosts," *New York Tribune*, n.d., Reel 3, HSB.

8. "Inez Milholland Is Wedded Abroad," *New York Press*, 16 July 1913, 5.

9. "Women in Historical Poses for Suffrage," *New York Times*, 18 January 1911, 9; "A Vision of Brave Women," program, Reel 2, HSB; and "Roosevelt Center of Suffrage Host," *New York Times*, 3 May 1913, 1.

10. See Karen Blair, "Pageantry for Women's Rights: The Career of Hazel MacKaye 1913–1923," *Theatre Survey* 31 (1990): 25–45.

11. "Six Periods of American Life," manuscript, MacKaye Family Papers, Special Collections, Dartmouth College Library, Hanover, N.H.; "Woman's Advance Told by Pageant," *New York Tribune*, 18 April 1914, 7.

12. Wallace Irwin and Inez Milholland, "Two Million Women Vote," *McClure's* 40 (January 1913): 251.

13. Mary Holland Kinkaid, "The Feminine Charms of the Woman Militant," *Good Housekeeping* 54 (February 1912): 153.

14. Speech, n.d., Folder 30, IMP.

15. "Speech to Dartmouth Men," n.d., Folder 30, IMP.

16. Speech, n.d., Folder 30, IMP.

17. "My Hopes for Suffrage," speech, n.d., Folder 30, IMP.

18. Speech, n.d., Folder 32, IMP.

19. "My Hopes for Suffrage," speech, n.d., Folder 30, IMP. For more on eugenics, see Linda Gordon, *Woman's Body, Woman's Right: Birth Control in America*, rev. ed. (New York: Penguin Books, 1990), 133–55.

20. IM to [?], n.d., Folder 26, IMP.

21. "From a Speech Delivered in the New York State Assembly Chamber, 1910," Folder 28, IMP.

22. Mary Ryan, *Womanhood in America: From Colonial Times to the Present* (New York: New Viewpoints, 1975), 246.

23. See "From a Speech Delivered at Columbia, Theatre, Poughkeepsie, 1909," Folder 28, IMP.

24. Speech to Dartmouth Club, n.d., Folder 30, IMP.

25. See Nancy Cott, *The Grounding of Modern Feminism* (New Haven, Conn.: Yale University Press, 1987), 276–83.

26. "Talked Suffrage at Smoker," *Kansas City Star*, 4 February 1912, n.p., Box 9, CP; flier, "Mass Meeting at Christ Church," Reel 2, HSB; unidentified newspaper clipping, Reel 3, HSB; "From a Speech Delivered in the New York State Assembly Chamber, 1910," Folder 28, IMP; "Woman Suffrage Wants Sacrifices," *New York Times*, 23 December 1910, 12; "1910 Speech to Women's Legislative League in Albany," Folder 28, IMP; and *New York Press* clipping, 18 March 1912, n.p., WSC-VC, Box 8, Folder 40.

27. "The Spokesman for Suffrage in America," *McClure's* 39 (July 1912): 335–37.

28. *New York Press* clipping, 24 January 1912, n.p., Box 8, Folder 40, WSC-VC.

29. *Springfield* [Mass.] *Republican*, 22 January 1912, n.p., Box 8, Folder 40, WSC-VC.

30. "The Spokesman for Suffrage in America," 336.

31. "Suffragist Talks to Genesee Diners," *New York Times*, 19 January 1913, pt. 2, 14.

32. "Talked Suffrage at Smoker," *Kansas City Star*, 4 February 1912, n.p., Box 9, CP.

33. Alva Belmont biography, manuscript, Box 9, Folder 290, Doris Stevens Papers, SL.

34. "Woman Suffrage Wants Sacrifices," 23 December 1910, *New York Times*, 12.

35. IM to AP, [November 4] 1913[?], Reel 5, NWP: SY.

36. "Report on the Philadelphia Convention," [1912], Folder 29, IMP.

37. "Mrs. Boissevain Heckled," *New York Times*, 21 March 1914, 1. See also "Heckles Miss Milholland," *New York Times*, 4 February 1912, pt. 2, 1.

38. "Miss Milholland Heckled by Antis," *New York Times*, 10 March 1913, 20.

39. "Other Paraders," *Woman's Journal*, 6 May 1911, 138–39.

40. Kinkaid, "Feminine Charms of the Woman Militant," 153.

41. Unidentified newspaper clipping, JAM.

42. IM to Louis Wiley, 9 May 1913; IM to Sarah Addington, [May 1913]; and Sarah Addington to JTM, [1937?]. All in JAM.

43. 24, 25, and 31 December 1908, and 1 January 1909, JEM Diaries.

44. Speech, n.d., Folder 29, IMP.

45. "Report on the Philadelphia Convention," Folder 29, IMP.

46. Irwin and Milholland, "Two Million Women Vote," 245.

47. "Report on the Philadelphia Convention," Folder 29, IMP.

48. Judith Schwarz, *Radical Feminists of Heterodoxy: Greenwich Village, 1912–1940* (Lebanon, N.H.: New Victoria Publishers, 1982), 9–10; Inez Haynes Irwin Papers, Reel 1, SL.

49. Inez Haynes Irwin, "The Adventures of Yesterday," 413, unpublished manuscript in Inez Haynes Irwin Papers, History of Women, Reel 974, SL.

50. Lois Rudnick, "The New Woman," in Adele Heller and Rudnick, *1915, the Cultural Moment: The New Politics, the New Woman, the New Psychology, the New Art, and the New Theatre in America* (New Brunswick, N.J.: Rutgers University Press, 1991), 73.

51. Schwarz, *Radical Feminists of Heterodoxy*, 13, 14, 91.

52. *New York Press*, 16 July 1913, n.p.

53. Isaac N. Stevens, *An American Suffragette* (New York: William Rickey and Co., 1911), 18.

54. Ibid., 17.

55. See Barbara Welter, *Dimity Convictions: The American Woman in the Nineteenth Century* (Athens: Ohio University Press, 1976), 21–41.

56. Max Eastman, *The Enjoyment of Living* (New York: Harper and Brothers, 1948), 320.

57. John Fox Jr. to IM, 21 November 1912, Folder 14, IMP.

58. [?] to IM, 6 March 1911, Folder 13, IMP.

59. [John Black] to IM, n.d., Folder 15, IMP.

60. "Upton Sinclair," in James J. Martine, *Dictionary of Literary Biography*, vol. 9: *American Novelists, 1910–1945, Part 3* (Detroit: Gale Research Co., 1981), 27; Floyd Dell, *Upton Sinclair: A Study in Social Protest* (New York: AMS Press, 1927), 103. See also Mary Craig Sinclair, *Southern Belle* (Phoenix: Sinclair Press, 1962), 173.

61. Mary Craig Sinclair to EB, n.d., Folder 18, IMP.

62. Upton Sinclair to IM, 14 August 1911, Folder 13, IMP.

63. See IM to Upton Sinclair, n.d., USP.

64. Upton Sinclair to IM, 1 June 1911, Folder 13, IMP; IM to Upton Sinclair, n.d., USP.

65. 25 June 1911, JEM Diaries.

66. Upton Sinclair to IM, 14 August 1911, Folder 13, IMP.

67. "Upton Sinclair Says Wife Has Left Him," *New York Times*, 24 August 1911, 1.

68. Upton Sinclair to IM, n.d., Folder 13, IMP.

69. See Edward L. Tucker, "John Fox Jr.," in Perry J. Ashley, ed., *Dictionary of Literary Biography*, vol. 9: *American Novelists, 1910–1945, Part II* (Detroit: Gale Research Co., 1983), 25–27.

70. Unidentified newspaper clipping, Box 9, FFP.

71. John Fox Jr. to IM, 16 November 1912 and 17 November 1912, Folder 13, IMP.

72. John Fox Jr. to IM, 23 November 1912, and John Fox Jr. to IM, n.d., Folder 14, IMP.

73. John Fox Jr. to IM, 21 November 1912, Folder 14, IMP.

74. John Fox Jr. to IM, 18 November 1912, Folder 14, IMP.

75. John Fox Jr. to IM, 23 November 1912, Folder 14, IMP.

76. 15 October 1912; 9, 11, 16 November 1912; and 27, 29 December 1912, JEM Diaries.

77. 27 December 1912 and 13 January 1912, JEM Diaries.

78. 25 December 1912, JEM Diaries.

79. John Fox Jr. to IM, n.d., Folder 13, IMP.

80. 8 December 1912, JEM Diaries.

81. John Fox Jr. to IM, n.d., Folder 14, IMP (emphasis in original).

8. Riot

1. "Plan Big Parade at Inauguration," *Woman's Journal*, 4 January 1913, 1.

2. AP interview, SOHC, 73; "Suffrage Parade," Report of the Committee on the District of Columbia, U.S. Senate, Pursuant to Sen. Resolution 499 of March 4, 1913, submitted by Mr. Jones, 29 May 1913, 63rd Congress, Report No. 53, 134.

3. "'The Most Beautiful and Dignified Thing': The Woman Suffrage Procession and Pageant, March 3, 1913," in Lucy Grace Barber, "Marches on Washington, 1894–1963: National Political Demonstrations and American Political Culture" (Ph.D. diss., Brown University, 1996, 106–107, 80).

4. 2 March 1913, JEM Diaries.

5. *New York Tribune*, 2 March 1913, 3; "5,000 of Fair Sex Ready to Parade," *Washington Post*, 3 March 1913, 1; "Beautiful Essex County Suffragette Denies Rumors," *Essex County Republican*, 7 March 1913, 1; "Vote as Aid to Beauty," *Washington Post*, 3 March 1913, 10.

6. "Suffrage Thousands Will March To-day," *New York American*, 2 March 1913, 3.

7. Official Program of the Woman's Suffrage Procession, Reel 49, NAWSA.

8. IM to Lucy Burns, 7 February 1913, and AP to IM, 12 February 1913, Reel 1, NWP: SY.

9. 25 January 1909, JEM Diaries; "5,000 Women March," *New York Times*, 4 March 1913, 1.

10. Martha Vicinus, "Male Space and Women's Bodies: The Suffragette Movement," in *Independent Women: Work and Community for Single Women* (Chicago: University of Chicago Press, 1985), 261, 266.

11. "5,000 Women March at Capital," *San Francisco Examiner*, 4 March 1913, 1; AP interview, SOHC, 78; "100 Are in Hospital," *Washington Post*, 4 March 1913, 10; and "Parade Protest Arouses Senate," *New York Times*, 5 March 1913, 8.

12. Sarah J. Moore, "Making a Spectacle of Suffrage: The National Woman Suffrage Pageant, 1913," *Journal of American Culture* 20 (Spring 1997): 94.

13. "Pioneering in Pageantry," unpublished manuscript, 9, HM.

14. 3 March 1913, JEM Diaries.

15. "Score the Police for Inefficiency," *Washington Evening Star*, 4 March 1913, 1, 12.

16. IM to AP, 17 March 1913, Reel 2, NWP: SY.

17. "Suffragette Counsel in Tong Man's Trial," *Call*, 1 March 1913, 1; "Suffragette as a Portia," *Los Angeles Times*, 11 March 1913, 1.

18. "Women to Protest against Treatment," *Call*, 6 March 1913, 2.

19. See "Mob Breaks Up Pageant," *Louisville Courier-Journal*, 4 March 1913, 1; "Police Must Explain," *Washington Post*, 6 March 1913, 3; "Say Police Urged Mob On in Insults to Women Hikers," *Chicago Tribune*, 7 March 1913, 1, 2; "She Cracked Him on Nose," *Los Angeles Times*, 16 March 1913, 1; "Say Police Urged Mob On in Insults to Women Hikers," *Chicago Tribune*, 7 March 1913, 1; "Parade Protest Arouses Senate," *New York Times*, 5 March 1913, 8; and "Tell Stories of Indignities," *Louisville Courier-Journal*, 7 March 1913, 1.

20. See Herbert Gans, *Deciding What's News: A Study of CBS Evening News, NBC Nightly News, Newsweek and Time* (New York: Vintage Books, 1980), 43–45.

21. "Anti-Suffragism Gets a Hard Blow," *New York Times*, 5 March 1913, 16. See also the following editorials: "Hoodlums vs. Gentlewomen," *Chicago Tribune*, 5 March 1913, 6; "Woman's Suffrage," *Raleigh News & Observer*, 6 March 1913, 4; "The Worms Turn," *Los Angeles Times*, 9 March 1913, pt. 2, 6; "Disgrace to the Capital," *New York Tribune*, 5 March 1913, 8; "How Differently We Do Things Here," *San Francisco Examiner*, 8 March 1913, 24; "Rowdyism in Washington," *Louisville Courier-Journal*, 13 March 1913, 4; and "Ruffians," *Atlanta Constitution*, 5 March 1913, 6. See also Moore, "Making a Spectacle of Suffrage," 79, 101, and Barber, "Marches on Washington."

22. Barber, "Marches on Washington," 132; Eleanor Flexner, *Century of Struggle: The Woman's Rights Movement in the United States* (Cambridge, Mass.: Belknap Press, Harvard University Press, 1959; reprint, New York: Atheneum, 1971), 262; "Put Suffrage before Senate," *Louisville Courier-Journal*, 16 March 1913, 3; and Inez Haynes Irwin, *The Story of the Woman's Party* (New York: Harcourt, Brace, and Co., 1921), 149.

23. "Suffrage Parade," Senate Report 53, xiii.

24. See Martin Green, *New York 1913: The Armory Show and the Paterson Strike Pageant* (New York: Charles Scribner's Sons, 1988), and David Levering Lewis, *W. E. B. Du Bois: Biography of a Race, 1868–1919* (New York: Henry Holt, 1993), 459–61.

25. Irwin, *The Story of the Woman's Party*, 31.

26. "Washington Mob Ruins the Parade of the Suffragists," *Atlanta Constitution*, 4 March 1913, 1; see "Mob Breaks Up Pageant," *Louisville Courier-Journal*, 4 March 1913, 1; "Mobs at Capitol Defy Police," *Chicago Tribune*, 4 March 1913, 1–2; "U.S. Cavalry Routs Mob," *Los Angeles Times*, 4 March 1913, 1; "Score the Police for Inefficiency," *Washington Evening Star*, 4 March 1913, 1; and "Excoriate Policemen," *Los Angeles Times*, 7 March 1913, 1.

27. "Suffrage Crusaders in Thrilling Pageant Take City by Storm," *Washington Evening Star*, 3 March 1913, 1. See also James McGovern, "The American Woman's Pre–World War I Freedom in Manners and Morals," *Journal of American History* 55 (September 1968): 326–27.

28. For more on Duncan, see Peter Kurth, *Isadora: A Sensational Life* (Boston: Little, Brown, 2001).

29. "Suffrage Crusaders in Thrilling Pageant Take City by Storm," *Washington Evening Star*, 3 March 1913, 1.

30. For more on the limits of beauty as power, see Barbara Sichtermann, *Femininity: The Politics of the Personal* (Minneapolis: University of Minnesota Press, 1986), 41–53, and Una Stannard, "The Mask of Beauty," in Vivian Gornick and Barbara Moran, eds., *Woman in Sexist Society* (New York: Basic Books, 1971), 118–30.

31. The marchers' vulnerability was similar to that experienced by British suffragettes who made a "sacrifice of their bodies" when they forced themselves into male space. See Vicinus, "Male Space and Women's Bodies," 247–80.

32. Liesbet van Zoonen, "Spectatorship and the Gaze," in *Feminist Media Studies* (London: Sage Publications, 1994), 87. For a discussion on other ways suffragists engaged the male gaze, see Shelley Stamp Lindsay, "*Eighty Million Women Want—?*: Women's Suffrage, Female Viewers and the Body Politic," *Quarterly Review of Film & Video* 16, no. 1 (1995): 1–22.

33. Martha Banta, *Imaging American Women: Idea and Ideals in Cultural History* (New York: Columbia University Press, 1987), 82.

34. Carrie Chapman Catt and Nettie Rogers Shuler, *Woman Suffrage and Politics: The Inner Story of the Suffrage Movement* (New York: Charles Scribner's Sons, 1923), 290–91.

35. "Government Disgrace, Asserts Suffragist," *New York Tribune*, 4 March 1913, 7.

36. "5,000 Women March at Capital," *San Francisco Examiner*, 4 March 1913, 1.

37. Linda Gordon, *Woman's Body, Woman's Right: Birth Control in America*, rev. ed. (New York: Penguin Books, 1990), 191.

38. Unidentified news clipping, Box 7, CP; "10,000 Marchers in Line," *New York Times*, 4 May 1913, 2; "Missing Their Opportunities," *Woman's Protest*, September 1912, 4; and speech, n.d., Folder 29, IMP.

39. See unsigned letter to Alice Stone Blackwell, 14 January 1913; AP to Mary Ware Dennett, 15 January 1913; AP to Alice Stone Blackwell, 15 January 1913; and Nellie Quander to AP, 17 February 1913. All in Reel 1, NWP: SY. Anna Howard Shaw to AP, 5 March 1913, Reel 2, NWP: SY.

40. See Paula Giddings, *When and Where I Enter: The Impact of Black Women on Race and Sex in America* (New York: Bantam, 1984), 161–62; "The Southern Question," in Aileen Kraditor, *The Ideas of the Woman Suffrage Movement, 1890–1920* (New York: Columbia University Press, 1965), 162–218; Rosalyn Terborg-Penn, "Discrimination against Afro-American Women in the Woman's Movement, 1830–1920," in Sharon Harley and Rosalyn Terborg-Penn, eds., *The Afro-American Woman: Struggles and Images* (Port Washington, N.Y.: Kennikat Press, 1978), 17–27; Rosalyn Terborg-Penn, *African American Women in the Struggle for the Vote, 1850–1920* (Bloomington: Indiana University Press, 1998), 110–12, 123–25, 161; and Marjorie Spruill Wheeler, *New Women of the New South: The Leaders of the Woman Suffrage Movement in the Southern States* (New York: Oxford University Press, 1993), 108–12.

41. "National Suffrage and the Race Problem," *Suffragist*, 14 November 1914, 3.

42. IM to EB, [?] April 1916, Folder 4, IMP; "Want Negresses to Have Ballot, but Not a Dance," *New York World*, 7 May 1911, 1–2.

43. Mary Church Terrell, *A Colored Woman in a White World* (reprint, New York: G. K. Hall, 1996), 212; "Living Tribute to Inez Milholland," *Adirondack Record-Elizabethtown Post*, 21 August 1924, 4.

44. "Howard Participates in the Suffragette and Inaugural Parades," *Howard University Journal*, 14 March 1913, 1; "Suffrage Paraders," *Crisis*, April 1913, 296. Another racist inci-

dent occurred when whites ordered Ida Wells-Barnett to march with other black women instead of the Illinois delegation. See Wanda Hendrickson, "Ida B. Wells-Barnett and the Alpha Suffrage Club of Chicago," in Marjorie Spruill Wheeler, *One Woman, One Vote: Rediscovering the Woman Suffrage Movement* (Troutdale, Ore.: NewSage Press, 1995), 263–76.

45. See Cherrie Moraga and Gloria Anzaldúa, *This Bridge Called My Back: Writings by Radical Women of Color* (Watertown, Mass.: Persephone Press, 1981); Angela Davis, *Women, Race, and Class* (New York: Random House, 1981); Bonnie Thornton Dill, "Race, Class, and Gender: Prospects for an All-Inclusive Sisterhood," *Feminist Studies* 9 (Spring 1983): 131–50; Gloria Hull, Patricia Bell Scott, and Barbara Smith, eds., *All the Women Are White, All the Blacks Are Men, but Some of Us Are Brave: Black Women's Studies* (Old Westbury, N.Y.: Feminist Press, 1982): Margarita Melville, ed., *Twice a Minority: Mexican-American Women* (St. Louis: C.V. Mosby Co., 1980); Phyllis Marynick Palmer, "White Women/Black Women: The Dualism of Feminist Identity and Experience in the United States," *Feminist Studies* 9 (Spring 1983): 151–70.

46. IM to EB, November 1913, Folder 2, IMP.

47. Document dated 14 April 1913, Appellate Division, Supreme Court, First Department, New York; "Miss Milholland a Lawyer," *New York Times*, 15 April 1913, 13.

48. "9,696 March for Cause of Women," *New York World*, 4 May 1913, 1; "City Officials Review Line in Men's Stand," *New York Tribune*, 4 May 1915, 3; "Crowds and Police Praised by Leader," *New York World*, 4 May 1913, 3; "10,000 Marchers in Suffrage Line," *New York Times*, 4 May 1913, 1; "Crowds Cheer Suffrage Host in Big Parade," *New York Evening Mail*, 3 May 1913, n.p., Reel 2, HSB; "Eyes to the Front Will Be the Parade Order," *New York Tribune*, 3 May 1913, 6; and *New York Sun*, 4 May 1913, 1.

49. "Calls Life Torture in Sing Sing Cells," *New York Times*, 12 May 1913, 4; "Designates J.W. Osborne," *New York Times*, 20 May 1913, 3; "Sing Sing Inquiry in June," *New York Times*, 25 May 1913, pt. 2, 3; and Mabel Ward Cameron, ed., *The Biographical Cyclopaedia of American Women*, vol. 1 (New York: The Halvord Publishing Co., 1924), 20.

50. 2 July 1913, JEM Diaries; "Thinning Out at Sing Sing," *New York Times*, 22 July 1913, 3; "Matter of the Inquiry into the Conditions of Sing Sing Prison, 1913," NYSA; and "Facts about Sing Sing," Folder 32, IMP.

9. Love

1. Max Eastman, *Love and Revolution* (New York: Random House, 1964), 80.

2. Louis Wilkinson, ed., *The Letters of Llewelyn Powys* (London: John Lake, The Bodley Head, 1943), 33.

3. Passport, Folder 39, IMP.

4. Joan Dash, *A Life of One's Own: Three Gifted Women and the Men They Married* (New York: Harper & Row, 1973), 161; "Eugen Boissevain, Retired Importer," *New York Times*, 31 August 1949, 23.

5. "Mr. Milholland Sends Blessing to Inez, Bride," *New York Mail*, 16 July 1913, n.p.; "29-Day Milholland Wooing," *New York American*, 16 July 1913, 1; and "Inez Milholland Wedded in Secret," *New York Times*, 16 July 1913, 1.

6. 2 and 12 July 1913, JEM Diaries.

7. Rex Barratt, *The Hey-day of the Great Atlantic Liners* (Redruth, England: Truran Publications), 17; Gordon Newell, *Ocean Liners of the 20th Century* (Seattle: Superior Publishing Co., 1963), 85.

8. Nicholas Cairis, *North Atlantic Panorama* (Middletown, Conn.: Wesleyan University Press, 1977), 32.

9. Franklin D. Roosevelt, "Queen with a Fighting Heart," *Sea Breezes* (1950), reprinted in Newell, *Ocean Liners*, 25.

10. "Mrs. Boissevain Proposed," *New York Times*, 25 November 1913, 3; "Wasn't Mrs. Boissevain's Secret a Corking One?" *San Francisco Chronicle*, 19 December 1915, 5.

11. IM to EB, 5 November 1913, and IM to EB, 20 April 1916, Folder 4, IMP.

12. IM to EB, 5 November 1913, Folder 2, IMP.

13. IM to JTM, telegram, 11 July 1913, JAM.

14. 15 July 1913, JEM Diaries.

15. "Inez Milholland a Bride," *New York American*, 15 July 1913, 1.

16. Ibid.; "Father Upset Plans of Inez Milholland," *New York Times*, 18 July 1913, 1; and "Inez Milholland a Suffragette Bride," *New York Sun*, 16 July 1913, 3.

17. 20 July 1913, JEM Diaries.

18. "Inez Milholland, Wed, Won't Leave Suffrage Course," *New York World*, 16 July 1913, 9.

19. 15 July 1913, JEM Diaries; unidentified newspaper clippings, JAM.

20. 12 July 1913, JEM Diaries.

21. 20 July 1913 and 12 July 1913, JEM Diaries.

22. "Mr. Milholland Sends Blessing to Inez, Bride," *New York Mail*, 16 July 1913, n.p., JAM.

23. "Father Upset Plans of Inez Milholland," *New York Times*, 18 July 1913, 1.

24. 21 July 1913, JEM Diaries.

25. 29 July 1913, JEM Diaries.

26. 31 July 1913, JEM Diaries.

27. 9 August 1913, JEM Diaries.

28. Nancy Milford, *Savage Beauty: The Life of Edna St. Vincent Millay* (New York: Random House, 2001), 270.

29. 10–12 August 1913, JEM Diaries.

30. 9 September 1913, JEM Diaries.

31. IM to EB, 14 October 1913, Folder 2, IMP.

32. See Michel Foucault, *The History of Sexuality* (New York: Pantheon Books, 1978), 3–4.

33. "The Liberation of a Sex," *McClure's* 40 (February 1913): 185.

34. "The Woman and the Man," *McClure's* 40 (April 1913): 192.

35. Allen Davis, "Crystal Eastman," in Edward James, Janet Wilson James, and Paul Boyer, eds., *Notable American Women, 1607–1950*, vol. 1 (Cambridge, Mass.: Belknap Press, Harvard University Press, 1971), 544.

36. Max Eastman, *The Enjoyment of Living* (New York: Harper and Brothers, 1948), 380.

37. See Lois Banner, *American Beauty* (Chicago: University of Chicago Press, 1984), 172–73; Carolyn Forrey, "The New Woman Revisited," *Women's Studies* 2 (1974): 47. Even Village playwrights emphasized such fulfillment through love and marriage in their work. June Sochen, *The New Woman in Greenwich Village, 1910–1920* (New York: Quadrangle Books, 1972), 34–35, 89–92.

38. Lynn D. Gordon, "The Gibson Girl Goes to College: Popular Culture and Women's Higher Education in the Progressive Era, 1890–1920," *American Quarterly* 39 (Summer 1987): 224; Barbara Kuhn Campbell, *The "Liberated" Woman of 1914: Prominent Women in the Progressive Era* (Ann Arbor: UMI Research Press, 1979), 76.

39. Leila J. Rupp, "Feminism and the Sexual Revolution in the Early Twentieth Century: The Case of Doris Stevens," *Feminist Studies* 15, no. 2 (Summer 1989): 296.

40. Ellen Kay Trimberger, "The New Woman and the New Sexuality," in Adele Heller and Lois Rudnick, eds., *1915, the Cultural Moment: The New Politics, the New Woman, the New Psychology, the New Art, and the New Theatre in America* (New Brunswick, N.J.: Rutgers University Press, 1991), 105.

41. Lois Palken Rudnick, *Mabel Dodge: New Woman, New Worlds* (Albuquerque: University of New Mexico Press, 1984), 96–97. Reed found himself in Dodge's shoes when the woman he later married, Louise Bryant, conducted a passionate affair with their friend Eugene O'Neill. See Mary Dearborn, *Queen of Bohemia: The Life of Louise Bryant* (Boston: Houghton Mifflin, 1996).

42. Ellen Kay Trimberger, ed., *Intimate Warriors: Portraits of a Modern Marriage, 1899–1944* (New York: Feminist Press, 1991), 33.

43. "The Liberation of a Sex," *McClure's* 40 (February 1913): 188; Max Eastman, *Great Companions: Critical Memoirs of Some Famous Friends* (New York: Farrar, Straus and Cudahy, 1959), 89.

44. "My Hopes of Suffrage," Folder 30, IMP.

45. "Mrs. Boissevain Dies on Coast," *Call*, 27 November 1916, 1.

46. See Robert K. Sarlos, "Jig Cook and Susan Glaspell: Rule Makers and Rule Breakers," in Heller and Rudnick, *1915, the Cultural Moment*, 250–59.

47. Phyllis Eckhaus, "Restless Women: The Pioneering Alumnae of New York University School of Law," 66 *New York University Law Review* (December 1991): 2009.

48. IM to EB, 3 November 1913, Folder 2, IMP.

49. John Demos, "The American Family in Past Time," *American Scholar* 43 (Summer 1974): 436–37; John D'Emilio and Estelle Freedman, *Intimate Matters: A History of Sexuality in America* (New York: Harper and Row, 1988), 68–69, 224. A 1918 study found that 40 percent of married women and 60 percent of unmarried women masturbated. Rosalind Rosenberg, *Beyond Separate Spheres: Intellectual Roots of Modern Feminism* (New Haven, Conn.: Yale University Press, 1982), 199.

50. IM to EB, [October 1913], Folder 2; IM to EB, [?] April 1916, Folder 4; EB to IM, [?] April 1916, Folder 8. All in IMP.

51. Allan Ross Macdougall, "Husband of a Genius," *Delineator*, October 1934, 40.

52. IM to EB, [October 1913], Folder 2, IMP; IM to EB, 3 November 1913, Folder 2, IMP (emphasis in original).

53. IM to EB, [October 1913], Folder 2, IMP.

54. Ibid.

55. Ibid.

56. IM to EB, 4 November 1913, Folder 2, IMP.

57. IM to EB, 5 November 1913, Folder 2, IMP.

58. IM to EB, 4 November 1913, Folder 2, IMP.

59. Allan Ross Macdougall, "Husband of a Genius," *Delineator*, October 1934, 40.

60. IM to EB, 18 April 1916, Folder 4, IMP.

61. EB to IM, 11 April 1916, Folder 6, IMP.

62. IM to EB, 17 April 1916, Folder 4, IMP.

63. IM to EB, 3 November 1913, Folder 2, IMP.

64. EB to IM, 8 April 1916, Folder 8, IMP.

65. EB to IM, 4 April 1916, Folder 8, IMP.

66. IM to EB, 14 and [?] April 1916, Folder 4, IMP.

67. IM to EB, 23 April 1916, Folder 4, IMP.

68. IM to EB, 17 April 1916, Folder 4, IMP.

69. IM to EB, [?] October 1913, Folder 2, IMP.

10. Marriage

1. IM to EB, 5 November 1913, Folder 2, IMP.

2. IM to EB, 13 November 1913, Folder 2, IMP.

3. "Alberta Hill to Put Bridal White over Suffrage Yellow," *New York Tribune*, 26 September 1915, 6.

4. "Wasn't Mrs. Boissevain's Secret a Corking One?" *San Francisco Chronicle*, 19 December 1915, 5.

5. See, for example, "Impossible to Be Both Wife and Artist," *Evening World*, 31 August 1916, 3; "The Most Difficult Problem of Modern Civilization," *Current Literature* 48 (January 1910): 58–61; Guglielmo Ferrero, "The New Woman and the Old," *Hearst's Magazine* 22 (July 1912): 70–78; and Jessie Lynch Williams, "The New Marriage," *Good Housekeeping* 58 (February 1914): 181–85.

6. Caroline Zilburg, ed., *Women's Firsts* (Detroit: Gale Research, 1997), 394.

7. Lynn D. Gordon, "The Gibson Girl Goes to College: Popular Culture and Women's Higher Education in the Progressive Era, 1890–1920," *American Quarterly* 39 (Summer 1987): 225; James McGovern, "The American Woman's Pre–World War I Freedom in Manners and Morals," *Journal of American History* 55 (September 1968): 320–21.

8. "The Most Difficult Problem of Modern Civilization," 58; William O'Neill, *Divorce in the Progressive Era* (New Haven, Conn.: Yale University Press, 1967), 20, 24–25. The divorce rate increased from 4.5 per 1,000 marriages in 1910 to 7.7 per 1,000 marriages in 1910. Ibid.

9. Mary Ryan, *Womanhood in America: From Colonial Times to the Present* (New York: New Viewpoints, 1975), 232.

10. IM, "The Woman and the Man," *McClure's* 40 (April 1913): 196. Her comment echoes the analysis of "sex parasitism" by influential feminist Olive Schreiner, whom Milholland admired. See Ruth First and Ann Scott, *Olive Schreiner* (New York: Schocken Books, 1980), 268–71.

11. IM to EB, 14 October 1913, Folder 2, IMP.

12. Ellen Kay Trimberger, "The New Woman and the New Sexuality," in Adele Heller and Lois Rudnick, *1915, the Cultural Moment: The New Politics, the New Woman, the New Psychology, the New Art, and the New Theatre in America* (New Brunswick, N.J.: Rutgers University Press, 1991), 108.

13. IM to EB, 13 April 1916, Folder 4, IMP.

14. EB to IM, [April 1916], Folder 8, IMP.

15. EB to IM, 9 April 1916, Folder 8, IMP.

16. Elizabeth Breuer, "Edna St. Vincent Millay," *Pictorial Review*, November 1931, 52.

17. EB to IM, 12 April 1916, Folder 8, IMP.

18. JTM to EB, 17 April 1916, Folder 4, IMP.

19. IM to EB, [?] May 1915, Folder 3, IMP.

20. IM to EB, 13 November 1913, Folder 2, IMP.

21. "Inez Milholland Becomes the Bride of Rich Hollander," *New York World*, 15 July 1913, n.p., JAM.

22. Gertrude Smith to IM, undated, Folder 21, IMP.

23. Karen Berger Morello, *The Invisible Bar: The Woman Lawyer in America to the Present* (New York: Random House, 1986), 198–200.

24. 27 May 1913 and 4 June 1913, Folder 21, IMP.

25. Speech, n.d., Folder 30, IMP.

26. IM to EB, 11 November 1913, Folder 2, IMP.

27. *Women Lawyers' Journal*, October 1914, 77.

28. See Virginia Sapiro, "Women, Citizenship and Nationality: Immigration and Naturalization Policies in the U.S.," *Politics and Society* 13, no. 1 (1984): 1–26.

29. "Mrs. Blatch Never to Vote," *New York Times*, 26 March 1913, 4. Blatch regained her citizenship when her husband died in 1915. "Mrs. Blatch Takes Oath," *New York Times*, 19 August 1915, 18.

30. "Suffragists Greet 'Dutchy' with Joy," *New York Tribune*, 1 November 1913, n.p., Reel 3, HSB.

31. Maurice Leon to IM, 28 October 1913, and 14 July 1914, Folder 20, IMP.

32. IM to Sen. James O'Gorman, 19 October 1914, and O'Gorman to IM, Folder 20, IMP.

33. Congress threw out the citizenship law with the passage of the Cable Act of 1922. Nancy Cott, *The Grounding of Modern Feminism* (New Haven, Conn.: Yale University Press, 1987), 98–99.

34. "Suffragists Greet 'Dutchy' with Joy," HSB.

35. "Mrs. Inez Milholland Boissevain Carries Last Appeal of Eastern Women to the Women Voters of the West," *Suffragist*, 7 October 1916, 7.

36. "Many Families May Envy the Workhorse," *New York Times*, 25 November 1913, 13; "Women after Johnson," *New York Times*, 12 December 1913, 10; and "Programme of Suffrage Events," *Women's Political World*, 17 December 1913, 5.

37. "One Woman's Reply to Another on the Subject of Suffrage," *New York World*, 14 December 1913, Editorial Section, 1.

38. Virginia Scharff, *Taking the Wheel: Women and the Coming of the Motor Age* (New York: Free Press, 1991), 84.

39. IM to EB, 3 and 11 November 1913, Folder 2, IMP.

40. IM to EB, 11 November 1913, Folder 2, IMP.

41. "Inez Milholland Returns," unidentified newspaper clipping, JAM; Mary Holland Kinkaid, "The Feminine Charms of the Woman Militant," *Good Housekeeping* 54 (February 1912): 152.

42. IM to EB, [?] November 1913, Folder 2, IMP.

43. IM to EB, 5 November 1913, Folder 2, IMP.

44. 8 November 1913, JEM Diaries.

45. IM to EB, 13 November 1913, Folder 2, IMP.

46. IM to EB, 5 November 1913, Folder 2, IMP.

47. 17 and 24 December 1913 and 30 July 1913, JEM Diaries.

48. IM to EB, 11 [?] November 1913, Folder 2, IMP.

49. Unidentified newspaper clippings, RSP.

50. Cott, *Grounding of Modern Feminism*, 163–65.

51. "Golden Rules of Housekeeping," unidentified newspaper clipping, JAM.

52. "Suffragists Greet 'Dutchy' with Joy," *New York Tribune*, 1 November 1913, Reel 3, HSB.

53. IM to EB, [November 1913], Folder 2, IMP.

54. Speech, n.d., Folder 29, IMP; IM to EB, 5 November 1913, Folder 2, IMP.

55. "Real Beauty Show in League Pageant," *New York Times*, 18 April 1914, 11.

56. "Suffragists Miss Glory of Parade," *New York Tribune*, 3 May 1914, n.p., and "Extracts from Some Suffrage Day Speeches," *New York American*, 3 May 1914, n.p., both on Reel 3, HSB.

57. "Society Satirized in Suffrage," *New York Times*, 19 February 1916, 9.

58. "C. E. Russell at Grant's Tomb," *New York Times*, 3 May 1914, pt. 2, 12.

59. "Jury of Women Finds for Wife," *New York Times*, 20 January 1915, 9.

60. Flier, Folder 27, IMP; "Suffrage Husbands Praise Their Wives," *New York Times*, 25 February 1915, 6.

61. EB to IM, 4 April 1916, Folder 8, IMP.

62. Floyd Dell, *Homecoming: An Autobiography* (Port Washington, N.Y.: Kennikat Press, 1969), 309.

63. Allan Ross Macdougall, "Husband of a Genius," *Delineator*, October 1934, 40.

64. See Eleanor Flexner, *Century of Struggle: The Woman's Rights Movement in the United States* (Cambridge, Mass.: Belknap Press, Harvard University Press, 1959; rev. ed. New York: Atheneum, 1971), 265–67.

65. "New York," *Suffragist*, 15 May 1915, 15.

66. "Congressional Union Deputation to Senator O'Gorman," *Suffragist*, 8 May 1915, 5; "Wall Street Derides the Suffragettes," *New York Times*, 28 February 1908, 7.

67. IM, "Judicial Destruction of Laws," *Women Lawyers' Journal*, April 1915, 51.

68. "Congressional Union Deputation to Senator O'Gorman," *Suffragist*, 8 May 1915, 5.

69. "Suffrage's Women Foes and Friends Throng Capitol," *New York Herald*, 10 February 1915, 6.

70. "Mrs. Boissevain Rejected Vaudeville," *New York Times*, 15 December 1914, 6.

71. 6 August 1909, JEM Diaries.

72. 31 May 1912, 16 September 1912, 26 December 1913, and 2 May 1915, JEM Diaries.

73. IM to JEM, n.d., JAM.

74. 19, 22, 25, and 28 May 1914, JEM Diaries.

75. EB to IM, 3 April 1916, Folder 8, IMP; EB to IM, 31 May 1915, Folder 6, IMP.

76. IM to EB, 20 October 1913, and 11 November 1913, Folder 2, IMP.

77. IM to EB, 18 and 23 October 1913, Folder 2, and EB to IM, 8 April 1916, Folder 8, IMP.

78. IM to The Committee, n.d., Folder 26, IMP; IM to JTM, 14 February 1905, JAM.

79. IM to EB, n.d., Folder 3, IMP.

80. IM to EB, [?] April 1916, Folder 4, IMP.

81. IM to EB, 23 April 1916, Folder 4, IMP.

82. Barbara Kuhn Campbell, *The "Liberated" Woman of 1914: Prominent Women in the Progressive Era* (Ann Arbor: UMI Research Press, 1979), 87–88.

83. "Speech Delivered at the Berkeley Lyceum for the League for Political Education in March 1911," Folder 28, IMP.

84. Speech, n.d., Folder 31, IMP.

85. Ellen Key, *Love and Marriage* (New York: G. P. Putnam's Sons, 1911), 144, 172, 217. See also Cott, *Grounding of Modern Feminism*, 46–47, and Leslie Fishbein, *Rebels in Bohemia: The Radicals of the Masses, 1911–1917* (Chapel Hill: University of North Carolina Press, 1982), 131–33.

11. Crusader

1. "Mrs. Belmont Heads Shop Union Fight," *New York Times*, 18 November 1913, 5.

2. Ralph Hower, *History of Macy's of New York, 1858–1919* (Cambridge, Mass.: Harvard University Press, 1983), 200, 202.

3. Robert Hendrickson, *The Grand Emporiums: The Illustrated History of America's Great Department Stores* (New York: Stein and Day, 1979), 324, 325.

4. Meredith Tax, *The Rising of the Women: Feminist Solidarity and Class Conflict, 1880–1917* (New York: Monthly Review Press, 1980), 98.

5. Susan Porter Benson, *Counter Cultures: Saleswomen, Managers, and Customers in American Department Stores, 1890–1940* (Urbana: University of Illinois Press, 1986), 128.

6. Lois Rudnick, "The New Woman," in Adele Heller and Rudnick, *1915, the Cultural Moment: The New Politics, the New Woman, the New Psychology, the New Art, and the New Theatre in America* (New Brunswick, N.J.: Rutgers University Press, 1991), 73.

7. Benson, *Counter Cultures*, 289.

8. See Kathy Peiss, *Cheap Amusements: Working Women and Leisure in Turn-of-the-Century New York* (Philadelphia: Temple University Press, 1986).

9. Mary K. Maule, "What Is a Shop-Girl's Life?" *World's Work* 14 (September 1907): 9314–15.

10. "Perkins Opposes Giving of Bonuses," *New York Times*, 11 February 1914, 6.

11. Speech manuscript, n.d., Folder 31, IMP.

12. Benson, *Counter Cultures*, 135.

13. "Does It Pay the Store?" *Harper's Weekly* 58 (30 May 1914): 14, 13.

14. See issues in "Report on the Philadelphia Convention," Folder 29, IMP.

15. Speech, n.d., Folder 29, IMP.

16. "Women Police Would Banish White Slavery," *New York Tribune*, 8 March 1913, 16.

17. "Tells Why Police Women Are Needed," *New York Times*, 7 March 1913, 20.

18. IM to AP, [4 November 1913?], Reel 5, NWP: SY.

19. David Mairn to IM, 12 August 1916, Folder 23, IMP; and Philip Friedman to IM, 8 May and 22 September 1916, Folder 21, IMP.

20. Frederick C. Howe, *The Confessions of a Reformer* (New York: Charles Scribner's Sons, 1925), 242.

21. For example, "Lefty's Widow Deals Blow to Becker Defense," *New York Times*, 16 May 1914, 4.

22. "Inez Milholland," *Suffragist*, 23 December 1916, 9.

23. IM to The Committee, n.d., Folder 26, IMP; John D'Emilio and Estelle Freedman, *Intimate Matters: A History of Sexuality in America* (New York: Harper and Row, 1988), 231–33; and Ellen Chesler, *Woman of Valor: Margaret Sanger and the Birth Control Movement in America* (New York: Simon and Schuster, 1992), 99, 103–104, 150.

24. Sarah Addington, "The Newspaper Woman, Who Is She, What Is She?" *New York Tribune*, 8 August 1915, pt. 4, 12.

25. *14th Census of the United States Taken in the Year 1920*, vol. IV: *Population, 1920 Occupations* (Washington, D.C.: U.S. Government Printing Office, 1921), 42: Women.

26. Elizabeth Frazer, "The Sob-Lady," *Good Housekeeping* 61 (September 1915): 316–24.

27. "Mr. Hearst's Tin Anniversary," *New York Times*, 29 April 1913, 9.

28. Program, New York Newspaper Association dinner, Folder 25, IMP; Speech, n.d., Folder 29, IMP.

29. Inez Haynes Irwin, "The Adventures of Yesterday," 282, unpublished manuscript, Inez Haynes Irwin Papers in "The History of Women," Reel 974, SL.

30. "Miss Milholland Barred," 18 May 1913, *New York Times*, pt. 2, 1.

31. Manuscript, n.d., Folder 33, IMP.

32. "The Futility of the Suppressive Idea," n.d., Folder 34, IMP.

33. Quoted in Matthew J. Bruccoli, *The Fortunes of Mitchell Kennerley, Bookman* (New York: Harcourt Brace Jovanovich, 1986), 68.

34. "Writers Turn Out for Book Trial," *New York Times*, 7 February 1914, 9; Bruccoli, *Fortunes of Mitchell Kennerley*, 72–73.

35. Peiss, *Cheap Amusements*, 160–61. The Supreme Court ruled the First Amendment protected films in *Bursyn v. Wilson*, 343 U.S. 495 (1951).

36. Inez Milholland, letter to editor, *New York Times*, 4 February 1914, 8.

37. Manuscript, n.d., Folder 33, IMP.

38. John Sumner, letter to editor, *New York Times*, 6 February 1914, 8.

39. "Professional Services," editorial, *New York Times*, 25 July 1914, 6.

40. 23, 24, 26 September 1915, JEM Diaries.

41. Manuscript, n.d., Folder 33, IMP.

42. Inez Milholland, "Censorship," *Crisis* 13 (January 1917): 116.

43. See Eastman, *Enjoyment of Living*, 464–73.

44. Marie Jenny Howe to Mr. Gerber, 12 February 1914, Reel 8, SOC; Eastman, *Enjoyment of Living*, 469–70.

45. "Hard Words for the Newspapers," *New York Times*, 6 March 1914, 20.

46. EB to IM, 31 May 1915, Folder 6, IMP.

47. Eastman, *Enjoyment of Living*, 521–22.

48. Emma Bugbee to EB, and Lillian Wald to EB, both 6 December 1916, Folder 19, IMP.

49. See Elizabeth A. Daniels and Barbara Page, "Suffrage as a Lever for Change at Vassar College," *Vassar Quarterly* 79 (1982): 31–35.

50. "Inez Milholland," *Suffragist*, 23 December 1916, 9.

51. Nancy Milford, *Savage Beauty: The Life of Edna St. Vincent Millay* (New York: Random House, 2001), 127.

52. Norman Brittin, *Edna St. Vincent Millay* (New York: Twayne Publishers, 1967), 38.

53. Mercedes M. Randall, *Improper Bostonian: Emily Greene Balch* (New York: Twayne Publishers, 1965), 134.

54. 13 June 1915, JEM Diaries.

55. 20 May 1915, JEM Diaries.

56. See Jean Beth Elshtain, *Jane Addams and the Dream of American Democracy* (New York: Basic Books, 2002), 223–24, and Linda Schott, *Reconstructing Women's Thoughts: The Women's International League for Peace and Freedom before World War II* (Stanford, Calif.: Stanford University Press, 1997), 40–46.

57. 14 July 1917, JEM Diaries.

58. IM to EB, 6 June 1915, Folder 3, IMP.

59. EB to IM, 5 June 1915, Folder 6, IMP.

60. EB to IM, 3, 29 May 1915, Folder 6, IMP.

61. EB to IM, [Summer 1915], Folder 7, IMP.

62. IM to EB, 6 June 1915, Folder 3, IMP.

63. EB to IM, [Summer 1915], Folder 7, IMP; JTM to IM, 22 May 1915, JAM.

64. IM to JTM, [May 1915], JAM; "Marconi Returns to Serve Italy," *New York Tribune*, 23 May 1915, 1; and IM to EB, n.d., Folder 3, IMP.

65. 22, 23 May 1915, JEM Diaries.

12. Italy

1. "Floating Dead Silence Prayer on Board Liner," *New York Tribune*, 17 May 1915, 2.

2. IM to JTM, [May 1915], JAM Papers; "St. Paul's Voyage a Nervous Trial," *New York Tribune*, 31 May 1915, 3; "Submarine Pursued St. Paul to Mersey," *New York Tribune*, 2 June 1915, 1.

3. EB to IM, 3 June 1915, Folder 6, IMP.

4. Mary Roberts Rinehart, "For King and Country: No Man's Land," *Saturday Evening Post* 187 (8 May 1915): 58. Her articles were collected in *Kings, Queens, and Pawns* (New York: Doran, 1915). See also Jan Cohn, *Improbable Fiction: The Life of Mary Roberts Rinehart* (Pittsburgh: University of Pittsburgh Press, 1980).

5. Fuller, her husband, and their baby drowned in a shipwreck within sight of New York's Fire Island on their return from Italy in 1850. Julia Edwards, *Women of the World: The Great Foreign Correspondents* (Boston: Houghton Mifflin Co., 1988), 21.

6. See "Emma Bugbee" in Barbara Belford, *Brilliant Bylines* (New York: Columbia University Press, 1986), 175–82.

7. Richard Kluger, *The Paper: The Life and Death of the "New York Herald Tribune"* (New York: Vintage Books, 1989), 210–11.

8. E. Alexander Powell, *Adventure Road* (New York: Doubleday and Co., 1954), 141–43.

9. IM to EB, [May 1915], Folder 3, IMP.

10. EB to IM, 31 May 1915, Folder 6, IMP.

11. EB to IM, [Summer 1915], Folder 7, IMP.

12. EB to IM, 31 May 1915, Folder 6, IMP.

13. Mary Craig Sinclair, *Southern Belle* (Phoenix, Ariz.: Sinclair Press, 1962), 169.

14. EB to IM, 3 June 1915, Folder 6, IMP.

15. EB to IM, 18 June 1915, Folder 6, IMP.

16. See Will Irwin, *The Making of a Reporter* (New York: G. P. Putnam's Sons, 1942).

17. "Warlike France Bustles While England Blusters," *New York Tribune*, 20 July 1915, 3.

18. IM to EB, 6 June 1915, Folder 3, IMP. Addams was in Rome with an international suffrage delegation visiting each of the belligerent nations to try to persuade them to mediate their differences. Jane Addams, *Peace and Bread in Time of War* (1922; reprint, Boston: G. K. Hall & Co., 1960), 16.

19. IM to JTM, 18 June 1915, JAM; EB to IM, [Summer 1915], Folder 7, IMP.

20. IM to EB, 6 June 1915, Folder 3, IMP.

21. "Warlike France Bustles While England Blusters," *New York Tribune*, 20 July 1915, 3.

22. "Italy's Heroic Response Is Blind War Hysteria," *New York Tribune*, 24 July 1915, 5.

23. "Italians' Loss Already Put at 100,000 Troops," *New York Tribune*, 15 July 1915, 2.

24. "Italians Press Assault along 75-Mile Front," *New York Tribune*, 21 July 1915, 7.

25. Folder 35, IMP. The U.S. commissioner of immigration wrote that she planned to study emigration from Europe under war conditions. Morne Howe, 22 May 1915, Folder 35, IMP.

26. "What Americans Are Doing to Help" and "What Italy Is Doing for Its War Sufferers," undated manuscripts, Folder 35, IMP.

27. IM to EB, [Summer 1916], Folder 35, IMP.

28. S. Sonnino, Ministry of Public Affairs, to U.S. Ambassador Thomas Nelson Page, 9 July 1915, Folder 35, IMP.

29. "Italy's Wounded," manuscript, Folder 35, IMP.

30. Ibid.

31. Irwin, *Making of a Reporter*, 341.

32. Untitled manuscript, Folder 35, IMP.

33. "Italy's Heroic Response Is Blind War Hysteria," *New York Tribune*, 24 July 1915, 5.

34. "National Vanity Led Italy to Enter War," *New York Tribune*, 26 July 1915, 6.

35. "What Americans Are Doing to Help," manuscript, Folder 35, IMP.

36. "Everything German, Even Names, Taboo," *New York Tribune*, 31 July 1915, 4.

37. "Italy's Wounded," manuscript, Folder 35, IMP.

38. "Italy's Sovereign," Folder 35, and untitled manuscript, Folder 36, IMP.

39. IM to EB, 6 June 1915, Folder 3, IMP.

40. See Max Eastman, *Child of the Amazons* (New York: Mitchell Kennerley, 1913).

41. IM to EB, [May 1915], Folder 3, IMP.

42. IM to JTM, [May 1915], JAM.

43. "Inez Milholland Boissevain," *Vassar Quarterly* 2 (February 1917): 1916.

44. IM to EB, 6 June 1915, Folder 3, IMP.

45. IM to EB, 16 June 1915, Folder 6, IMP.

46. EB to IM, 17 June 1915, Folder 6, IMP.

47. EB to IM, 18 June 1915, Folder 6, IMP.

48. EB to IM, 17 June 1915, Folder 6, IMP.

49. See Linda Gordon, *Woman's Body, Woman's Right: Birth Control in America*, rev. ed. (New York: Penguin Books, 1990), 191–93.

50. Leila J. Rupp, "Feminism and the Sexual Revolution in the Early Twentieth Century: The Case of Doris Stevens," *Feminist Studies* 15, no. 2 (Summer 1989): 293.

51. EB to IM, 9 April 1916 and 15 April 1916, Folder 8, IMP.

52. EB to IM, [April 1916], Folder 8, IMP.

53. "Eugen Boissevain Sails for Italy," *New York Times*, 27 June 1915, pt. 2, 2; IM to EB, 20 April 1916, Folder 4, IMP.

54. IM to EB, 17 August 1915, Folder 3, IMP; "Polite but Firm to Mrs. Boissevain," *New York Times*, 28 September 1915, 1.

55. Il Secratrio Generale to IM, 15 August 1915, Folder 35, IMP.

56. "One Day in the War Zone," manuscript, Folder 36, IMP.

57. 23 August 1915, Folder 16, IMP.

58. "Guido" to IM, 27 August 1915, Folder 16, IMP.

59. EB to IM, [Summer 1915], Folder 7, IMP.

60. EB to IM, 3 April 1916, Folder 8, IMP.

61. "Polite but Firm to Mrs. Boissevain," *New York Times*, 28 September 1915, 1.

62. Irwin, *Making of a Reporter*, 341–42.

63. IM to EB, 8 August 1915, Folder 3, IMP.

64. "Mrs. Boissevain Could Stop War," *New York Tribune*, 28 September 1915, 8.

13. Pacifist

1. IM to EB, 8 August 1915, Folder 3, IMP.

2. "Suffragists to Ask Mayor for Meeting," unidentified newspaper clipping, CP.

3. IM to EB, [?] April 1916, Folder 4, IMP.

4. Mary A. Hill, *Charlotte Perkins Gilman: The Making of a Radical Feminist, 1860–1896* (Philadelphia: Temple University Press, 1980), 296.

5. Manuscript, n.d., Folder 32, IMP.

6. "Soldiers Tired of War," *New York Times*, 29 October 1915, 4.

7. "'Suffrage and Education,'" *Brooklyn Daily Eagle*, 1 November 1915, 22; "5,000 Women Will Watch Polls Today," *New York Tribune*, 2 November 1915, 1, 6.

8. Speech, n.d., Folder 29, IMP.

9. Eleanor Flexner, *Century of Struggle: The Woman's Rights Movement in the United States* (Cambridge, Mass.: Belknap Press, Harvard University Press, 1959; rev. ed., New York: Atheneum, 1971), 271.

10. Robert Lacey, *Ford: The Men and the Machine* (Boston: Little, Brown, and Co., 1986), 18, 103–10.

11. Barbara S. Kraft, *The Peace Ship: Henry Ford's Pacifist Adventure in the First World War* (New York: Macmillan Publishing Co., 1978), 37, 55; "Henry Ford to Push World-wide Campaign for Universal Peace," *Detroit Free Press*, 22 August 1915, 1, 6.

12. See Olive Schreiner, *Women and Labour* (London, 1911); Ruth First and Ann Scott, *Olive Schreiner* (New York: Schocken Books, 1980), 271–72, 282–84; and Linda Schott, *Reconstructing Women's Thoughts: The Women's International League for Peace and Freedom before World War II* (Stanford, Calif.: Stanford University Press, 1997), 43–44.

13. Harriet Hyman Alonso, *Peace as a Women's Issue: A History of the U.S. Movement for World Peace and Women's Rights* (Syracuse, N.Y.: Syracuse University Press, 1993), 54–55.

14. Kate Richards O'Hare, quoted in June Sochen, *Movers and Shakers; American Women Thinkers and Activists, 1900–1970* (New York: Quadrangle, 1973), 59. In 1919, O'Hare was sentenced to five years in federal prison for speaking out against the war and served thirteen months. Ibid.

15. IM to Crystal Eastman, 18 October 1916, WPP. Blanche Wiesen Cook, ed., *Crystal Eastman on Women and Revolution* (New York: Oxford University Press, 1978), 17. After the United States entered the war, Eastman and her followers briefly published the anti-war *Four Lights* newspaper until the government banned it. See Erika Kuhlman, "Women's Ways in War: The Feminist Pacifism of the New York City Woman's Peace Party," *Frontiers* 18 (June–August 1997): 80–100.

16. *New York Tribune*, 22 May 1915, 1.

17. Barbara J. Steinson, *American Women's Activism in World War I* (New York: Garland Publishing Co., 1982), 49–50, 58; Jane Addams, *The Second Twenty Years at Hull-House* (New York: Macmillan Co., 1930), 125; and Alonso, *Peace as a Women's Issue*, 66–67. See also Jane Addams, Emily Balch, and Alice Hamilton, *Women at The Hague* (New York: Macmillan, 1915).

18. Jane Addams, *Peace and Bread in Time of War* (1922; reprint, Boston: G. K. Hall & Co., 1960), 27–28.

19. Kraft, *Peace Ship*, 64–65, 67.

20. Anne Wiltsher, *Most Dangerous Women: Feminist Peace Campaigners of the Great War* (London: Pandora, 1985), 160–61; Louis P. Lochner, *America's Don Quixote: Henry Ford's Attempt to Save Europe* (London: Kegan Paul, Trench, Trubner, and Co., 1924), 33; and Kraft, *Peace Ship*, 86. See also, "Ford Peace Expedition May Be Made a Joke by Allies and America," *Washington Times*, 3 December 1915, 14.

21. Carol Gelderman, *Henry Ford, the Wayward Capitalist* (New York: Dial Press, 1981), 109, 112.

22. "Ford Recants on General Strike," *Call*, 2 December 1915, 1–2.

23. "One Woman's Reply on the Subject of Suffrage," *New York World*, 14 December 1913, Editorial Section, 1.

24. "Mrs. Boissevain Accepts," *New York Times*, 30 November 1915, 6.

25. Itinerary, HF.

26. Lella Secor Florence, "The Ford Peace Ship and After," in *We Did Not Fight: 1914–18 Experiences of War Resisters* (London: Cobden-Sanderson, 1935), 97.

27. "As the Ship Sails," *Call*, 3 December 1915, 6; "Peace Envoys Depart on Oscar II, Bearing Call to End Conflict," *Call*, 4 December 1915, 1; and Reel 1, HF.

28. Kraft, *Peace Ship*, 99, 111, 117, 121.

29. Reel 1, HF.

30. IM to EB, [December 1915], Folder 3, IMP.

31. Kraft, *Peace Ship*, 9–11.

32. IM to EB, [December 1915], Folder 3, IMP.

33. John D. Barry, "Bulletin Writer Tells of Split," *San Francisco Bulletin*, 21 December 1915, 1.

34. "'Cat and Dog Fight' Aboard Peace Ship," *Washington Star*, 20 December 1915, 2.

35. Kraft, *Peace Ship*, 136.

36. IM to EB, [December 1915], Folder 3, IMP.

37. IM to EB, [21 December 1915], Folder 3, IMP.

38. IM to EB, [December 1915], Folder 3, IMP.

39. Kraft, *Peace Ship*, 149–50.

40. Lacey, *Ford*, 144.

41. Rosika Schwimmer to Henry Ford, 15 January 1916, Accession 79, Box 9, Henry Ford Museum and Greenfield Village Research Center, Detroit, Mich.

42. Speech, n.d., Folder 29, IMP.

43. IM to EB, [December 1915], Folder 3, IMP.

44. Ibid.

45. "Ford to Rejoin Party," *San Francisco Bulletin*, 27 December 1915, 1; Florence, "Ford Peace Ship and After," 109; and Kraft, *Peace Ship*, 158, 162.

46. IM to Members and Secretary of the General Committee of the Ford Peace Expedition, [26 December 1915], Box 4, FPP.

47. See "Inez Boissevain Quits," *San Francisco Bulletin*, 27 December 1915, 1.; "Ford Party in Dispute, Mrs. Boissevain Leaves," *New York Times*, 26 December 1915, pt. 2, 1; and Meeting Minutes of Committee of Administration, Reel 2, HF.

48. Committee of Seven to Mrs. Boissevain, ca. 27 December 1915, Container 8, Folder "Ford Peace Expedition (Dec. 19, 1915–Jan. 15, 1916)," FPP.

49. James W. Gerard, *My Four Years in Germany* (New York: George H. Doran Co., 1917), 298; manuscript, n.d., Folder 34, IMP.

50. 2 January 1916, JEM Diaries.

51. IM to EB, 10 January 1916, Folder 3, IMP.

52. IM to Crystal Eastman, 18 October 1916, WPP.

53. Steinson, *American Women's Activism in World War I*, 112, 398.

54. "The Expedition in Holland," *Survey*, 12 February 1916, 585; Lochner, *America's Don Quixote*, 121, 225.

55. IM to EB, [?] April 1916, Folder 4, IMP.

56. EB to IM, 15 April 1916, Folder 8, IMP.

57. JTM to EB, 17 April 1916, Folder 4, IMP.

58. IM to EB, [?] April 1916; IM to EB, 17 April 1916, Folder 4, IMP.

59. EB to IM, 12 April 1916, Folder 8, IMP.

60. Jan Boissevain to IM, [?] April 1916, Folder 8, IMP.

61. EB to IM, 21 April 1916, Folder 8, IMP.

62. IM to EB, 9 April 1916, Folder 4, IMP.

63. IM to EB, 20 April 1916, Folder 4, IMP.

64. IM to EB, 17 April 1916, Folder 4, IMP (emphasis in original).

65. EB to IM, 12 April 1916, Folder 8, IMP.

66. IM to EB, 25 April 1916, Folder 5, IMP.

67. Mabel Vernon Interview, 68–69, SOHC.

68. AP to Mrs. John (Elizabeth) Rogers, 16 March 1916, Reel 25, NWP: SY.

69. AP to Mary Beard, 18 March 1916, Reel 25, NWP: SY.

70. Mary Beard to AP, 20 March 1916, Reel 25, NWP: SY.

71. IM to Mary Beard, [1916?], Reel 237, NWP: SY.

72. IM to EB, [?] and 12 April 1916, Folder 4, IMP.

73. IM to EB, 12 April 1916, Folder 4, IMP.

74. IM to AP, [April 1916], Reel 36, NWP: SY.

75. IM to EB, [?] April 1913 Folder 4, IMP.

76. Speech, n.d., Folder 29, IMP.

77. Unidentified newspaper clipping, Folder 40, IMP.

78. IM to Judge Louis Gibbs, 10 April 1916, Folder 21, IMP.

79. 24 April 1916, IM to EB, Folder 4, IMP.

80. IM to EB, [?] April 1916, Folder 4, IMP.

14. Execution

1. Craig Brandon, *The Electric Chair: An Unnatural American History* (Jefferson, N.C.: McFarland and Co., 1999), 9, 156.

2. William J. Bowers, *Executions in America* (Lexington, Mass.: Lexington Books, 1974), 303–304.

3. "Charles Stielow," *Independent*, 21 August 1916, 258.

4. Misha Appelbaum to Rose Pastor Stokes, 4 April 1916, RPS.

5. "Want Murderess Spared," *New York Times*, 7 November 1913, 6; "Disgrace to Hang Mrs. Wakefield, Say Suffrage Lawyers," unidentified newspaper clipping, JAM.

6. IM to Assemblymen, n.d., Folder 22, IMP; and Maurice Bloch to IM, 24 February 1915, Folder 22, IMP.

7. "Assail Court for Women," *New York Times*, 20 May 1916, 17.

8. "Women Lawyers Volunteer Free Service in the Night Court and Pave Way for 'Public Defender,'" *New York Tribune*, 7 July 1915, 7.

9. IM to EB, 17 April 1917, Folder 4, IMP.

10. Frederick C. Howe, *The Confessions of a Reformer* (New York: Charles Scribner's Sons, 1925), 242.

11. David Mairn to IM, 12 August 1916, Folder 23, IMP; Philip Friedman to IM, 8 May and 22 September 1916, Folder 21, IMP.

12. 20 June 1916, JEM Diaries.

13. Speech, n.d., Folder 32, IMP.

14. Inez Milholland Boissevain, "Another Point of View," *Women Lawyers' Journal*, January 1915, 30.

15. IM to EB, 16 April 1916, Folder 4, IMP; "A Mount Airy Bohemian Tour," *Croton Gazette*, 22–28 July 2001, C7.

16. Eleanor Flexner, *Century of Struggle: The Woman's Rights Movement in the United States* (Cambridge, Mass.: Belknap Press, Harvard University Press, 1959; rev. ed., New York: Atheneum, 1971), 276. The twelve states were Arizona, California, Colorado, Idaho, Illinois (presidential only), Kansas, Montana, Nevada, Oregon, Utah, Washington, and Wyoming.

17. "Closing Session of the Woman's Party Convention," *Suffragist*, 24 June 1916, 6.

18. Editorial, *New York Times*, 14 July 1916, 10.

19. Ida Tarbell, "Organized Women in Dramatic Phase in Political Flurry," *New York World*, 8 June 1916, 4. The five parties were the Democrats, Republicans, Progressives, Socialists, and Communists.

20. "Closing Sessions of the Woman Party's Convention," *Suffragist*, 17 June 1916, 7; "Suffrage First," *Suffragist*, 17 June 1916, 4.

21. "Last Women's Session," *Chicago Tribune*, 8 June 1916, 17; Mabel Vernon Interview, SOHC, 60.

22. Warden Osborne testified in Albany for the abolition of the death penalty. "Death Chair Horror Overcomes Osborne," *New York Times*, 4 March 1915, 7.

23. "A Feminine 'Sherlock Holmes,'" *Literary Digest* 55 (7 July 1917): 50–52.

24. Frank Marshall White, "Where There Are Women There's a Way," *Good Housekeeping* 67 (August 1918): 54–56; "The Girl That God Did Not Forget," unidentified clipping, Folder 50, IMP.

25. Ishbel Ross, *Ladies of the Press: The Story of Women in Journalism by an Insider* (New York: Harper and Brothers, 1936), 117–18.

26. "Stielow's Fate Rests with Court, Seeking New Trial," *Buffalo Times*, n.d., Folder 43, IMP.

27. "Report to the Attorney General Appointed to Investigate the Murders of Charles Phelps and Margaret Wolcott, 1917," NYSA; White, "Where There Are Women There's a Way," 56; and "Says Detective in Stielow Case Was Trapped," *Buffalo Evening News*, 15 July 1916, 1. Although the *Good Housekeeping* account has Milholland charming the information out of the detective, court records say the undercover detectives interviewed him. 160 N.Y.S. 555, 562.

28. "Stielow to Die, Cole's Decision," *Buffalo Evening News*, 26 July 1916, 1.

29. "The Girl That God Did Not Forget," unidentified clipping, Folder 50, IMP; Ethel M. Stielow to Papa, n.d., Folder 24, IMP.

30. Fred M. Parson, M.D., to Warden George Kirchwey, 9 June 1916, Folder 24, IMP.

31. Copy of Charles Stielow statement, Folder 24, IMP.

32. "Seeking Chance for Stielow to Show Innocence," *Buffalo Evening News*, 27 July 1916, 15.

33. White, "Where There Are Women There's a Way," 56.

34. "Mrs. Stielow to Ask Whitman to Save Husband," *Buffalo Evening News*, 28 July 1916, 1–2.

35. White, "Where There Are Women There's a Way," 56.

36. "Mrs. Stielow to Ask Whitman to Save Husband," *Buffalo Evening News*, 28 July 1916, 1–2.

37. "The Girl That God Did Not Forget," unidentified clipping, Folder 50, IMP.

38. White, "Where There Are Women There's a Way," 130.

39. Ibid., 130; "The Girl That God Did Not Forget," unidentified clipping, Folder 50, IMP; "Supreme Court Stays Execution of Stielow as Prison Attendants Prepare to Lead Condemned Murderer to Electric Chair," *Buffalo Evening News*, 29 July 1916, 1; and "Third Degree a Peril," *New York World*, 14 September 1916, 3.

40. Christine Lunardini, *From Equal Suffrage to Equal Rights: Alice Paul and the National Woman's Party, 1910–1928* (New York: New York University Press, 1986), 67–69; "Women to Plan Active Campaign," *New York Tribune*, 31 July 1916, 11.

41. AP to Joy Webster, 27 September 1916, Alice Paul Papers, Box 17, Folder 256, SL; 22, 27 September 1916, JEM Diaries.

42. AP to Anne Martin, 24 October 1916, Reel 35, NWP: SY.

43. IM to Mrs. Weed, [?] September 1916, Reel 36, NWP: SY.

44. IM to EB, 8 October 1916, Folder 5, IMP.

45. 21 November 1911, JEM Diaries; Mabel Ward Cameron, ed., *The Biographical Cyclopaedia of American Women*, vol. 1 (New York: Halvord Publishing Co., 1924), 22; "Vida Milholland, Lyric Soprano," flier, JAM Papers; and 20 June 1916, JEM Diaries.

46. EB to IM, 31 May 1915, Folder 6, IMP.

47. IM to EB, 6 October 1916, Folder 5, IMP.

48. Adrian Anderson, "President Wilson's Politician: Albert Sidney Burleson of Texas," *Southwestern Historical Quarterly* 77, no. 3 (1974): 339–54. According to Milholland family lore, years earlier Milholland had accused Burleson of exploiting African American laborers on his cotton plantation. As postmaster general, Burleson did systematically fire, demote, and segregate black postal workers. "Albert Sidney Burleson," in Allen Johnson, ed., *Dictionary of American Biography* (New York: Charles Scribner's Sons, 1927), 74. Milholland was convinced Burleson was out to destroy him. 14 December 1916, JEM Diaries.

49. IM to EB, 6 October 1916, Folder 5, IMP.

15. Campaign

1. "Mrs. Boissevain Off Today," *New York Times*, 4 October 1916, 4.

2. 3 November 1916, JEM Diaries; IM to EB, 6 October 1916, Folder 5, IMP.

3. 7 October 1916, JEM Diaries (written 23 September 1917).

4. 5 October 1916, JEM Diaries (written 23 September 1917).

5. 10 November 1917, JEM Diaries.

6. VM to AP, 30 October 1916, Reel 35, NWP: SY; IM to EB, 6 and 8 October 1916, Folder 5, IMP.

7. "Mrs. Inez Milholland Boissevain Carries Last Appeal of Eastern Women to the Women Voters of the West," *Suffragist*, 7 October 1916, 7.

8. Katherine Morey to AP, 13 October 1916, Reel 15, NWP: SY. The main difference between the CU and the Woman's Party of Western Voters was that members of the latter possessed the vote. Paul in effect ran both organizations in tandem, although Anne Martin chaired the Woman's Party. Within a year, they merged the two groups into the National Woman's Party.

9. "Appeal to the Women Voters," Folder 29, IMP.

10. "Last Appeal from Unenfranchised Women," *Suffragist*, 14 October 1916, 7; IM to EB, 8 October 1916, Folder 5, IMP.

11. IM to EB, 8 October 1916, Folder 5, IMP.

12. Doris Stevens to Beulah Amidon, 16 October 1916, Reel 34, NYP: SY.

13. IM to EB, 9 October 1916, Folder 5, IMP.

14. VM to AP, 30 October 1916, Reel 35, NWP: SY.

15. See Amelia Fry, "Along the Suffrage Trail," *American West* 6 (January 1969): 16–25.

16. "Here's Sisterly Gossip about Mrs. Boissevain, the Suffrage Speaker," *Idaho Statesman*, 18 October 1916, 5.

17. VM Report, [October 1916], Reel 37, NWP: SY.

18. IM to EB, 9 October 1916, Folder 5, IMP.

19. "Here's Sisterly Gossip about Mrs. Boissevain, the Suffrage Speaker," *Idaho Statesman*, 18 October 1916, 5; "Oust Wilson, Women Urge," *Idaho Statesman*, 10 October 1916, 1.

20. Memorial Tribute to Inez Milholland Boissevain, Reel 35, NWP: SY.

21. IM to EB, 9 October 1916, Folder 5, IMP.

22. "Here's Sisterly Gossip about Mrs. Boissevain, the Suffrage Speaker," *Idaho Statesman*, 18 October 1916, 5.

23. IM to AP, [4 November 1913?], Reel 5, NWP: SY.

24. Speech, n.d., Folder 30, IMP.

25. IM to EB, 17 October 1916, Folder 5, IMP.

26. "Twenty-Eight States Will Greet the Women's Hughes Campaigners," *World*, 1 October 1916, 6; "Wilson's Yellow Is a Silent Whip to Golden Special," *World*, 18 October 1916, 2; and "Facts About Hughesettes Luxurious Stumping Tour," *World*, 5 November 1916, 20.

27. "Women Voters Hear Eastern Appeal," *Suffragist*, 28 October 1916, 4.

28. "Appeal to the Women Voters," Folder 29, IMP.

29. Speech, n.d., Folder 30, IMP.

30. IM to EB, 9 October 1916, Folder 5, IMP; Sara Bard Field Interview, 355, SOHC.

31. IM to EB, 12 October 1916, Folder 5, IMP.

32. "Message from Unenfranchised Carried to Oregon and Washington," *Suffragist*, 21 October 1916, 4.

33. Margaret Whittemore to AP, 14 October 1916, Reel 15, NWP-SY.

34. Report from VM, 11 October 1916, Reel 34, NWP: SY.

35. "Life Work Was Not Completed," *Portland Evening Telegraph*, 27 November 1916, sec. 2, 1.

36. IM to EB, 9 October 1916, Folder 5, IMP.

37. JEM to AP, n.d., Reel 34, NWP: SY.

38. IM to EB, 12 October 1916, Folder 5, IMP.

39. Ida Finney Mackrille to Doris Stevens, 14 October 1916, Reel 15, NWP: SY.

40. VM Report, 13 October 1916, Reel 15, NWP: SY.

41. Vivian Pierce to AP, 22 October 1916, Reel 34, NWP: SY.

42. Abby Scott Baker to AP, 20 October 1916, Reel 34, NWP: SY; AP to Maud Younger, 21 October 1916, Reel 34, NWP: SY.

43. Press release, n.d., Reel 91, NWP: SY.

44. AP Interview, 339, SOHC (emphasis in original).

45. VM to AP, 30 October 1916, Reel 35, NWP: SY; IM to EB, 12 October 1916, Folder 5, IMP.

46. IM to EB, 12 October 1916, Folder 5, IMP.

47. "Inez Milholland," in Mabel Ward Cameron, ed., *The Biographical Cyclopaedia of American Women*, vol. 1 (New York: Halvord Publishing Co., 1924), 21.

48. VM Report, 13 October 1916, Reel 15, NWP: SY.

49. Agnes Campbell to AP, Reel 34, NWP: SY.

50. IM to EB, 12 October 1916, Folder 5, IMP.

51. Abby Scott Baker to AP, 12 October 1916, Reel 15, NWP: SY.

52. IM to EB, 15 October 1916, Folder 5, IMP; "Stielow Must Die Is Court Decision, Denying New Trial," *World*, 12 October 1916, 24; and *People v. Stielow*, 161 N.Y.S. 599 (1916).

53. EB to IM, 17 October 1916, Folder 9, IMP.

54. EB to IM, 20 October 1916, Folder 9, IMP.

55. "Message from Unenfranchised Carried to Oregon and Washington," *Suffragist*, 21 October 1916, 4.

56. IM to EB, 12 October 1916, Folder 5, IMP.

57. "Urges Women of West to Show Power of Their Votes," *Spokane Spokesman Review*, 14 October 1916, 1.

58. "Big Crowd Hears Mrs. Boissevain," *Spokane Daily Chronicle*, 14 October 1916, 2.

59. VM to AP, 30 October 1916, Reel 35, NWP: SY; IM to EB, 17 October 1916, Folder 5, IMP.

60. IM to EB, 17 October 1916, Folder 5, IMP; press release, 24 October 1916, Reel 34, NWP-SY.

61. Jane Pincus to AP, 15 October 1916, Reel 34, NWP: SY.

62. AP to IM, IM to AP, both 16 October 1916, Reel 34, NWP: SY.

63. Mabel Vernon to Doris Stevens, 14 October 1916, Reel 15, NWP: SY.

64. Vivian Pierce to AP, 15 and 21 October 1916, Reel 34, NWP: SY.

65. Harriot Stanton Blatch to Elsie Hill, 13 October 1916, Reel 15, NWP: SY.

66. Elsie Hill to Jessie Hardy MacKaye, 14 October 1916, Reel 15, NWP: SY; Katherine Morey to AP, 17 October 1916, Reel 34, NWP: SY.

67. IM to EB, 20 October 1916, Folder 5, IMP.

68. "Women Voters Hear Eastern Appeal," *Suffragist*, 28 October 1916, 4; "Woman's Party Leaders at a Luncheon and a Rally in the Orpheum," *Ogden Standard*, 17 October 1916, 2; and IM to EB, 20 October 1916, Folder 5, IMP.

69. "Rally Is Held by the Woman's Party," *Salt Lake City Tribune*, 18 October 1916, 16.

70. IM to EB, 20 October 1916, Folder 5, IMP; "Women Voters Hear Eastern Appeal," *Suffragist*, 28 October 1916, 4.

71. IM to EB, 20 October 1916, Folder 5, IMP.

72. VM Reports, 9 and 21 October 1916, Reel 34, NWP: SY; IM to EB, 20 October 1916, Folder 5, IMP; and Anne Martin speech, 21 December 1916, Reel 36, NWP: SY.

73. VM Reports, 9 and 21 October 1916, Reel 34, NWP: SY; "Women Voters Hear Eastern Appeal," *Suffragist*, 28 October 1916, 4; "Noted Suffragist Cordially Received," *Nevada State Journal*, 21 October 1916, 4; and "Mrs. Boissevain Exposes Falsity of Democrats," *Reno Evening Gazette*, 21 October 1916, 3.

74. IM to EB, 8, 17, 15 October 1916, Folder 5, IMP.

75. IM to EB, 8 October 1916, Folder 5, IMP.

76. EB to IM, 17 October 1916, Folder 9, IMP.

77. IM to EB, 20 October 1916, Folder 5, IMP.

78. VM Report, 21 October 1916, Reel 34, NWP: SY.

79. VM Report, [1916?], Reel 37, NWP: SY.

80. "Eastern Appeal Carried to Women Voters," *Suffragist*, 4 November 1916, 4; VM to AP, 30 October 1916, Reel 35, NWP: SY; and VM Report, [1916?], Reel 37, NWP: SY.

81. Doris Stevens to IM, 19 October 1916, Reel 34, NWP: SY.

82. Doris Stevens to IM, 23 October 1916, Reel 35, NWP: SY.

83. IM to EB, 8 and 15 October 1916, Folder 5, IMP.

84. EB to IM, 17 October 1916, Folder 9, IMP.

85. EB to IM, 18 October 1916, Folder 9, IMP.

86. Beulah Amidon to Doris Stevens, 19 October 1916, Reel 34, NWP: SY.

87. Beulah Amidon to Doris Stevens, 24 October 1916, Reel 35, NWP: SY.

88. Doris Stevens to Beulah Amidon, 19 October 1916, Reel 34, NWP: SY.

89. VM to AP, 30 October 1916, Reel 35, NWP: SY.

90. Beulah Amidon to Doris Stevens, 24 October 1916, Reel 35, NWP: SY; Beulah Amidon to Anne Martin, 15 December 1916, Reel 36, NWP-SY; and "Faints at Her Highest Point," *Los Angeles Times*, 24 October 1916, pt. 2, 5.

16. Martyr

1. "Noted Feminist Speaker Faints, Then Continues," *Los Angeles Examiner*, 24 October 1916, 3; "Faints at Her Highest Point," *Los Angeles Times*, 24 October 1916, pt. 2, 5.

2. "Indefatigable," *Los Angeles Times*, 28 October 1916, pt. 2, 4.

3. IM to AP, 23 October 1916, Reel 34, NWP: SY; VM to AP, 30 October 1916, Reel 35, NWP: SY.

4. AP to Doris Stevens, 23 and 24 October 1916, Reel 34, NWP: SY.

5. IM to AP and AP to IM, both 23 October 1916, and three telegrams from Paul to IM, 24 October 1916. All Reel 34, NWP: SY.

6. AP to Anne Martin, 24 October 1916, Reel 34, NWP: SY.

7. AP to Emily Perry, 29 October 1916, and AP to Crystal Eastman, 28 October 1916, Reel 35, NWP: SY.

8. AP to Crystal Eastman, Mrs. St. Clair Thompson to Iris Calderhead, and AP to Vivian Pierce, all 28 October 1916, Reel 35, NWP: SY; AP to Jessie Hardy MacKaye, 25 October 1916, Reel 34, NWP: SY.

9. "Mrs. Inez Boissevain Is Operated On Here," *Los Angeles Times*, 27 October 1916, pt. 2, 1; Dr. Catherine Lynch to AP, 25 October 1916, Reel 34, NWP: SY.

10. VM to AP, 30 October 1916, Reel 35, NWP: SY. Milholland actually may have suffered from chronic leukemia, cancer of the blood cells, whose symptoms are similar to those of aplastic, or pernicious, anemia but which was more difficult to diagnose in the 1910s. See "Cancer.gov: What You Need to Know About Leukemia," www.hcnih.gov/cancer/wyntk/leukemia. Accessed 31 January 2002.

11. "Mrs. Inez Boissevain Is Operated On Here," *Los Angeles Times*, 27 October 1916, pt. II, 1.

12. Beulah Amidon to AP, 28 October 1916, Reel 35, NWP: SY.

13. "Hearts Torn for Mrs. Boissevain," *Los Angeles Times*, 14 November 1916, pt. 2, 3.

14. Julia Hurlburt to AP, 18 November 1916, Reel 35, NWP: SY.

15. George Held to IM, 31 October 1916; Dr. Millicent Cosgrove to IM, 1 November 1916; and Misha Appelbaum to EB, 17 November 1916. All Folder 17, IMP. William Seeley to IM, Folder 23, IMP.

16. Minnie Kauffmann to IM, 9 November 1916; [?] to VM, 12 November 1916; "A well-wisher" to IM, 12 November 1916; H. F. Frasse to EB, n.d.; [?] to EB, 27 November 1916; David White to EB, 18 November 1916; and [?] to EB, 18 November 1916. All Folder 17, IMP.

17. "Miracle Is Claimed for Suffragist," *Los Angeles Examiner*, 23 November 1916, 1.

18. 26 October 1916, 26 and 31 October 1916, 4.

19. "Woman's Party Orator Makes Final Appeal," *Chicago Tribune,* 6 November 1916, 1.

20. 12 November 1916, JEM Diaries; "Inez Milholland under Knife," *Los Angeles Examiner,* 9 November 1916, 7.

21. "Blood Transfusion Aids Mrs. Boissevain," *New York Tribune,* 10 November 1916, 5; "Suffrage Victory Causes Mrs. Boissevain to Rally," *New York World,* 9 November 1916, 5.

22. Eleanor Flexner, *Century of Struggle: The Woman's Rights Movement in the United States* (Cambridge, Mass.: Belknap Press, Harvard University Press, 1959; rev. ed., New York: Atheneum, 1971), 277.

23. "Inez Milholland Is Still Critically Ill," *Los Angeles Examiner,* 11 November 1916, 1; "Hearts Torn for Mrs. Boissevain," *Los Angeles Times,* 14 November 1916, pt. 2, 3; and 22 February 1915, JEM Diaries.

24. 13 November 1916, JEM Diaries; "Parents Cannot See Inez Milholland," *Los Angeles Examiner,* 13 November 1916, 3; and "Hearts Torn for Mrs. Boissevain," *Los Angeles Times,* 14 November 1916, pt. 2, 3.

25. 13, 14 November 1916, JEM Diaries; Margaret Waddell to EB, 15 November 1916, Folder 17, IMP.

26. "Inez Milholland Undergoes Fourth Blood Transfusion," *Los Angeles Examiner,* 15 November 1916, 1.

27. "Mrs. Boissevain Close to Death," *New York Tribune,* 16 November 1916, 4.

28. 16 November 1916, JEM Diaries.

29. "Pleurisy Sets In," *Los Angeles Times,* 16 November 1916, pt. 2, 1.

30. 17 November 1916, JEM Diaries; "Mrs. Boissevain Is Better," *New York Times,* 20 November 1916, 6; and "Miracle Is Claimed for Suffragist," *Los Angeles Examiner,* 23 November 1916, 1.

31. Beulah Amidon, "Inez Milholland," *Suffragist,* 24 November 1917, 9.

32. "Stielow Again Sentenced to Die," *New York Tribune,* 26 October 1916, 7; Frank Marshall White, "Where There Are Women There's a Way," *Good Housekeeping* 67 (August 1918): 131.

33. 13, 15 November 1916, JEM Diaries.

34. 18 November 1916, JEM Diaries.

35. 17 November 1916, JEM Diaries.

36. 18 November 1916, JEM Diaries.

37. "Miracle Is Claimed for Suffragist," *Los Angeles Examiner,* 23 November 1916, 1; 23 November 1916, JEM Diaries.

38. "Death Claims Inez Milholland-Boissevain," *Los Angeles Examiner,* 26 November 1916, 1, 2.

39. "Mrs. Boissevain Felt No Fear," *Los Angeles Examiner,* 27 November 1916, 3.

40. 12 November 1921, JEM Diaries.

41. Max Eastman, *The Enjoyment of Living* (New York: Harper and Brothers, 1948), 572.

42. 25 November 1917, JEM Diaries.

43. Death certificate, 28 November 1916, California Office of Vital Records.

44. 26 November 1916, JEM Diaries; "Mrs. Boissevain Felt No Fear," 3.

45. "Mrs. Boissevain's Body Now Home," *New York Tribune,* 3 December 1916, 8.

46. "Service Here for Mrs. Boissevain," *New York Times,* 3 December 1916, pt. 1, 3; "Burial Near Old Home," *Plattsburgh Daily Press,* 4 December 1916, 4; 29 November 1916, JEM Diaries.

47. "Women Mourn Mrs. Boissevain; Plan Memorial," *New York Tribune*, 28 November 1916, 9; Mary Spencer Blackford to Dr. John H. Holmes, 20 December 1916, Reel 36, NWP: SY.

48. "Mrs. Boissevain's Body Now Home," *New York Tribune*, 3 December 1916, 8.

49. "Receiving Blotter, Sing Sing Prison," NYSA; White, "Where There Are Women There's a Way," 131; and "Saves Life of Stielow," *New York Times*, 4 December 1916, 6.

50. 28 August 1912, 30 May 1915, and unidentified newspaper clipping, JEM Diaries.

51. *Elizabethtown Post*, 14 August 1919, n.p., JAM.

52. 4 December 1916, JEM Diaries.

53. "Mrs. Boissevain's Body Now Home," *New York Tribune*, 3 December 1916, 8; 22 September 1912 and 4 December 1916, JEM Diaries. Although townspeople voted to rename the mountain Mt. Inez, the U.S. Department of the Interior Geological Survey never officially approved the name change from Mt. Discovery. "Mount Renamed Inez," *New York Times*, 12 December 1916, 7.

54. "Her Long Journey Ended," *Plattsburgh Daily Press*, 6 December 1916, 4.

55. "J. A. Milholland Weds," *New York Times*, 24 July 1917, 11.

56. "Women Mourn Mrs. Boissevain; Plan Memorial," *New York Tribune*, 28 November 1916, 9.

57. Sara Bard Field to Lucy Burns, 4 December 1916, Reel 36, NWP: SY.

58. "Will Rest in Adirondacks," *Los Angeles Times*, 27 November 1916, pt. 2, 1.

59. "Miss Martin Pays Tribute to the Late Suffragette," *Reno Evening Gazette*, 27 November 1916, 8.

60. *Adirondack Record*, 1 December 1916, 1, 7.

61. "Mrs. Boissevain Dies in Hospital," *New York Tribune*, 27 November 1916, 1.

62. "Inez Milholland," *Suffragist*, 23 December 1916, 9; Emma Bugbee to EB, 6 December 1916, Folder 18, IMP.

63. Flier, Reel 36, NWP: SY; "Meeting Honors Mrs. Boissevain," *New York Tribune*, 22 December 1916, 9.

64. Remarks of Crystal Eastman, 21 December 1916, Reel 36, NWP: SY.

65. "Ship Body Today," *Los Angeles Times*, 28 November 1916, pt. 2, 1; "Inez Boissevain to Be Buried Here," *New York Times*, 27 November 1916, 11.

66. "Inez Milholland Boissevain," *Call*, 28 November 1916, 6; "Two Friends," *Crisis* 13 (January 1917): 115; and "Press Comments on the Life and Work of Inez Milholland," *Suffragist*, 9 December 1916, 10.

67. *Women Lawyers' Journal*, December 1916, 21.

68. Resolution of NAACP, 2 January 1917, Reel 13, NAACP; Resolution of Women's Trade Union League, Reel 2, WTUL. Civic Club of New York to Eugen Boissevain, 5 December 1916, and Heterodoxy Club to Eugen Boissevain, 14 December 1916, Folder 19, IMP.

69. "Repetitions," in Carl Sandburg, *Cornhuskers* (New York: Henry Holt and Co., 1918), 47.

70. Marjory Nelson, "Ladies in the Street: A Sociological Analysis of the National Woman's Party, 1910–1930" (Ph.D. diss., State University of New York at Buffalo, 1976), 99.

71. VM to AP, 30 October 1916, Reel 35, NWP: SY.

17. Icon

1. Anne Martin to Beulah Amidon, 14 December 1916, Reel 36, NWP: SY.

2. Beulah Amidon to Anne Martin, 15 December 1916, Reel 36, NWP: SY.

3. Anne Martin Speech, 21 December 1916, Reel 36, NWP: SY.

4. Memorial Program, 1 January 1917, Reel 37, NWP: SY; Sara Bard Field Interview, 360, SOHC.

5. Anne Martin to Alice Carpenter, 17 December 1916, Reel 36, NWP: SY.

6. AP to Elizabeth Rogers, 17 December 1916, Reel 36, NWP: SY. The *Suffragist* published an Inez Milholland memorial number devoted entirely to her on 23 December 1916.

7. "Pay Tribute to Mrs. Boissevain," *Philadelphia Ledger*, 26 December 1916, n.p.

8. 24 December 1916, JEM Diaries.

9. "The National Memorial Service in Memory of Inez Milholland," *Suffragist*, 30 December 1916, 7; JEM to AP, 22 December 1916, Reel 36, NWP: SY; and "Boissevain Memorial in Capitol Ends in Vote Appeal," *Call*, 26 December 1916, 3.

10. "The National Memorial Service in Memory of Inez Milholland," *Suffragist*, 30 December 1916, 7.

11. Inez Haynes Irwin, *The Story of the Woman's Party* (New York: Harcourt, Brace, 1921), 22; AP Interview, 170, SOHC.

12. "Memorial Address," *Suffragist*, 30 December 1916, 5.

13. 25 December 1917, JEM Diaries.

14. Resolution, [1916 N?], Reel 36, NWP: SY.

15. "To the President and Congress," *Suffragist*, 30 December 1916, 6.

16. Ethel Adamson to AP, 21 December 1916, and Agnes Morey to AP, 22 December 1916, Reel 36, NWP: SY. "Suffragists Do Honor to Inez Milholland," *New York World*, 26 December 1916, 7.

17. "Tribute to Inez Boissevain Was Greatest Ever Paid to Woman," *Evening Mail*, 26 December 1916, 4.

18. "The National Memorial Service in Memory of Inez Milholland," *Suffragist*, 30 December 1916, 7.

19. See Haig Bosmajian, "The Abrogation of the Suffragists' First Amendment Rights," *Western Speech* 38 (1974): 218–32.

20. AP to President Wilson, 1 January 1917, Reel 37, NWP: SY.

21. Thomas Brahany to AP and AP to Thomas Brahany, both 4 January 1917, Reel 37, NWP: SY; "Inez Milholland Boissevain," *Suffragist*, 2 December 1916, 6.

22. Doris Stevens, *Jailed for Freedom* (New York: Boni and Liveright, 1920), 54.

23. Sara Bard Field Interview, 360, SOHC; Stevens, *Jailed for Freedom*, 56.

24. Stevens, *Jailed for Freedom*, 59.

25. 9 January 1917, JEM Diaries.

26. "President Ignores Suffrage Pickets," *New York Times*, 11 January 1917, 3.

27. Stevens, *Jailed for Freedom*, 75–79; Irwin, *Story of the National Woman's Party*, 208; and "Suffragists Girdle White House in Rain," *New York Times*, 5 March 1917, 3.

28. "White House 'Riot' Broken Up by Police," *New York Times*, 5 July 1917, 9; "13 Suffragists Jailed in Riots at White House," *Washington Post*, 5 July 1917, 2.

29. Stevens, *Jailed for Freedom*, 365. A total of 218 women from twenty-six states were arrested, and 97 went to jail. Eleanor Flexner, *Century of Struggle: The Woman's Rights Movement in the United States* (Cambridge, Mass.: Belknap Press, Harvard University Press, 1959; rev. ed., New York: Atheneum, 1971), 285.

30. Letter to the editor, *New York Times*, 9 July 1917, 8.

31. 8 July 1917, JEM Diaries.

32. Irwin, *Story of the Woman's Party*, 262–63.

33. See Sally Hunter Graham, "Woodrow Wilson, Alice Paul, and the Woman Suffrage Movement," *Political Science Quarterly* 98 (Winter 1983–84): 665–79.

34. "Miss Paul Describes Feeding by Force," *New York Times*, 10 December 1909, 1.

35. AP to Dora Lewis, [?] November 1917, Reel 53, NWP: SY.

36. 6 November 1917, n.p., MFP.

37. "John E. Milholland's Protest," *New York Evening Post*, 7 November 1917, 3.

38. "Suffrage Pickets Freed from Prison," *New York Times*, 28 November 1917, 13.

39. 9 December 1917, JEM Diaries.

40. Stevens, *Jailed for Freedom*, 246.

41. 1 January 1918, JEM Diaries; "John E. Milholland's Protest," *New York Evening Post*, 7 November 1917, 3.

42. "Suffragists Again Attack the President," *New York Times*, 7 August 1918, 1.

43. Irwin, *Story of the Woman's Party*, 387.

44. "Singing Prison Songs, Militants Invade," *Los Angeles Evening Herald*, 27 February 1919, 1; "Prison Special Arouses South," *Suffragist*, 8 March 1919, 4; "The Prison Special," *Suffragist*, 15 March 1919, 8–9; and "The Prison Special through the West," *Suffragist*, 27 March 1919, 7–8.

45. For accounts of the NWP's militant campaign, see Linda Ford, *Iron-Jawed Angels: The Suffrage Militancy of the National Woman's Party, 1912–1920* (Lanham, Md.: University Press of America, 1991); "Picketing: Women's First Battle for First Amendment Rights," in Linda Lumsden, *Rampant Women: Suffragists and the Right of Assembly* (Knoxville: University of Tennessee Press, 1997), 114–43; and Christine Lunardini, *From Equal Suffrage to Equal Rights: Alice Paul and the National Woman's Party, 1910–1928* (New York: New York University Press), 1986.

46. June Sochen, *The New Woman in Greenwich Village, 1910–1920* (New York: Quadrangle Books, 1972), 18.

47. Ibid., 146.

48. Martha Patterson, "'Survival of the Best Fitted'; Selling the American New Woman as Gibson Girl, 1895–1910." *ATQ* 9 (March 1995): 87.

49. Quoted in "Press Comments on the Life and Work of Inez Milholland," *Suffragist*, 9 December 1916, 10.

50. "In Memory of Inez Milholland," flier, LTH. See Susan Becker, *The Origins of the Equal Rights Amendment: American Feminism between the Wars* (Westport, Conn.: Greenwood Press, 1981).

51. See Lois Banner, *American Beauty* (Chicago: University of Chicago Press, 1984), 279–80; Patricia Erens, "The Flapper: Hollywood's First Liberated Woman," in Lawrence R. Broer and John D. Walther, eds., *Dancing Fools and Weary Blues: The Great Escape of the Twenties* (Bowling Green, Ohio: Bowling Green State University Popular Press, 1990), 130–39; and "The Flapper," in Carolyn Kitch, *The Girl on the Magazine Cover: The Origins of Visual Stereotypes in American Mass Media* (Chapel Hill: University of North Carolina Press, 2001), 121–35.

52. Banner, *American Beauty*, 16. See also ibid., 269–70.

53. For discussions on how feminism fared in the 1920s, see Carolyn Anne Bonard, "The Women's Movement in the 1920s: American Magazines Document the Health and Progress of Feminism," in David Abrahamson, ed., *The American Magazine: Research Perspectives and Prospects* (Ames: Iowa State University Press, 1995), 231–40; "Part One," in William Henry Chafe, *The American Woman: Her Changing Social, Economic, and Political Roles, 1920–1970* (New York: Oxford University Press, 1972): 25–132; Nancy

Cott, "Feminist Politics in the 1920s: The National Woman's Party," *Journal of American History* 71 (June 1984): 43–68; Estelle Freedman, "The New Woman: Changing Views of Women in the 1920s," *Journal of American History* 61 (September 1974): 372–93; Kitch, *Girl on the Magazine Cover*, 182–84; J. Stanley Lemons, *The Woman Citizen: Social Feminism in the 1920s* (Urbana: University of Illinois Press, 1973); Rayna Rapp and Ellen Ross, "The Twenties' Backlash: Compulsory Heterosexuality, the Consumer Family, and the Waning of Feminism," in Amy Swerdlow and Hanna Lessinger, eds., *Class, Race, and Sex: The Dynamics of Control* (Boston: G. K. Hall, 1983), 93–107; Mary Ryan, *Womanhood in America: From Colonial Times to the Present* (New York: New Viewpoints, 1975), 253–303; Lois Scharf and Joann Jensen, eds., *Decades of Discontent: The Women's Movement, 1920–1940* (Westport, Conn.: Greenwood Press, 1983); and "*The New Woman?*" in Sochen, *New Woman in Greenwich Village*, 118–51.

54. Program, LTH. The pageant was originally scheduled on the August 6 anniversary of Inez's birth. "Inez Milholland Masque," *New York Times*, 27 January 1924, 23. The pageant hit a snag at a service at Inez's graveside the morning of the performance, when Paul infuriated John Milholland by refusing to acknowledge two African Americans he had invited to speak. He charged the NWP with racism. "Protest Made by Negroes," *New York Times*, 19 August 1924, 3.

55. The original oil painting by an unknown artist hangs in NWP headquarters in the Sewall-Belmont House National Historic Site in Washington, D.C. The party slogan is "Forward into Light," and its logo remains an illustration of Milholland based on the painting.

56. "Equal Rights for Women Pageant," *Essex County Republican*, 8 August 1924, 1. See also Mike Peterson, "Suffragette Remembered," *Plattsburgh Press-Republican*, 15 August 1999, C1, C12.

57. "Living Tribute to Inez Milholland," *Adirondack Record–Elizabethtown Post*, 21 August 1924, 1, 4.

Epilogue

1. 17 May 1919, JEM Diaries.

2. "The Birthday of Inez Milholland," unidentified newspaper clipping, 1 September 1917, JAM; "In Honor of 'Our Inez,'" *Elizabethtown Post*, 14 August 1919, 4; "A Memorial Exercise over Inez's Grave," 21 November 1920, JAM; and 18 January 1917 and 7 August 1921, JEM Diaries. The NWP held services in Washington on the anniversary of her death. 23 November 1919, JEM Diaries.

3. JTM to Mary Austin, 12 November 1932, APP. Austin likely met Inez in 1912–13, when Austin also moved in Greenwich Village's feminist circle. T. M. Pearce, *Mary Hunter Austin* (New York: Twayne Publishers, 1965), 15.

4. See Frank Pavey to VM, 2 June 1925, JAM; 16, 28 April 1921, 25 December 1922, and 13 July 1923, JEM Diaries.

5. "Would Buy Mail/ Tubes," *New York Times*, 2 March 1918, 19.

6. "Post Office Bill Passed," 17 May 1918, *New York Times*, 12; Albert B. Rossdale, "The Problem of the Mails," *The Forum* 68 (20 July 1922): 630. See also "The Hamstrung Postal Service," *Nation* 107 (10 August 1918): 139, and "A Crowning Appeal for the Pneumatic Mail Tube Service," reprint from the *New York American*, n.d., JAM.

7. "Message from the President of the United States Vetoing H.R. 7237," 29 June 1918. 65th Congress, 2d Session, Doc. No. 1206.

8. "The Postal Tube Veto," *New York Times*, 1 July 1918, 10.

9. 13 July 1923, JEM Diaries.

10. 31 December 1923, and Memoranda, 1924, JEM Diaries.

11. "Milholland," *Crisis*, September 1925, 215. See also "John E. Milholland, Underground Mail Tube Builder, Dead," *New York Tribune*, 30 June 1926, 15; "John Milholland, Editor and Public Benefactor," *Fourth Estate*, 4 July 1925, n.p.; "Keeping Faith," *Elizabethtown Record-Post*, n.d., 2; "Memorial Service to the Late John E. Milholland," NAACP; "County Convention Program, Essex County Sunday School Association"; "The 'Sage of Meadowmount,'" *Empire State Leader*, n.d.; "Milholland Funeral Largely Attended," *Elizabethtown Record-Post*, 9 July 1925, n.p.; "John Henry Elmer Milholland," *Oracle*, n.d., 118; and "John E. Milholland," *Sun*, 1 July 1925, n.p. All in JAM.

12. "Milholland Funeral Largely Attended"; John E. Milholland will, 10 January 1925, ECCH; and 21 July 1917, 10 February 1918, 23 January 1919, JEM Diaries.

13. Certificate of Death, 15 February 1939, New York City Department of Records and Information Services, Municipal Archives.

14. Author interview with Judith Galamian, July 1998; and VM to John Deming, 9 December 1950, JAM. The Meadowmount School of Music continues to attract more than two hundred young string musicians from around the world each summer.

15. "John Milholland, Banker, 56, Dead," *New York Times*, 3 April 1949, 77.

16. "To Assail Death Penalty," *New York Times*, 20 January 1917, 4.

17. Vida became her father's private secretary in 1919. 2 January 1919, JEM Diaries.

18. Those causes included prison reform, civil rights, the Socialist Party, the People's Council, the Friends of Irish Freedom, and the Emergency Peace Federation. "Vida Milholland," in Mabel Ward Cameron, ed., *The Biographical Cyclopaedia of American Women*, vol. 1 (New York: Halvord Publishing Co., 1924), 22; "Vida Milholland, Lyric Soprano," flier, JAM.

19. 5 October 1919, JEM Diaries.

20. VM to Mabel Vernon, 12 November 1952, VMP. See also Peg Hamilton to Mabel Vernon, 13 November 1952, VMP.

21. "Miss Vida Milholland," 2 December 1952, *New York Times*, 36.

22. Floyd Dell, *Homecoming: An Autobiography* (Port Washington, N.Y.: Kennikat Press, 1969), 308; Max Eastman, *Love and Revolution* (New York: Random House, 1964), 8; and Max Eastman, *Great Companions: Critical Memoirs of Some Famous Friends* (New York: Farrar, Straus, and Cudahy, 1959), 86.

23. Eastman, *Love and Revolution*, 80, 183; letter to author from The New-York Historical Society, 25 January 2001; Dell, *Homecoming*, 308.

24. Joan Dash, *A Life of One's Own: Three Gifted Women and the Men They Married* (New York: Harper and Row, 1973), 165.

25. "Eugen Boissevain," *New York Times*, 31 August 1949, 23. For more on the Millay-Boissevain marriage, see Nancy Milford, *Savage Beauty: The Life of Edna St. Vincent Millay* (New York: Random House, 2001).

26. "Honored as Pioneer," *Washington Post*, 19 November 1923, 2; "The Immortal American Trinity," Box 88, Folder 1160, APP.

27. Norma Millay, ed., *Collected Poems* (New York: Harper and Row, 1956), 627. Millay originally titled the sonnet "The Pioneers." Author interview with Elizabeth Barnett, 13 November 2002. "Take up the Song" is also the title of a play about Milholland by John Tepper Marlin, great-nephew of Eugen Boissevain. "From Economist to Playwright," *New York Times*, 12 July 1998, sec. 14, 6.

BIBLIOGRAPHY

Primary Sources

Archives

The Papers of Harriot Stanton Blatch. Manuscripts Division, Library of Congress, Washington, D.C. Microfilm edition.

Centre for Migration Studies at the Ulster American Folk Park, Omagh, Northern Ireland.

Cullen Papers. Sophia Smith Collection. Smith College, Northampton, Mass.

W. E. B. Du Bois Papers. Special Collections and Archives, W. E. B. Du Bois Library, University of Massachusetts, Amherst, Mass.

Crystal Eastman Papers. Arthur and Elizabeth Schlesinger Library on the History of Women in America, Radcliffe Institute for Advanced Study, Harvard University, Cambridge, Mass.

Essex County Historical Society, Elizabethtown, N.Y.

Fabian Society Archives, Archives Division of British Library of Political & Economic Science, London School of Economics and Political Science, London, England.

Henry Ford Museum and Greenfield Village Research Center, Detroit, Mich.

Henry Ford Peace Expedition. Swarthmore College Peace Collection. Swarthmore College, Swarthmore, Pa.

The Papers of the Ford Peace Plan. Library of Congress, Washington, D.C.

Genealogy and Local History Division, New York Public Library, New York, N.Y.

Dorothy Smith Gruening (Recollections, sound recording). Arthur and Elizabeth Schlesinger Library on the History of Women in America, Radcliffe Institute for Advanced Study, Harvard University, Cambridge, Mass.

Harvard University Archives, Cambridge, Mass.

Howard University Archives, Howard University, Washington, D.C.

Inez Haynes Irwin Papers, 1872–1945. Arthur and Elizabeth Schlesinger Library on the History of Women in America, Radcliffe Institute for Advanced Study, Harvard University, Cambridge, Mass.

Jersey City Historical Society, Jersey City, N.J.

Lewis Historical Records. Town Historian, Lewis, N.Y.

Local Studies Collection of The Royal Borough of Kensington & Chelsea Libraries, London, England.

President A. Lawrence Lowell's Papers, 1909–1914. Harvard University Archives, Cambridge, Mass.

MacKaye Family Papers. Special Collections, Dartmouth College Library, Hanover, N.H.

Inez Milholland Papers, 1906–1916. Arthur and Elizabeth Schlesinger Library on the History of Women in America. Radcliffe Institute for Advanced Study, Harvard University, Cambridge, Mass. Microfilm edition.

John A. Milholland Papers. Private collection.

John E. Milholland Papers. Ticonderoga Historical Society, Ticonderoga, N.Y.

Vida Milholland Folders. Swarthmore College Peace Collection. Swarthmore College, Swarthmore, Pa.

National American Woman Suffrage Association Papers. Microfilm edition, Sanford, N.C.: Microfilm Corp. of America, 1979.

National Association for the Advancement of Colored People Papers. Library of Congress, Washington, D.C. Microfilm edition.

National Woman's Party Papers: The Suffrage Years, 1913–1920. Library of Congress. Microfilm edition, Glen Rock, N.J.: Microfilm Corp. of America, 1979.

National Woman's Party Papers, 1913–1974. Library of Congress. Microfilm edition, Glen Rock, N.J.: Microfilm Corp. of America, 1977–78.

New York State Archives, Albany, N.Y.

New York University Archives, New York, N.Y.

New-York Historical Society, New York, N.Y.

Alice Park Papers. The Huntington Library, San Marino, Calif.

Passaic County Historical Society, Paterson, N.J.

Paterson Local History Department, Paterson Public Library, Paterson, N.J.

Alice Paul Papers. Arthur and Elizabeth Schlesinger Library on the History of Women in America, Radcliffe Institute for Advanced Study, Harvard University, Cambridge, Mass.

Public Records Office of Northern Ireland, Belfast, Northern Ireland.

Upton Sinclair Papers. Manuscripts Department, Lilly Library, Indiana University, Bloomington, Ind.

Socialist Collections in the Tamiment Library, 1872–1956. New York University, New York, N.Y. Microfilm edition.

Doris Stevens Papers. Arthur and Elizabeth Schlesinger Library on the History of Women in America, Radcliffe Institute for Advanced Study, Harvard University, Cambridge, Mass.

Rose Pastor Stokes Papers. Tamiment Library, New York University, New York, N.Y.

Suffragette Fellowship Collection of Museum of London, Fawcett Library, London, England.

Suffragists Oral History Collection. University of California, Berkeley. Microfiche edition, Sanford, N.C. Microfilming Corp. of America, 1980.

Vassariana Collection. Vassar College, Poughkeepsie, N.Y.

John Wanamaker Papers. Historical Society of Pennsylvania, Philadelphia, Pa.

Woman Suffrage Collection. Fawcett Library, London, England.

Woman Suffrage Collection. Vassar College, Poughkeepsie, N.Y.

Collected Records of Woman's Peace Party, 1914–1920. Swarthmore College Peace Collection, Swarthmore College, Swarthmore, Pa.

Matilda Young Papers. Duke Special Collections, Duke University, Durham, N.C.

Works by Inez Milholland

"Another Point of View." *Women Lawyers' Journal*, January 1915, 30.

"Censorship." *Crisis* 13 (January 1917): 116.

"The Changing Home." *McClure's* 40 (March 1913): 206–19.

"Does It Pay the Store?" *Harper's Weekly* 58 (May 30, 1914): 12–14.

"Everything German, Even Names, Taboo." *New York Tribune*, 31 July 1915, 4.

"If Women Voted." Unpublished skit, IMP.

"Italy's Heroic Response Is Blind War Hysteria." *New York Tribune*, 24 July 1915, 5.

"Judicial Destruction of Laws." *Women Lawyers' Journal*, April 1915, 51.

"The Liberation of a Sex." *McClure's* 40 (February 1913): 181–88.

"My Conversion to Woman Suffrage." *Woman Voter*, January 1917, 13.

"National Vanity Led Italy to Enter War." *New York Tribune*, 26 July 1915, 6.

"Submarine Pursued St. Paul to Mersey." *New York Tribune*, 2 June 1915, 1.

"The Suffrage Question in England." *Vassar Miscellany* 37 (October 1907): 27–30.
"Two Million Women Vote." *McClure's* 40 (January 1913): 241–51 (with Wallace Irwin).
"Warlike France Bustles While England Blusters." *New York Tribune*, 20 July 1915, 3.
"The Woman and the Man." *McClure's* 40 (April 1913): 185–96.

Contemporary Sources

Addams, Jane. *Peace and Bread in Time of War.* 1922. Reprint, Boston: G. K. Hall and Co., 1960.
———. *The Second Twenty Years at Hull-House.* New York: Macmillan Co., 1930.
Addams, Jane, Emily Balch, and Alice Hamilton. *Women at The Hague.* New York: Macmillan, 1915.
"After Vassar, What?" *Outlook*, 30 June 1915, 518–23.
Annual Report of the Postmaster-General for the Fiscal Year Ending June 30, 1893. Washington, D.C.: GPO, 1893.
Archer, William. "The American Drama Revisited." *Independent* 62 (June 27, 1907): 1519–25.
Balsan, Consuelo Vanderbilt. *The Glitter and the Gold.* New York: Harper and Brothers, 1952.
Batcheller, B. *The Pneumatic Despatch Tube System of the Batcheller Pneumatic Tube Co.* Philadelphia: J. B. Lippincott Co., 1897.
Blatch, Harriot Stanton, and Alma Lutz. *Challenging Years: The Memoirs of Harriot Stanton Blatch.* New York: G. P. Putnam's Sons, 1940.
Bradwell v. Illinois, 83 U.S. (16 Wall.) 130, 141 (1872).
Breuer, Elizabeth. "Edna St. Vincent Millay." *Pictorial Review*, November 1931, 2, 50–54, 57.
Byrns, Elinor. "I Resolve to Be Restless." *Independent*, 10 January 1916, 50–51.
Catt, Carrie Chapman, and Nettie Rogers Shuler. *Woman Suffrage and Politics: The Inner Story of the Suffrage Movement.* New York: Charles Scribner's Sons, 1923.
"Crystal Eastman." *Nation* 127 (8 August 1928): 124.
Deland, Margaret. "The Change in the Feminine Ideal." *Atlantic Monthly* 105 (March 1910): 292, 289.
Dell, Floyd. *Homecoming: An Autobiography.* Port Washington, N.Y.: Kennikat Press, 1969.
———. *Upton Sinclair: A Study in Social Protest.* New York: AMS Press, 1927.
Dorr, Rheta Childe. *What Eight Million Women Want.* Boston: Small, Maynard and Co., 1910.
Doty, Madeline. *Society's Misfits.* New York: Century Co., 1916.
Du Bois, W. E. B. *The Amenia Conference: An Historic Negro Gathering.* Troutbeck Leaflet No. 8. Amenia, N.Y.: Privately printed at Troutbeck Press, 1925.
———. *The Autobiography of W. E. B. Du Bois.* New York: International Publishers, 1968.
———. "National Committee on the Negro." *Survey*, 12 June 1909, 407–408.
Eastman, Max. *Child of the Amazons.* New York: Mitchell Kennerley, 1913.
———. *The Enjoyment of Living.* New York: Harper and Brothers, 1948.
———. *Great Companions: Critical Memoirs of Some Famous Friends.* New York: Farrar, Straus, and Cudahy, 1959.
———. *Love and Revolution.* New York: Random House, 1964.
Ellis, Havelock. *Man and Woman: A Study of Human Secondary Sexual Characteristics*, 5th ed. New York: Charles Scribner's Sons, 1915.

Fawcett, Waldon. "The United States Postal Service in the Twentieth Century." *Harper's Weekly* 45 (February 1901): 130–31.

"A Feminine 'Sherlock Holmes.'" *Literary Digest* 55 (7 July 1917): 50–52.

Ferrero, Guglielmo. "The New Woman and the Old." *Hearst's Magazine* 22 (July 1912): 70–78.

"The First Year out of College." *Vassar Alumnae Magazine,* 2 (November 1910), 10–14, and (January 1911), 45–46.

Frazer, Elizabeth. "The Sob-Lady." *Good Housekeeping* 61 (September 1915): 316–24.

Freeman, Joseph. *An American Testament: A Narrative of Rebels and Romantics.* New York: Farrar and Rinehart, 1936.

Gerard, James W. *My Four Years in Germany.* New York: George H. Doran Co., 1917.

Gilman, Charlotte Perkins. *Women and Economics: A Study of the Economic Relations Between Men and Women as a Factor in Social Evolution.* Boston, 1898.

Grand, Sarah. "The New Aspect of the Woman Question." *North American Review* 158 (March 1894): 270–76.

"The Hamstrung Postal Service." *Nation* 107 (10 August 1918): 139.

Hapgood, Hutchins. *A Victorian in the Modern World.* 1939. Reprint, Seattle: University of Washington Press, 1972.

Harlan, Louis R., and Raymond W. Smock, eds. *The Booker T. Washington Papers,* 13 vols. Urbana: University of Illinois Press, 1981.

Herrick, Hugh M., ed. *William Walter Phelps: His Life and Public Services.* New York: Knickerbocker Press, 1904.

Hill, Joseph. *Women in Gainful Occupations 1870 to 1920: A Study of the Trend of Recent Changes in the Numbers, Occupational Distribution, and Family Relationship of Women reported in the Census as Following a Gainful Occupation,* Census Monograph 9. Washington, D.C.: United States Printing Office, 1929.

Howe, Frederick C. *The Confessions of a Reformer.* New York: Charles Scribner's Sons, 1925.

"Inez Milholland Boissevain." *Vassar Quarterly* 2 (February 1917): 1916.

Irwin, Inez Haynes. *The Story of the Woman's Party.* New York: Harcourt, Brace and Co., 1921.

Irwin, Will. *The Making of a Reporter.* New York: G. P. Putnam's Sons, 1942.

Key, Ellen. *Love and Marriage.* New York: G. P. Putnam's Sons, 1911.

Kinkaid, Mary Holland. "The Feminine Charms of the Woman Militant." *Good Housekeeping* 54 (February 1912): 146–55.

Koven, Anna de. "The Athletic Woman." *Good Housekeeping* 55 (August 1912): 148–57.

Lattimore, Florence L. "Aboard the Oscar II." *Survey,* 15 January 1916, 457–60.

———. "The Expedition in Holland." *Survey,* 12 February 1916, 584–85.

Lochner, Louis P. *America's Don Quixote: Henry Ford's Attempt to Save Europe.* London: Kegan Paul, Trench, Trubner and Co., 1924.

Macdougall, Allan Ross. "Husband of a Genius." *Delineator,* October 1934, 21, 40.

———, ed. *The Letters of Edna St. Vincent Millay.* New York: Harper and Brothers, 1952.

Malkiel, Theresa. *The Diary of a Shirtwaist Striker.* New York: Co-operative Press, 1910. Reprint, Ithaca, N.Y.: ILR Press, School of Industrial and Labor Relations, Cornell University, 1990.

Marconi, Degna. *My Father: Marconi.* London. Frederick Muller, 1962.

Marot, Helen. "A Woman's Strike: An Appreciation of the Shirtwaist Makers of New York." *Proceedings of the Academy of Political Science in the City of New York, 1910*, no. 1 (1910): 119–28.

Maule, Mary K. "What Is a Shop-Girl's Life?" *World's Work* 14 (September 1907): 9311–16.

Milholland, John A. "Autobiography." Unpublished manuscript edited by John Tepper Marlin, copy in author's possession.

Milholland, John E. "The Preservation of Fort Ticonderoga by Town Ownership." Undated speech, New York Public Library.

"The Most Difficult Problem of Modern Civilization." *Current Literature* 48 (January 1910): 58–61.

O'Hare, Kate Richards. "The Wounded Who Do Not Fight." *Social Revolution* 11 (October 1914): 7.

"Opening of the Pneumatic Tube Service in New York City." *Scientific American* 77 (16 October 1897): 243.

Oppenheimer, Mary S. "The Suffrage Movement and the Socialist Party." *New Review* 3 (December 1915): 359–60.

Ovington, Margaret White. "The National Association for the Advancement of Colored People." *Journal of Negro History* 9 (April 1924): 107–16.

Pankhurst, Christabel, *Unshackled: The Story of How We Won the Vote*. London: Hutchinson, 1959.

Pankhurst, E. Sylvia. *The Suffragette: The History of the Women's Militant Suffrage Movement, 1905–1910*. Boston: Woman's Journal, 1911.

———. *The Suffragette Movement*. London: Longmans, Green and Co., 1932.

People v. Stielow, 160 N.Y.S. 555 (1916).

People v. Stielow, 161 N.Y.S. 599 (1916).

"Pneumatic Pains," *Time* 31 (10 January 1938): 45–46.

Powell, E. Alexander. *Adventure Road*. New York: Doubleday and Co., 1954.

Robinson, Lelia J. "Women Lawyers in the United States." *Green Bag* 2 (1890): 10–32.

Ross, Ishbel. *Ladies of the Press: The Story of Women in Journalism by an Insider*. New York: Harper and Brothers, 1936.

Rossdale, Albert B. "The Problem of the Mails." *Forum* 68 (20 July 1922): 624–30.

Sandburg, Carl. *Cornhuskers*. New York: Henry Holt and Co., 1918.

Schneiderman, Rose, and Lucy Goldthwaite. *All for One*. New York: Paul S. Eriksson, 1967.

Schreiner, Olive. *Women and Labour*. New York: Frederick A. Stokes, 1911.

Sinclair, Mary Craig. *Southern Belle*. Phoenix, Ariz.: Sinclair Press, 1962.

"The Spokesman for Suffrage in America." *McClure's* 39 (July 1912): 335–37.

Stealey, Orlando O. *Twenty Years in the Press Gallery*. New York: by the author, Publishers Printing Co., 1906.

Stevens, Doris. *Jailed for Freedom*. New York: Boni and Liveright, 1920.

Stevens, George A. *New York Typographical Union Number Six*. Albany: New York State Department of Labor, 1912.

Stevens, Isaac N. *An American Suffragette*. New York: William Rickey and Co., 1911.

"Suffrage Parade." Report of the Committee on the District of Columbia, U.S. Senate, Pursuant to Sen. Resolution 499 of March 4, 1913, submitted by Mr. Jones, May 29, 1913, 63rd Congress, Report No. 53.

Sumner, Mary Brown. "The Spirit of the Strikers." *Survey* 23 (22 January 1910): 550–55.

Terrell, Mary Church. *A Colored Woman in a White World*. Reprint, New York: G. K. Hall, 1996.

Ticknor, Caroline. "The Steel Engraving Lady and the Gibson Girl." *Atlantic Monthly* 88 (July 1901): 105–108.

Tompkins, Leslie J. "The University Law School." *New York University Law Review* 4 (1927): 35–50.

United States Census, 1850, 1855, 1860, 1870, Town of Lewis, Essex County, N.Y.

Vorse, Mary Heaton. *A Footnote to Folly: The Reminiscences of Mary Heaton Vorse.* New York: Farrar and Rinehart, 1935.

White, Frank Marshall. "Where There Are Women, There's a Way." *Good Housekeeping* 67 (August 1918): 54–56, 130–31.

Wilkinson, Louis, ed. *The Letters of Llewelyn Powys.* London: John Lake, The Bodley Head, 1943.

Williams, Jessie Lynch. "The New Marriage." *Good Housekeeping* 58 (February 1914): 181–85.

Witte, Mabel E. "Women in Law." *Vassar Alumnae Monthly* 2 (January 1911): 42–44.

Young, Elva Hulburd. "The Law as a Profession for Women." *Publications of the Association of Collegiate Alumnae,* series 3, no. 5 (February 1902): 15–23.

Periodicals

Call (New York)
Crisis (New York)
New York Times
New York Tribune
Progressive Women (Chicago)
Suffragist (Washington, D.C.)
Ticonderoga [N.Y.] *Sentinel*
Vassar Miscellany (Poughkeepsie, N.Y.)
Votes for Women (London)
Woman Citizen (New York)
Woman Voter (New York)
Woman's Journal (Boston)
Women Lawyers' Journal (New York)
Women's Political World (New York)

Secondary Sources
Books

Adams, Herbert. *John Wanamaker.* Vol. 1. New York: Harper and Brothers, 1926.

Adickes, Sandra. *To Be Young Was Very Heaven: Women in New York before the First World War.* New York: St. Martin's Press, 1997.

Alonso, Harriet Hyman. *Peace as a Women's Issue: A History of the U.S. Movement for World Peace and Women's Rights.* Syracuse, N.Y.: Syracuse University Press, 1993.

Appel, Joseph H. *The Business Biography of John Wanamaker: Founder and Builder.* New York: Macmillan and Co., 1930.

Ashley, Perry J., ed., *Dictionary of Literary Biography,* vol. 9: *American Novelists, 1910–1945, Part II.* Detroit: Gale Research Co., 1983.

Atkinson, Diane. *Suffragettes in the Purple, White, and Green: London 1906–14.* London: Museum of London, 1992.

Banner, Lois. *American Beauty.* Chicago: University of Chicago Press, 1984.

Banta, Martha. *Imaging American Women: Idea and Ideals in Cultural History.* New York: Columbia University Press, 1987.

Barratt, Rex. *The Hey-day of the Great Atlantic Liners.* Redruth, England: Truran Publications, 1983.

Becker, Susan. *The Origins of the Equal Rights Amendment: American Feminism between the Wars.* Westport, Conn.: Greenwood Press, 1981.

Begbie, Harold. *The Life of General William Booth, the Founder of the Salvation Army.* New York: Macmillan Co., 1920.

Belford, Barbara. *Brilliant Bylines.* New York: Columbia University Press, 1986.

Benson, Susan Porter. *Counter Cultures: Saleswomen, Managers, and Customers in American Department Stores, 1890–1940.* Urbana: University of Illinois Press, 1986.

Berger, John. *Ways of Seeing.* London: British Broadcasting Co., 1972.

Bowers, William J. *Executions in America.* Lexington, Mass.: Lexington Books, 1974.

Brandon, Craig. *The Electric Chair: An Unnatural American History.* Jefferson, N.C.: McFarland and Co., 1999.

Brittin, Norman. *Edna St. Vincent Millay.* New York: Twayne Publishers, 1967.

Bruccoli, Matthew J. *The Fortunes of Mitchell Kennerley, Bookman.* New York: Harcourt Brace Jovanovich, 1986.

Buhle, Mari Jo. *Women and American Socialism, 1870–1920.* Urbana: University of Illinois Press, 1981.

Cairis, Nicholas. *North Atlantic Panorama.* Middletown, Conn.: Wesleyan University Press, 1977.

Cameron, Mabel Ward, ed. *The Biographical Cyclopaedia of American Women.* Vol. 1. New York: Halvord Publishing Co., 1924.

Campbell, Barbara Kuhn. *The "Liberated" Woman of 1914: Prominent Women in the Progressive Era.* Ann Arbor: UMI Research Press, 1979.

Chafe, William Henry. *The American Woman: Her Changing Social, Economic, and Political Roles, 1920–1970.* New York: Oxford University Press, 1972.

Chesler, Ellen. *Woman of Valor: Margaret Sanger and the Birth Control Movement in America.* New York: Simon and Schuster, 1992.

Churchill, Allen. *The Improper Bohemians: A Recreation of Greenwich Village in Its Hey-day.* New York: E. P. Dutton and Co., 1959.

Cohn, Jan. *Improbable Fiction: The Life of Mary Roberts Rinehart.* Pittsburgh: University of Pittsburgh Press, 1980.

Cole, Margaret. *The Story of Fabian Socialism.* Stanford, Calif.: Stanford University Press, 1961.

Collier, Richard. *The General Next to God: The Story of William Booth and the Salvation Army.* New York: E. P. Dutton and Co., 1965.

Cook, Blanche Wiesen, ed. *Crystal Eastman on Women and Revolution.* New York: Oxford University Press, 1978.

Cott, Nancy. *The Grounding of Modern Feminism.* New Haven, Conn.: Yale University Press, 1987.

Daniels, Elizabeth A. *Bridges to the World: Henry Noble MacCracken and Vassar College.* Clifton Corner, N.Y.: College Avenue Press, 1994.

Dash, Joan. *A Life of One's Own: Three Gifted Women and the Men They Married.* New York: Harper and Row, 1973.

Davis, Angela. *Women, Race, and Class.* New York: Random House, 1981.

Dearborn, Mary. *Queen of Bohemia: The Life of Louise Bryant.* Boston: Houghton Mifflin, 1996.

Decter, Midge. *Shoulder to Shoulder: A Documentary.* New York: Alfred A. Knopf, 1975.

D'Emilio John, and Estelle Freedman. *Intimate Matters: A History of Sexuality in America.* New York: Harper and Row, 1988.

Drachman, Virginia G. *Women Lawyers and the Origins of Professional Identity in America: The Letters of the Equity Club, 1887 to 1890.* Ann Arbor: University of Michigan Press, 1993.

DuBois, Ellen Carol. *Feminism and Suffrage: The Emergence of an Independent Women's Movement in America, 1848–1869.* Ithaca, N.Y.: Cornell University Press, 1978.

———. *Harriot Stanton Blatch and the Winning of Woman Suffrage.* New Haven, Conn.: Yale University Press, 1997.

Duncan, Bingham. *Whitelaw Reid: Journalist, Politician, Diplomat.* Athens: University of Georgia Press, 1975.

Dye, Nancy Schrom. *As Equals and as Sisters: Feminism, the Labor Movement, and the Women's Trade Union League of New York.* Columbia: University of Missouri Press, 1980.

Edwards, Julia. *Women of the World: The Great Foreign Correspondents.* Boston: Houghton Mifflin Co., 1988.

Elshtain, Jean Beth. *Jane Addams and the Dream of American Democracy.* New York: Basic Books, 2002.

Emery, Edwin, and Michael Emery. *The Press and America: An Interpretive History of the Mass Media.* 8th ed. Boston: Allyn and Bacon, 1996.

Enstad, Nan. *Ladies of Labor, Girls of Adventure: Working Women, Popular Culture, and Labor Politics at the Turn of the Twentieth Century.* New York: Columbia University Press, 1999.

Filene, Peter. *Him/Her/Self: Gender Identities in Modern America.* 3rd ed. Baltimore: Johns Hopkins University Press, 1998.

Finnegan, Margaret. *Selling Suffrage: Consumer Culture and Votes for Women.* New York: Columbia University Press, 1999.

First, Ruth, and Ann Scott. *Olive Schreiner.* New York: Schocken Books, 1980.

Fishbein, Leslie. *Rebels in Bohemia: The Radicals of the Masses, 1911–1917.* Chapel Hill: University of North Carolina Press, 1982.

Flexner, Eleanor. *Century of Struggle: The Woman's Rights Movement in the United States.* Cambridge, Mass.: Belknap Press, Harvard University Press, 1959. Reprint, New York: Atheneum, 1971.

Folkerts, Jean, and Dwight Teeter. *Voices of a Nation: A History of Mass Media in the United States.* 3rd ed. Boston: Allyn and Bacon, 1998.

Foner, Philip. *Women and the American Labor Movement: From the First Trade Unions to the Present.* New York: Free Press, 1979.

Ford, Linda. *Iron-Jawed Angels: The Suffrage Militancy of the National Woman's Party, 1912–1920.* Lanham, Md.: University Press of America, 1991.

Foucault, Michel. *The History of Sexuality.* New York: Pantheon Books, 1978.

Frankel, Noralee, and Nancy S. Dye, eds. *Gender, Class, Race, and Reform in the Progressive Era.* Lexington: University Press of Kentucky, 1991.

Gans, Herbert. *Deciding What's News: A Study of CBS Evening News, NBC Nightly News, Newsweek and Time.* New York: Vintage Books, 1980.

Gaunt, William. *Kensington and Chelsea.* London: B. T. Batsford, 1975.

Gelderman, Carol. *Henry Ford: The Wayward Capitalist.* New York: Dial Press, 1981.

Giddings, Paula. *When and Where I Enter: The Impact of Black Women on Race and Sex in America.* New York: Bantam, 1984.

Gillon, Edmund Vincent, ed. *The Gibson Girl and Her America: The Best Drawings of Charles Dana Gibson.* New York: Dover, 1969.

The Girls' Public Day School Trust 1872–1972: A Centenary Review. London: Girls' Public Day School Trust, 1972.

Glennon, Lorraine, ed. *Our Times: The Illustrated History of the 20th Century.* Atlanta: Turner Publishing, 1995.

Gluck, Sherna, ed. *From Parlor to Prison: Five American Suffragists Talk about Their Lives—An Oral History.* New York: Vintage Books, 1976.

Gold, Joyce. *From Trout Stream to Bohemia: Greenwich Village—A Walking Guide through History.* New York: Old Warren Road Press, 1996.

Goldsmith, Barbara. *Other Powers: The Age of Suffrage, Spiritualism, and the Scandalous Victoria Woodhull.* New York: Alfred A. Knopf, 1998.

Gordon, Linda. *Woman's Body, Woman's Right: Birth Control in America.* Rev. ed. New York: Penguin Books, 1990.

Gosnell, Harold F. *Boss Platt and His New York Machine: A Study of the Political Leadership of Thomas C. Platt, Theodore Roosevelt, and Others.* New York: Russell and Russell, 1969.

Gray, Mary Peck. *Carrie Chapman Catt: A Biography.* New York: The H. W. Wilson Company, 1944.

Green, Martin. *New York 1913: The Armory Show and the Paterson Strike Pageant.* New York: Charles Scribner's Sons, 1988.

Hale, Nathan. *Freud and the Americans.* New York: Oxford University Press, 1971.

Harlan, Louis R. *Booker T. Washington: The Wizard of Tuskegee, 1901–1915.* New York: Oxford, 1983.

Harris, Barbara J. *Beyond Her Sphere: Women and the Professions in American History.* Westport, Conn.: Greenwood Press, 1978.

Harris, Jacqueline L. *History and Achievement of the NAACP.* New York: Franklin Watts, 1992.

Heller, Adele, and Lois Rudnick, eds. *1915, the Cultural Moment: The New Politics, the New Woman, the New Psychology, the New Art, and the New Theatre in America.* New Brunswick, N.J.: Rutgers University Press, 1991.

Hendrickson, Robert. *The Grand Emporiums: The Illustrated History of America's Great Department Stores.* New York: Stein and Day, 1979.

Herrick, Hugh M., ed. *William Walter Phelps: His Life and Public Services.* New York: Knickerbocker Press, 1904.

Hershey, Burnet. *The Odyssey of Henry Ford and the Great Peace Ship.* New York: Taplinger Publishing Co., 1967.

Hill, Mary A. *Charlotte Perkins Gilman: The Making of a Radical Feminist, 1860–1896.* Philadelphia: Temple University Press, 1980.

Hirsh, Jeff. *Manhattan Hotels, 1880–1920.* Dover, N.H.: Arcadia Publishing, 1997.

Honey, Maureen, ed. *Breaking the Ties That Bind: Popular Stories of the New Woman, 1915–1930.* Norman: University Press of Oklahoma, 1992.

Horn, Max. *The Intercollegiate Socialist Society, 1905–1921: Origins of the Modern American Student Movement.* Boulder, Colo.: Westview Press, 1979.

Howe, Irving. *Socialism and America*. San Diego: Harcourt Brace Jovanovich, 1985.

Hower, Ralph. *History of Macy's of New York, 1858–1919*. Cambridge, Mass.: Harvard University Press, 1983.

Hughes, Langston. *Fight for Freedom: The Story of the NAACP*. New York: W. W. Norton and Co., 162.

Hull, Gloria, Patricia Bell Scott, and Barbara Smith, eds. *All the Women Are White, All the Blacks Are Men, but Some of Us Are Brave: Black Women's Studies*. Old Westbury, N.Y.: Feminist Press, 1982.

James, Edward, Janet Wilson James, and Paul Boyer, eds. *Notable American Women, 1607–1950*. Vols. 1, 2. Cambridge, Mass.: Belknap Press, Harvard University Press, 1971.

Janeway, Elizabeth. *Man's World, Woman's Place: A Study in Social Mythology*. New York: William Morrow and Co., 1971.

Jennings, Peter, and Todd Brewster. *The Century*. New York: Doubleday, 1998.

Jolly, W. P. *Marconi*. New York: Stein and Day, 1972.

Jones, Theodore Francis, ed. *New York University, 1832–1932*. New York: New York University Press, 1933.

Kamm, Josephine. *Indicative Past: A Hundred Years of the Girls' Public Day School Trust*. London: George Allen and Unwin, 1971.

Kerber, Linda. *Women of the Republic: Intellect and Ideology in Revolutionary America*. Chapel Hill: University of North Carolina Press, 1980.

Kitch, Carolyn. *The Girl on the Magazine Cover: The Origins of Visual Stereotypes in American Mass Media*. Chapel Hill: University of North Carolina Press, 2001.

Kluger, Richard. *The Paper: The Life and Death of the "New York Herald Tribune."* New York: Vintage Books, 1989.

Kraditor, Aileen. *The Ideas of the Woman Suffrage Movement, 1890–1920*. New York: Columbia University Press, 1965.

Kraft, Barbara S. *The Peace Ship: Henry Ford's Pacifist Adventure in the First World War*. New York: Macmillan Publishing Co., 1978.

Kurth, Peter. *Isadora: A Sensational Life*. Boston: Little, Brown, 2001.

Lacey, Robert. *Ford: The Men and the Machine*. Boston: Little, Brown and Co., 1986.

Lane, Ann J. *The Brownsville Affair: National Crisis and Black Reaction*. Port Washington, N.Y.: Kennikat Press, 1971.

Lemons, J. Stanley. *The Woman Citizen: Social Feminism in the 1920s*. Urbana: University of Illinois Press, 1973.

Lewis, David Levering. *W.E.B. Du Bois: Biography of a Race, 1868–1919*. New York: Henry Holt, 1993.

Leyburn, James G. *The Scotch-Irish: A Social History*. Chapel Hill: University of North Carolina Press, 1962.

Lumsden, Linda. *Rampant Women: Suffragists and the Right of Assembly*. Knoxville: University of Tennessee Press, 1997.

Lunardini, Christine. *From Equal Suffrage to Equal Rights: Alice Paul and the National Woman's Party, 1910–1928*. New York: New York University Press, 1986.

MacKenzie, Midge. *Shoulder to Shoulder: A Documentary*. New York: Alfred A. Knopf, 1975.

MacKenzie, Norman, and Jeanne MacKenzie. *The Fabians*. New York: Simon and Schuster, 1977.

Marks, Patricia. *Bicycles, Bangs, and Bloomers: The New Woman in the Popular Press*. Frankfort: University Press of Kentucky, 1990.

Masini, Giancarlo. *Marconi*. New York: Marsilio Publishers, 1976.

Matthews, Glenna. *The Rise of Public Woman: Woman's Power and Woman's Place in the United States, 1630–1970*. New York: Oxford University Press, 1992.

McBriar, A. M. *Fabian Socialism and English Politics, 1884–1918*. Cambridge: Cambridge University Press, 1966.

Meier, August. *Negro Thought in America, 1880–1915*. Ann Arbor: University of Michigan Press, 1969.

Melville, Margarita, ed. *Twice a Minority: Mexican-American Women*. St. Louis: C.V. Mosby Co., 1980.

Milford, Nancy. *Savage Beauty: The Life of Edna St. Vincent Millay*. New York: Random House, 2001.

Millay, Norma, ed. *Collected Poems*. New York: Harper and Row, 1956.

Miller, Kerby A. *Emigrants and Exiles: Ireland and the Irish Exodus to North America*. New York: Oxford University Press, 1985.

Moraga, Cherrie, and Gloria Anzaldúa. *This Bridge Called My Back: Writings by Radical Women of Color*. Watertown, Mass.: Persephone Press, 1981.

Morello, Karen Berger. *The Invisible Bar: The Woman Lawyer in America to the Present*. New York: Random House, 1986.

Morgan, H. Wayne. *From Hayes to McKinley: National Party Politics, 1877–1896*. Syracuse: Syracuse University Press, 1969.

Morris, Edmund. *The Rise of Theodore Roosevelt*. Rev. ed. New York: The Modern Library, 2001.

Muncy, Robyn. *Creating a Female Dominion in American Reform, 1890–1935*. New York: Oxford University Press, 1991.

Newell, Gordon. *Ocean Liners of the 20th Century*. Seattle: Superior Publishing Co., 1963.

O'Neill, William. *Divorce in the Progressive Era*. New Haven, Conn.: Yale University Press, 1967.

———. *Everyone Was Brave: The Rise and Fall of Feminism in America*. Chicago: Quadrangle Books, 1969.

———. *The Last Romantic: A Life of Max Eastman*. New York: Oxford University Press, 1978.

Orleck, Annelise. *Common Sense and a Little Fire: Women and Working-Class Politics in the United States, 1900–65*. Chapel Hill: University of North Carolina Press, 1995.

Painter, Nell Irvin. *Standing at Armageddon: The United States, 1877–1919*. New York: W. W. Norton Co., 1987.

Parry, Albert. *Garrets and Pretenders: A History of Bohemianism in America*. New York: Covici-Friede, 1933. Rev. ed., New York: Dover Publications, 1960.

Pearce, T. M. *Mary Hunter Austin*. New York: Twayne Publishers, 1965.

Pease, Edward R. *The History of the Fabian Society*. London: Frank Cass and Co., 1963.

Peiss, Kathy. *Cheap Amusements: Working Women and Leisure in Turn-of-the-Century New York*. Philadelphia: Temple University Press, 1986.

Plum, Dorothy A., and George B. Dowell. *The Great Experiment: A Chronicle of Vassar*. Poughkeepsie, N.Y.: Vassar College, 1961.

Raeburn, Anita. *The Militant Suffragettes*. London: Michael Joseph, 1973.

Randall, Mercedes M. *Improper Bostonian: Emily Greene Balch*. New York: Twayne Publishers, 1964.

Rosenberg, Rosalind. *Beyond Separate Spheres: Intellectual Roots of Modern Feminism.* New Haven, Conn.: Yale University Press, 1982.

Ross, B. Joyce. *J. E. Spingarn and the Rise of the NAACP, 1911–1939.* New York: Atheneum, 1972.

Rudnick, Lois Palken. *Mabel Dodge: New Woman, New Worlds.* Albuquerque: University of New Mexico Press, 1984.

Ryan, Mary. *Womanhood in America: From Colonial Times to the Present.* New York: New Viewpoints, 1975.

Sandeen, Eric, ed. *The Letters of Randolph Bourne: A Comprehensive Edition.* Troy, N.Y.: Whitston Publishing Co., 1981.

Scharf, Lois, and Joann Jensen, eds. *Decades of Discontent: The Women's Movement, 1920–1940.* Westport, Conn.: Greenwood Press, 1983.

Scharff, Virginia. *Taking the Wheel: Women and the Coming of the Motor Age.* New York: Free Press, 1991.

Schott, Linda. *Reconstructing Women's Thoughts: The Women's International League for Peace and Freedom before World War II.* Stanford, Calif.: Stanford University Press, 1997.

Schwarz, Judith. *Radical Feminists of Heterodoxy: Greenwich Village, 1912–1940.* Lebanon, N.H.: New Victoria Publishers, 1982.

Sichtermann, Barbara. *Femininity: The Politics of the Personal.* Minneapolis: University of Minnesota Press, 1986.

Simon, Kate. *Fifth Avenue: A Very Social History.* New York: Harcourt Brace Jovanovich, 1978.

Smith-Rosenberg, Carroll. *Disorderly Conduct: Visions of Gender in Victorian America.* New York: Alfred A. Knopf, 1985.

Sochen, June. *Movers and Shakers: American Women Thinkers and Activists, 1900–1970.* New York: Quadrangle, 1973.

———. *The New Woman in Greenwich Village, 1910–1920.* New York: Quadrangle Books, 1972.

Socolofsky, Homer, and Allan B. Spetter. *The Presidency of Benjamin Harrison.* Lawrence: University Press of Kansas, 1987.

Solomon, Barbara Miller. *In the Company of Educated Women.* New Haven, Conn.: Yale University Press, 1985.

Stansell, Christine. *American Moderns: Bohemia New York and the Creation of a New Century.* New York: Henry Holt and Co., 2000.

Stein, Leon. *The Triangle Fire.* Philadelphia: J. B. Lippincott Co., 1962.

Steinson, Barbara J. *American Women's Activism in World War I.* New York: Garland Publishing Co., 1982.

Suleiman, Susan Rubin. *The Female Body in Western Culture.* Cambridge, Mass.: Harvard University Press, 1986.

Tax, Meredith. *The Rising of the Women: Feminist Solidarity and Class Conflict, 1880–1917.* New York: Monthly Review Press, 1980.

Terborg-Penn, Rosalyn. *African American Women in the Struggle for the Vote, 1850–1920.* Bloomington: Indiana University Press, 1998.

Trimberger, Ellen Kay, ed. *Intimate Warriors: Portraits of a Modern Marriage, 1899–1944.* New York: Feminist Press, 1991.

Van Zooten, Liesbet. *Feminist Media Studies.* London: Sage Publications, 1994.

Vicinus, Martha. *Independent Women: Work and Community for Single Women.* Chicago: University of Chicago Press, 1985.

Wagner, Sally Roesch. *A Time of Protest: Suffragists Challenge the Republic, 1870–1877.* Carmichael, Calif.: Sky Carrier Press, 1988.

Walker, Annabel, with Peter Jackson. *Kensington and Chelsea: A Social and Architectural History.* London: John Murray, 1987.

Weaver, John D. *The Senator and the Sharecropper's Son: Exoneration of the Brownsville Soldiers.* College Station: Texas A&M University Press, 1997.

Wedin, Carolyn. *Inheritors of the Spirit: Mary White Ovington and the Founding of the NAACP.* New York: John Wiley and Sons, 1997.

Welter, Barbara. *Dimity Convictions: The American Woman in the Nineteenth Century.* Athens: Ohio University Press, 1976.

Wertheim, Arthur Frank. *The New York Little Renaissance: Iconoclasm, Modernism, and Nationalism in American Culture, 1890–1917.* New York: New York University Press, 1976.

Wheeler, Marjorie Spruill. *New Women of the New South: The Leaders of the Woman Suffrage Movement in the Southern States.* New York: Oxford University Press, 1993.

Whyte, Frederic. *The Life of W. T. Stead.* Vol. 2. London: Jonathan Cape, 1925.

Wiltsher, Anne. *Most Dangerous Women: Feminist Peace Campaigners of the Great War.* London: Pandora, 1985.

Woloch, Nancy. *Women and the American Experience.* New York: Alfred A. Knopf, 1984.

Yoder, Jon A. *Upton Sinclair.* New York: Frederick Ungar Publishing Co., 1975.

Zilburg, Caroline, ed. *Women's Firsts.* Detroit: Gale Research, 1997.

Articles

Anderson, Adrian. "President Wilson's Politician: Albert Sidney Burleson of Texas." *Southwestern Historical Quarterly* 77, no. 3 (1974): 339–54.

Baker, Paula. "The Domestication of Politics: Women and American Political Society, 1780–1920." *American Historical Review* 89 (June 1984): 620–47.

Bennett, Alma J. "A Critic's Response to Stage Representations of the 'New Woman' during the Progressive Era." *American Transcendental Quarterly* 10 (September 1996): 219–31.

Blair, Karen. "Pageantry for Women's Rights: The Career of Hazel MacKaye, 1913–1923." *Theatre Survey* 31 (1990): 25–45.

"Boissevain, Inez Milholland." In *The National Cyclopaedia of American Biography.* Vol. 16. 216–17. New York: James T. White and Co., 1945.

Bonard, Carolyn Anne. "The Women's Movement in the 1920s: American Magazines Document the Health and Progress of Feminism." In David Abrahamson, ed., *The American Magazine: Research Perspectives and Prospects,* 231–40. Ames: Iowa State University Press, 1995.

Bosmajian, Haig. "The Abrogation of the Suffragists' First Amendment Rights." *Western Speech* 38 (1974): 218–32.

Bzowski, Frances Diodato. "Spectacular Suffrage; or, How Women Came Out of the Home and into the Streets and Theaters of New York City to Win the Vote." *New York History* 76 (1995): 57–94.

Chapman, Mary. "Women and Masquerade in the 1913 Suffrage Demonstration in Washington." *Amerikastudien* 44 (1999): 343–55.

Cookingham, Mary E. "Bluestockings, Spinsters and Pedagogues: Women College Graduates, 1865–1910." *Population Studies* 39 (November 1984): 349–64.

Cott, Nancy. "Feminist Politics in the 1920s: The National Woman's Party." *Journal of American History* 71 (June 1984): 43–68.

Crofts, Daniel W. "The Warner-Foraker Amendment to the Hepburn Bill: Friend or Foe of Jim Crow." *Journal of Southern History* 39 (1973): 345–58.

Daniels, Elizabeth, and Barbara Page. "Suffrage as a Lever for Change at Vassar College." *Vassar Quarterly* 79 (1982): 31–35.

Demos, John. "The American Family in Past Time." *American Scholar* 43 (Summer 1974): 422–46.

Dill, Bonnie Thornton. "Race, Class, and Gender: Prospects for an All-Inclusive Sisterhood." *Feminist Studies* 9 (Spring 1983): 131–50.

DuBois, Ellen. "Working Women, Class Relations, and Suffrage Militance: Harriot Stanton Blatch and the New York Woman Suffrage Movement, 1894–1909." *Journal of American History* 74 (1987): 34–58.

Eckhaus, Phyllis. "Restless Women: The Pioneering Alumnae of New York University School of Law." *New York University Law Review* 66 (December 1991): 1996–2007.

———. "Vita: Inez Milholland." *Harvard Magazine* (November–December 1994): 50.

Elshtain, Jean Beth. "Aristotle, the Public-Private Split, and the Case of the Suffragists." In Jean Beth Elshtain, ed., *The Family in Political Thought*, 51–65. Amherst: University of Massachusetts Press, 1982.

Erens, Patricia. "The Flapper: Hollywood's First Liberated Woman." In Lawrence R. Broer and John D. Walther, eds., *Dancing Fools and Weary Blues: The Great Escape of the Twenties*, 130–39. Bowling Green, Ohio: Bowling Green State University Popular Press, 1990.

Florence, Lella Secor. "The Ford Peace Ship and After." In Julian Bell, ed. *We Did Not Fight: 1914–18 Experiences of War Resisters*, 97–128. London: Cobden-Sanderson, 1935.

Forrey, Carolyn. "The New Woman Revisited." *Women's Studies* 2 (1974): 37–56.

Freedman, Estelle. "The New Woman: Changing Views of Women in the 1920s." *Journal of American History* 61 (September 1974): 372–93.

———. "Separatism as Strategy: Female Institution Building and American Feminism, 1870–1930." *Feminist Studies* 5 (Fall 1979): 512–49.

Fry, Amelia. "Along the Suffrage Trail." *American West* 6 (January 1969): 16–25.

Gordon, Lynn D. "The Gibson Girl Goes to College: Popular Culture and Women's Higher Education in the Progressive Era, 1890–1920." *American Quarterly* 39 (Summer 1987): 211–30.

Graham, Sally Hunter. "Woodrow Wilson, Alice Paul, and the Woman Suffrage Movement." *Political Science Quarterly* 98 (Winter 1983–84): 665–79.

Hall, Robert F. "Women Have Been Voting Ever Since." *Adirondack Life* 2 (Winter 1971): 46–49.

Hendrickson, Wanda. "Ida B. Wells-Barnett and the Alpha Suffrage Club of Chicago." In Marjorie Spruill Wheeler, ed., *One Woman, One Vote: Rediscovering the Woman Suffrage Movement*, 263–76. Troutdale, Ore.: NewSage Press, 1995.

Jacoby, Robin Miller. "The Women's Trade Union League and American Feminism." *Feminist Studies* 3 (1975): 126–40.

Kryder, LeeAnne Giannone. "Self-Assertion and Social Commitment: The Significance of Work to the Progressive Era's New Woman." *Journal of American Culture* 6 (1983): 25–30.

Kuhlman, Erika. "Women's Ways in War: The Feminist Pacifism of the New York City Woman's Peace Party." *Frontiers* 18 (June–August 1997): 80–100.

Law, Sylvia A. "Crystal Eastman: NYU Law Graduate." *New York University Law Review* 66 (1963): 1963–95.

Lindsay, Shelley Stamp. *"Eighty Million Women Want—?*: Women's Suffrage, Female Viewers and the Body Politic." *Quarterly Review of Film & Video* 16, no. 1 (1995): 1–22.

McGerr, Michael. "Popular Style and Women's Power, 1830–1930." *Journal of American History* 77 (December 1990): 864–85.

McGovern, James. "The American Woman's Pre–World War I Freedom in Manners and Morals." *Journal of American History* 55 (September 1968): 315–33.

Mezzacappa, Dale. "Vassar College and the Suffrage Movement." *Vassar Quarterly* 69 (Spring 1973): 2–9.

Moore, Sarah J. "Making a Spectacle of Suffrage: The National Woman Suffrage Pageant, 1913." *Journal of American Culture* 20 (Spring 1997): 89–103.

Palmer, Phyllis Marynick. "White Women/Black Women: The Dualism of Feminist Identity and Experience in the United States." *Feminist Studies* 9 (Spring 1983): 151–70.

Patterson, Martha. "'Survival of the Best Fitted': Selling the American New Woman as Gibson Girl, 1895–1910." *ATQ* 9 (March 1995): 73–87.

Quinn, Peter. "The Tragedy of Bridget Such-a-One." *American Heritage* 48 (December 1997): 37–51.

Rapp, Rayna, and Ellen Ross. "The Twenties' Backlash: Compulsory Heterosexuality, the Consumer Family, and the Waning of Feminism." In Amy Swerdlow and Hanna Lessinger, eds., *Class, Race, and Sex: The Dynamics of Control*, 93–107. Boston: G. K. Hall, 1983.

Rinehart, Mary Roberts. "For King and Country: No Man's Land," *Saturday Evening Post* 187 (May 8, 1915): 57–58, 61–62.

Rupp, Leila J. "Feminism and the Sexual Revolution in the Early Twentieth Century: The Case of Doris Stevens." *Feminist Studies* 15, no. 2 (Summer 1989): 289–309.

Sanger, Carol. "Curriculum Vitae (Feminae): Biography and Early American Women Lawyers." *Stanford Law Review* 46 (May 1994): 1245–81.

Sapiro, Virginia. "Women, Citizenship and Nationality: Immigration and Naturalization Policies in the U.S." *Politics and Society* 13, no. 1 (1984): 1–26.

Sledge, John. "Alva Smith Vanderbilt Belmont." *Alabama Heritage* (Spring 1997): 6–17.

Smart, James G. "Information Control, Thought Control: Whitelaw Reid and the Nation's News Services." *The Public Historian* 3 (Spring 1981): 23–42.

Smith-Rosenberg, Carroll, and Charles Rosenberg. "The Female Animal: Medical and Biological Views of Woman and Her Role in 19th-Century America." *Journal of American History* 60 (1973–74): 332–56.

Stannard, Una. "The Mask of Beauty." In Vivian Gornick and Barbara Moran, eds., *Woman in Sexist Society*, 118–30. New York: Basic Books, 1971.

Terborg-Penn, Rosalyn. "Discrimination against Afro-American Women in the Woman's Movement, 1830–1920." In Sharon Harley and Rosalyn Terborg-Penn, eds., *The Afro-American Woman: Struggles and Images*, 17–27. Port Washington, N.Y.: Kennikat Press, 1978.

Tucker, Edward L. "John Fox Jr." In *Dictionary of Literary Biography*. Vol. 9, 25–27. Detroit: Gale Research Co., 1981.

Dissertations and Theses

Barber, Lucy Grace. "Marches on Washington, 1894–1963: National Political Demonstrations and American Political Culture." Ph.D. diss., Brown University, 1996.

Beals, Polly A. "Fabian Feminism: Gender, Politics and Culture in London, 1880–1930." Ph.D. diss., Rutgers, The State University of New Jersey, New Brunswick, N.J., 1989.

Bland, Sidney. "Techniques of Persuasion: The National Woman's Party and Woman Suffrage, 1913–1919." Ph.D. diss., George Washington University, 1972.

Herman, Debra. "College and After: The Vassar Experiment in Women's Education, 1861–1924." Thesis, Stanford University, 1979.

Nelson, Marjory. "Ladies in the Street: A Sociological Analysis of the National Woman's Party, 1910–1930." Ph.D. diss., State University of New York at Buffalo, 1976.

Richwine, Keith. "The Liberal Club: Bohemia and the Resurgence in Greenwich Village, 1912–1918." Ph.D. diss., University of Pennsylvania, 1968.

INDEX

Page numbers in italics refer to illustrations.

suffrage activities, 35, 39; in suffrage protests, 179; at Vassar, 31

Millay, Edna St. Vincent, 117, 188; "To Inez Milholland," 188, 238n27

Miller, Spencer, 147

Minor, Robert, 145

Miss America pageant, 184

Montana, 152, 157, 158, 159

Moore, Alexander, 10

Moore, Robert, 10

Morgan, Anne, 50, 52, 61

Morgan, J. P., 50

Motherhood, 108–109

Motion pictures, 114, 115

Mott, Lucretia, 188

Mt. Discovery (Mt. Inez), 17, 171, 234n53

Mrs. Warren's Profession, 55

Much Ado about Nothing, 33

Mulholland (Milholland), John, 10–11

NAACP. *See* National Association for the Advancement of Colored People

Nation, 56

National American Woman Suffrage Association (NAWSA), 3, 48, 181, 182; Congressional Committee, 106; Congressional Union, 65; conventions, 66, 75, 76, 82; and Inez Milholland, 88; and race, 89; Washington, D.C., parade, 81, 85, 88, 89

National Association for the Advancement of Colored People (NAACP), 25, 59, 89, 115–116

National Woman's Party (NWP), 178, 179, 180, 181, 182, 184, 188, 229n8, 237n54

NAWSA. *See* National American Woman Suffrage Association

Nelson, Marjory, 173

Nevada, 152, 160, 161

New Deal, 112

New Jersey, 71, 136

New Women: agency of, 5–6, 76; athleticism, 30, 41; beginnings of, 5; and birth control, 113; characteristics of, 5–7; class, 5, 6, 41, 59; clothing, 87; and college, 29, 36; complexities

of, 7, 22, 79, 102, 127, 131, 182–184; and death of Inez Milholland, 172; and driving, 50; families, 28; and "Gibson girl," 41, 182; independence of, 6, 7, 79, 118–119, 127; and journalism, 113; and law, 63; and marriage, 96–97, 98, 102; in mass media, 7–8, 30, 64; and motherhood, 108–109; in 1920s, 184; and pacifism, 118; and prostitution, 112; race, 5, 6, 41, 59; and religion, 39; Second Wave feminism, 192n25; and self realization, 6–7, 37, 63, 65, 76, 111, 131, 182; sexuality, 41, 55–56, 77, 87, 88, 96, 97, 109, 128; in shirtwaist strike, 45, 46, 49, 50, 52, 60; significance of, 6–7, 54, 55, 182; and social responsibility, 61, 64; and suffrage, 75, 76, 145; and work, 5, 61, 64, 67, 102, 127; World War I, 118. *See also* Wells-Barnett, Ida

New York American, 34, 84, 93

New York Board of Child Welfare, 147

New York City Men's League for Equal Suffrage, 72

New York Commission for the Relief of Widowed Mothers, 147

New York Evening Mail, 177

New York Evening World, 147

New York Newspaper Association, 113

New York Press, 74

New York Press Club, 113

New York Society for the Suppression of Vice, 115

New York state, 65; and capital punishment, 143–144; 1915 suffrage referendum, 106, 131–132; 1917 suffrage referendum, 132

New York State Assembly, 73

New York Sun, 70, 90

New York Times, 36, 41, 49, 51, 84, 86, 95, 115, 146, 166, 179

New York Tribune, 12, 14, 82, 120, 121–122, 124, 125, 126, 169

New York Typographical Union Number Six, 14

New York University, 11, 55; School of Law, 56, 64

LINDA J. LUMSDEN is Associate Professor in the School of Journalism and Broadcasting at Western Kentucky University, where she teaches journalism and women's studies. She is author of *Rampant Women: Suffragists and the Right of Assembly* and *Adirondack Craftspeople.*